Za
Mozambique &
Malawi

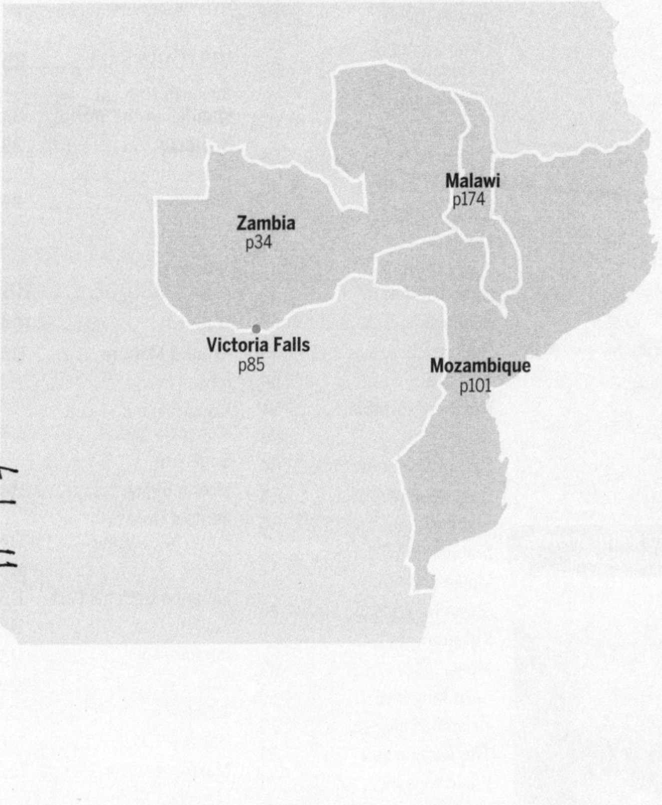

Mary Fitzpatrick, James Bainbridge,
Trent Holden, Brendan Sainsbury

PLAN YOUR TRIP

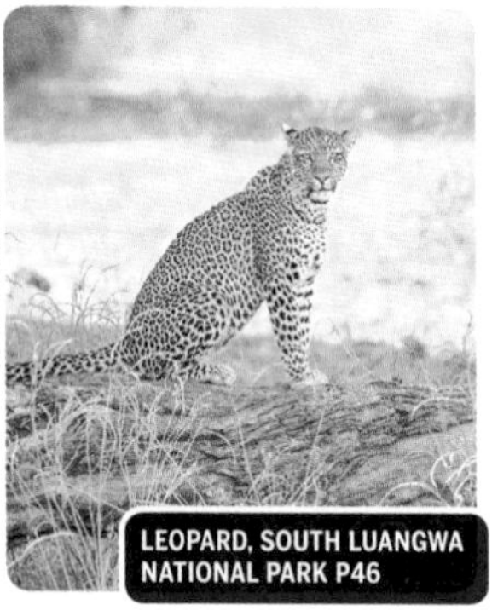

PHILIP LEE HARVEY/LONELY PLANET ©

LEOPARD, SOUTH LUANGWA NATIONAL PARK P46

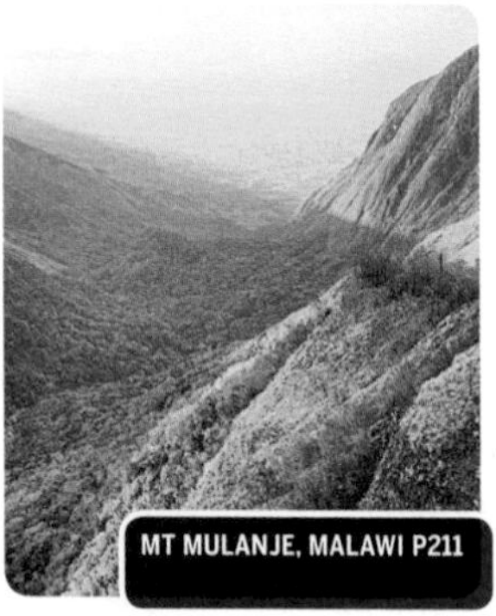

JONATHAN GREGSON/LONELY PLANET ©

MT MULANJE, MALAWI P211

ON THE ROAD

Contents

SURVIVAL GUIDE

SPECIAL FEATURES

Welcome to Zambia, Mozambique & Malawi

Zambia's wildlife and waterfalls, Malawi's lake and mountains, Mozambique's islands and beaches: each country has its own personality. Focus on exploring one, or sample all three.

Wildlife

Zambia's wildlife-filled plains are legendary, from South Luangwa National Park in the southeast to Kafue National Park in the west. With their remoteness, species diversity and fine network of camps, the country's protected areas offer outstanding wildlife watching for those willing to meet the challenge of getting there and around. Mozambique and Malawi also offer some treats. Highlights include Mozambique's lovely Gorongosa National Park, which is also a prime birding destination, and Malawi's Liwonde National Park, with its hippos and crocs.

Landscapes

Diverse and beautiful landscapes captivate visitors at every turn. A highlight is Zambia's (and Zimbabwe's) thundering Victoria Falls, one of the continent's iconic images and a Unesco World Heritage Site. Raft the rapids or stand on the spray-misted sidelines: the wildness, power and magnificence of the falls are unforgettable. Along the coast, the azure waters and the islands of Mozambique's Bazaruto and Quirimbas Archipelagos are mesmerising. Inland, marvel at the mist-covered peaks of Mt Mulanje in Malawi and vast tracts of bush bordering the Zambezi River in southern Zambia.

Beaches

Mozambique's coastline is one of Africa's longest and most alluring, from the windswept dunes of Ponta d'Ouro to the languid archipelagos and palm-fringed beaches of the north. There are many islands, including magical Mozambique Island and enchanting Ibo. The country's history and culture are tied to the sea, and most visitors focus on the coast, travelling from one beach to the next. Inland, Lake Malawi, with its backdrop of lush mountains rising from the lakeshore, is a fixture in Southern African travel itineraries.

Cultures

Wherever you go, immerse yourself in the everyday beauty, realities and vibrancy of Southern African life and take advantage of opportunities for community-based tourism. In English-speaking Zambia and Malawi, local culture is often readily accessible, and both countries offer cultural-tourism activities. In Mozambique, Maputo's excellent dance and cultural scenes, complemented by local walking tours, provide a jumping-off point for getting acquainted with local vibes. Throughout, it will likely be encounters with Zambians, Malawians and Mozambicans that will make your visit to the region unforgettable.

Why I Love Zambia, Mozambique & Malawi

By Mary Fitzpatrick, Writer

The sense of space and light, the rugged bush interior and the magnificent Indian Ocean coastline are what first captured my imagination when visiting this region. The colourful mix of cultures and languages further drew me in. Now, after spending extended periods in southern Africa, both living and travelling, the gracious welcome offered by so many people and the many friends I have met combine with the region's landscapes and nature to make this corner of Africa one of my favourites.

For more about our writers, see p256.

Above: Camping under the stars, South Luangwa National Park (p46), Zambia

Zambia, Mozambique & Malawi

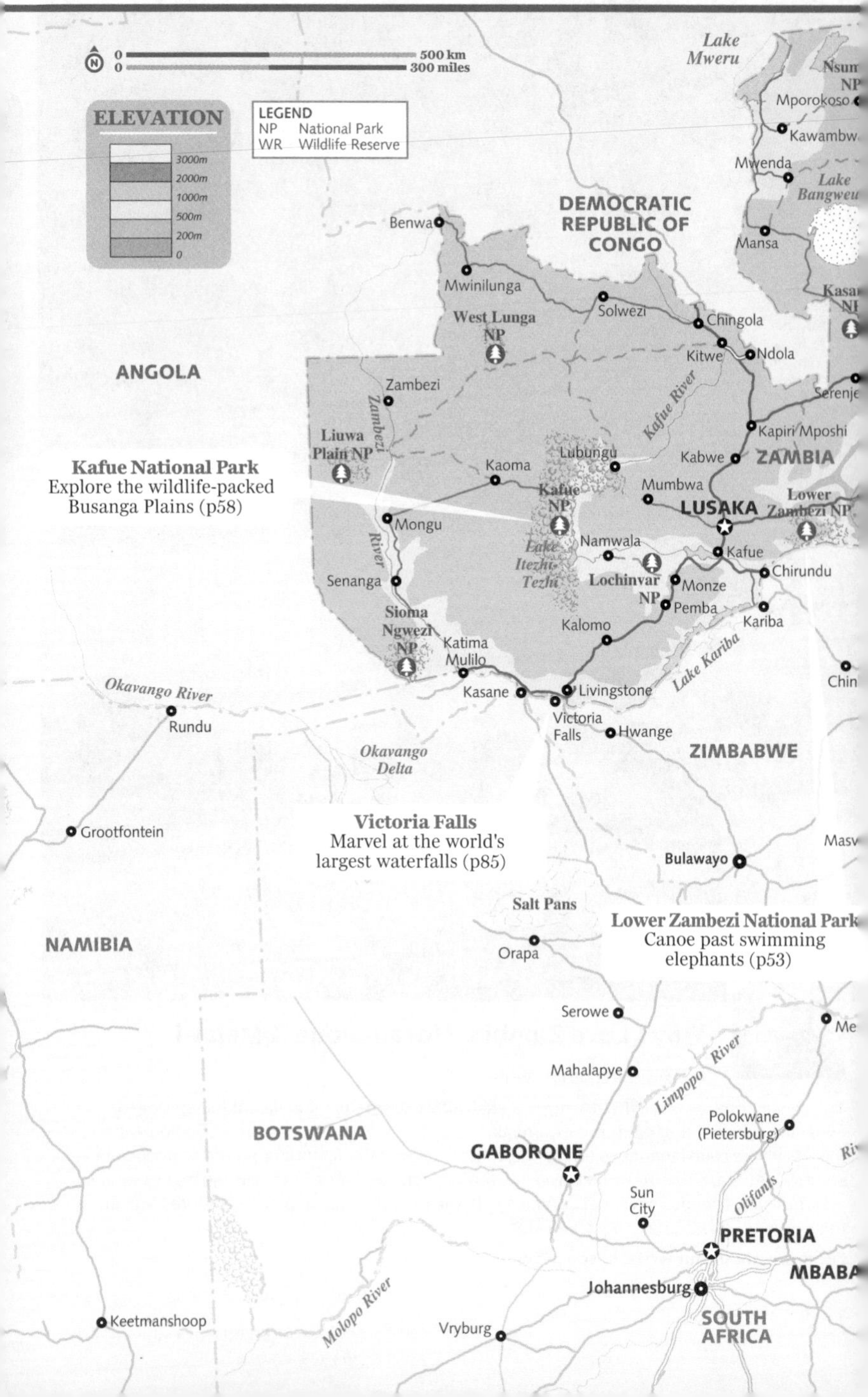

0 500 km
0 300 miles
ELEVATION
3000m
2000m
1000m
500m
200m
0
LEGEND
NP National Park
WR Wildlife Reserve
Kafue National Park
Explore the wildlife-packed Busanga Plains (p58)
Victoria Falls
Marvel at the world's largest waterfalls (p85)
Lower Zambezi National Park
Canoe past swimming elephants (p53)
DEMOCRATIC REPUBLIC OF CONGO
ANGOLA
ZAMBIA
ZIMBABWE
NAMIBIA
BOTSWANA
SOUTH AFRICA
LUSAKA
GABORONE
PRETORIA
Lake Mweru
Lake Bangweulu
Mporokoso
Kawambwa
Mwenda
Mansa
Benwa
Mwinilunga
Solwezi
Chingola
Kitwe
Ndola
West Lunga NP
Zambezi
Zambezi River
Liuwa Plain NP
Kaoma
Lubungu
Kafue River
Kapiri Mposhi
Serenje
Kabwe
Mumbwa
Kafue NP
Lower Zambezi NP
Mongu
Lake Itezhi-Tezhi
Namwala
Kafue
Chirundu
Senanga
Lochinvar NP
Monze
Pemba
Kariba
Sioma Ngwezi NP
Kalomo
Katima Mulilo
Lake Kariba
Kasane
Livingstone
Victoria Falls
Hwange
Okavango River
Rundu
Okavango Delta
Grootfontein
Bulawayo
Salt Pans
Orapa
Serowe
Mahalapye
Limpopo River
Polokwane (Pietersburg)
Sun City
Olifants
Johannesburg
Molopo River
Vryburg
Keetmanshoop

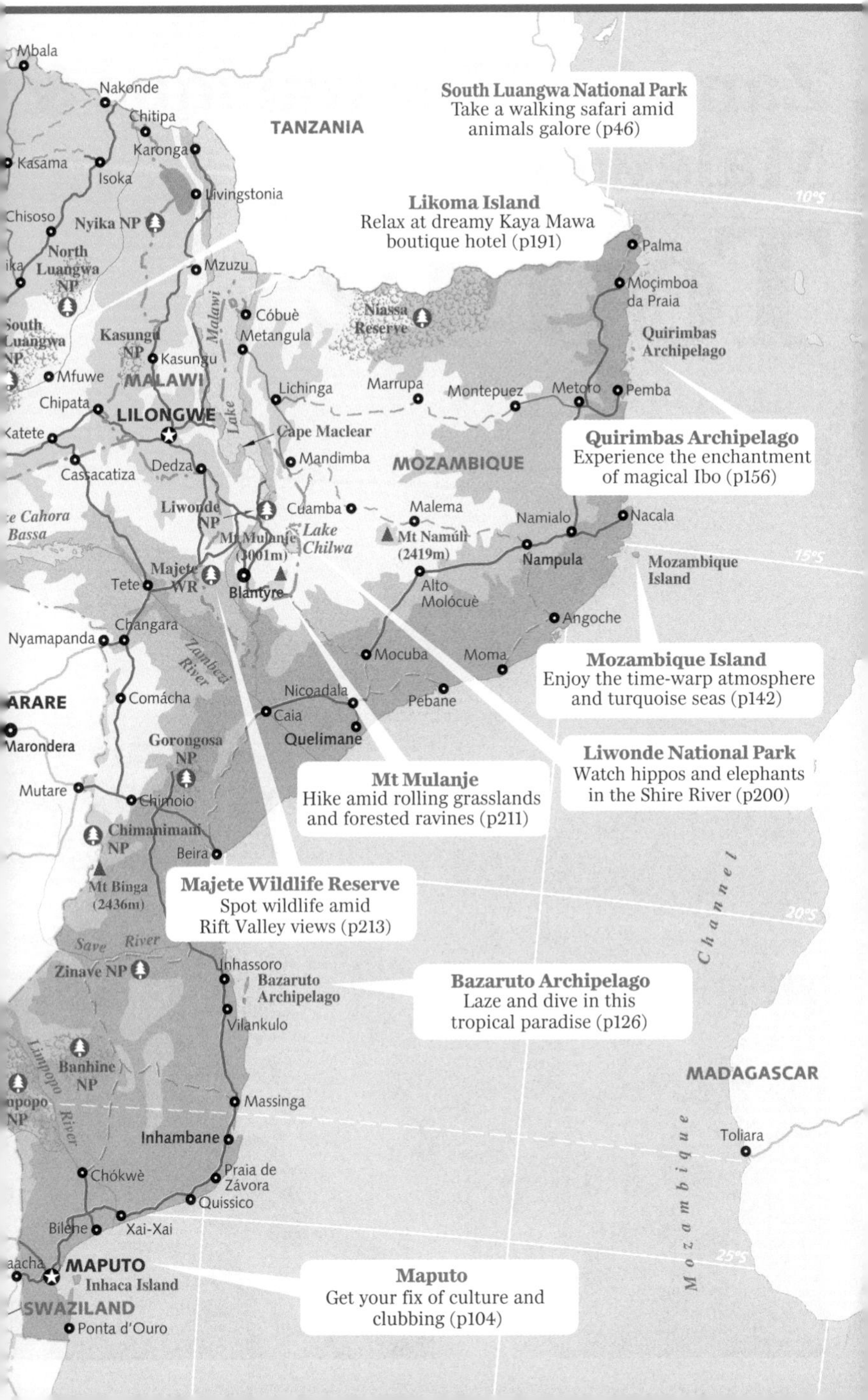
South Luangwa National Park
Take a walking safari amid animals galore (p46)
Likoma Island
Relax at dreamy Kaya Mawa boutique hotel (p191)
Quirimbas Archipelago
Experience the enchantment of magical Ibo (p156)
Mozambique Island
Enjoy the time-warp atmosphere and turquoise seas (p142)
Liwonde National Park
Watch hippos and elephants in the Shire River (p200)
Mt Mulanje
Hike amid rolling grasslands and forested ravines (p211)
Majete Wildlife Reserve
Spot wildlife amid Rift Valley views (p213)
Bazaruto Archipelago
Laze and dive in this tropical paradise (p126)
Maputo
Get your fix of culture and clubbing (p104)
TANZANIA
MALAWI
LILONGWE
MOZAMBIQUE
MADAGASCAR
SWAZILAND
MAPUTO
Mbala
Nakonde
Chitipa
Karonga
Kasama
Isoka
Livingstonia
Chisoso
Nyika NP
North Luangwa NP
Mzuzu
Kasungu NP
Kasungu
Mfuwe
Chipata
Katete
Cassacatiza
Dedza
Lake Malawi
Cóbuè
Metangula
Niassa Reserve
Lichinga
Marrupa
Montepuez
Metoro
Pemba
Palma
Moçimboa da Praia
Quirimbas Archipelago
Cape Maclear
Mandimba
Cuamba
Malema
Mt Namúli (2419m)
Namialo
Nacala
Nampula
Mozambique Island
Liwonde NP
Mt Mulanje (3001m)
Lake Chilwa
Majete WR
Tete
Blantyre
Alto Molócuè
Angoche
Changara
Nyamapanda
Zambezi River
Mocuba
Moma
Pebane
Nicoadala
Caia
Quelimane
Comácha
Marondera
Gorongosa NP
Mutare
Chimoio
Chimanimani NP
Beira
Mt Binga (2436m)
Save River
Zinave NP
Inhassoro
Bazaruto Archipelago
Vilankulo
Banhine NP
Limpopo River
Massinga
Inhambane
Chókwè
Praia de Závora
Quissico
Bilene
Xai-Xai
Inhaca Island
Ponta d'Ouro
Toliara
Mozambique Channel
10°S
15°S
20°S
25°S

Zambia, Mozambique & Malawi's Top 12

1

Devil's Pool, Victoria Falls (Zambia)

1 The mighty Victoria Falls (p90) offers many viewpoints, but none so gut-wrenching as from the aptly named Devil's Pools. From mid-August to January, daredevils can swim out to this natural infinity pool that is literally at the top of the falls. Test your nerve by leaping in where the water will carry you to the edge, only to be stopped by the natural barrier on the lip of this sheer and massive curtain of water. Lap it up while peeking over the edge for the ultimate bird's-eye view.

Mozambique Island (Mozambique)

2 There are no crowds and few vehicles, but Mozambique Island (p142) is hardly silent. Echoes of its past mix with the squawking of chickens, the sounds of children playing and the calls of the muezzin to remind you that the island is still very much alive. Wander along cobbled streets, past graceful plazas rimmed by once-grand churches and stately colonial-era buildings. This Unesco World Heritage Site, with its time-warp atmosphere and backdrop of turquoise seas, is a Mozambique highlight, and is not to be missed.

Cycling past the Igreja da Misericórdia (p143), Mozambique Island

Lower Zambezi National Park (Zambia)

3 Floating down one of Africa's great rivers – Zimbabwe's sandy banks on one side, Zambia's Lower Zambezi National Park (p53) on the other – gives you a front-row seat to a menagerie of wildlife: hippos surface with warning calls, crocodiles scuttle through grass, elephants slosh their way between islands and fierce tiger fish tempt anglers. Whether travelling by canoe or motorised boat, you'll be hypnotised by the languidly flowing river and pastel-coloured sunsets.

South Luangwa National Park (Zambia)

4 On a walking safari, stroll through the bush single file behind a rifle-carrying scout. No engine sounds break the music of the bush, and no barriers stand between you and the wildlife. Listen to scurrying in the underbrush as you focus on the little things, then pause in the shade of an acacia tree, gaze over wide plains filled with munching grazers and immerse yourself in the magnificent wildness that is South Luangwa National Park (p46).

3

4

Bazaruto Archipelago (Mozambique)

5 Brilliant hues of turquoise and jade laced with shimmering white sandbanks, dolphins cavorting in the swells and dugongs grazing in the shallows, graceful dunes, pink flamingos, shoals of fish, brilliant corals and swaying palm trees – this is the Bazaruto Archipelago (p126), a world-class marine park and the quintessential tropical paradise for anyone seeking a getaway. Stay for a while in one of the handful of luxury lodges or sail over from the mainland for a day on a dhow. Either way, you'll undoubtedly wish your visit was longer.

Liwonde National Park (Malawi)

6 Set in dry savannah and woodland, this small reserve (p200) punches way above its weight with a staggering animal population including thousands of elephants, hippos and crocs. Stay in the beguilingly romantic Mvuu Camp beside the Shire River, listening to passing elephants and snuffling hippos as you fall asleep in your cosy cabana. Then get up early and enjoy a dawn walk and boat ride past some very territorial hippos.

Likoma Island (Malawi)

7 A visit to Likoma Island (p191) is unforgettable: think Caribbean waters, friendly locals, rustling palm trees and a sense that everything can wait until tomorrow. Once you've witnessed the extraordinary Cathedral of St Peter, get down to chilling in the country's nicest hostel, Mango Drift. Alternatively, stay at the heavenly Kaya Mawa, on a crescent beach with powder-fine sand, with perfectly calibrated service and rooms designed around the island's natural rock formations. Remember Bond villain Scaramanga's pad? You've found it. Cathedral of St Peter

8

9

JONATHAN GREGSON/LONELY PLANET ©

10

Mt Mulanje (Malawi)

8 At an elevation of 3002m, the Mulanje massif (p211) towers above the surrounding landscape of rolling grasslands, forested ravines and tea plantations. It's also a paradise for hikers and climbers, with a series of cabins for overnighting in during longer treks. Imagine montane forest a-croak with frogs, rocky outcrops and clear mountain streams for refilling your bottle. This is among the most dramatic scenery in the country. But be warned: you have to earn it. The only way up is on foot.

Kafue National Park (Zambia)

9 Imagine a small, extremely diverse country, but with animals substituted for people – this is western Zambia's Kafue National Park (p58). On the Busanga Plains in the north, the vistas open up to the horizon, with herds of grazers congregating as far as you can see. The park's south feels worlds away, with mysterious riverine landscapes, jungle-clad islands, fast-moving rapids and meandering channels. North or south, there are few visitors in this land where the wild things roam. Rondavel (hut) in Kafue National Park

Quirimbas Archipelago (Mozambique)

10 Idyllic islands strewn across azure seas, dense mangrove channels opening onto pristine patches of soft, white sand, dhows silhouetted against the horizon, and magical Ibo Island, with its silversmiths, fort and crumbling mansions – the remote Quirimbas Archipelago (p156) is a time and place apart, accessed with difficulty and left behind with regret. Whether you dive and snorkel amid the coral and fish, wander Ibo's sand lanes, relax in a luxury lodge or explore on a dhow, the archipelago never fails to enchant.

[M]aputo (Mozambique)

11 Maputo (p104) is Mozambique's pulse point, its economic centre, cultural [he]art and historical treasure trove, with [an] intoxicating vibe and a stunning setting [ov]erlooking Maputo Bay. Wide, jacaranda- [an]d flame-tree-lined streets flow from the [qu]ieter upper part of town down into the [bu]stling, low-lying *baixa*. Shady sidewalk [ca]fes offer an ideal spot to watch the pass[in]g scene, and the city's pulsating nightlife, [go]od shopping, rewarding museums and [wid]e array of restaurants all beckon, making [an]y visit here a pleasure.

Majete Wildlife Reserve (Malawi)

12 The brightest star in Malawi's ever-improving network of parks and reserves is the lovely Majete (p213) – 700 sq km of riverine valleys and miombo (woodland) in the southwestern Rift Valley. Sip sundowners under the watchful eyes of hippos and crocs in the river below, dodge buffaloes and elephants on a boating safari, and ensconce yourself in luxurious boutique-style digs at wonderful Mkulumadzi Camp (pictured, below). Majete – a conservation model for others to follow – is home to the Big Five, including Malawi's first reintroduced lion pride.

11

12

Need to Know

For more information, see Survival Guide (pp78, 165, 218)

Currencies

Zambia Zambian kwacha (ZMW)
Mozambique Mozambican new metical (Mtc)
Malawi Malawian kwacha (MK)

Languages

Zambia English, African languages
Mozambique Portuguese, African languages
Malawi English, African languages

Money

ATMs are found in cities and major towns. Away from cities, credit cards aren't often accepted (or involve surcharges).

Visas

All Mozambique visas should be arranged in advance. Otherwise, single-entry visas, where required, are available at major international airports and at many land borders.

Driving

Drive on the left in all three countries.

When to Go

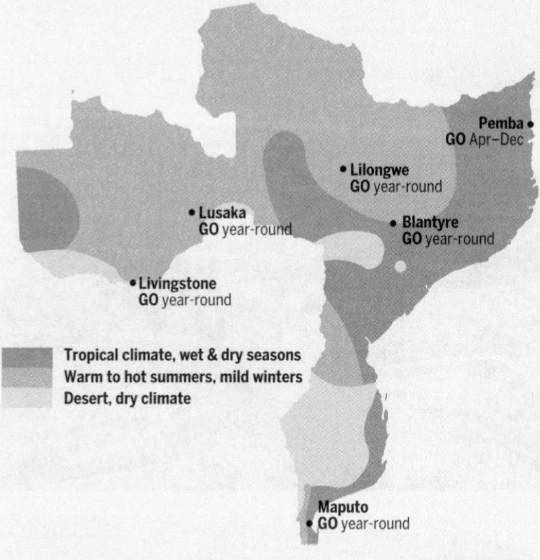

High Season
(Jun–Oct)

➡ Weather throughout is cooler and dry.

➡ August can be crowded, with higher prices.

➡ Animal spotting is easiest from August to October, due to sparse foliage and animals congregating around dwindling water sources.

Shoulder
(Apr, May, Nov & Dec)

➡ An ideal travel time, with green landscapes, though watch for muddy (or impassable) roads, especially in April, before the rains have dried out.

➡ Peak-season prices from mid-December to mid-January and at Easter.

Low Season
(Jan–Mar)

➡ Heavy rains make secondary roads muddy and some areas inaccessible.

➡ It seldom rains all day, every day; landscapes are lush and green.

Useful Websites

BBC News – Africa (www.bbc.com/news/world/africa) Keeping a finger on Southern Africa's pulse.

Club of Mozambique (www.clubofmozambique.com) Mozambique news and tourism info.

Integrated Regional Information Network (www.irinnews.org/afrique/southern-africa) Regional humanitarian news.

Lonely Planet (www.lonelyplanet.com) Destination information, hotel bookings, traveller forum and more.

RoundTrip Foundation (www.roundtripfoundation.org.au) Turn your travel in Southern Africa into sustainable change for local communities.

Safari Bookings (www.safaribookings.com) Online safari-planning resource with a focus on sustainable travel.

Important Numbers

In all three countries, mobile numbers are six digits plus a four-digit provider code. There are no central police or other emergency numbers.

Zambia country code	☎260
Mozambique country code	☎258
Malawi country code	☎265
International access code (all)	☎00

Mobile Phones

Local SIM cards can be used in (unlocked) European and Australian phones; others must be set to roaming. Starter packs and top-up vouchers are widely and inexpensively available.

Exchange Rates

For exchange rates, see p79 (Zambia), p167 (Mozambique) and p220 (Malawi). Current exchange rates are at www.xe.com.

Your Daily Budget

The following provides a rough guideline. Malawi tends to be cheaper, Zambia and Mozambique pricier.

Budget: Less than US$50

- Room in basic budget guesthouse: US$10–30
- Local-style meal: less than US$5
- Ask about low-season and children's discounts

Midrange: US$50–200

- Double room in midrange hotel: US$50–150
- Meal in Western-style restaurant: US$15–20
- Wildlife safari: from US$150 per person per day
- Vehicle rental: from US$80 per day

Top End: More than US$200

- Upmarket hotel room: from US$150
- All-inclusive safari packages: from US$200 per person per day

Arriving in Zambia, Mozambique & Malawi

Lusaka International Airport (p43; Zambia) Taxis to centre: ZMW200 to ZMW250.

Maputo International Airport (p112; Mozambique) Taxis to centre: Mtc400 to Mtc500.

Lilongwe International Airport (p221; Malawi) Taxis to centre: US$35.

What to Pack

Binoculars and a field guide

Torch (flashlight) There's no electricity in the bush.

Mosquito repellent, net and malaria prophylaxis

Zoom lens and extra storage chips

Travel insurance

Wind- and waterproof jacket

Yellow-fever-vaccination certificate

Visa card For accessing cash at ATMs.

Portuguese phrasebook For visiting Mozambique.

For much more on **getting around**, see pp83, 171, 223

If You Like...

Wildlife

Zambia is the big wildlife-watching drawcard, but Mozambique and Malawi have their own allure.

South Luangwa National Park Abundant wildlife, wonderful scenery and walking safaris. (p46)

Kafue National Park A vast wilderness known especially for its wildlife-packed Serengeti-like grasslands. (p58)

Lower Zambezi National Park Canoe safaris, riverine vistas, swimming elephants and fantastic scenery. (p53)

Gorongosa National Park Antelope, elephants and a sublime setting. (p131)

Liwonde National Park Crocs, hippos and elephants in an enchanting Shire River location. (p200)

Kasanka National Park Swamplands and sitatungas, plus the mind-blowing bat migration in November. (p65)

Majete Wildlife Reserve Reintroduced lions, along with crocs, elephants and rhinos in one of Malawi's best reserves. (p213)

Beaches

The region's best beaches are in Mozambique, where you'll find fine white sand, dunes, palms and a languid ambience. Inland, Lake Malawi's tranquil shoreline has been drawing travellers for decades.

Tofo A lovely arc of white sand with azure waters, and surfing and diving opportunities with manta rays and whale sharks. (p120)

Chidenguele High, vegetated dunes back a long, wide beach that stretches to the horizon in both directions. (p118)

Pomene A stunning estuarine setting and rewarding birding are among the draws at this often-overlooked spot on the southern Mozambique coast. (p123)

Ponta d'Ouro Mozambique's southernmost tip features a long, dune-fringed beach with reliable surf and the chance to spot dolphins. (p114)

Bazaruto Archipelago Idyllic islands are rimmed by relaxing beaches and turquoise waters abounding in marine life. (p126)

Vilankulo Horseback riding along the beach and kitesurfing are among the highlights of the coastline around Vilankulo. (p124)

Lake Malawi Cape Maclear, with its golden sands and exclusive Mumbo Island, is just one of many enjoyable spots along the Lake Malawi shoreline. (p149)

Lake Tanganyika Perfect white sandy beaches line this expansive lake, with its crystal-clear waters and tropical fish. (p69)

Chilling Out

Whether it's laid-back backpacker vibes, upmarket island-lodge pampering or bush-camp chic, Zambia, Mozambique and Malawi have relaxation down to a fine art.

Nkwichi Lodge Spend a night here, or three, revelling in the remoteness, snorkelling in crystal-clear waters and kayaking past quiet coves. (p151)

Bazaruto Archipelago Lodges Take your pick – all are lovely patches of luxury amid the stunning, natural setting of Bazaruto Archipelago National Park. (p126)

Lake Kariba Spend a few low-key days at this beautiful artificial lake enjoying sunset cruises and walks along the dam wall. (p56)

Likoma Island This jewel in Lake Malawi has sublime crescent bays, views across the water to Mozambique and a delightfully slow pace. (p191)

Nkhata Bay Chill out in a reed hut on the beach at one of Malawi's classic down-time destinations. (p189)

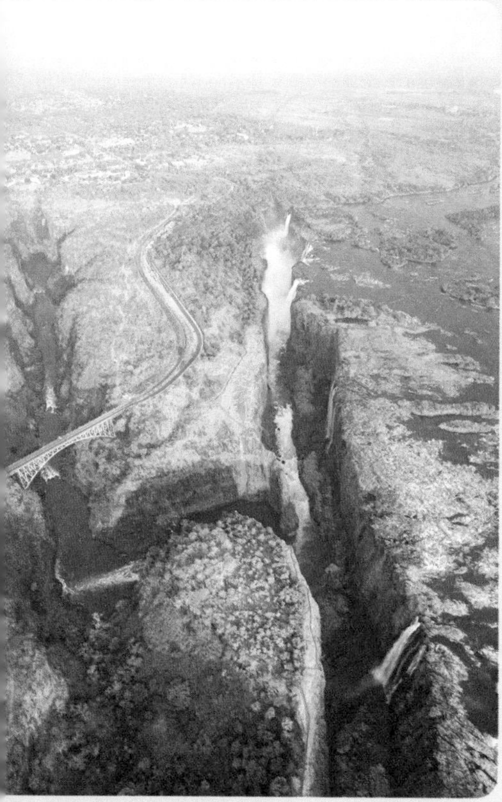

p: Aerial view of Victoria Falls (p85) over the chasm separating Zambia and mbabwe

ottom: Street view, Maputo (p104), Mozambique

Lake Tanganyika Laze on the pristine sands of this serene lake in between snorkelling and kayak trips. (p69)

History & Culture

Early Bantu-speaking migrants, later influxes from Arabia, India and the Orient, and European colonialists – all have left their mark on the region's history and cultures.

Mozambique Island Step back through the centuries in this historical treasure trove and cultural melting pot. (p142)

Ibo Island With its fortress, silversmiths and crumbling colonial-era mansions, Ibo Island is caught in an enchanting time warp. (p156)

Livingstonia Stroll around the old stone buildings for a glimpse of this 19th-century Scottish mission's fascinating past. (p184)

Maputo Whether it's taking a walking tour through lively Mafalala neighbourhood, exploring the bustling *baixa* (old town) or watching for revolutionary-themed murals, the Mozambique capital's history is present at every turn. (p104)

Kungoni Centre of Culture & Art Malawian history and culture come alive here, especially in the vibrant murals of the Chamare Museum. (p196)

Kuomboka Ceremony Now that there's a road out here, there's no excuse to miss this annual ritual of the Lozi people of western Zambia. (p63)

Shiwa Ng'andu A 1920s English mansion in the middle of the Zambian bush is something that has to be seen to be believed. (p67)

Landscapes & Nature

In all three countries, diversity and beauty will surround you.

Mutinondo Wilderness Mutinondo offers wide vistas and soul-stirring landscapes dotted with huge purple-hued inselbergs and laced with meandering rivers. (p66)

Inhambane This Mozambican province's long coastline is known for its palm-fringed beaches, its flamingos and waterbirds, and its picturesque dhows. (p118)

Victoria Falls Thundering Victoria Falls is one of the most breathtaking natural spectacles on earth. (p85)

Mt Mulanje This towering hulk of twisted granite – Malawi's 'Island in the Sky' – rises up majestically from the surrounding plains, and offers lovely scenery and easy access. (p211)

Viphya Plateau Sweeping valleys and cool forests are the highlights of this stunning highland area. (p192)

Nyika Plateau Enjoy Nyika Plateau's grasslands and wildflowers on a multiday guided hike from Livingstonia. (p185)

Ngonye Falls This remote, 1km-wide chain of waterfalls, rapids and rocky islands is stunningly beautiful. (p63)

Adventure & Offbeat Travel

Few regions are so ideally suited to adventure travel as this one. In Zambia, almost anywhere outside Lusaka is remote, while northern Mozambique is one of the continent's last travel frontiers. Malawi is tamer, but has some quirky gems.

Northern Mozambique Sail by dhow past remote islands or venture into trackless bush in the interior. (p138)

Chimanimani Mountains Get to know local culture while hiking through lush, seldom-visited forest areas. (p133)

Kalambo Falls Hike to the top of Africa's second-highest single-drop waterfall. (p70)

Vwaza Marsh Wildlife Reserve Off Malawi's mainstream tourist track, this intriguing reserve is awash with buffaloes, elephants and hippos. (p186)

Liuwa Plain National Park These remote grasslands host vast herds of wildebeest and exceptionally large and numerous hyenas. (p62)

Mt Namúli Fit hikers will enjoy this challenging but scenic peak well off the beaten track near Gurúè. (p138)

Month by Month

TOP EVENTS

Kusefya Pangwena, August (Zambia)

Lake of Stars Music Festival, October (Malawi)

Mt Mulanje Porters Race, July (Malawi)

Marrabenta Festival, February (Mozambique)

Festival Azgo, May (Mozambique)

January

January throughout the region is warm, wet and ideal for birding. Despite the humidity and the rains, the early part of the month still sees many visitors enjoying the New Year's peak-season holiday period.

Viphya Orchid Weekend (Malawi)

Among the forests of the Viphya Plateau, Luwawa Forest Lodge has a calendar of annual events that begins with a weekend focusing on the plateau's profuse orchids. (p193)

February

The rains are now in full force, with the occasional tropical storm and high humidity along the coast. Secondary roads are muddy, and getting around away from main roads can be a challenge.

Gwaza Muthini (Mozambique)

This early-February celebration in Marracuene (25km north of Maputo) commemorates colonial resisters who lost their lives in the 1895 Battle of Marracuene. It also marks the start of the season of *ukanhi*, a traditional brew made from the fruit of the *canhoeiro* (marula) tree.

Marrabenta Festival (Mozambique)

To hear *marrabenta* – Mozambique's national music – at its best, don't miss the annual Marrabenta Festival. It's held mostly in Maputo but also takes place in Beira, Inhambane and several other locations. The timing is set to coincide with Marracuene's Gwaza Muthini commemorations. (p105)

N'cwala (Zambia)

The Ngoni people hold this thanksgiving or 'first fruits' festival in late February near Chipata in eastern Zambia. There's plenty of food, dance and music for celebrating the approaching end of the rainy season and to pray for a successful harvest.

April

The long rains are tapering off, with green landscapes everywhere and still-muddy roads. Visitor numbers increase in connection with the Easter holidays. Birding is at its best, and Victoria Falls is swathed in spray.

Kuomboka (Zambia)

Kuomboka is celebrated by the Lozi people of western Zambia at the end of the rainy season to mark the journey of their *litunga* (king) from his compound on the Zambezi flood plains to higher ground. Dates vary. (p63)

May

Cooler, drier weather throughout the region makes May a delightful time to travel, although secondary roads may still be difficult to negotiate in some areas.

Festival Azgo (Mozambique)

This Maputo-based extravaganza has become Mozambique's largest arts and culture festival, featuring artists from Mozambique as well as elsewhere in the region. (p105)

June

The entire region is now settling in to enjoy the cool, dry weather. June is generally a comfortable, uncrowded time to travel, although the sea along the southernmost coast can be windy and choppy.

Luwawa International Mountain Bike Race (Malawi)

Running along the ridges of the Viphya Mountains, this tough 50km race is popular with experienced South African riders. Like them, after crossing the finish line you can tackle the three-day wilderness trail down to Lake Malawi.

Ibo Island Day (Kueto Siriwala) (Mozambique)

June 24 marks the feast of St John the Baptist, which is now celebrated with great gusto as Kueto Siriwala ('to not forget your roots') day on Ibo Island in Mozambique's Quirimbas Archipelago. Events include traditional music and dance, and dhow races.

July

Prime wildlife-watching season is just around the corner, with the weather continuing to be cool and dry. Humpback whales have reached Mozambican waters on their migration up from Antarctica.

Lake Malawi International Sailing Marathon (Malawi)

This week-long June–July sailing extravaganza on Lake Malawi – claimed by promoters to be one of the longest freshwater sailing competitions in the world – covers about 500km, from Mangochi in the south to the Chintheche Strip in the north.

Mt Mulanje Porters Race (Malawi)

Originally only for Mt Mulanje porters, this 22km rocky run across rivers and gorges to the 2500m-high Chambe Plateau now has an international following. Hikers typically take around 13 hours to finish the route; the runners do it in three. (p211)

August

Humpback whales are now readily spotted along much of the Mozambican coast. Although dolphins are seen year-round, August tends to be particularly favourable for sightings. Along the coast, hotels may fill, with peak-season prices.

Kusefya Pangwena (Zambia)

At Kusefya Pangwena, northern Zambia's Bemba people celebrate their 1830s victory over the marauding Ngoni with a program of music, drama and dance. The festival is held near Kasama over four days in August.

Chamare Day (Malawi)

Mua's Kungoni Centre of Culture & Art is fascinating year-round, but this celebration of Malawian culture sends it into overdrive, with performances of Chewa, Yao and Ngoni song, dance and theatre. Courses on history and culture are also offered in this century-old Roman Catholic mission.

Cape Maclear Triathlon (Malawi)

Inaugurated in 2015, this swimming, cycling and running contest includes both the lake and the national park, and the weekend in late August puts Cape Maclear in a party mood. Proceeds go to local NGOs and charities.

September

Clear, dry weather, minimal foliage and dwindling rivers make September one of the best months for wildlife watching, as animals congregate around scarce water sources.

☆ Kugoma (Mozambique)

This festival (http://kugomashortfilms.wixsite.com/kugoma) showcases short films from throughout the Southern Africa region, with many free screenings and discussion forums held in and around Maputo.

October

Prime wildlife-watching season continues into dry, warm October, with water sources scarce and wildlife plentiful. It's an ideal time to travel – very hot in the interior, but moderate along the coast and with jacarandas abloom in the highlands.

☆ Lake of Stars Music Festival (Malawi)

One of the region's largest spectacles, this three-day music festival features live acts from around Africa and Europe. It takes place in a different lakeshore venue each year, with proceeds benefiting charity. (p217)

☆ Likoma Festival (Malawi)

Malawi's largest desert island brings the party to its shores by organising a barbecue- and music-packed lake cruise from Monkey Bay, for a weekend of cultural performances and beach sports.

November

November marks the end of the dry season and the start of the hottest weather before the rains arrive. With the start of the rains come muddy roads, as well as calving season for many animals.

Mafalala Festival (Mozambique)

Held annually between late October and late November, this festival showcases Maputo's rich artistic and cultural legacy, focusing especially on the city's lively Mafalala neighbourhood. See www.iverca.org.

December

Along the coast, changing winds have brought calmer seas. Whale-shark sightings tend to be particularly good now, during the height of summer. Diving conditions are also optimal, with calmer seas and warmer temperatures.

Plan Your Trip
Itineraries

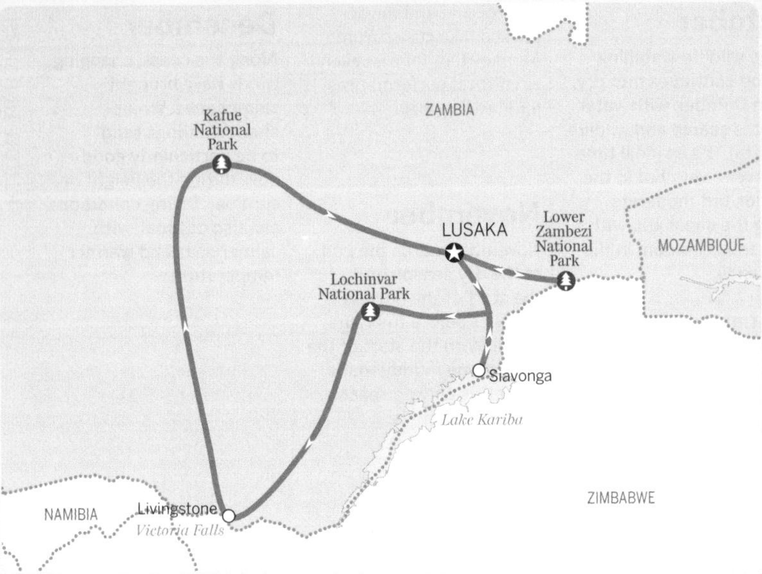

2 WEEKS Wildlife & Waterfalls

This itinerary encompasses several of the region's highlights: wildlife, the majestic Victoria Falls and Lake Kariba, one of the world's largest artificial lakes.

Start in **Lusaka**, Zambia's gateway. Then journey southeast to **Lower Zambezi National Park**, one of Africa's finest wilderness regions, to spot wildlife along the Zambezi.

Navigate southwest to **Siavonga** on sparkling Lake Kariba and relax by the water. From Siavonga, retrace your steps northwest towards Kafue junction, before continuing westwards to the wetlands at **Lochinvar National Park**, renowned for birding and its lechwe population. Overnight at the Moorings Campsite.

The next stop is historic **Livingstone**, gateway to thundering **Victoria Falls**, where you can do some canoe trips or white-water rafting. Next head northeast to **Kafue National Park** via its south Dundumwezi Gate. Spend the first night at Konkamoya Lodge overlooking Lake Itezhi-Tezhi, then a few days heading north into the park for excellent birding and wildlife. From here it's a day's travel back to Lusaka.

MAKSYM KALYTA/SHUTTERSTOCK ©

Top: Victoria Falls (p85)

Bottom: Lodge restaurant, Kafue National Park (p58), Zambia

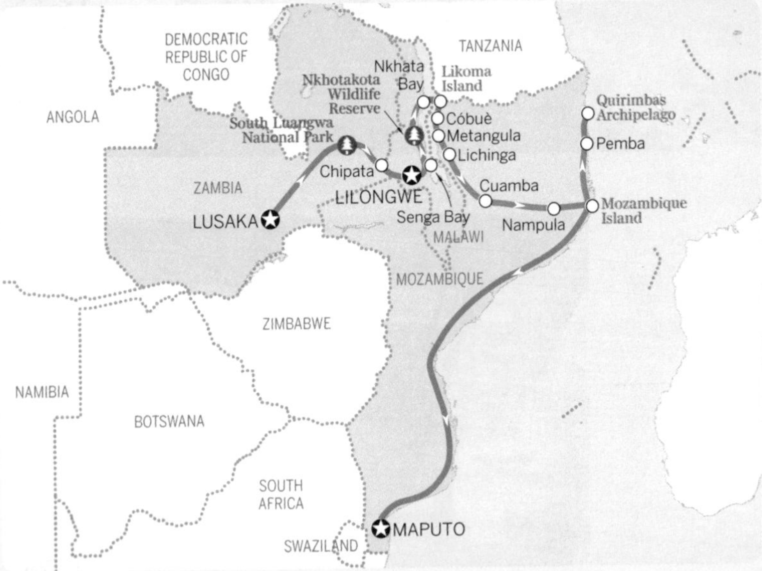
DEMOCRATIC REPUBLIC OF CONGO
TANZANIA
ANGOLA
Nkhata Bay
Likoma Island
Nkhotakota Wildlife Reserve
Quirimbas Archipelago
Cóbuè
Metangula
Lichinga
Pemba
South Luangwa National Park
Chipata
LILONGWE
ZAMBIA
Cuamba
LUSAKA
Senga Bay
Nampula
Mozambique Island
MALAWI
MOZAMBIQUE
ZIMBABWE
NAMIBIA
BOTSWANA
SOUTH AFRICA
MAPUTO
SWAZILAND

PHILIP LEE HARVEY/LONELY PLANET ©

JACOJVR/GETTY IMAGES ©

Top: Lionesses and cubs, South Luangwa National Park (p46), Zambia
Bottom: Low tide at Pemba (p151), Mozambique

6 WEEKS Zambia, Mozambique & Malawi Sampler

Exploring all three countries in a single trip makes for an excellent journey. Given the distances involved, it's best to plan out a general route in advance, and to allow a bit of extra time just in case.

Start in **Lusaka**, getting your bearings and becoming acquainted with this low-key capital, before taking a flight (or enduring a long bus journey) to **South Luangwa National Park**. This is one of Zambia's premier parks, with an incredible density of animals. Plan on at least three days here, taking in night drives, daytime wildlife drives and a walking safari or two before continuing on via the busy but agreeable town of **Chipata** to the Zambia–Malawi border, from where it's just over 100km to **Lilongwe**. Stop to grab some Malawian kwacha and have a good meal before continuing east to meet the mighty Lake Malawi in laid-back **Senga Bay**, which has some good beachfront lodges. While exploring the lake, don't miss a detour to **Nkhotakota Wildlife Reserve**, which offers an accessible experience of the bush with the chance of seeing elephants, antelope and even lions.

Nkhata Bay, with its chilled vibe and many water-based activities, is the perfect place to relax and take a diving course. From here, catch the ferry to **Likoma Island** to explore the lake's crystal waters, visit the historic cathedral and enjoy the serene island pace. From Likoma, it's straightforward to continue over to **Cóbuè**, a short sail away on Mozambique's wild northwestern lake coast. Once in Cóbuè, you could continue by pre-arranged charter boat to lovely Nkwichi Lodge, or make your way south towards **Metangula** and on to **Lichinga**. Spend a day or two in Lichinga, with its jacarandas and cool temperatures, before travelling to **Cuamba**, starting point of the classic 10-hour train ride east to **Nampula**. Nampula, in turn, is the jumping-off point for magical **Mozambique Island**, a Unesco World Heritage Site and Africa highlight, with its cobbled streets, colonial-era architecture and constant backdrop of turquoise seas. You'll likely want to linger at least two or three days here, perhaps longer, before heading north to **Pemba** and the **Quirimbas Archipelago**, or south towards **Maputo**.

3 WEEKS Beaches & Islands

Mozambique has some of the most enticing coastline on the continent. Combine exploration of its northern highlights with visits to Lake Malawi's alluring islands and inland beaches for an adventurous but relaxing itinerary.

The beach town of **Pemba**, in northern Mozambique, makes a good starting point. Spend a few days here getting acclimatised and enjoying the vibe. Don't miss nearby **Murrébuè**, with its kitesurfing, quiet, white sand and turquoise-hued ocean vistas. Next, set off for enchanting **Ibo Island**, a regional highlight, with its massive star-shaped fort, its silversmiths and its crumbling colonial-era mansions. After wandering and enjoying Ibo's pace, charter a dhow for several days to explore one of the other nearby islands in the **Quirimbas Archipelago**. Quirimbas Island is a good place to start: you can walk here from Ibo at low tide with a guide, and then return by boat. Once you manage to tear yourself away from the charms of the archipelago, turn south – the most straightforward route will take you via Pemba – to the crowded regional hub of **Nampula**. If you arrive early enough in Nampula, it's possible to avoid overnighting here, continuing the same day on to **Mozambique Island**. Plan at least several days exploring this Unesco World Heritage Site.

Once back on the mainland, you will need to pass through Nampula for an overnight, before catching the train west to **Cuamba**. The ride isn't anywhere near the coast, but it's scenic and offers fascinating glimpses of local life. After an overnight in Cuamba (where the train arrives late afternoon), continue into Malawi via the Mandimba border post, and then travel straight on to Lake Malawi. **Cape Maclear** makes a convenient first stop, with many options for snorkelling, kayaking and relaxing.

From Cape Maclear, the route turns north towards the scenic beachside outpost of **Nkhata Bay**, with its fine selection of lodges, kayaking, swimming and diving. From Nkhata Bay, it's possible to detour to beautiful **Chizumulu Island** and **Likoma Island**, where the highlights are the scenery, the local life, the relaxed pace and Likoma's historic cathedral. Once you've had your fill, travel south to **Blantyre** for a day or two getting acquainted with the city before heading home.

DOC STAR/500PX ©

JOHN SEATON CALLAHAN/GETTY IMAGES/FLICKR OPEN ©

Top: Lake Malawi at Cape Maclear (p196
Bottom: Old church on Mozambique Island (p142)
Mozambiqu

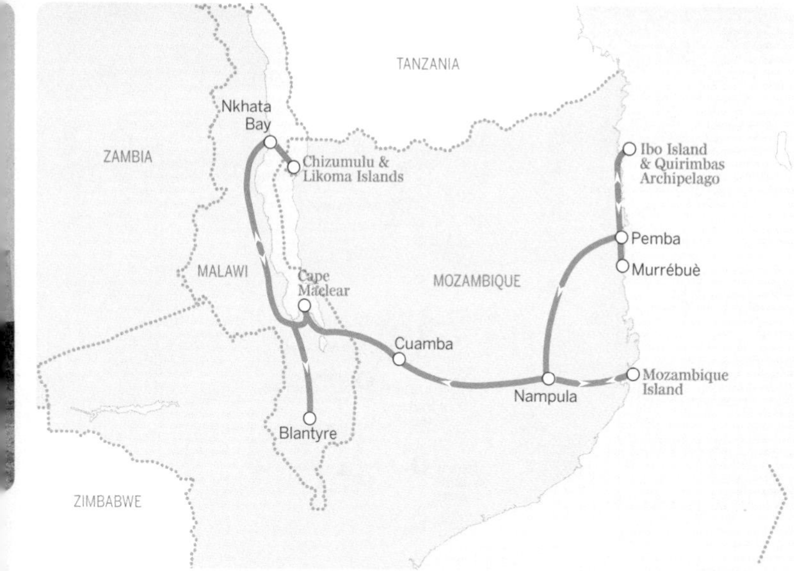

TANZANIA
ZAMBIA
MALAWI
MOZAMBIQUE
ZIMBABWE
Nkhata Bay
Chizumulu & Likoma Islands
Cape Maclear
Cuamba
Blantyre
Nampula
Mozambique Island
Ibo Island & Quirimbas Archipelago
Pemba
Murrébuè

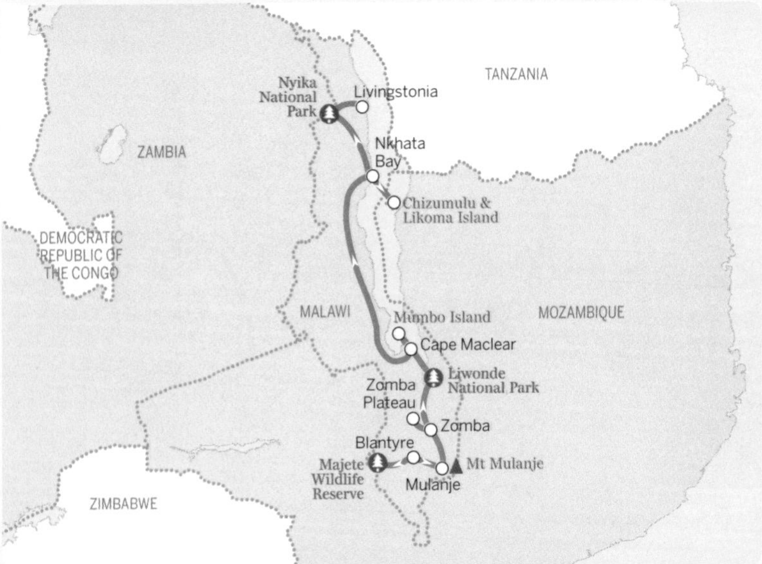
TANZANIA
Nyika National Park
Livingstonia
ZAMBIA
Nkhata Bay
Chizumulu & Likoma Island
DEMOCRATIC REPUBLIC OF THE CONGO
MALAWI
Mumbo Island
MOZAMBIQUE
Cape Maclear
Liwonde National Park
Zomba Plateau
Zomba
Blantyre
Majete Wildlife Reserve
Mt Mulanje
Mulanje
ZIMBABWE

JONATHAN GREGSON/LONELY PLANET ©

LMSPENCER/SHUTTERSTOCK ©

Top: Elephant, Liwonde National Park (p200), Malawi
Bottom: Nkhata Bay (p189), Malawi

4 WEEKS Malawi Odyssey

Whether you start in the north or south, this is the ultimate Malawi journey, taking in mountains, wilderness, historical riches and the lake with its beaches. It's best done in a month, to allow time for side trips, but in a pinch you could squeeze it into three weeks.

Fly into **Blantyre** and spend a day or so acclimatising, while getting to grips with local history at the Museum of Malawi and the Society of Malawi Library & Archive. If you have time, you could make an easy detour southwest to **Majete Wildlife Reserve** for a few days of pampered wildlife watching, before continuing to **Mulanje** for a multiday hike across **Mt Mulanje**, the country's highest peak. Recover by spending time in an old planter's house on one of southern Malawi's many tea estates, and head north to the colonial gem of **Zomba**. Here, enjoy a day or two of walking on the misty **Zomba Plateau**, perhaps finding time for a horseback trot to the plateau's viewpoints and waterfalls.

From Zomba, make your way north to nearby **Liwonde National Park**, its lovely scenery dominated by the wide, meandering Shire River. There are hippos and crocs aplenty, various antelope species and zebras, as well as canoe, riverboat and walking safaris on offer. When your binoculars are exhausted, head for the lake and the resort village of **Cape Maclear**. Budget at least three days here, with an overnight visit to **Mumbo Island** in Lake Malawi National Park and time kayaking and swimming with the brilliantly coloured fish.

Next, make your way up the lakeshore to **Nkhata Bay**, Malawi's other famous lakeside resort. As in Cape Maclear, you can snorkel, kayak, take a PADI course at the local dive school, and hang out at the beach bar. From Nkhata Bay you could detour to **Chizumulu Island** and **Likoma Island**, or continue north to lovely **Nyika National Park**, the country's largest, to explore wild, flower-carpeted grasslands reminiscent of the Yorkshire moors on foot or by mountain bike. Finally, it's time to plunge into history at **Livingstonia**, a quiet hilltop town that provides a glimpse of Malawi's colonial-era past. From Livingstonia, continue north into Tanzania (and from there to Zambia), or retrace your steps south, perhaps continuing to Mozambique or Zambia.

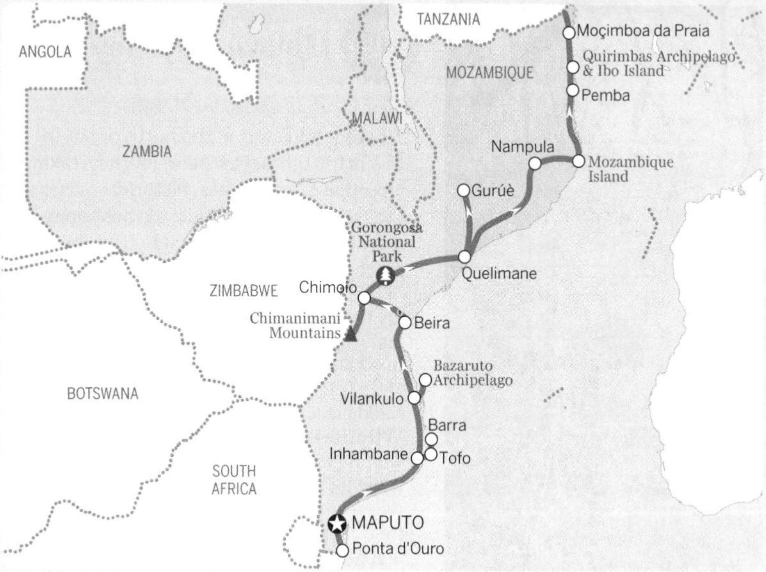

2 MONTHS

Mozambique Grand Tour

To explore Mozambique from south to north (north to south works just as well) in a grand overland tour, allow at least two months. With more limited time, it's easy enough to choose sections from the following itinerary, perhaps taking a flight or two to break up the longer stretches.

Note that as of late 2016, political skirmishes in central Mozambique have made overland travel difficult in some areas. Check for updates on government travel websites.

Starting in the far south, spend time enjoying the wonderful beach at **Ponta d'Ouro** before continuing on to the lively, culture-packed capital of **Maputo**. Here, the many museums, sidewalk cafes, restaurants and craft shops will keep you busy for at least several days.

Continue north to **Inhambane**, with its flamingos, dhows and wonderful nearby beaches, including **Tofo** and **Barra**. Further north, **Vilankulo** is an amenable spot and also the springboard to the **Bazaruto Archipelago**, with its diving and upmarket lodges.

From Vilankulo, continue north to **Beira**, spending a day or two in this old port city before heading west to **Chimoio**, the best base for organising hiking in the **Chimanimani Mountains**. Allow four days or more, including transport, for the excursion. Once back in Chimoio, make your way northeast to lovely **Gorongosa National Park**. For all stops in this part of central Mozambique, get an update on the security situation before setting your plans.

The route continues north via **Quelimane**, with its nearby beaches and coconut plantations, and bustling, crowded **Nampula** to **Mozambique Island** – a gem of a place, where it's easy to spend at least two or three days taking in the sights. A recommended diversion en route is to scenic, mountainous **Gurúè**, with its cool climate, jacarandas, tea plantations and hiking.

Continue north to **Pemba** and the nearby beaches before travelling to the **Quirimbas Archipelago**. All the islands are lovely, with **Ibo** a highlight. Sail back to the mainland, and continue north to **Moçimboa da Praia** – a pleasant stop for a day or three – and on into Tanzania.

Countries at a Glance

Zambia, Mozambique and Malawi combine to make an alluringly diverse destination. With at least a month, you could sample all three countries in one trip. But getting around takes time, and it's better to focus on getting to know one or two areas in depth rather than trying to take in too much on one visit.

For wildlife, Zambia tops the list, with vast tracts of animal-filled bush. Majestic Victoria Falls is another major draw, and one of the continent's highlights. For culture, Malawi is one of the most accessible destinations. It's also a relatively easy introduction to Southern Africa for first-time visitors. Mozambique offers outstanding beaches, idyllic islands and – in the north – the chance for real adventure travel.

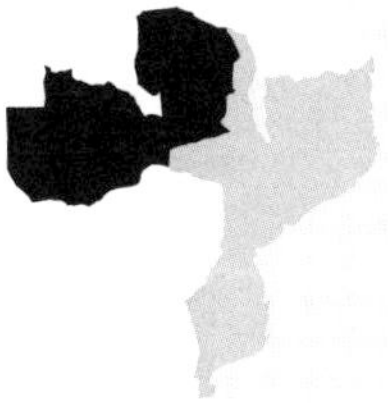

Zambia

Safaris
Adventure
Waterfalls

Wildlife

A wealth of animals and a network of bush camps make Zambia one of Southern Africa's most alluring wildlife-watching destinations. South Luangwa National Park is the highlight, but there are many more, including Kafue and Lower Zambezi National Parks.

Remote Destinations

Outside Lusaka almost everywhere in Zambia is bush. While the country can be difficult to get around, this remoteness is one of Zambia's main draws. Once you're out in the wild, the logistical hassles fade away as the raw beauty of Zambia's landscapes takes over.

Victoria Falls

The world's largest waterfall assaults the senses: get drenched by the spray, fill your ears with its roar and feast your eyes on its magnificence. Whether you raft the rapids, cruise the Zambezi or simply stand awestruck on the sidelines, Victoria Falls is one of Africa's unforgettable destinations.

p34

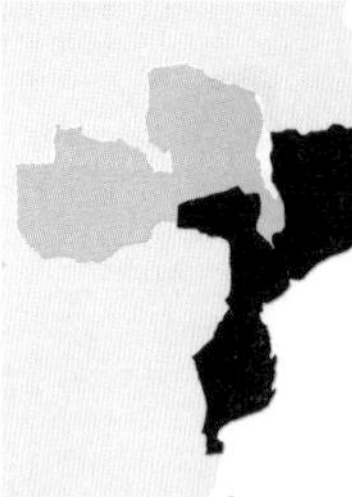

Mozambique

Beaches
Culture & History
Adventure

Islands & Archipelagos

From the pounding surf and windswept dunes of Ponta d'Ouro to the turquoise waters and powdery white sand of the Quirimbas Archipelago, Mozambique offers some of the continent's best beaches. Fringing the coastline are alluring archipelagos and magical islands, with Mozambique Island at the top of the list.

Local Culture & History

After being suppressed by war, Mozambique's colourful cultures have come back with full force. Sample this vibrancy in Maputo, with its array of dance, theatre and other cultural offerings. Follow history's footsteps at Mozambique Island and Ibo Island.

Frontier Travel

Northern Mozambique is one of the continent's last adventure frontiers. Sail on a dhow to magical islands, relax on pristine beaches or track wildlife in the interior. Adventure is everywhere.

p101

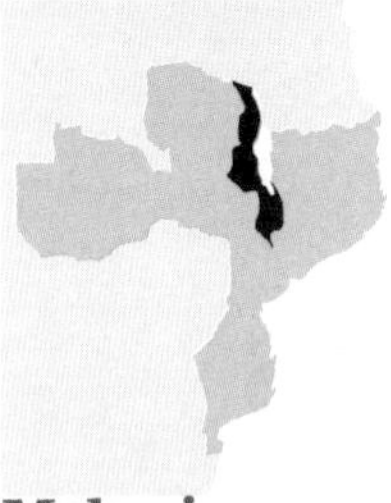

Malawi

Nature
Beaches
Landscapes

Wildlife

With three major reserves (Majete, Liwonde and Nkhotakota) managed by the excellent African Parks, Malawi now has lions, as well as representatives of the rest of the 'Big Five'. Add to this some fine safari lodges and the country merits packing your binoculars.

Lakeshore Beaches

Lake Malawi offers relaxing beaches and mountain-backed panoramas. Cape Maclear – a legendary backpacker hang-out – is one of the most popular spots to appreciate the lake. Nkhata Bay is another, and there are many more.

Plateaus, Waterfalls & Tea Plantations

From the forests and valleys of the Viphya Plateau to the wildflowers and grasslands of the Nyika Plateau and the waterfall-riven slopes of the Zomba Plateau and Livingstonia, Malawi's landscapes are stunning. In the far south, make time for the granite massif and emerald-green tea plantations in the Mulanje area.

p174

On the Road

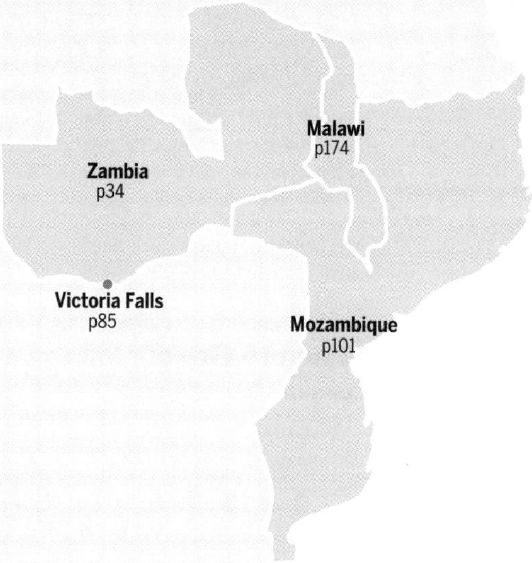

Zambia

POP 15.5 MILLION

Includes ➡

Best Places to Sleep

- Chizombo (p48)
- Chiawa Camp (p55)
- Kapishya Hot Springs Lodge (p67)
- Ndole Bay Lodge (p70)
- Mukambi Plains Camp (p59)

Best Places to Eat

- Sugarbush Cafe (p39)
- Courtyard Café (p72)
- Luangwa Bridge Camp (p46)
- Thorn Tree Guesthouse (p68)

Why Go?

The rewards of travelling in Zambia are those of exploring remote, mesmerising wilderness as full of an astonishing diversity of wildlife as any part of Southern Africa. Adventures undertaken here will lead you deep into the bush where animals, both predators and prey, wander through unfenced camps, where night-time means swapping stories around the fire and where the human footprint is nowhere to be seen. Where one day you can canoe down a wide, placid river and the next raft through the raging rapids near world-famous Victoria Falls.

Though landlocked, three great rivers – the Kafue, the Luangwa and the Zambezi – flow through Zambia, defining both its geography and the rhythms of life for many of its people. For the independent traveller, however, Zambia is a logistical challenge, because of its sheer size, dilapidated road network and upmarket facilities. For those who do venture here, the relative lack of crowds means an even more satisfying journey.

When to Go

Lusaka

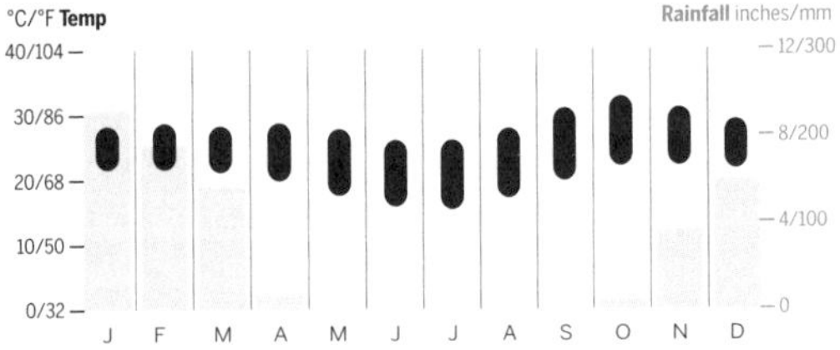

Late May–early Oct Dry season, with prime wildlife viewing; tourist high season.

Jun–Aug Dry, cooler temperatures and sometimes frosty nights.

Nov–Apr Blooming landscapes during the rainy ('emerald') season. Wildebeest and bat migration.

LUSAKA

All roads lead to Lusaka, the geographic, commercial and metaphorical heart of Zambia. However, the nation's capital and largest urban zone, with its mishmash of dusty tree-lined streets, bustling African markets, Soviet-looking high-rise blocks and modern commerce, doesn't easily justify exploration by the casual visitor. There are no real attractions, grand museums to drool over or historical treasures to unearth. Nonetheless, for some, the city's genuine African feel, cosmopolitan populace and quality restaurants and accommodation are reason enough to spend a night or two. If you feel like letting loose, expat bars and the home-grown nightclub scene will see you through to the wee hours.

Sights

Lusaka National Park NATIONAL PARK
(☎0955 472433; adult/child US$30/15) The idea of seeing a rhino in the wild just 15km from the capital seems absurd, but this new national park (opened in 2015) allows you to do just that. Set over 46 sq km, it's home to eland, zebra, giraffe and wildebeest, among others. But it's the white rhino that brings people here. While you'll be able to tick it off from the list of Big Five, most likely you'll see them in their holding pen, so it can feel more like a zoo than national park.

Lilayi Elephant Nursery WILDLIFE RESERVE
(☎0211-840435; www.lilayi.com; adult/child/under 12yr ZMW50/20/free; ⏲11.30am-1pm) On the southern outskirts of town is this elephant nursery set up by Game Rangers International (a Zambian conservationist NGO), which works with rescuing and rehabilitating orphaned elephants in Kafue National Park. You can see them being fed from 11am to 1.30pm daily; Monday is free entry. You can also do wildlife drives on its 650-hectare property. There's a lovely restaurant and lodge where, if you're staying, you can get a behind-the-scenes look at the elephants.

Presidential Burial Site National Monument MAUSOLEUM
(Embassy Park; adult/child US$15/7; ⏲8.30am-4.30pm) This mausoleum is where the late Zambian presidents Levy Patrick Mwanawasa (1948–2008), Frederick Chiluba (1943–2011) and Michael Sata (1937–2014) are buried. Remarkably both Mwanawasa and Sata died while in office; the latter's tomb will be completed in 2018. It's an interesting enough sight, but the US$15 entry is a bit steep, though does include a guided tour.

Henry Tayali Visual Arts Centre GALLERY
(www.henrytayaliartgallery.wordpress.com; Showgrounds, Lion Lane; ⏲9am-5pm Mon-Fri, to 4pm Sat & Sun) A lovely space exhibiting quality contemporary works by local artists, and all are for sale.

Namwandwe Gallery GALLERY
(☎0976 608538, 0977 549802; www.namwandwe.com; Leopards Hill Rd; by donation; ⏲8am-6pm) Featuring the impressive private collection of businessman and patron of the arts John Kapotwe, Namwandwe is hands-down the best in the country for contemporary Zambian art. The gallery space is within his private home (an attraction in itself) and features paintings, sculptures, masks and fabrics by both established and up-and-coming artists. It's located 15km southeast of the city centre.

Lusaka National Museum MUSEUM
(Nasser Rd; adult/child US$5/3; ⏲9am-4.30pm) This big square box of a building resembling a Soviet-era Moscow ministry has upstairs galleries displaying exhibits on urban culture and Zambian history as well cultural, ethnographic and archaeological displays. Contemporary Zambian paintings and sculpture are shown downstairs.

Lusaka City Market MARKET
(Lumumba Rd; ⏲7am-5pm) Fronted by the chaotic and congested eponymously named bus station, as well as a veritable Maginot Line of sidewalk vendors, reaching the entrance to the Lusaka City Market is an achievement in and of itself. Unfortunately, while large, lively and packed to the rafters, the clothing and housewares sold in the warren of stalls aren't of much interest to the average traveller.

Sleeping

★ **Natwange Backpackers** HOSTEL $
(☎0966 303816, 0977 886240; www.natwangebackpackers.com; 6808 Kapuka Rd; dm/s/d incl breakfast with shared bathroom US$12/30/40;) In quiet residential street, this lovely and secure home offers a relaxed atmosphere for independent travellers. Rooms are clean, though can be a little cramped, and all share bathrooms. It has plenty of lawn with fruit trees and a nice little pool and gym. There are several lounge areas to

Zambia Highlights

1 South Luangwa National Park (p46) Bushwalking like a detective following the tracks of wild animals.

2 Zambezi River (p53) Paddling a canoe down this mighty river past pods of hippos, menacing-looking crocs and thirsty elephants.

3 Kafue National Park (p58) Spotting leopards in this behemoth wilderness area where wildlife dreams unfold amid stunning landscapes.

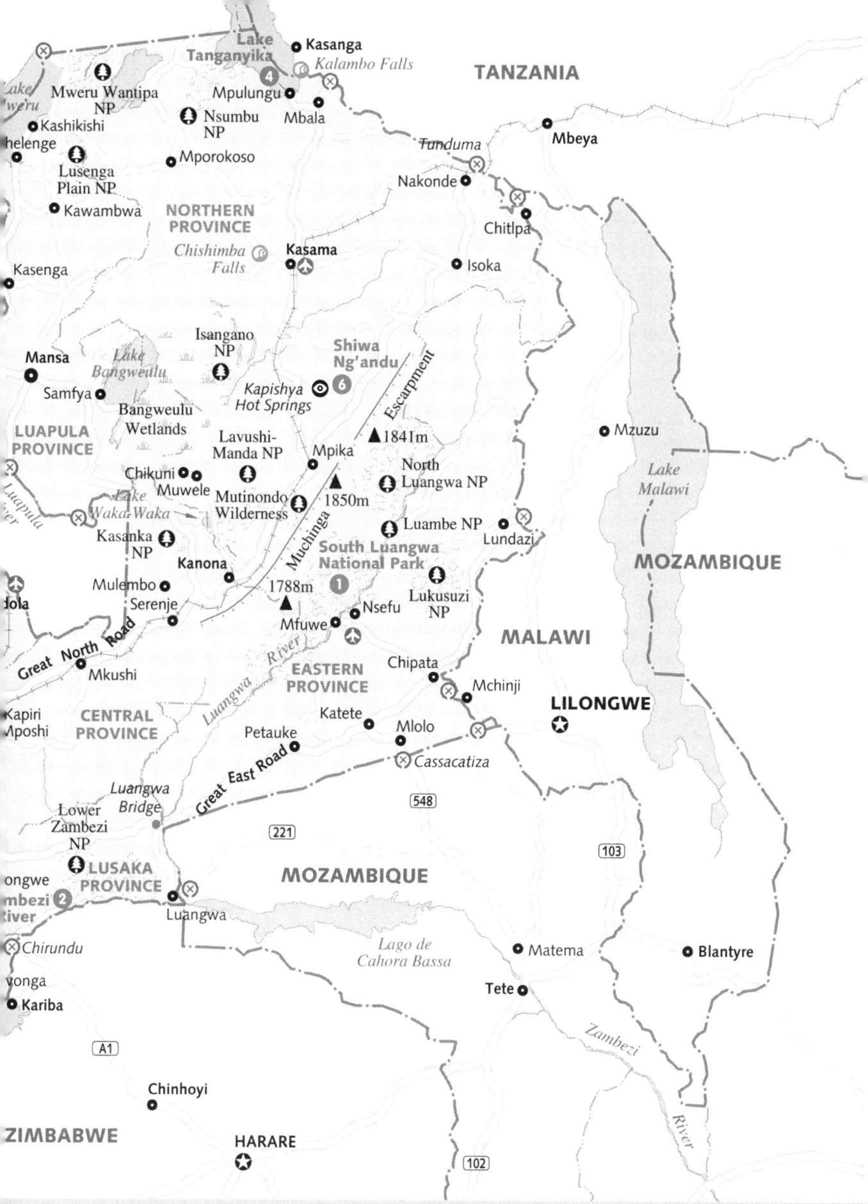

4 Lake Tanganyika (p69) Lazing on white sandy beaches and snorkelling with tropical fish on this beautiful lake in the country's far north.

5 Liuwa Plain National Park (p62) Witnessing the wildebeest migration unfold at Zambia's 'mini Serengeti'.

6 Shiwa Ng'andu (p67) Taking a step back in time and a leap to another continent at a remarkably well-preserved English manor estate.

hang out, and a fully equipped kitchen for self-caterers.

Tanuger Travels HOSTEL $
(☎0972 662588; www.tanuger.com; cnr Sibweni & Chigwilizano Rds; dm US$15, r US$60, with shared bathroom US$40;) Set up by a bunch of local female friends, this funky and vibrant hostel offers a homely, social and relaxed atmosphere. There's plenty of artwork about, including graffiti-splashed walls, plus a swimming pool, firepit, giant chess board and free pool table. Its members-only bar is one of the liveliest in town, and a great place to meet travellers and locals alike.

Lusaka Backpackers HOSTEL $
(☎0977 805483; www.lusakabackpackers.com; 161 Mulombwa Cl; 4-/8-bed dm US$12/15, r US$55, with shared bathroom US$40; @) One of the more established and respected backpackers in Lusaka, this place is deservedly popular with those on a budget. The centrepiece of activity is the patio area out front with a small pool and a tiki bar, which can get lively and loud, especially on weekends. Nearby is also its Wanderers Lodge, which offers cheaper rooms and camping.

Wanderers Lodge HOSTEL $
(☎0971 763508; www.wandererslusaka.com; 848 Lagos Rd, Rhodes Park; camping US$5, dm/s/d US$10/25/30;) The sister lodge to the popular Lusaka Backpackers, this centrally located lodge offers some of cheapest rooms in town, along with camping facilities.

Eureka Camping Park CAMPGROUND, CHALET $
(☎0977 803051, 0966 822448; www.eurekacamp.com; Kafue Rd; camping US$14, dm US$20, r from US$60, with shared bathroom from US$40;) The grassy campsite here, shaded by big trees, is popular with overlanding groups. The security is good, while the swimming pool and bar (which sells burgers and breakfasts) are nice touches. There are braai facilities for cooking and charcoal for sale. Chalets are cool and comfortable and modelled on the traditional thatch hut. It's about 12km south of the city centre.

Kilimanjaro Country Lodge LODGE $$
(☎0955 611779, 0975 838461; www.kilimanjarozambia.com; Leopards Hill Rd; s/d incl breakfast US$85/100, mains ZMW50-100; ⌚cafe 7am-8pm;) A good out-of-town option – especially for groups and families – around 7.5km east of the city centre, Kilimanjaro consists of several well-kept, low-slung buildings on a manicured lawn. The 11 rooms are spacious and simply furnished and management is responsive to any requests. A perk is free laundry for guests staying more than a night.

Bongwe Barn GUESTHOUSE $$
(☎0973 589419; www.bongwesafaris.com/guesthouse.html; 609 Zambezi Rd, Roma; r US$55-75;) If you've outgrown the whole backpacker scene, but still want something informal and homely – and social, if inclined – then Bongwe's your place. Run by UK expat Stacey, the staff here are exceptionally friendly and helpful, and rooms (some of which share bathrooms) are spotless and spacious. There's a stocked kitchen, couches in the living room and a sparkling pool to relax by.

Pioneer Camp CAMPGROUND, CHALET $$
(☎0966 432700; www.pioneercampzambia.com; Palabana Rd, off Great East Rd; camping US$10, chalet with shared/private bathroom from US$88/132;) An isolated 25-acre camp, surrounded by bird-rich woodland, Pioneer is the accommodation of choice for many expats living outside Lusaka, especially those with an early flight out of the country. Most of the widely dispersed and simply furnished thatch-roofed chalets have flagstone floors, small verandas and large bathrooms. The well-kept facilities for campers are up the front next to the small plunge pool.

★**Latitude 15 Degrees** BOUTIQUE HOTEL $$$
(☎0211-268802; http://15.latitudehotels.com; Leopards Lane, Kabulonga; s/d incl breakfast US$244/297;) Lusaka's best accommodation is this fashionable hotel with an architecturally designed building that resembles a chic contemporary gallery. Its rooms are plush with king-sized beds, standalone tubs, coffee makers, fast wi-fi, cable TV and plenty of art decorating its walls. Guests also have access to the 'Other Side' executive members-only lounge. Its **restaurant** (mains ZMW140-180; ⌚7-10am, noon-3pm & 6-9.30pm) is also very popular. It's just off Leopards Hill Rd.

Wayside Bed & Breakfast GUESTHOUSE $$$
(☎0211-273439; www.wayside-guesthouse.com; 39 Makeni Rd, Makeni; s/d incl breakfast US$80/120;) This upmarket and peaceful guesthouse is one of the best in Lusaka, with only a handful of snug en-suite rooms. It used to be a farm and today the sizeable grounds are devoted to the owners' love

of gardening, and really are magnificent. Three rooms in a separate cottage have air-conditioning and there's a lounge with TV and comfortable couches.

Southern Sun Ridgeway HOTEL $$$
(0211-251666; www.southernsun.com; cnr Church Rd & Independence Ave; s/d incl breakfast US$169/204;) Deservedly popular with in-the-know expats and a coterie of international business and government types, the Southern Sun is a no-brainer for those seeking an affordable low-key, comfortable city-centre option. Rooms are tastefully done in muted tones. A quality restaurant, pub, small gym, large outdoor pool area and free wi-fi round out the offerings.

Eating

★**Deli** CAFE, BAKERY $
(Lunzua Rd, Rhodes Park; mains from ZMW25, coffee ZMW14; 7am-4pm Mon-Fri, 8.30am-12.30pm Sat;) Boasting the best barista in Lusaka (the winner of an international competition) as well as an enviable garden setting, the Deli is a good place to plant yourself for a few hours. The sophisticated kitchen turns out all-day breakfasts like eggs and French toast, speciality sandwiches like Asian pork meatball and classics like pastrami, wood-fired pizzas and homemade ice cream.

Gigibontà GELATERIA $
(Foxdale Court, Zambezi Rd; from ZMW16) Around the back of Foxdale Court shopping centre, this small outlet makes delicious homemade gelato using fresh ingredients, with 26 flavours to choose from. Proceeds go towards funding local community projects.

Zambean Coffee CAFE $
(6 Nyati Close, Rhodes Park; coffee/sandwiches from ZMW17/70; 8.30am-4pm Mon-Fri, to 1pm Sat;) Run by a couple of friendly Zimbabwean expats, this lovely little garden cafe is a great spot to grab a well-made Zambian coffee, a quality breakfast and gourmet sandwiches on home-baked breads. They also have a good list of South African wines.

Lusaka Garden Club CAFE $
(off Nangwenya Rd, Showgrounds; coffee ZMW12, mains ZMW50; 8am-5pm Mon-Sat) A lovely little garden oasis within the Showgrounds that's a nice to spot to relax with a filter coffee, an Aussie lamington, sandwich, or heartier meat and *nshima* dishes.

★**Sugarbush Cafe** INTERNATIONAL, ORGANIC $$
(0967 648761; www.facebook.com/sugarbushcafezam; Leopards Hill Rd, Sugarbush Farm; breakfast ZMW40-75, mains ZMW75-120; 8am-5pm Tue-Sat, 8.30am-4.30pm Sun;) This picture-postcard idyllic cafe is worth every kwacha of the journey it takes to get here. Chill out for an afternoon at one of the picnic tables munching on homemade bread and pastries, salads made with organic homegrown vegetables, and expertly prepared sandwiches, pasta and meat dishes, as well as a glass of wine, or Pimms by the jug.

Casa Portico ITALIAN $$
(0211-250111; 27 Ngumbo Rd, Longacres; mains from ZMW85; 7am-10pm Mon-Thu, to midnight Fri & Sat, to 8pm Sun) Italian owned and operated, this garden restaurant offers as authentic cuisine as you'll get outside Italy. There's homemade pastas (go the tagliatelle ragu), home-baked panini, and imported Italian cheeses and meats. It's a good spot, too, for a glass of Prosecco or well-made Negroni cocktails.

Marlin STEAK $$
(0211-252206; Los Angeles Blvd, Longacres Roundabout; mains ZMW85-110; noon-2.30pm & 7-10pm Mon & Wed-Sat, noon-2.30pm Tue) Housed in the colonial-era Lusaka Club with decor that probably hasn't been touched since the '60s, this wood-panelled favourite serves some of the best steaks in Lusaka. While it does serve gargantuan portions of every cut of meat under the sun, most guests come for the aged fillet with mushroom or pepper sauce. Reservations are strongly recommended.

Drinking & Nightlife

★**Bongwe Pub & Grill** PUB
(www.facebook.com/bongwebarn; 609 Zambezi Rd, Roma; 2pm-late) A favourite watering hole for many locals, expats and tourists (and basically anyone who likes a drink) is this tropical dive bar, set in an open-air shack centred around a palm tree. There's a pool table, sports on the TV and always someone around for a chat. On Fridays it's usually pumping and regularly has local bands and DJs.

Sky Bar BAR
(www.facebook.com/roma.sky.bar.lusaka; Foxdale Court, Zambezi Rd; 2pm-midnight) A decent rooftop bar atop of Foxdale Court shopping centre, Sky Bar attracts a young crowd

Lusaka

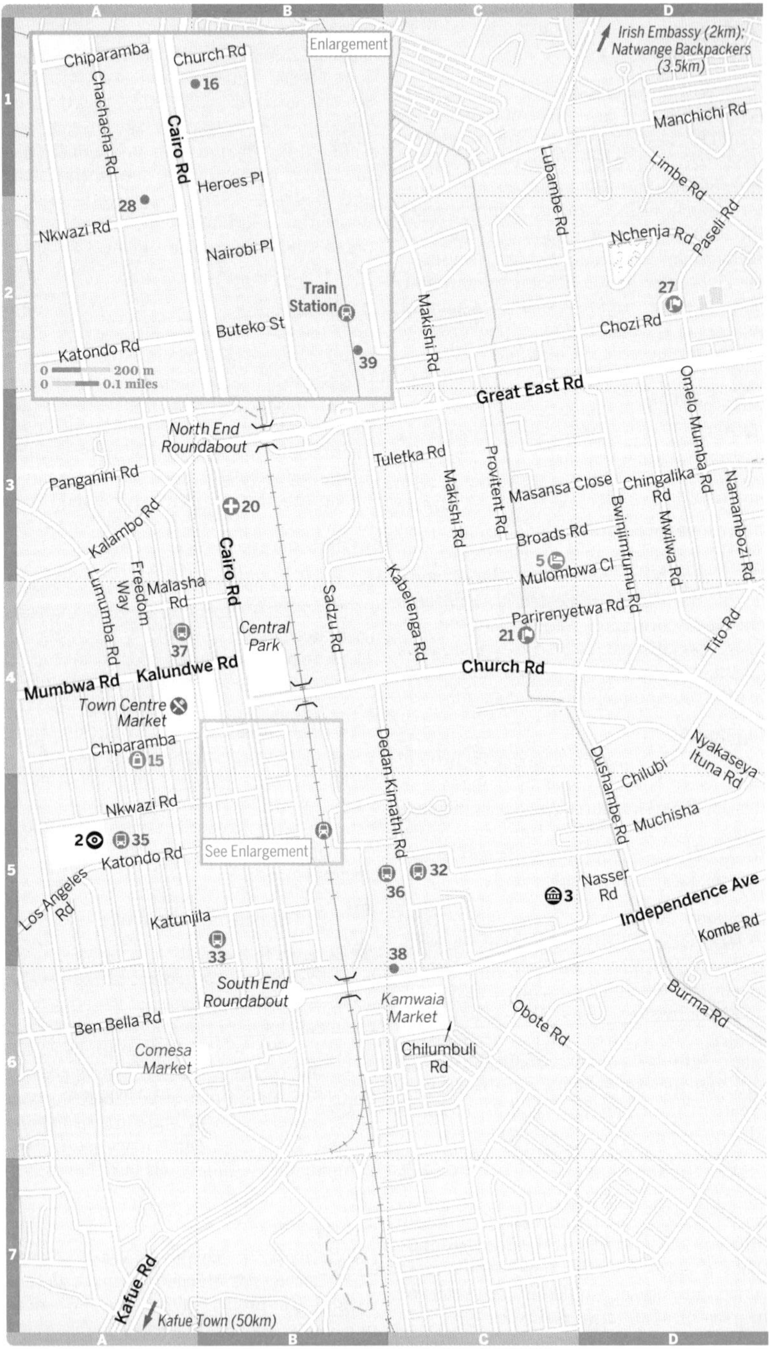

A
B
C
D
1
2
3
4
5
6
7
Enlargement
Chiparamba
Church Rd
16
Chachacha Rd
Cairo Rd
Heroes Pl
28
Nkwazi Rd
Nairobi Pl
Train Station
Buteko St
Katondo Rd
39
0 200 m
0 0.1 miles
Irish Embassy (2km); Natwange Backpackers (3.5km)
Manchichi Rd
Lubambe Rd
Limbe Rd
Nchenja Rd
Paseli Rd
27
Chozi Rd
Makishi Rd
Omelo Mumba Rd
Great East Rd
North End Roundabout
Tuletka Rd
Panganini Rd
Provitent Rd
Masansa Close
Chingalika Rd
Namambozi Rd
20
Makishi Rd
Bwinjimfumu Rd
Kalambo Rd
Broads Rd
Mwilwa Rd
Cairo Rd
5
Mulombwa Cl
Freedom Way
Malasha Rd
Sadzu Rd
Kabelenga Rd
Lumumba Rd
Central Park
Parirenyetwa Rd
21
Tito Rd
37
Mumbwa Rd
Kalundwe Rd
Church Rd
Town Centre Market
Chiparamba
15
Dedan Kimathi Rd
Dushambe Rd
Chilubi
Nyakaseya Ituna Rd
Nkwazi Rd
Muchisha
2
35
See Enlargement
Katondo Rd
32
Los Angeles Rd
36
Nasser Rd
3
Independence Ave
Katunjila
33
Kombe Rd
38
South End Roundabout
Kamwaia Market
Obote Rd
Burma Rd
Ben Bella Rd
Chilumbuli Rd
Comesa Market
Kafue Rd
Kafue Town (50km)

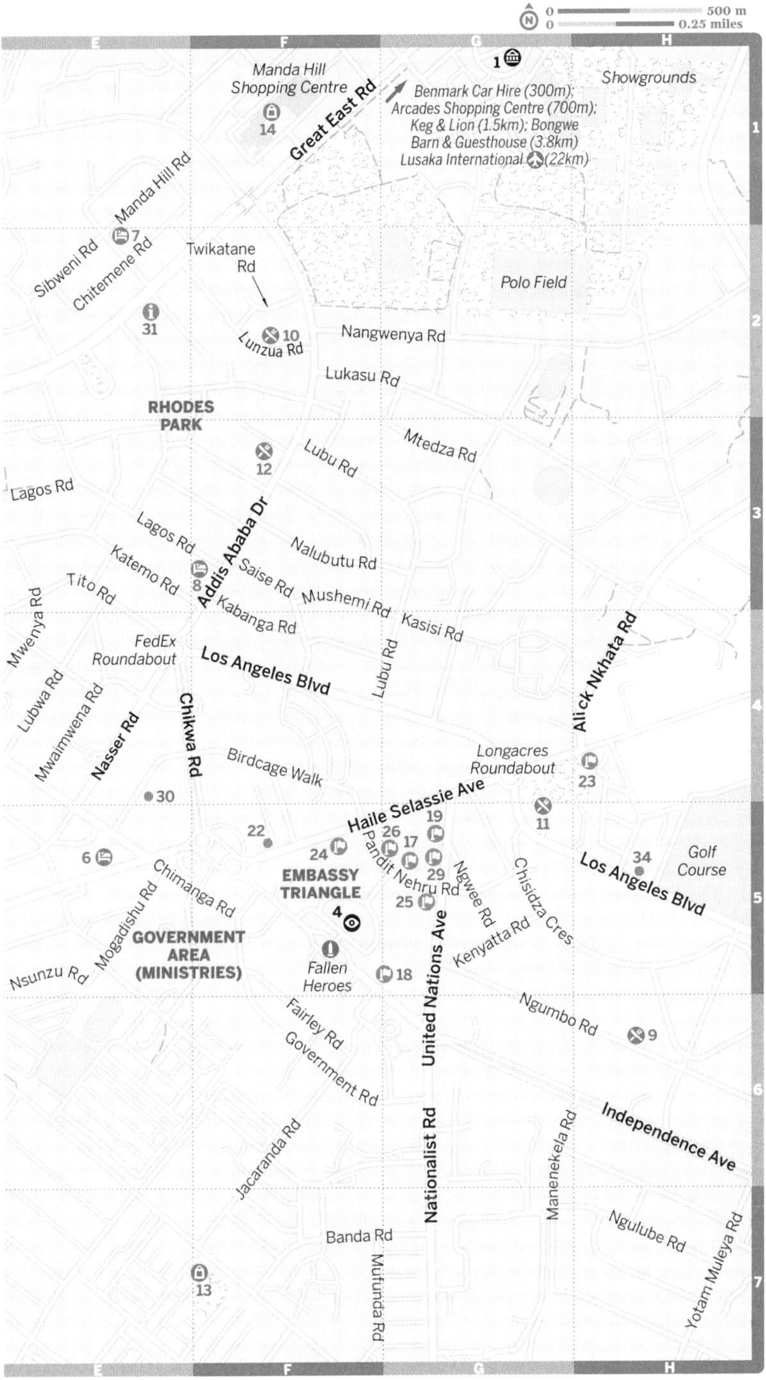
0 500 m
0 0.25 miles
Manda Hill Shopping Centre
Great East Rd
Benmark Car Hire (300m); Arcades Shopping Centre (700m); Keg & Lion (1.5km); Bongwe Barn & Guesthouse (3.8km) Lusaka International (22km)
Showgrounds
Manda Hill Rd
Sibweni Rd
Chitemene Rd
Twikatane Rd
Polo Field
Lunzua Rd
Nangwenya Rd
Lukasu Rd
RHODES PARK
Mtedza Rd
Lubu Rd
Lagos Rd
Addis Ababa Dr
Nalubutu Rd
Katemo Rd
Saise Rd
Mushemi Rd
Tito Rd
Kabanga Rd
Kasisi Rd
Mwenya Rd
FedEx Roundabout
Los Angeles Blvd
Lubu Rd
Alick Nkhata Rd
Lubwa Rd
Mwaimwena Rd
Nasser Rd
Chikwa Rd
Birdcage Walk
Longacres Roundabout
Haile Selassie Ave
Pandit Nehru Rd
EMBASSY TRIANGLE
Ngwee Rd
Chisidza Cres
Golf Course
Chimanga Rd
Mogadishu Rd
GOVERNMENT AREA (MINISTRIES)
Nsunzu Rd
Fallen Heroes
Kenyatta Rd
United Nations Ave
Ngumbo Rd
Fairley Rd
Government Rd
Independence Ave
Jacaranda Rd
Nationalist Rd
Manenekela Rd
Ngulube Rd
Banda Rd
Mufunda Rd
Yotam Muleya Rd
E
F
G
H
1
2
3
4
5
6
7
1
4
6
7
8
9
10
11
12
13
14
17
18
19
22
23
24
25
26
29
30
31
34

Lusaka

Sights
- 1 Henry Tayali Visual Arts Centre G1
- 2 Lusaka City Market A5
- 3 Lusaka National Museum C5
- 4 Presidential Burial Site National Monument F5

Sleeping
- 5 Lusaka Backpackers C3
- 6 Southern Sun Ridgeway E5
- 7 Tanuger Travels E2
- 8 Wanderers Lodge F3

Eating
- 9 Casa Portico H6
- 10 Deli F2
- Lusaka Garden Club ..... (see 1)
- 11 Marlin G5
- 12 Zambean Coffee F3

Shopping
- Bookworld ..... (see 14)
- 13 Kabwata Cultural Village F7
- 14 Manda Hill Shopping Centre F1
- 15 Salaula Clothing Market A4

Information
- 16 Bimm Travel Agency B1
- 17 Botswanan High Commission G5
- 18 British High Commission G5
- 19 Canadian High Commission G5
- 20 Corpmed B3
- 21 Democratic Rebublic of Congo Embassy C4
- 22 Department of Immigration F5
- 23 Dutch Embassy H4
- Finland Embassy ..... (see 23)
- 24 German Embassy F5
- 25 Kenyan High Commission G5
- 26 Malawian High Commission G5
- 27 Mozambican Embassy D2
- River Safari Company ..... (see 5)
- 28 Steve Blagus Travel A2
- Swedish Embassy ..... (see 23)
- 29 Tanzanian High Commission G5
- 30 Voyagers E4
- 31 Zambia Tourism Agency E2
- Zimbabwean High Commission ..... (see 23)

Transport
- 32 Buses for Zimbabwe C5
- 33 City Bus Station B5
- 34 Corporate Air H5
- CR Holdings ..... (see 36)
- Falcon ..... (see 36)
- Insight ..... (see 36)
- Jonda Bus Tours ..... (see 36)
- Juldan ..... (see 36)
- KOBS Coach Service ..... (see 36)
- 35 Lusaka City Market Bus Station A5
- 36 Lusaka Inter-City Bus Station C5
- Mazhandu Family Bus Services ..... (see 36)
- 37 Millennium Bus Station A4
- Mwayera Buses ..... (see 32)
- Power Tools ..... (see 36)
- Shalom Bus ..... (see 36)
- Taqwa ..... (see 36)
- 38 Tazara House C6
- 39 Train Station B2
- Zambia-Botswana Express ..... (see 36)
- Zupco ..... (see 32)

for DJs spinning house, hip hop and R&B tracks.

Keg & Lion SPORTS BAR
(☎0211-377824; East Gate Mall, Great East Rd; ⏲11am-late) Despite its uninspired shopping mall location, this South African chain pub has three beers on tap, does excellent pub food and has all the sports you need on the TV.

Shopping

Salaula Clothing Market CLOTHING
(Lumumba Rd; ⏲9am-6pm) For those with a love of secondhand clothes shopping, absolutely don't miss this market in downtown Lusaka. Known locally as the *salaula* trade (a local word meaning 'to pick through a pile'), it has block after block of stalls selling Western charity clothing all divided into heaped piles of specific items. From designer labels to vintage clothing, it's all here.

Kabwata Cultural Village ARTS & CRAFTS
(Burma Rd; ⏲7am-6pm) A popular shopping stop for tourists, this open-air market comprises thatch-roofed huts and stalls selling carvings, baskets, masks, drums, fabrics and more. Prices are cheap because you can buy directly from the workers who live here. There's usually cultural performances (ZMW30) held on weekends around 2pm. It's southeast of the city centre.

Sunday Market MARKET
(Arcades Shopping Centre, Great East Rd; ⏲9am-6pm Sun) This weekly market, held in the car park at the Arcades Shopping Centre, features Lusaka's best range of handicrafts, especially wood carvings, curios made from malachite and African prints. Bargaining

is expected, though it's a relaxed, low-pressure affair.

Bookworld BOOKS
(www.bookworldzambia.com; Manda Hill Shopping Centre, Great East Rd; 9am-6pm) Stocks a good selection of Zambia-specific nonfiction and cultural books, as well as fiction, international magazines and newspapers.

Manda Hill Shopping Centre SHOPPING CENTRE
(Great East Rd) The swish Manda Hill Shopping Centre has all the usual retail, restaurants and banks you get in shopping malls.

Information

IMMIGRATION

Department of Immigration (0211-252622; www.zambiaimmigration.gov.zm; Kent Building, Haile Selassie Rd)

INTERNET ACCESS

I-Zone Internet (Arcades Shopping Centre, Great East Rd; 9am-9pm) Reliable, fast internet access, plus printing facilities.

MEDICAL SERVICES

Corpmed (0211-222612; Cairo Rd; 24hr) Located behind Barclays Bank. Has a doctor on duty 24 hours and is probably the city's best-equipped facility. Also runs its own ambulance service.

Specialty Emergency Services (737; www.ses-zambia.com) For evacuations. Has bases in Lusaka, Livingstone and Kitwe but operates throughout the country. Also has ambulances and in-patient care.

MONEY

Banks (Barclays and others) and bureaux de change are located in Arcades, Levy Junction and Mana Hill shopping centres, along Cairo Rd and elsewhere in Lusaka, such as on Haile Selassie Ave.

SAFE TRAVEL

Like most African cities, pickpockets take advantage of crowds, so be alert in the markets and bus stations and along the busy streets immediately west of Cairo Rd. Take care of your mobile phone and bring along only the cash you need in your pockets. Soweto Market, only a few blocks from the city markets on Lumumba Rd, in particular is notorious for robbery and pickpockets (if in a car, wind windows up and lock doors); there is a township nearby with a bad reputation. At night, most streets are dark and often empty, so even if you're on a tight budget, take a taxi.

The suburb of Rhodes Park, between Cairo Rd and Embassy Triangle, which is quite upmarket during the week, takes on a sleazy twist at weekends when prostitutes display their wares at night, especially along Mwilwa Rd.

TOURIST INFORMATION & TRAVEL AGENCIES

Bimm Travel Agency (0211-220641; www.bimmzambia.com; Shop 3, Luangwa House, Cairo Rd) Located just south of the post office, this agency is reliable and locally run. It can also arrange car hire. There's another branch at Levy Junction.

Bush Buzz (0978 773930, 0977 801374; www.bush-buzz.com) Organises trips to Kafue, Lower Zambezi and South Luangwa National Parks.

Steve Blagus Travel (0211-227739; www.sbltravel.com; 24 Nkwazi Rd; 8am-4pm Mon-Fri, to 11.30am Sat) The agency for Amex and a dozen upmarket lodges/camps; also organises regional and domestic tours.

Voyagers (0211-253064; www.voyagerszambia.com; Suez Rd; 8am-5pm Mon-Fri, to 11am Sat) Perhaps the most popular agency in Zambia (with other offices in Ndola, Chingola and Kitwe), Voyagers arranges flights and hotel reservations, and partners with Europcar for car hire.

Zambia Tourism Agency (0211-229087; www.zambiatourism.com; 1st fl, Petroda House, Great East Rd; 8am-1pm & 2-5pm Mon-Fri) Information and maps of Lusaka are limited, but has an excellent website.

Getting There & Away

AIR

Lusaka International Airport is about 20km northeast of the city centre. Taxis between the airport and central Lusaka cost anywhere from ZMW200 to ZMW250. There's no airport bus but the upmarket hotels send minibuses (usually for a fee) to meet international flights, so you may be able to arrange a ride into town with the minibus driver (for a negotiable fee).

Arriving at the airport there are ATMs, foreign-exchange booths, car-rental offices and mobile-phone companies selling SIM cards. For departures, once through security for international flights, there's a restaurant and basic bar, and a couple of shops selling curios.

BUS & MINIBUS

Domestic

From a tourist point of view, the only real bus station you'll need to worry about is the **Lusaka Inter-City Bus Station** (Dedan Kimathi Rd). Here you can find a bus to all long-distance destinations in Zambia and across the border.

A range of buses from different companies cover most tourist destinations (all leaving from this bus station unless otherwise stated) – we've quoted the highest prices because they represent the best companies, with the most comfortable buses (two-storey with reclining seats). It's certainly worth double-checking the schedules and booking your tickets one or two days before you leave.

Much less safe are the buses and minibuses from in front of the massive and chaotic **Lusaka City Market Bus Station** (Lumumba Rd), which leave for nearby towns such as Kafue (not to be confused with the national park; ZMW30, one hour, 10 to 15 daily), Chirundu (ZMW55, 2½ hours, five to seven daily), Siavonga (ZMW70, three hours, three to five daily) and Luangwa Bridge (ZMW95, four hours, one or two daily); destinations are more or less signposted. To add to the confusion, minibuses to places not far south of Lusaka also leave from the **City Bus Station** (Kulima Towers Bus Station; off Chachacha Rd), also called the Kulima Towers Station. So it's possible to get to Kafue, Chirundu and Siavonga from here too.

Minibuses heading to the north (eg the Manda Hill Shopping Centre) depart from the **Millennium Bus Station** (Malasha Rd).

Copperbelt

Juldan (Lusaka Inter-City Bus Station), **Power Tools** (☎0960 812019; Lusaka Inter-City Bus Station) and **Mazhandu Family** (☎0977 805064; Lusaka Inter-City Bus Station) buses, among others, go to Copperbelt destinations such as Ndola (ZMW85, four hours, five daily) and Kitwe (ZMW90, five hours, five daily); Kapiri Mposhi (ZMW60, 2½ hours, five daily) is also reached along this route.

East Zambia

Travelling east, many companies operate services to Chipata (ZMW160), the road link for South Luangwa or Malawi; **Jonda Bus Tours** (☎0977 412616; Lusaka Inter-City Bus Station) has departures from 5am.

Northeast

Tracking northeast, Juldan and Power Tools are two of the better companies, making a beeline for Serenje (ZMW145, five to six hours), Mpika (ZMW160, 10 hours), Kasama (ZMW130, 14 hours, four daily) and Mpulungu (ZMW180, 18 hours, four daily).

Southwest

Heading southwest, as you'd expect, there are plenty of buses to Livingstone (ZMW120, six to seven hours, at least seven daily) with either Mazhandu Family or **Shalom** (☎0977 414932; Lusaka Inter-City Bus Station) being the recommended bus services. It's best to purchase the ticket the day before or phone ahead of time to get seat details.

West Zambia

Heading west, catch an 8am Juldan or Shalom bus through Kafue National Park and onto Mongu (ZMW130, eight hours); for Kafue camps just off the highway, it's ZMW120 and three hours.

International

All buses mentioned here (unless stated otherwise) leave from the Lusaka Inter-City Bus Station.

Botswana

Zambia-Botswana Express (☎0977 800042, 0966 800042; Lusaka Inter-City Bus Station) has buses to Gaborone (ZMW300, 22 hours, Sunday and Wednesday at 9pm) via Kasane and Francistown; Mazhandu Family has a 5am departure for the border at Kazungula.

East Africa

Falcon (☎0977 212516, 0977 945874; Lusaka Inter-City Bus Station) and **Taqwa** (☎0977 157763; Lusaka Inter-City Bus Station) both make the run to Dar es Salaam (ZMW500, 27 hours, six weekly), Tanzania, but services can be haphazard (and the train is a more interesting and adventurous experience). For the pathologically masochistic, you can even board Nairobi- (ZMW900) and Kampala (Uganda)-bound buses, which take two to three days.

Malawi

For Malawi, there's no direct service to Blantyre, but **KOBS Coach Service** (☎0955 714545; Lusaka Inter-City Bus Terminal) has five services a week to Lilongwe (ZMW220, 10 hours, 4.30am), where you can change buses.

Namibia

Insight (☎0976 599441; Lusaka Inter-City Bus Station) has buses to Windhoek (ZMW550, 24 hours) departing at 5.30am.

South Africa

For South Africa, buses cost around ZMW450 for the journey that heads to Johannesburg (18 to 24 hours) via Livingstone, Harare, Masvingo and Pretoria.

Shalom departs daily at 9am, while Mazhandu Family, **CR Holdings** (Lusaka Inter-City Bus Station) and Juldan also have services through the week.

Zimbabwe

Buses heading to Zimbabwe leave just across from the Lusaka Inter-City bus station. **Mwayera Buses** (www.facebook.com/mwayerabuses; Dedan Kimathi Rd, opp Lusaka Inter-City Bus Station) head via Chirundu, while **Zupco** (opp Lusaka Inter-City Bus Station, Dedan Kimathi Rd) goes via Siavonga border crossings. It's US$20 to Harare (eight hours via Chirundu) and US$10 to Siavonga (three hours). There are usually around three buses per day.

TRAIN

The train travelling to Livingstone (economy/business/sleeper class ZMW70/90/135, 14 hours), via Choma, leaves Lusaka at 7am on Saturday and Tuesday, and arrives in Livingstone at the ungodly hour of 2am. Quite simply, it's not worth it. But if you insist, tickets are available from the reservations office inside the **train station** (☎0961 195353; btwn Cairo & Dedan Kimathi Rds). Get there early and be prepared for hustle and bustle. Slow, 'ordinary' trains to Ndola (standard class ZMW40, 12 hours), via Kapiri Mposhi (ZMW25, eight hours), depart Friday and Monday at 7pm.

The Tazara train runs between Kapiri Mposhi and Dar es Salaam (Tanzania) on Tuesday (ZMW334) at 4pm and Friday (ZMW278) at 2pm, taking 38 to 48 hours. Get tickets from **Tazara House** (☎0979 484980; 2nd Fl, Tazara House, off Independence Ave; ⊙8am-5pm Mon-Fri).

ℹ Getting Around

CAR & MOTORCYCLE

The roads can get extremely clogged around Lusaka at peak traffic times. Speed limits are enforced in and around the city. Do not park your vehicle on the streets unless you have someone to keep an eye on it for you; hotels, restaurants and shopping centres all have guarded car parks. If you drive around at night, you increase the risk of an accident or carjacking; after dark, leave the car at your hotel and take a taxi.

Several international car-rental companies have counters at the airport, including **Avis** (☎airport 0211-271020; www.avis.com) and **Europcar/Voyagers** (☎0212-620314; www.europcarzambia.com). **Benmark Transways & Car Hire** (☎0211-292192; ben@benmarkcarhire.com; cnr Parliament & Great East Rds) rents out cars for travel within Lusaka for around US$35 per day.

If you want a car and driver to help get you around Lusaka, you're better off hiring a taxi for the day; your lodge will be able to recommend a trusted driver for around US$40 to US$50 a day, depending on how much distance you will cover.

LOCAL TRANSPORT

Local minibuses run along Lusaka's main roads, but there are no route numbers or destination signs, so the system is difficult to work out. There is also a confusing array of bus and minibus stations.

Otherwise it is possible to flag down a minibus along a route. For instance, from the South End Roundabout, the 'Kabulonga' minibus goes along Independence Ave to Longacres Roundabout and then heads back towards the city along Los Angeles Blvd and Church Rd; the 'Chakunkula' or 'Chelston' minibus shuttles down Kafue Rd to Kafue town; and the 'Chilanga' minibus heads to Chilanga, via Kafue Rd. The standard fare is ZMW2 to ZMW3.

TAXI

Official taxis can be identified by the numbers painted on the doors and their colour – light blue – but hundreds of unofficial taxis also cruise the streets (you'll hear them honk their horn as they go past you on the street, looking for business).

Official taxis can be hailed along the street or found at ranks near the main hotels and markets. Fares are negotiable, but if you're unsure, ask at your accommodation first for an approximate price; always agree on the fare before setting out.

EASTERN ZAMBIA

Eastern Zambia contains a couple of the country's wilderness gems. It's a sparsely populated region with one long highway, the Great East Rd, meandering out to the border with Malawi and onto Lilongwe. The two key national parks of the Luangwa Valley complement each other beautifully: stunning South Luangwa is the most set-up park for tourism in Zambia, as well as being one of the best in the region for wildlife watching and the most accessible park for budget tourists in Zambia; North Luangwa is wild and difficult to reach – access is usually by private charter flights – and spectacular for exploring on foot. Splitting the two parks is the lesser visited Luambe National Park, under new private management and one to look out for with animal numbers on the rise.

Chipata

The primary commercial and urban centre in this eastern district, Chipata is a fast-growing, traffic-clogged town in a valley surrounded by a fertile agricultural region. For travellers, it's simply a stop on the way to South Luangwa National Park or Malawi, which is only 30km away. There are a few decent accommodation options, petrol stations, ATMs and several large shopping malls with restaurant chains and supermarkets to stock up on food and other supplies.

Deans Hill View Lodge CAMPGROUND, LODGE $
(☎0216-223698; www.deanshillviewlodge.com; Plot 3278, Kanjala Hill, Fort Jameson; camping/

WORTH A TRIP

GREAT EAST ROAD: FROM LUSAKA TO CHIPATA

The Great East Rd crosses the Luangwa River on a large suspension bridge about half-way between Lusaka and Chipata. There are several places en route to break your trip.

Tikondane Community Centre (☎0979 176960; www.tikondane.org; Katete; camping/dm/r US$5/6/25, s/d with shared bathroom from US$10/15; 📶) This grassroots initiative does wonderful work in assisting to empower local communities. It's a great place to hang around and help out as a volunteer. Otherwise you can spend the night at its Tiko Lodge, which offers camping, dorms and basic rooms in various configurations. The food here is another reason to stop by, with intriguing local dishes on offer.

Luangwa Bridge Camp (☎0977 395037; www.bridgecampzambia.com; Feira Rd; camping/r US$10/85, meals ZMW95-175; ⏲8am-9pm) A great place to break up the drive between Lusaka and Chipata, Luangwa Bridge Camp offers a good menu and drinks list, and scenic spot overlooking the river. It does filtered Zambian coffee, cold drinks, burgers, pizzas and steaks, as well as gourmet items such as deep-fried crumbed camembert or a tempura prawn burger with onion rings.

dm/d ZMW60/100/300, s/d with shared bathroom ZMW150/250; 📶) This laid-back lodge is perched at the top of a hill with great views of the valley and Chipata below. Simple rooms are set in a two-storey stone-and-thatch chapel-like building. The shared ablutions are kept clean, and camping is out on a nice big sloping garden. Meals are served in a cosy dining area with bar, or there's a kitchen for self-caterers.

Mama Rula's CAMPGROUND, LODGE **$$**
(☎0965 790225, 0977 790226; www.mamarulas.com; camping US$10, s/d incl breakfast US$32/60, s/d with shared bathroom US$15/30; @) Owned and operated by a South African/Zimbabwean family, this long-running operation is in a leafy compound around 4km out of Chipata along the road to Mfuwe. Simply furnished rooms with mosquito nets are in a low-slung building; nearby are small but clean cheaper rooms with shared bathroom facilities and a campsite popular with overland groups. Its social bar is Chipata's best spot for a beer.

Meals (T-bone steaks or schnitzel with chips and salad around ZM60 to ZMW120) are served in the bar festooned with South African rugby flags. Transport to and from town is ZMW50, or ZMW100 to the border.

Getting There & Away

The main **bus station** is located in the tangle of streets about 1.5km north of the town centre.

Of the handful of bus companies offering services to Lusaka, Johabie (ZMW160, seven hours, 4am and 7am) is easily the most recommended. Touts from competing companies can be very aggressive in trying to steer you, or rather manhandle you, towards their waiting vehicle.

Buses also leave here to Mfuwe (around ZMW50, 2½ hours, 1.30pm) for South Luangwa National Park. A taxi to Mfuwe (ZMW450, three-plus hours) is another option.

It's best to arrive an hour early to guarantee a seat; always choose the bus closest to being filled, otherwise you might have a long, uncomfortable wait.

KOBS Coach Service has departures to Lilongwe, Malawi (ZMW80, four hours) at 5.30am pretty much daily (except Thursday and Sunday).

Minibuses (ZMW25) for the Malawi border depart from 7am to 5pm from the **Puma petrol station** (Great East Rd) on the main drag in town; otherwise, a taxi should run at around ZMW100 (30 minutes). Once you've passed through Zambian customs (open 24 hours), it's a few minutes' walk to the Malawian entry post. From the border crossing you can catch a shared taxi to nearby Mchinji (MK300) before getting a minibus all the way to Lilongwe.

South Luangwa National Park

For scenery, variety and density of animals, **South Luangwa National Park** (per person/self-drive vehicle US$25/30; ⏲6am-6pm) is one of the best parks in Zambia, if not Africa. Impalas, pukus, waterbucks, giraffes and buffaloes wander on the wide-open plains; leopards, of which there are many in the park, hunt in the dense woodlands; herds of elephants wade through the marshes; and hippos munch serenely on Nile cabbage in the Luangwa River. The bird life is a highlight: about 400 species have been recorded – large birds like snake eagles, bateleurs and ground hornbills are normally easy to spot.

South Luangwa National Park

South Luangwa National Park

Top Sights
1 South Luangwa National Park A2

Sleeping
2 Chamilandu Bushcamp A3
3 Chizombo.......................................A1
4 Croc Valley.....................................A1
5 Flatdogs Camp................................A1
6 Kawaza Village B2
7 Luwi Bush Camp..............................A1
8 Marula Lodge..................................A1
9 Mfuwe Lodge...................................A1
10 Nkonzi Camp..................................A1
11 Nkwali..A2
12 Nsefu Camp...................................B2
Track & Trail River Camp............(see 8)
13 Wildlife Camp A2
14 Zungulila......................................A3

Eating
Dorphil Restaurant ....(see 8)

Shopping
15 Tribal Textiles...............................B2

The focal point is Mfuwe, an uninspiring though more prosperous than average village with shops as well as a petrol station and market. Around 1.8km further along is **Mfuwe Gate**, the main entrance to the park, where a bridge crosses the Luangwa River.

Much of the park is inaccessible because of rains between November and April.

Activities

All lodges/camps run excellent day or night wildlife drives and some have walking safaris (June to November). These activities are included in the rates charged by the upmarket places, while the cheaper lodges/camps can organise things with little notice. A three-hour morning or evening wildlife drive normally costs around US$40, while a wildlife walk is about US$50.

Budget Safaris

While South Luangwa is one of the easier parks to navigate for those without their own vehicle, an all-inclusive safari is still an excellent way to see the park. The following offer some more affordable safaris:

Jackalberry Safari (www.jackalberrysafaris.net; 3-/4-/5-day safari per person US$645/995/1195) Popular all-inclusive multiday safaris that offer top value for money with stays at its lovely, remote Nkonzi Camp.

Edward Selfe Photography Safaris (☎0976 750967; www.edwardselfephotography.com; 6 days from US$2870) One for budding wildlife photographers, these tours are run by an experienced nature photographer.

River Safari Company (☎in South Africa 021-426 2838; www.riversafaricompany.com; 161 Mulombwa Cl; 3-/4-day safari per person US$545/695) Budget safaris run out of Lusaka Backpackers.

Kiboko Safaris (☎0975 713820; www.kiboko-safaris.com; 4-day safari per person US$515) Operating out of Lilongwe, Malawi; offers multiday trips in its tented camp along the Luangwa River.

Sleeping

Most lodges and camps in South Luangwa are along the banks of the river; those deep in the park are all-inclusive and at the very top end price-wise.

Budget travellers will be treated to some of the best-value accommodation in Africa, where you don't need to spend a cashload for waterfront views or wildlife encounters.

Many lodges close during the rainy season (November to April), but those around Mfuwe open year-round.

Around Mfuwe Gate

★Marula Lodge LODGE $
(☎0216-246073; www.marulalodgezambia.com; Mfuwe; dm US$10, dome tents per person US$15, r from US$40;) Occupying a stretch of riverfront with plenty of lawn, Marula offers one of the best choices in the park for budget travellers. Options include waterfront domed tents, upstairs dorm rooms with a view and some charming, comfortable chalets with private bathroom. The shared bathroom for those in the tents and dorms offers a unique experience in a wonderful circular open-air structure built around a lovely mahogany tree.

There's also a self-catering kitchen, an atmospheric thatched restaurant/bar serving up Western mains, and an inviting swimming pool that makes it worth hanging around another day.

Croc Valley LODGE $
(☎0216-246074; www.crocvalley.com; camping/safari tent US$12/15, r from US$40, with shared bathroom from US$25; @) One of several places catering to independent travellers along this stretch of the river, Croc Valley offers great options. In a sprawling compound set under a tangle of trees lining the riverbank, there's both camping and good-value 'backpacker rooms' with shared amenities. Otherwise it has air-conditioned safari tents of varying levels of luxury and more standard tents with open-air, thatch-walled bathrooms.

Wildlife Camp LODGE, CAMPGROUND $
(☎0216-246026; www.wildlifecamp-zambia.com; camping US$12, safari tent s/d US$55/90, chalet s/d US$85/136;) This spacious, secluded spot about 5km southwest of Mfuwe village is popular with both overland groups and independent travellers. There are nine simple stone-and-thatch chalets (two with basic kitchenettes), five airy tented ones and a big, open area for campers with its own bar and pool area. Its tented camps have some of the best views in the park.

Track & Trail River Camp CHALET, CAMPGROUND $$
(☎0977 600556, 0974 244850, in Lusaka 0211-246020; www.trackandtrailrivercamp.com; camping US$12.50, s/d all-inclusive US$495/850;) Set on a riverfront property about 400m east of Mfuwe Gate, Track & Trail offers varying levels of luxurious chalets and lovely camping grounds shaded by a giant African fig. Its pool with elevated deck and lounge chairs overlooking the river is one of the park's finest.

Flatdogs Camp TENTED CAMP $$
(☎0216-246038; www.flatdogscamp.com; safari tents U$52-97, all-inclusive chalets per person US$395; @) On a large, leafy property along a kilometre of riverfront, Flatdogs has 11 safari tents of varying features. All are well kept and have outdoor showers. Groups of four can consider the 'tree house' (US$405), which has two open-air bedrooms overlooking a flood plain frequented by all manner of wildlife (a telescope is on hand for stargazing).

Kawaza Village HUT $$
(www.kawazavillage.co.uk; per person day visit incl lunch US$20, overnight per person with full board US$70) This enterprise run by the local Kunda people gives tourists the opportunity to visit a real rural Zambian village while helping the local community. Four rondavels (each sleeps two) with open-air reed showers and long-drop toilets are reserved for visitors who are encouraged to partake in village life, learning how to cook *nshima* (maize porridge), attending church services and visiting schools.

Mfuwe Lodge LODGE $$$
(☎0216-245041; www.bushcampcompany.com; per person all-inclusive US$545;) Laid out along an enviable stretch of a well-trafficked oxbow lagoon only 2km from the Mfuwe Gate, this resort-like lodge, one of the largest, is also certainly one of the nicest and most well run. The 18 separate cottages (12 face the lagoon and six the hippo pool) are imaginatively designed with private verandas (and hanging wicker 'basket chairs') and colourful bathrooms with big windows.

★Chizombo LODGE $$$
(☎0216-246025; www.normancarrsafaris.com/camps/chinzombo; per person all-inclusive US$1300;) One of the park's most exquisite lodges, Chizombo offers luxury villas done out in designer soft white tones, with spacious, breezy and immaculate areas furnished with a classy vintage decor. Each of the six villas has its own massive decking area with a sofa and private plunge pool overlooking the wildlife-viewing areas.

SOUTH LUANGWA'S FLORA & FAUNA

The lifeblood of South Luangwa park is the wide Luangwa River, which rises in far north-eastern Zambia, near the Malawi border, and flows southward for 800km through the broad Luangwa Valley. Although it flows all year, it gets very shallow in the dry season (May to October) when vast midstream sandbanks are exposed – usually covered in groups of hippos or crocodiles basking in the sun. Steep exposed banks mean animals prefer to drink at the park's numerous oxbow lagoons, formed as the river continually changes its course, and this is where wildlife viewing is often best, especially as the smaller waterholes run dry.

Vegetation ranges from open grassy plains to the strips of woodland along the riverbank, dominated by large trees including ebony, mahogany, leadwood and winterthorn, sometimes growing in beautiful groves. As you move away from the river onto higher ground, the woodland gets denser and finding animals takes more patience.

Not that you'll ever be disappointed by Luangwa's wildlife. The park is famous for its buffalo herds, which are particularly large and dramatic when they congregate in the dry season and march en masse to the river to drink. Elephant numbers are also very healthy, even though ivory poaching in the 1980s had a dramatic effect on the population. This park is also a great place to see lions and leopards (especially on night drives), and local specialities include Cookson's wildebeest (an unusual light-coloured subspecies) and the endemic Thornicroft's giraffe, distinguished from other giraffes by a dark neck pattern.

Even the zebras here are unusual; called Crawshay's zebras, their stripes are thin, numerous and extend down to the hooves, under the belly, with no shadow stripe – they are an intermediate form between the 'standard' East African form and the extra-stripy subspecies in Mozambique.

There's a stunning variety wildlife on the plains; the numerous antelope species include bushbuck, waterbuck, kudu, impala and puku. Roan antelopes, hartebeests and reedbucks are also here, but encountered less often.

Luangwa's population of wild dogs, one of the rarest animals in Zambia (and Africa), seems to be on the increase, especially around the Mfuwe area from November to January; there has been a resurgence in numbers around the Nsefu sector as well. An organisation that works to protect and rehabilitate wild dog populations is the Zambia Carnivore Programme (www.zambiacarnivores.org) – healthy packs require huge areas to roam for their nomadic lifestyles, and it is trying to open up a viable corridor for the dogs between South Luangwa and the Lower Zambezi National Parks.

The birdlife in South Luangwa is also tremendous. As small lagoons dry out, fish writhe in the shallows and birds mass together as 'fishing parties'. Pelicans and yellow-billed storks stuff themselves silly, and become so heavy they can't fly. Herons, spoonbills and marabou storks join the fun, while grasses and seeds around the lagoons attract a moving coloured carpet of queleas and Lilian's lovebirds. Other ornithological highlights are the stately crowned cranes and the unfeasibly colourful Carmine bee-eaters, whose migration here every August is one of the world's great wildlife spectacles – some visitors come just to see these flocks of beautiful birds busy nesting in the sandy riverbanks.

The **South Luangwa Conservation Society** (CLS; ☎ in South Africa 096 2492386; www.slcszambia.org) helps to protect this wonderful natural heritage through its anti-poaching efforts, with regular patrols throughout the park.

Southern Camps

Zungulila LODGE $$$

(☎ 0216-245041; www.bushcampcompany.com; per person all-inclusive US$720; ⌚ Jun-Dec) Imagine a *Vogue* shoot with an *Out of Africa* theme and you'll have the sophisticated design aesthetic of this camp. Spacious safari tents evoke colonial-era fantasies with copper-plated taps and Middle Eastern rugs; each has its own sun deck with tiny circular plunge pool and outdoor shower. Zungulila's decadent signature treats are the sundowners enjoyed barefoot in folding chairs in the shallow river.

BUSHCAMP COMPANIES

Only a handful of companies offer lodging within the park proper, primarily in what are generally referred to as 'bush camps'. Despite the misleading name, these are very comfortable, ranging from simple thatch-roofed chalets to stylishly furnished tents with gold-plated taps and plunge pools. Most have only three to five rooms and offer customised itineraries that take guests to multiple camps by vehicle or on foot.

Bushcamp Company (www.bushcampcompany.com) Sophisticated and expertly managed Bushcamp operates six uniquely designed camps (Bilimungwe, Chamilandu, Chindeni, Kapamba, Kuyenda and Zungulila), which are all in the southern section of the park, as well as its base **Mfuwe Lodge** (p48).

Norman Carr Safaris (www.normancarrsafaris.com) Operates five somewhat more rustic camps (Chizombo, Kakuli, Luwi, Mchenja and Nsolo) mainly in the remote sections of the park; its base is at Kapani Lodge.

Robin Pope Safaris (www.robinpopesafaris.net) With its base at **Nkwali** (p50) not far south of Mfuwe Gate, Robin Pope Safaris operates three camps (Luangwa River Camp, Nsefu and Tena Tena), several remote mobile walking camps in the north sector of the park and two houses for rent (Robin's House and Luangwa Safari House).

The other companies in the park that are the highly recommended: **Remote Africa** (www.remoteafrica.com; Chikoko, Mwaleshi and Tafika) in the northern section run by John and Carol Coppinger; **Sanctuary Retreats** (www.sanctuaryretreats.com; Chichele and Puku Ridge) and **Shenton Safaris** (www.kaingo.com; Mwamba and Kaingo).

Chamilandu Bushcamp LODGE $$$
(☎0216-245041; www.bushcampcompany.com; per person all-inclusive US$720; ⏲mid-Jun–Nov) Built along the banks of the Luangwa River, Chamilandu Bushcamp's stilted thatch-and-reed chalets are utterly exposed to the elements; they have no fourth wall, only three sides of expert carpentry work. You'll never want to spend more time in a bathroom! Sunrise offers another revelation when the true brilliance of the camp's design comes to light. It's a two-hour drive south of Mfuwe.

Northern Camps

Nkwali LODGE $$$
(☎0216-245090; www.robinpopesafaris.net; per person all-inclusive US$665; 🏊) A long-standing, classic Luangwa lodge, Nkwali has just six small cottages with delightful open-air bathrooms. They're all very comfortable but with no unnecessary frills, which gives a feel of the bush – rustic but also quite classy. If you're after privacy, the two-bedroom Safari House has traditional African decor and a private guide, hostess and chef!

Nsefu Camp LODGE $$$
(www.robinpopesafaris.net; per person all-inclusive US$835) Luangwa's first tourist camp (now protected as a historic monument) has an excellent location smack bang in the middle of the Nsefu sector on an open plain awash with wildlife and with hot springs nearby. The stylishly furnished rondavels retain a 1950s atmosphere (along with the rest of the camp), complete with brass taps in the bathrooms and good-sized windows with river views.

★**Luwi Bush Camp** LODGE $$$
(☎0216-246015, 0216-246025; www.normancarrsafaris.com/camps/luwi; per person all-inclusive US$840) One of Norman Carr Safari's original remote luxury wilderness camps in South Luangwa, Luwi nails the rustic:luxury ratio with each of its open-plan thatch-and-reed chalets overlooking the plains. It's dismantled at the end of each season to minimise environmental impact.

★**Nkonzi Camp** TENTED CAMP $$$
(☎0966 411320; www.jackalberrysafaris.net; 3 days per person all-inclusive US$610; ⏲June 1–Oct 31) Run by Jackalberry Safaris, Nkonzi is a bush camp within the national park that offers a wonderful (and relatively more affordable) wilderness experience; it's excellent value for those looking to spend a few days on safari. The seasonal site offers tented accommodation with double bed and attached open-air bathrooms constructed from reed material. Rates include activities led by experienced owner/guide Gavin Opie.

Eating

Dorphil Restaurant INTERNATIONAL $
(☎0216-246196; mains ZMW25; ⏰6am-9pm) Highly recommended by area expats and one of the few places to eat in the village of Mfuwe is friendly Dorphil Restaurant. The owner/chef Dorika prepares samosas, spring rolls, T-bones with *nshima* and pizza, served at a few outdoor tables under a thatch roof.

Shopping

Tribal Textiles ARTS & CRAFTS
(☎0216-245137; www.tribaltextiles.co.zm; ⏰7am-4.30pm) This enterprise employs a team of local artists to produce, among other things, bags, wall hangings, bed linens and sarongs, much of which are sold abroad. Tribal Textiles has some striking original designs and it's quite a refined place to shop or take a short (free) tour around the factory.

Getting There & Away

AIR

Many people reach South Luangwa by air. Mfuwe Airport is about 20km southeast of Mfuwe Gate and served by Proflight (www.proflight-zambia.com), with several daily flights from Lusaka (from US$150 one way). A flight to Lower Zambezi was introduced in late 2016. **Ulendo Airlink** (☎in Malawi 01-794638; www.flyulendo.com) flies from Lilongwe (Malawi) to Mfuwe.

At Mfuwe Airport's little terminal there's a bureau de change, Barclays Bank and Zanaco ATMs, and a cafe by the car park where you can grab a coffee and meal while waiting for your flight. Almost every lodge meets clients at the airport (the charge is often included in the room rates). Otherwise a taxi to locations near the Mfuwe gate should cost around ZMW80.

BUS

There are several buses from Mfuwe village for Chipata (around ZMW50) and Lusaka (ZMW220); Jonada Bus is probably the most reliable. Note that when you arrive there's a facility for you to call your lodge to pick you up as it's not safe to walk due to the prevalence of wildlife.

Shared taxi and minibuses are other options and depart from the **BP petrol station** early in the morning, typically before 7am.

CAR

While the vast majority of visitors come and go using the main park entrance at Mfuwe, the Chifungwe Gate is an option if arriving/departing from the north of the country via Mpika. The route is open during the dry season only, and passes over the Muchinga Escarpment along a steep rocky track, which you'll need to pass along at a snail's pace – hence it's one for experienced 4WD drivers only. The turnoff to Chifungwe is signed about 40km south of Mpika along the Great North Rd, from where it's a further 50km or so to the gate. All up expect the journey from Mpika to Mfuwe to take six to seven hours.

If you're heading to or arriving to Luambe or North Luangwa national parks, you'll take the Chikwinda Gate and follow a track along the east side of the Luangwa River. There are several river crossings, so it's only passable during the dry season and again for experienced 4WD drivers only.

For alternative routes to Mfuwe Gate, be sure to call ahead to enquire about the state of the roads.

Getting Around

For independent drivers, South Luangwa is probably the easiest park to access (with the exception of Kafue) and to drive around. A limited section of all-weather gravel roads are in excellent condition near Mfuwe Gate and there's

WORTH A TRIP

LUAMBE NATIONAL PARK

Despite the relative proximity of North and South Luangwa National Parks, driving between them is long and hard, and it would take over 11 hours if you were to try the trip in one go. However, most who venture this route stop after around six hours in small **Luambe National Park** (entry US$35, per vehicle US$20).

A destination in its own right, Luambe is a great option for those wanting to see the same animals as South Luangwa, minus the crowds. Though tiny in size, it's one of the country's oldest parks, gazetted in 1938.

Luambe Camp (☎in South Africa 072 298 0777; www.luambe.com; Luambe National Park; per person all-inclusive US$395; ⏰Apr-Nov) is the place to stay in the northwest pocket of the park, only 3km off the roadway on the Luangwa River. It's run by a team of passionate conservationists aiming to put the park back on to the tourist map.

It's another five hours or so from here to Buffalo camp in North Luangwa.

lots of smaller tracks. You should be able to pick up a very basic map at the gate. The bush opens up off the side of the roads (even early after the rainy season in May), making wildlife spotting fairly easy, especially along the river.

If you're not staying at an all-inclusive place and you want to arrange a 4WD (up to nine people; around US$125 per 24 hours) for wildlife viewing or to explore villages in the area contact Ben Koobs, the owner of **Personal Touch** (☎0978 459965, 0966 602796; www.tptouch.com).

Be aware that it's never entirely safe to walk anywhere in the park (even within your lodge you'll need to be highly vigilant) as there are no fenced boundaries, so wildlife roams freely inside and out of the park.

North Luangwa National Park

This **park** (admission US$20, self drive US$25; ⏲6am-6pm) is large, wild and spectacular, but nowhere near as developed or set up for tourism as its southern counterpart. The big draw of North Luangwa is its walking safaris, where you can get up close to the wildlife in a truly remote wilderness.

The range of wildlife in North Luangwa is similar to South Luangwa's (except there are no giraffes), and the park is particularly famous for its small population of black rhino and huge buffalo herds (sometimes up to 1000-strong), which in turn attract large numbers of lions and hyenas. The bush here is dense in places, so the animals are slightly harder to see than at South Luangwa, and there are very few tracks for vehicles, so the emphasis is firmly on walking.

North Luangwa's eastern boundary is the Luangwa River, but the heart of the park is the Mwaleshi River – a permanent watercourse and vital supply for wildlife.

There is no public transport to North Luangwa. Most guests fly in and out on charter flights arranged by their lodge (typical price per person from Mfuwe to one of the airstrips is ZMW1000 one way); the result is that only several hundred people visit the park each year.

If you are coming to the park independently remember that you need to be well set-up with a fully equipped, high-clearance 4WD, and your accommodation prebooked. Also, get advice regarding the state of the roads into the park and make sure you've got maps that cover the area (and GPS); they should be supplemented by a map of the park, usually available at Mano Gate and detailing where you're allowed to drive.

Mwaleshi Camp CAMPGROUND **$$$**
(☎0216-246185; www.remoteafrica.com; per person all-inclusive from US$710; ⏲Jun 15–Oct 31) A top-notch operation – at once luxurious, in terms of care from the staff, and relaxed. It's a bush camp with accommodation in four charmingly simple chalets made from reeds and thatch with open-roofed bathrooms. Walking is the main activity and that's a fortunate thing once you've tasted the excellent food. Spotted hyenas are commonly seen in this area, as are buffaloes and, of course, lions.

Buffalo Camp LODGE **$$$**
(☎0976 970444; www.shiwasafaris.com; per person self-catering/all-inclusive US$100/280) Located in the south of the park, Buffalo Camp is a quiet, secluded place. It's good value (and unusually welcomes children) and the six traditional-style thatch-roofed chalets overlook the river. Book ahead for the 'self-catering rates', normally only available when there's a paucity of guests on the all-inclusive package. Transfers for those without vehicles are usually possible from Kapishya Lodge or Mpika (maximum four people).

SOUTHERN ZAMBIA

This region is a real highlight of Zambia with some wonderful natural attractions. There are great national parks, the Lower Zambezi in particular highly regarded for both its wildlife (especially elephants) and its scenic landscape. The area is also home to the remote Lochinvar National Park, renowned for its pristine wetlands. Then there's the massive Lake Kariba, with Siavonga's sandy beaches and Chikanka Island (smack in the middle of the lake) providing fascinating views of the night sky and a glimpse of the 60 elephants that make their way between the islands. If you're lucky enough to see a storm roll in over the steely waters from Zimbabwe, it'll be an experience you'll long remember. Siavonga offers the chance to experience the more rural side of the country.

Chirundu

This dusty and bedraggled border town is on the main road between Lusaka and Harare. The only reason to stay here is if you're going on to Zimbabwe or planning to explore the

Lower Zambezi National Park. Other than a few shops and bars, as well as a Barclays Bank with ATM and a number of moneychangers, there's little else to note.

That said, west of town, near the Siavonga turnoff, is the **Fossil Forest**. From a sign on the main road, paths lead through the bush. At first, things are pretty uninspiring, but further in huge trunks of petrified trees are visible, complete with age rings and grains of bark now preserved as stone.

Minibuses leave regularly for Chirundu from Lusaka (ZMW40, three hours, five to seven daily). To reach Siavonga (on Lake Kariba) from Chirundu, catch a minibus towards Lusaka, get off at the obvious turnoff to Siavonga and wait for something else to come along.

There is no petrol station in town. Gwabi Lodge and Kiambi Safaris have a couple of fuel pumps, but there is a limited supply, so it's safer to stock up in Lusaka or Kafue.

Wagtail River Club LODGE **$**
(☎0965 623067, 0979 279468; www.wagtailrivercamp.com; camping US$10, r per person US$45, with shared bathroom US$20;) The former Zambezi Breezers has been rebadged as Wagtail River Club, but it's the exact same place. It still boasts a wonderful grassy spot overlooking the Zambezi River and is still run by the same Dutch owner. It's only 6km from Chirundu, and has a variety of accommodation including a wide lawn for riverbank camping, and simple, clean tented chalets with small decks.

Gwabi Lodge CAMPGROUND, CHALET **$$**
(☎0966 345962; www.gwabiriverlodge.com; camping/stone tents US$9/14, s/d chalets from US$54/88;) This long-running lodge owned by a Zimbabwean family is set on large, leafy grounds 12km northeast of Chirundu. There's a well-equipped camping ground (popular with overland backpackers) and solid stone-floor chalets with TVs. The highlight is the lovely elevated outlook over the Kafue River, with the decking area in front of the restaurant providing a great spot to observe birds and hippos.

Lower Zambezi National Park

One of the country's premier wildlife-viewing areas, the **Lower Zambezi National Park** (adult/self-drive vehicle US$25/30; 6am-6pm) covers a large stretch of wilderness area along the northeastern bank of the Zambezi River. Several smaller rivers flow through the park, which is centred on a beautiful flood plain alongside the Zambezi, dotted with acacias and other large trees, and flanked by a steep escarpment on the northern side, covered with thick miombo woodland. On the opposite bank, in Zimbabwe, is Mana Pools National Park, and together the parks constitute one of Africa's finest wildlife areas.

The best wildlife viewing is on the flood plain and along the river itself. Mammal species include elephant, puku, impala, zebra, buffalo, bushbuck, leopard, lion, cheetah and wild dog, and more than 400 bird species have been recorded.

The best time to visit is May to October; however, temperatures average around 40°C in the latter half of October.

Activities

Canoe Safari

One of the best ways to see the Lower Zambezi is by canoe safari.

Drifting silently in a canoe past the riverbank allows you to get surprisingly close to birds and animals without disturbing them. Nothing beats getting eye-to-eye with a drinking buffalo, or watching dainty bushbuck tiptoe towards the river's edge. Excitement comes as you negotiate a herd of grunting hippos or hear a sudden 'plop' as a croc you hadn't even noticed slips into the water nearby.

Most of the camps and lodges have canoes, so you can go out with a river guide for a few hours. Longer safaris are even more enjoyable; ask your lodge what is available.

Wildlife Watching

Most lodges offer wildlife-viewing activities by boat or by safari vehicle and are not fenced. Keep in mind, however, that while theoretically on offer, most of the lodges in the Game Management Area (GMA), especially those closer to Chirundu than to Chongwe Gate, don't take their wildlife drives in the park proper.

The main entrance is at **Chongwe Gate** along the southwestern boundary. The southwestern sector of the park is the easiest to reach and the most scenic, and has excellent wildlife viewing, so as you might expect, it's a popular area. As you go further into the central part of the park, the surroundings become wilder and more open

Lower Zambezi National Park

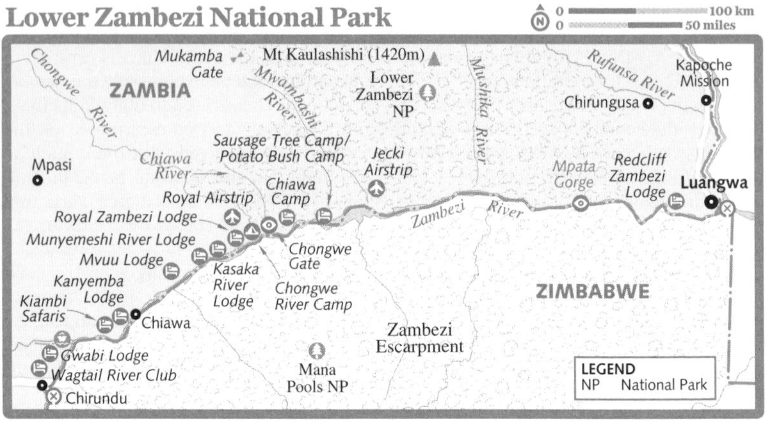

and there's more chance of having the place to yourself. Although the park is technically open all year, access is impossible in the rainy season and most lodges close down from at least mid-December to the end of February.

The elephant population was ravaged by poaching until the early 1990s, but thanks to the efforts of Conservation Lower Zambezi (www.conservationlowerzambezi.org), an organisation funded by the area's lodges and private grants, they are making a strong comeback now, with the surrounding Chiwa Game Management Area particularly dense with elephants. However, despite regular anti-poaching flights and regular ZAWA patrols, illegal hunting remains a big concern. Hence here you'll likely find elephants more on the aggressive side, so take absolute care if you're driving, especially given the road is tight.

The eastern part of the park is different in character as here the hills are close to the Zambezi and there's virtually no flood plain. The park's eastern boundary is the dramatic **Mpata Gorge** where the steep hillsides plunge straight into the river, and the only access is by boat.

Sleeping

All lodges here are found stretched out along the banks of the Zambezi river. Here you'll find some of the most stunning luxury safari lodges in Zambia; however, budget travellers also have some lovely camping options in the GMA leading into the park, which likewise has plenty of wildlife.

Munyemeshi River Lodge LODGE $

(0979 565646, 0211-231466; www.munyemeshi.co.zm; r ZMW450;) An affordable waterfront lodge close to the park, Munyemeshi's stone-and-thatch chalets are rough around the edges, but at these prices you can't be too choosy. It was undergoing renovations at the time of research, so call ahead to see if it's going to remain as a budget lodge. There's no restaurant, so it's one for self-caterers, with a fully equipped kitchen on hand.

Kiambi Safaris CAMPGROUND, CHALETS $$

(0977 876003, 0977 186106; www.kiambi.com; camping US$12, tent rental US$28, chalets s/d with full board from US$208/306;) This well-run and atmospheric operation at the confluence of the Zambezi and Kafue Rivers has a smattering of different, relatively affordable accommodation options. Set in attractive, verdant surrounds, chalets and cottages are comfortable and characterful. Campsites come with a powerpoint and firepit, and a tent if you don't have one. The social restaurant and bar is another highlight.

Mvuu Lodge CAMPGROUND, TENTED CAMP $$

(0966 363762, in South Africa 012-660 5369; www.mvuulodge.com; camping US$28, tented camping US$38, luxury tent per person all-inclusive US$175) A large, leafy property with an informal vibe, Mvuu is built on the edge of the tree-lined riverbank. Comfortable elevated safari tents with balconies are on either side of a casual lounge and dining area. The communal campfire encourages guests to share their tales of leopard and lion sightings.

★**Chiawa Camp** CHALET $$$
(☎0211-261588; www.chiawa.com; per person all-inclusive US$1120; ⏰mid-Apr–mid-Nov; @📶🏊) In a spectacular position at the confluence of the Chiawa and Zambezi Rivers, this luxurious lodge inside the park was the first in the Lower Zambezi. As a pioneer in this area, the owner Grant Cummings knows the park intimately and his guiding expertise is highly regarded. The large walk-in canvas-thatch tents feature pine-clad private bathrooms.

The bar-lounge has an upstairs deck with majestic views over the river and there's a viewing platform high up in the trees.

The food is top notch and for the romantics among you (and honeymooners), candlelit private tables can be set up in the bush, on a boat or, at full moon, on a sand bar in the middle of the river.

Chiawa's sister camp, **Old Mindoro**, is a classic old-school safari bush camp unlike anything else in the park and receives rave reviews.

★**Royal Zambezi Lodge** TENTED CAMP $$$
(☎0979 486618; www.royalzambezilodge.com; per person all-inclusive from US$990; ⏰year-round; 📶🏊) The epitome of luxury bush mixed with a colonial-era vibe, Royal is only a short drive to the eponymous airstrip as well as Chongwe Gate. Despite its understated opulence – think brass fixtures, claw-footed tubs and private day beds on decks overlooking the river – it's unpretentious and exceptionally friendly. Its bar built around the trunk of a sausage tree is a well-received feature.

In addition, there's a full-service spa (the only one on the Zambezi) and a small pool, essentially in the river; rest your elbows on the edge and you might see a hippo glide by only a few feet away. Kids and families are welcome and there are discounts in the 'green' season when rains tend to be heavy and quick; although wildlife drives might be impossible, canoe trips are still on and there are few other visitors around.

Chongwe River Camp TENTED CAMP $$$
(☎0968 351098, 0973 965851; www.chongwe.com; per person all-inclusive US$725; ⏰Apr–mid-Nov; 📶🏊) Right on the Chongwe River that marks the boundary between the GMA and the national park, this camp has an enviable position with plenty of wildlife around the camp but without the park fees. The confluence of the Zambezi is within view and a menagerie of wildlife grazes on a spit of grassland with the park's escarpment in the background – an absolutely Edenic view.

Getting There & Away

AIR

Proflight (☎0211-271032; www.proflight-zambia.com) has daily flights between Lusaka and Royal Airstrip (30 minutes; in the GMA just a few kilometres west of Chongwe Gate) and Jeki Airstrip (40 minutes; in the heart of the park). Almost every guest staying at one of the top-end lodges in the park flies into and out of Jeki, while Royal is very convenient for the lodges near Chongwe Gate. All include transfers from the airstrip.

From 2017 Proflight will also offer flights between Lower Zambezi and Mfuwe in South Luangwa National Park, which will make life considerably easier for those heading between the two parks.

Charter flights are also available with Nkwazi Air (www.ngwaziaircharters.com).

CAR

Uncomfortable minibuses run from Lusaka to Chirundu; departures run throughout the morning, but you have to sort out transport from town to your accommodation.

There's no public transport to Chongwe Gate, nor anything to the eastern and northern boundaries, and hitching is very difficult. Most people visit the park on an organised tour, and/or stay at a lodge that offers wildlife drives and boat rides as part of the deal. The lodges also arrange transfers from Lusaka – generally a minivan to Chirundu and then boat to the lodge (rates and travel times vary depending on the distance from Chirundu).

There are also tracks via the north for those heading to the eastern side of the park but these are far less used: there's an approach road accessed from the Great East Rd, 100km east of Lusaka, that will take you to Mukanga Gate; and there's a track from Leopards Hill in Lusaka, which is earmarked for improvement, though this could be many years in the future. Seek local advice before attempting either of these routes.

For budget travellers, ask at **Bongwe Barn** (p38) and **Lusaka Backpackers** (p38) in Lusaka or **Jollyboys** (p91) in Livingstone for deals on budget safaris into the Lower Zambezi.

Getting Around

Remember that you'll need a well-equipped 4WD to access and get around the park. You must drive slowly in the GMA area and the park itself – watch especially for elephants along the roadside at all times. There are several loops inside the park for wildlife viewing, but these change

WORTH A TRIP

KARIBA DAM

Lake Kariba was formed in the 1960s, its waters held back by the massive Kariba Dam, built to provide electricity for Northern and Southern Rhodesia (later Zambia and Zimbabwe) and as a symbol of the Central African Federation in the days before independence. Today Kariba measures 280km long by 12km to 32km wide, with an area of over 5500 sq km, making it one of the largest artificial lakes in the world. Underground power stations on both sides of the dam produce over 1200 megawatts between them.

As well as being a source of power, Lake Kariba is an important commercial fishing centre. Small sardine-like fish called *kapenta* were introduced from Lake Tanganyika, and they thrived in the new mineral-rich waters. In recent years overfishing has led to a decline in catches, but some rigs still operate, and you'll often see their lights twinkling on the horizon.

A visit to the dam wall with your own wheels is quite straightforward. Head down to the Zimbabwean border crossing at Siavonga/Kariba; it's a few kilometres from the wall. Enter the immigration building (on the right-hand side down some stairs as you face the border gate). Tell them that you just want to visit the wall and that you are coming back to Zambia and not going onto Zimbabwe. They will give you a stamped pass to the dam wall and ask you to leave some ID behind (driving licence or passport are OK). At the gate, show them your pass and you'll be let through. From here it's a short drive or walk to the wall. Once there, park your car and walk out over the wall: the views are spectacular and it's well worth the trip – particularly if you admire gargantuan engineering projects. You should be allowed to take pictures of the wall but not the power station. Remember that the authorities don't like cameras around here and have a fear of terrorism or sabotage to the dam. So do what they tell you. On the way back, surrender your pass at the border gate, and don't forget to pick up your ID from immigration.

from year to year, especially after the rainy season, so pick up a guide at any of the gates.

One adventurous way to visit the park is by canoe along the Zambezi. Most lodges offer two- or three-day canoe trips, with stops at seasonal camps along the river or makeshift camps on midstream islands.

For fuel in the park, Kiambi Safaris generally has petrol and diesel; otherwise Gwabi Lodge is the closest option.

Lake Kariba

Beyond Victoria Falls, the Zambezi River flows through the Batoka Gorge then enters the waters of Lake Kariba. Formed behind the massive Kariba Dam, this is one of the largest artificial lakes in the world. It's enormous, and a spectacular sight with the silhouettes of jagged Zimbabwean peaks far across its shimmering waters. For those who make it here, this remoteness is the very attraction.

The main base for activities on and around the lakeshore is Siavonga, which is a small town with accommodation. Sinazongwe, almost halfway between Livingstone and Siavonga, is even less set up for tourism. Only 17km away across the water, closer to Zimbabwe (150m away) than Zambia, is Chete (27 sq km), the largest island on the lake. It has lions, leopards, elands, waterbucks, bushbucks, impalas and kudus, and of course hippos and crocs, as well as an astonishing variety of birds – but no roads or accommodation.

Siavonga

Siavonga, the main town and resort along the Zambian side of Lake Kariba, has a location to be envied. Set among hills and verdant greenery, just a few kilometres from the massive Kariba Dam, views of the lake pop up from many vantage points, especially from the lodges. Yet, as it is set up primarily for the conference/business market and wealthy urban Zambians (especially from Lusaka) who tear down here towing their sleek boats and stay in their holiday bungalows, independent travellers without their own wheels might not find enough upside to offset the challenges of a visit. The lodges can organise activities in and around the lake, including boat trips to the dam wall, sunset cruises, fishing trips, longer-distance boat trips and one-day to four-night canoe safaris on the Zambezi.

Minibuses from Lusaka (ZMW70, three hours, three to five daily) leave when bursting to capacity for Siavonga and the nearby border. Alternatively get a bus towards Chirundu and get dropped off at the Siavonga turnoff; from here take a local pickup (ZMW15) the rest of the way.

Leaving Siavonga, minibuses depart from near the market. There are no official taxis in Siavonga, but your hotel can arrange a car to the border; otherwise, minibuses head here as well.

Eagles Rest CAMPGROUND, CHALET **$$**
(☎0967 688617, 0978 869126; www.eaglesrestresort.com; camping/tent hire US$1025, s/d/tr incl breakfast US$50/75/90; ❄ 🏊) While it's all a little bit tired and in need of a refurb, this laid-back beachfront resort is still the best spot for independent travellers. It has its own little sandy area (no swimming, however), pool and beach bar. It's the only campsite around town, and its chalets are spacious with stone floors and great decking outside with patio furniture overlooking the lake.

Lake Kariba Inns HOTEL **$$**
(☎0977 770480, 0211-511290; www.karibainns.com; s/d from ZMW825/945; ❄ @ 📶 🏊) With a commanding hilltop location with lush gardens (home to some roaming zebra) and lake views, this hotel has relatively luxurious rooms (some with verandas) and is a good choice if you don't mind sharing space with conference attendees. The restaurant (buffet ZMW150) and sports bar overlook the pool area, which is itself perched high above the lake.

Sinazongwe

Near the southwestern end of Lake Kariba and far from its cousin Siavonga at the other end of the lake, Sinazongwe is a small Zambian town used by *kapenta* fishers as an outpost. The centre of town is actually up on a hill away from the lake's edge and the whole area has little tourism footprint. It's a lovely place to come to get away from it all.

Ask in Choma for minibuses that can take you to Sinazongwe. By car, head to Batoka, just north of Choma. From here take the turnoff to Maamba. After about 50km look for the turn-off to Sinazongwe; the town is a short distance down this dirt road. All up it's around a 5½-hour drive from Lusaka. Note: if visiting during the rainy season, you'll need a 4WD.

WORTH A TRIP

CHIKANKA ISLAND CAMP

Chikanka Island Camp (☎0976 667752; www.lakeview-zambia.com; camping ZMW100, s/d incl breakfast ZMW750/1350; 🏊) is located on a beautiful private island 18km from Sinazongwe – it's mostly wooded, with impala, kudu, zebra, bushbuck and the occasional elephant dropping in. Crocs and hippos patrol the shores, so don't even think about taking a dip.

The camp features a mix of stone-and-thatch chalets with views overlooking the lake. Fishing for tiger fish and bream is a big draw, as are boat trips and wildlife safaris to Chete Island. Campers are welcome to pitch a tent. Meals are available to order or there's braai facilities for self-caterers.

To get here you'll need to transfer from its sister accommodation Lakeview Lodge at Sinazongwe on the mainland, a 40-minute boat trip (ZMW950).

Lakeview Lodge LODGE **$$**
(☎0976 667752; www.lakeview-zambia.com; camping ZMW100, s/d incl breakfast ZMW420/714; 🏊) A kilometre from the town of Sinazongwe, Lakeview Lodge has comfortable chalets with ceiling fans and a secluded terrace overlooking the lake and verdant grounds. There's also a campsite to pitch a tent, as well as a pool, small beach area and a braai, making it a good spot to chill out for a few days.

Choma

This busy market town, the capital of the Southern Province, is strung out along the highway 188km northeast of Livingstone. Most visitors zip through on their way to Lusaka or Livingstone, but Choma is a convenient stopover or staging post for trips to the southern section of Kafue National Park or to Lake Kariba. Other than the **museum** (adult/child US$5/3; ⏰9am-4pm) there's not much to distinguish the town, but it has all of the facilities and services travellers need, including a Spar supermarket, international banks with ATMs, internet, a couple of petrol stations and decent accommodation.

All daily buses and trains between Livingstone and Lusaka stop at Choma. The bus to either Lusaka or Livingstone is ZMW60 or ZMW75 and there are many departures throughout the day.

Leon's Lodge LODGE $
(☎0978 666008; off Livingstone Rd; r ZMW250-450; ❄) Marked by two enormous stone carved lions out front, and rather luxurious-looking thatched chalets, Leon's has clean and large rooms that come with satellite TV and fridge. There's a small bar and restaurant on site, both of which are rarely attended to, consistent with what is fairly patchy service across the board. It's along a backstreet running parallel with the main road.

New Choma Hotel HOTEL $
(☎0213-220836; Livingstone-Lusaka Rd; r incl breakfast ZMW175-250; ❄) Far from flash, this gritty hotel nonetheless has a convenient central location along the main strip. Rooms are spacious and have TV, fridge and air-con. At its rear is a great Indian restaurant and bar, which can get noisy at night, however.

Lochinvar National Park

This small, 410 sq km **park** (adult US$10; ⏲6am-6pm), northwest of Monze, consists of grassland, low wooded hills and the seasonally flooded Chunga Lagoon – all part of a huge, impressive wetland site called the Kafue Flats. You may see buffalo, wildebeest, zebra, kudu and some of the 30,000 Kafue lechwe residing in the park. Bushbuck, oribi, hippo, jackal, reedbuck and common waterbuck are also here. Lochinvar is a haven for birdlife too, with more than 400 species recorded.

While all safaris in the park are self-drive, you're likely to be able to arrange for a ranger to accompany you for around US$20. The network of tracks around the park is still mostly overgrown, with only the track from the gate to Chunga Lagoon reliably open.

Moorings Campsite CAMPGROUND $
(☎0977 521352; www.mooringscampsite.com; camping/tent rental US$8/15, chalet s/d US$30/50) This is perhaps the most beautifully landscaped campsite in Zambia. It's a lovely secluded spot on an old farm with plenty of grass and there are open-walled thatch rondavels scattered around the campsite and a braai next to them for cooking. It's perhaps the best place to break a journey between Lusaka and Livingstone, or to access Lochinvar National Park.

WESTERN ZAMBIA

When it comes to tourism, west Zambia doesn't do things by half measures: it's either wildly popular or just plain wild.

At one end of the spectrum is Victoria Falls. Being one of Africa's most famous attractions – combined with a world-class outdoor adventure scene – it's home to the country's tourism industry. The other big hitter is Kafue National Park, one of the continent's largest parks and a truly magnificent spot with all the big animals, and a thousand different landscapes.

Conversely, in the bulk of this vast west region you'll be hard pressed to see a single traveller. It's by far Zambia's least-visited area, which for many is its very appeal. It has huge tourism potential, however, with thundering waterfalls and remote wilderness areas such as Liuwa Plain National Park. Barotseland is also here, home to the Lozi people and the site of the colourful Kuomboka, Zambia's best-known traditional ceremony.

Kafue National Park

Covering more than 22,500 sq km, **Kafue National Park** (adult/vehicle US$20/15; ⏲6am-6pm) is the largest in Zambia and one of the biggest in the world. With terrain ranging from the lush riverine forest of the Kafue River to the vast grassland of the Busanga Plains, the park rewards wildlife enthusiasts with glimpses of various carnivores and their nimble prey. There's a good chance of sighting lions and leopards, and, if you're lucky, cheetahs in the north of the park, plus elephants, zebras and numerous species of antelope. There are some 500 species of birds too.

The main route into the park is via the sealed highway running between Lusaka and Mongu, which loosely divides the park into its northern and southern sectors. Kafue is one of the few parks in Zambia that's easily accessible by public transport, with a handful of camps just off the highway.

For a budget safari into the park, check with Lusaka Backpackers (p38) and Bongwe Barn (p38) in Lusaka, or the **Mobile Safari Company** (☎0963 005937; www.wild-kafue.com; 2 nights/3 days from US$425) based in Livingstone.

Sleeping

Northern Sector

★ **Mayukuyuku** CAMPGROUND, TENTED CAMP $$$
(☎0972 179266, 0977 721284; www.kafuecamps.com; Northern Sector; camping US$25, all-inclusive chalet per person US$495;) This rustic bush camp, small and personal, is in a gorgeous spot on the river with a well-landscaped camping area and four tastefully furnished thatch-roofed safari tents. Each of the latter has hammocks, chairs and table out the front and great outdoor bathrooms (even campers get open-air toilets and showers). If you don't have your own gear, you can rent tents (US$15/30 small/large tent).

★ **Mukambi Plains Camp** TENTED CAMP $$$
(☎0974 424013; www.mukambisafaris.com; Northern Sector; per person all-inclusive US$775, minimum 5-night stay; 15 Jul-Oct) The approach to this bucolic oasis, basically an island just 7km from the park's northern border, is made all the more dramatic by the wooden walkway over a prairie of 'floating grass'. The four simply but comfortably outfitted safari tents succeed in the exact balance between luxury and offering a safari experience, and feature outdoor bathrooms with bucket showers.

Southern Sector

Chibila Camp LODGE $
(☎0211-251630; www.conservationzambia.org/camps-and-lodges; Southern Sector; r member/non-member ZMW100/150) Just outside the park in the GMA, Chibila offers three basic, bargain-priced rooms that overlook Lake Itezhi-tezhi. Rooms come with attached bathroom, and while you need to bring along your own food, the team here are happy to cook it up for you. It's a peaceful spot among woodland and boulders, where plenty of hyrax dart about.

There are no wildlife drives on offer here, so you'll either need your own wheels or you can arrange safaris with one of the neighbouring lodges, including Hippo Bay Bush Camp or New Kalala Camp.

Hippo Bay Bush Camp CAMPGROUND, CHALET $$
(☎0962 841364; www.hippobaycamp.com; Southern Sector; camping US$20, chalets US$60-100) Hippo Bay is easily one of the best budget options in south Kafue. It has six rustic, well-priced thatched reed chalets with attached bathroom, or a campsite with flush toilets and hot water. There's a braai and firewood to cook meals, but otherwise you can drive to its nearby sister Konkamoya Lodge for meals (breakfast/lunch US$15, dinner US$30) and drinks. Wildlife drives cost US$35.

New Kalala Camp CAMPGROUND, CHALET $$
(☎0211-290914, 0979 418324; www.newkalala.com; camping/tent hire ZMW100/200, s/d from ZMW500/700;) Just outside the park boundary in the GMA is this locally run place with large, bland chalets in a rocky setting overlooking beautiful Lake Itezhi-Tezhi. There's a choice of thatched chalets or new concrete rondavels; the latter have lake views. All come with TV, fridge and air-con. The campsite is separate from the lodge in a patch of shady trees.

★ **KaingU Safari Lodge** CAMPGROUND, TENTED CAMP $$$
(☎in Lusaka 0211-256992; www.kaingu-lodge.com; Southern Sector; camping US$20-25, tented camping with full board & 2 activities US$450; Apr-Dec;) Set on a magical stretch of the Kafue River, this lodge overlooks a primordial stretch of lush islands among the rapids, with delightful birdwatching. The four tastefully furnished Meru-style tents are raised on rosewood platforms with stone bathrooms and large decks to enjoy the view. There are also three campsites, each with its own well-kept thatch ablution and braai facilities.

Mukambi Safari Lodge CHALET $$$
(☎0974 424013; www.mukambi.com; Southern Sector; per person with full board US$350;) Easily the most accessible of the Kafue lodges and easy to reach from Lusaka, Mukambi makes a great base to explore the park. Tastefully designed rondavels with Adirondack-style chairs on each front porch are set back from the riverfront on a lawn with a manicuring assisted by visiting hippos in the evenings. Activities such as wildlife drives and boat cruises are additional (US$45).

Konkamoya Lodge CHALET $$$
(☎0962 841364; www.konkamoya.com; Southern Sector; per person all-inclusive US$500; mid-

Kafue National Park

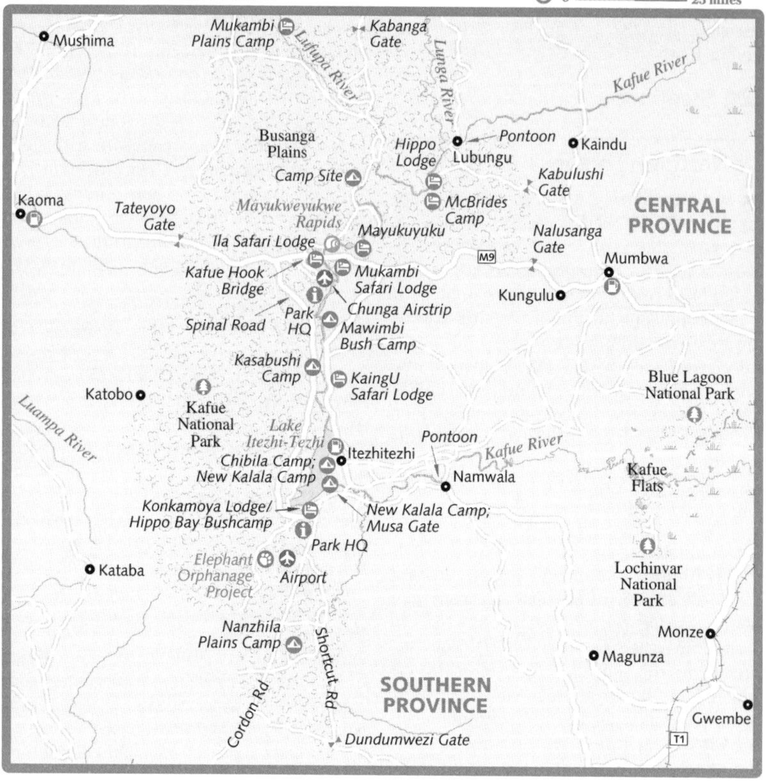

Jun–mid-Nov;) One of the best lodges in the southern sector, Konkamoya has a wonderful location on the southern shores of Lake Itezhi-Tezhi. Enjoy dramatic views of skeletal tree trunks rising from the water and grassy plains that attract plenty of wildlife. Its enormous and luxurious stilted safari tents come with wicker furniture and panoramic outlooks.

Kasabushi Camp CAMPGROUND, CHALET **$$$**
(0971 807226; www.kasabushi.wordpress.com; Southern Sector; camping US$20, tent hire US$15-20, chalet per person all-inclusive US$350; chalets May-Dec, campsite year-round) Run by husband-and-wife team Andy and Libby, Kasabushi gets great reviews for both its tranquil riverside campsite and luxury chalets. Separated from the campsite, its two rosewood chalets are thoughtfully and lovingly designed and open directly to the river. The camping area has wonderful views and atmospheric outdoor showers. There's also a natural rock swimming pool built into the riverbank.

Getting There & Away

Most guests of the top-end lodges/camps fly in on chartered planes.

Given there's a sealed road passing through the centre of the park, you can easily catch a Mongu-bound bus here from Lusaka (ZMW120, 3½ hours). On the highway ask to be let off either near Mukambi Safari Lodge (contact Mukambi for pick-up; only a couple hundred metres away wildlife roams free) or Mayukuyuku (arrange pick-up from the highway for US$35). For a ride back to Lusaka, wait out by Hook Bridge or the stop by Mukambi between 11am and 11.30am. Juldan or Shalom are two of the more recommendable bus companies.

Alternatively, take the slow daily bus, or one of the more regular minibuses from Lusaka to Itezhitezhi village (ZMW75, four hours). From the village bus stop wait around for a lift (because of the number of wild animals, it's not safe to hike).

If you're driving, be aware that the tsetse flies in the park are horrendous. It pays to have air-conditioning so you can close the windows.

There are several gates, but the main ones are: Nalusanga Gate (200km from Lusaka), along the eastern boundary; Dundumwezi Gate for the southern sector, accessed from the town of Kalomo if coming from Livingstone or Choma; Kabanga Gate if entering or exiting from the north; and Tateyoyo Gate for either sector if you're coming from the west. Rangers are also stationed at the two park headquarters: one at Chunga Camp and another 8km south of Musa Gate, at the southern end of Lake Itezhi-Tezhi.

For those heading south from the main road, the newly upgraded Spinal Rd is by far the best option. If coming from Lusaka it's accessed off the Lusaka–Mongu highway about 10km after the Kafue Hook Bridge (or 82km from Nalusanga Gate); look for the sign to Chunga. To get to the lodges along the eastern side of the Kafue River, you'll have to take a boat trip across (inclusive in the rates); otherwise from June to November there's a very rough, though scenic, dirt track that mostly hugs the eastern bank of the river.

Mongu

The largest town in Barotseland, and the capital of the Western Province, is on high ground overlooking the flat and seemingly endless Liuwa Plain. This is a low-key town with plenty of activity on the streets but little to draw travellers outside of the annual Kuomboka ceremony, when thousands flock here and room prices skyrocket.

The town is quite spread out with no real centre and the highlight is the spectacular panoramic view over the flood plains. From a harbour on the southwestern outskirts of town, an 8km canal runs westwards to meet a tributary of the Zambezi. The river port is a settlement of reed-and-thatch buildings, where local fishers sell their catch, and it's a good spot for people-watching as longboats glide down the river transporting people and goods to nearby villages.

Sights

While in Mongu itself there isn't much to see, you can head to Limulunga, 15km north of town, for an interesting little museum and the palace of the litunga (the king of the Lozi). Otherwise head to the main palace of the litunga in the village of Lealui, 15km northwest of Mongu.

Nayuma Museum MUSEUM

(Limulunga; adult/child US$5/2.50; 8am-4.30pm) This small, dusty museum has some good info on the Lozi people, the litunga (Lozi king) and Kuomboka ceremony. It has various artefacts and cultural exhibits, as well as a large model of the *nalikwanda* boat used in the Kuomboka. There are some fascinating shots of royal pageantry in a black-and-white photo exhibition titled, 'A Retrospective in the Forties' by Max Gluckman. It also has interesting pictures of the historical line of the litungas.

Lealui Palace PALACE

(Lealui; by appointment Mon-Fri) FREE Lealui village is the site of the main palace of the litunga (king of the Lozi). The palace is a large single-storey Lozi house, built with traditional materials (wood, reeds, mud and thatch); it was being renovated at the time of research and was scheduled to reopen 2017. Avoid visiting on weekends when the *litunga's* kotu (court) is closed, because you need permission from his *indunas* (advisors) to get a close look at the palace and even to take photos.

Sleeping

Country Lodge LODGE $

(0977 222216; countrylodge@iconnect.zm; 3066 Independence Ave; r incl breakfast ZMW250-600;) Close to the centre of town, this modern and well-run place sees its fair share of conferences, weddings and the like. The rooms are plainly decorated but come with amenities like satellite TV and nice modern bathrooms. There's a bar and restaurant onsite.

Greenview Guesthouse CAMPGROUND, GUESTHOUSE $

(0217-221029; www.limagarden.com; Limulunga Rd; camping per person ZMW80, s/d from ZMW70/200;) Located next to the church, chalets here sleep two people and are fantastic value; newer ones come with air-conditioning, shiny tiled floors and DSTV. Spacious inside and set in nice, grassy grounds with views of the flood plains, they may well be the best deal in Mongu. It's on the road to Limulunga; keep an eye out for the sign on the left.

Shopping

Mumwa Craft Association ARTS & CRAFTS

(0964 015014; Lusaka Rd; 7.30am-6pm Mon-Sat) A visit here is well worth your time.

Proceeds from sales of expertly made basketry and woodcarvings – at low prices – are ploughed back into the local communities that produce them. Located next to the Total petrol station on the road to Lusaka.

Liuwa Plain National Park

About 100km northwest of Mongu, near the Angolan border, **Liuwa Plain National Park** (☎0964 168394; liuwa@africanparks.co.zm; adult/child US$30/10) is 3600 sq km of true wilderness. The remote park is characterised by expanses of flat, grassy flood plains, and is most famous for the second-largest wildebeest migration in Africa; in the wet season you'll find a wall-to-wall gathering of herds.

The park is also notable for having one of the highest population densities of hyena in the world, as well as a stunning variety of birdlife. Other wildlife include lion, cheetah, wild dog, zebra, buffalo, lechwe, wildebeest, tsessebe and Roan antelope.

Since 2004 the park has been managed by African Parks (www.african-parks.org), an international organisation that assists governments in funding conservation projects and reviving animal numbers across Africa.

A sizeable community of Lozi people live both within and around the park, and you'll pass several of their villages en route, characterised by their thatched rondavels.

Most visitors are here to see the November migration of wildebeest, which congregate here in vast numbers that turn the park into a 'mini Serengeti'. Although it's often called a migration, in reality the wildebeest are here year-round, so it's more a meander from one sector of the park to another. While November is undoubtedly the best time to visit, you can see them at other times in the northern part of the park in large numbers.

Liuwa Plain is accessible from May/June to December. However the best time to go is November, just after the rains start (the later the better). Leave before the flood waters rise, however, or you'll be stuck for months.

Sleeping

For completely self-sufficient travellers, there are five well-maintained campsites in the park.

Sikhale Camp Site CAMPGROUND $
(www.african-parks.org/the-parks/liuwa-plain; per person US$ adult/child US$15/7) In the far northern part of the park, Sikale is the place to camp for those wanting to see wildebeest during the drier months. Lions also often head up this way. There's no running water or flush toilets, so you'll need to be totally self-sufficient. It's about a 4½-hour drive from Kalabo.

Katoyana CAMPGROUND $
(www.african-parks.org/the-parks/liuwa-plain; camping adult/child US$15/7) One of Liuwa's best campsites is this lovely shaded spot that's well placed for the wildebeest gatherings, as well as for spotting birdlife, hyenas and lions. It's a 2½-hour drive from the main gate at Kalabo.

Getting There & Away

The new pristine tarmac road from Mongu to the park's headquarters in Kalabo (70km, 45 minutes) has drastically improved accessibility to the park. At Kalabo you need to cross the river via the rope-pulled pontoon (per vehicle ZMW40); from that point it's 12km to the park boundary. There is no petrol in Kalabo, so be sure to fill up in Mongu and carry a full jerry can.

Access to Liuwa Plain National Park is restricted from around May to December. Despite a network of tracks, Liuwa is serious 4WD territory; a lot of the tracks are very sandy, wet or both. Although the trackless, featureless, endless plains appear benign, it's also very easy to get lost. Taking a scout with you is highly recommended and also financially assists the national park; this can be organised at the park headquarters. A GPS is advisable.

Senanga

Senanga has a real 'end of the line' feel, particularly if you've come from Lusaka. That said, the main street can be surprisingly lively, especially in the evening, and the views of the Zambezi are beautiful. It is the best place to break up a journey between Mongu and Ngonye Falls or Sesheke.

Minibuses and pickups run between Senanga and Mongu (ZMW50, two hours) several times a day. For Livingstone it's an 8½-hour bus journey (ZMW140), departing daily at 3pm apart from Sundays.

Senanga Safaris CHALET $
(☎0976 020143; r incl breakfast ZMW200-350; 🍽) The best accommodation in Senanga are these comfortable rondavels with splendid views over the Zambezi plains. It's spoiled only by the giant satellite TV dish in the garden. The bar sells cold beer and the res-

taurant serves stock-standard meals, where staff are for the most part disinterested.

Ngonye Falls

Located about 130km north of Sesheke are the **Ngonye Falls** (Sioma Falls; entry US$5, vehicle US$15; ⏲6am-6pm), a 1km-wide chain of waterfalls, rapids and rocky islands cutting across the Zambezi River. It's beautiful and very impressive and would be a major attraction if it wasn't so difficult to reach. Imagine something almost as majestic as Victoria Falls, but with almost no other person (local or foreign) in sight. It's worth visiting anytime of the year, but it peaks around June to July.

Wildlife is being introduced to the area of the park surrounding the falls, including zebra and sitatunga among others.

While it's easy to get a view of the falls, getting a really good view is much harder as you need to get out onto an island in front of the falls – ask at the National Parks office if there are any boats that might take you there. Otherwise Ngonye River Camp (p63) can arrange boat trips.

Sleeping

Ngonye River Camp LODGE $
(☎0975 144820; www.ngonyerivercamp.com; per person camping US$10, tented camping from US$15, chalet US$35) This scenic camp on the sandy banks of the Zambezi, about 5km from Ngonye Falls, is a laid-back spot where you can pitch a tent (or hire one of theirs) or stay in a chalet. They offer boat trips to the falls as well as canoeing trips, fishing and village tours. Meals are available and there's complimentary filter coffee.

Campsite CAMPGROUND $
(camping US$10) A lovely campsite, just a five-minute walk from the falls, with hot-water showers, toilets and a shelter for food preparation. There's a camp attendant to provide firewood and light campfires.

Getting There & Away

The falls are reached along a nice stretch of tarmac running from Sesheke to Sioma, which

KUOMBOKA CEREMONY

The Kuomboka (literally, 'to move to dry ground') is probably one of the last great Southern African ceremonies. It is celebrated by the Lozi people of western Zambia, and marks the ceremonial journey of the *litunga* (the Lozi king) from his dry-season palace at Lealui, near Mongu, to his wet-season palace on higher ground at Limulunga. It usually takes place in late March or early April, and sometimes ties in with Easter. The dates are not fixed, however; they're dependent on the rains. In fact, the Kuomboka does not happen every year and is not infrequently cancelled because of insufficient flood waters; the 2012 ceremony was called off because it's against Lozi tradition to hold the Kuomboka under a full moon. While the new road here means the journey by boat is no longer necessary, tradition dictates the ceremony continues as is – though since there's a road a lot more people come to watch!

In 1933 a palace was built by Litunga Yeta III on permanently dry ground at the edge of the plain at a place called Limulunga. Although the Kuomboka was already a long-standing tradition, it was Yeta III who first made the move from Lealui to Limulunga a major ceremony.

Central to the ceremony is the royal barge, the *nalikwanda*, a huge wooden canoe, painted with black-and-white stripes, that carries the *litunga*. It is considered a great honour to be one of the hundred or so paddlers on the *nalikwanda*, and each paddler wears a headdress of a scarlet beret with a piece of a lion's mane and a knee-length skirt of animal skins. Drums also play a leading role in the ceremony. The most important are the three royal war drums, *kanaona*, *munanga* and *mundili*, each more than one-metre wide and said to be at least 170 years old.

The journey from Lealui to Limulunga takes about six hours. The *litunga* begins the day in traditional dress, but during the journey changes into the full uniform of a British admiral, complete with regalia and ostrich-plumed hat. The uniform was presented to the *litunga* in 1902 by the British King, Edward VII, in recognition of the treaties signed between the Lozi and Queen Victoria.

links up to Senanga. Plenty of buses ply the route – but you'll need to make sure they're Sioma-bound, as the road splits just before the new Sioma bridge.

The falls themselves are also easily accessible, less than 1km east of the main road. If driving, for the falls follow the signs to Sioma when you reach the split in the road, from where it's a further 5km over the new bridge.

Sesheke

The sleepy border town of Sesheke is a handy base for those crossing the border to Namibia (via the bridge to Katima Mulilo), or onward travel to northwest Zambia.

Buses link Sesheke with Natakindi Rd in Livingstone (ZMW70, three hours, two daily), usually at 7am and 5pm. Occasional minibuses also link Sesheke with Katima Mulilo, otherwise it's a ZMW15 taxi ride to the Nambian border which is open 6.30am to 6pm.

★ **Brenda's Best & Baobab Bar** CAMPGROUND, CHALET $
(☎0963 786882; brendasbaobab@gmail.com; Mulambwe St; camping ZMW50, s/d incl breakfast ZMW200/300) Run by the friendly Brenda and her Dutch husband, this relaxed guesthouse is easily the best place to stay in Sesheke. The thatch-roofed double-storey chalets are built around a lovely lawn and a massive baobab overlooking fantastic views of the Zambezi.

NORTHERN ZAMBIA

Those with a spirit of adventure and who love wild, open spaces will be at home in Zambia's untamed north. The region starts after the 'Pedicle', the slice of DRC territory that juts sharply into Zambia, almost splitting it in two. From here onwards the old Great North Rd shoots its way straight up to Tanzania, passing national parks, vast wilderness areas and waterfalls along the way.

Attractions in the north include Lake Tanganyika where you can relax on white sandy beaches; Kasanka National Park, to watch the spectacular bat migration; Mutinondo Wilderness, a vast area of whaleback hills, rivers and valleys so untouched you feel almost like you have been transported to a prehistoric era; and the eerie Shiwa Ng'andu, a grand English mansion buried deep in the Zambian bush with a relaxing hot springs on tap.

Serenje

Serenje is a relatively uninspiring rural town spread out around the Great North Rd. The only reason for travellers to pass through is for a convenient refuelling stop or to spend the night on the way to more exciting destinations.

There are two main hubs in the town: the turnoff at the junction, with a petrol station, a couple of shops and a few basic restaurants; and the town centre, 3km north of the Great North Rd, with a bank, the bus station and some lodges.

All buses between Lusaka (ZMW90, five hours) and Kasama (ZMW90, five hours) pass through Serenje. Most of the big buses stop beside the petrol station at the junction with the Great North Rd, while minibuses stop in town.

Mapontela Inn GUESTHOUSE $
(☎0979 587262; r ZMW180-235; ⊙restaurant 7am-9pm) Located along the main road in the centre of town is this charming guesthouse that's the best in Serenje. Opening out onto the leafy courtyard are a number of homely brick cottage rooms with fans and spotless bathrooms. The attached restaurant (meals ZMW35 to ZMW70), with a patio overlooking the street, serves tasty staples and is a good a place to sample Zambian food.

Kasanka National Park

One of Zambia's least-known wilderness areas and a real highlight of a visit to this part of the country is the privately man-

FIBWE HIDE

A trip to Kasanka isn't complete without viewing the park from the heights of the **Fibwe Hide**, a 15-minute drive from Wasa Lodge. Ascend 20m up an old mahogany tree via a rickety wooden ladder to a platform where you can sit and watch the swamps below. Come at dawn and dusk for the best chance of spotting sitatungas.

Pontoon Campsite (www.kasankanationalpark.com; camping US$20) and **Kasanka Conservation Centre** (camping ZMW59, dm/r ZMW99/190) are good budget bets.

aged **Kasanka National Park** (☎in South Africa 072-298 0777; www.kasankanationalpark.com; adult US$8; 6am-6pm). At just 390 sq km, it's pretty small compared to most African parks, it doesn't have a huge range of facilities and it sees very few visitors – and this is what makes it special. There are no queues of jeeps to get a look at a leopard here; instead, you'll discover great tracts of miombo woodland, evergreen thicket, open grassland and rivers fringed with emerald forest, all by yourself.

Kasanka is most famous for its fruit bat migration in November and December, which sees up to 10 million of the nocturnal creatures arrive. The park is also known for its swampland, and this is the terrain to see the park's shy and retiring star, the sitatunga.

For sleeping, Pontoon Campsite and Kasanka Conservation Centre are good budget bets.

★ **Wasa Lodge** LODGE $$

(☎in South Africa 072-298 0777; www.kasankanationalpark.com; per person self-catering chalets US$70, all-inclusive US$420) Doubling as the park headquarters, accommodation here consists of thatched bungalows overlooking Lake Wasa. Larger chalets are airy and cool with wide balconies and lovely stone showers. There are multiple vantage points – including the deck of the large bar and dining area – to look out over the swamp to spot hippos, puku and sometimes even sitatungas.

Getting There & Away

From Lusaka, take a bus (ZMW130) in the direction of Mansa, or take any bus from Lusaka to Serenje and change onto a minibus (ZMW45) for Mansa. After turning off the Great North Rd, ask the driver to drop you at Kasanka National Park (near Mulembo village), not at Kasanka village, which is much further away. From the gate to Wasa Lodge is 12km; you can radio Wasa Lodge for a lift. It is also possible to charter a taxi from Serenje directly to Wasa Lodge; ZMW200 is about what you can expect to pay.

If you have your own vehicle, continue north along the Great North Rd from Serenje for 36km, then turn left onto the road towards Mansa. It's then 55km on a good road to the Kasanka entrance gate, clearly signposted on the left. There is no fuel available in the park, so stock up at Serenje.

There's an airstrip used for charter flights arranged through **Skytrails Charters** (☎0979 337206; www.skytrailszambia.com), which is based there. For further information and prices, contact the Kasanka Trust (www.kasanka.com).

OFF THE BEATEN TRACK

KASANKA TO THE GREAT NORTH ROAD DRIVE

Drivers with a taste of adventure (and time on their side) may like to take the 'back route' from Kasanka direct to the Great North Rd, which winds past several attractions, including a memorial to explorer David Livingstone and lovely Lake Waka-Waka. The roads are generally in poor condition, so you'll need a 4WD or high-clearance vehicle.

In between Kasanka National Park and the Bangweulu Wetlands is the **Nakapalayo Tourism Project** (☎0977 561714; r incl full-board & activities per person US$60, r only & activities per person US$40), a community initiative that allows tourists to experience life in a real Zambian village. Visitors can camp or stay in huts with double beds and mosquito nets. Activities revolve around village life and include learning how to pound cassava, meeting local healers and bush walks to learn about traditional uses for plants and trees.

Bangweulu Wetlands

The **Bangweulu Wetlands** (www.african-parks.org/the-parks/bangweulu; adult ZMW50) is a watery wilderness of lakes, seasonally flooded grasslands, swamp and unspoiled miombo woodland that lies 50km to the north of Kasanka. This rarely visited part of Zambia is the only place in Africa to see major numbers of black lechwes (antelopes with long, curved antlers). Bangweulu is also known for its birds. Some 400 species have been noted, and a particular highlight for twitchers is the strange and rare shoebill stork.

It's one of several national parks run by African Parks. During the rainy season, be sure to call ahead to enquire about accessibility into the area.

June to July is the best time to see the lechwe herds as the waters have begun receding, leaving vast plains of fresh green grass.

Nsobe Camp CAMPGROUND $
(www.african-parks.org; camping ZMW50; ⏲ May-Jan) This is a basic campsite with braai area, hot showers, flush toilets and a couple of thatched cooking shelters. Note it's closed February to April.

Nkondo Safari Camp TENTED CAMP $
(www.african-parks.org; per person ZMW250) Open year-round, Nkondo offers a comfortable self-catering option with safari tents with attached bathroom. There's a common kitchen to cook up meals. It's set among miombo woodlands with plenty of wildlife about.

Shoebill Island Camp CAMPGROUND $$$
(www.african-parks.org) This camp rests in the heart of the wetlands and is splendidly positioned on a tiny permanent island with only birds, hippos, lechwes and the occasional passing fisher for company. It was closed from 2016 for a refurb with plans of reopening mid-2017.

Getting There & Away

The only way into the wetlands is by 4WD or chartered plane. Dirt roads lead here from Kasanka via Lake Waka-Waka and the Nakapalayo Tourism Project. The Chikuni ranger post and Nsobe Camp are 65km on from Nakapalayo, and from here it's another 10km to Shoebill Island Camp if it's dry. (In the wet, you'll have to travel this last stretch by boat.) You will definitely need a fully equipped 4WD to attempt this trip as the going is tough. Set off from Kasanka in the early morning in order to reach Bangweulu before it gets dark. You can also get here along the Great North Rd via Lavushi Manda National Park; the African Parks team can provide a detailed information sheet about getting to the wetlands.

Samfya

Perched on the western shore of Lake Bangweulu, about 10km east of the main road between Mansa and Serenje, is Samfya, a small and dusty trading centre with little going for it except for its excellent white sandy beaches on the western shores of this beautiful lake. In the local language *bangweulu* means 'where the water meets the sky' and if you watch the lake at sunset, when the lake and hazy clouds both turn the same shade of blue, it's not hard to see why. Though locals are insistent it's safe to swim, the occasional crocodile is known to pass by.

Samfya is regularly served by minibuses from Serenje (ZMW95, five hours). Buses from Lusaka (ZMW120, 12 hours) may drop you in town or at the junction 10km away, from where local pickups shuttle passengers to and fro.

Samfya Beach Hotel HOTEL $
(☎0969 121916; camping ZMW100, r ZMW200-500) Sitting on Cabana Beach, this place has a pretty good location but the rooms are small and have very basic bathrooms. Camping is an affordable option for those with a tent. As of late 2016 it was undergoing a much-needed renovation. Take the first turning on the left in town and it's about 2km north of the centre.

Mutinondo Wilderness

This is one of the most stunning places in northern Zambia. Mutinondo is a beautiful 100-sq-km wilderness littered with whaleback hills or inselbergs: huge, sweeping hulks of stone in varying shades of black, purple, green and brown. The landscape here feels unspoiled and ancient.

It's beautiful walking country and there are more than 60km of wilderness trails. Scramble to the top of one of those great granite beasts and it is easy to imagine a time when Stone Age hunters wandered the endless valleys, woodland and rivers below.

The network of rivers and waterfalls at Mutinondo are incredibly clear and calm, and safe to swim in (and to drink). Canoes are also available.

Mammal sightings are rare here, although Mutinondo is an important birding destination. There are about 345 species here including plenty of rare specimens that are difficult to find outside the country. Notable are the Ross's turaco, Anchieta's sunbird and the bar-winged weaver.

The turnoff to Mutinondo is 164km past Serenje heading north on the Great North Rd. It's signposted to the right; Mutinondo is 25km down a 2WD-friendly track. Travelling by bus from Lusaka, ask for a ticket to Kalonje Railway Station (ZMW150, six hours). Road transfers for a maximum of five people can be arranged from the Great North Rd turnoff (ZMW290). There's also an airstrip at nearby Mpika for charter flights, from where the team at Mutinondo can pick up guests for US$125.

Mayense Campsite CAMPGROUND $
(www.mutinondozambia.com; camping US$8-15, rondavel US$35-45, tented camping US$100) This

fantastic campsite offers a user-friendly spot to pitch a tent. Each pitch has cooking areas and bird-proof cupboards to protect supplies. The large, open-air showers (constructed out of sustainable materials) have hot water, sinks have framed pieces of information to read while teeth-brushing, and the eco-toilets have magazines to browse and strategically placed slots for views over the bush.

★ **Mayense Camp** LODGE $$$
(☎0978 198198; www.mutinondozambia.com; s/d all-inclusive from US$145/260; 📶) Built into the hillside are Mayense's individually designed chalets, each with outstanding views. All are beautiful in their simplicity and blend in seamlessly with their natural environment. Some are built into the granite rocks, with a huge handmade bath with a view, while others are open to the elements so it feels as if you're sleeping in the wild.

Mpika

Mpika is a busy crossroads town on the Great North Rd. The old road (M1) runs north to Kasama and Mpulungu, while the newer road (T2) runs northeast to the Tanzanian border at Nakonde. It is a good supply stop, and can also serve as a base to tackle South or North Luangwa national parks if you have a 4WD.

Buses and minibuses stop at the junction where the Kasama road and the Great North Rd divide. Destinations include Lusaka (ZMW140 to ZMW160, 9½ hours), Kasama (ZMW80), Serenje (ZMW85) and Mpulungu (ZMW110). There are also daily services to Nakonde on the Tanzanian border, but the buses usually pass through around midnight on their way from Lusaka.

Mpika's huge and impressive Tazara train station is about 7km southwest of the town centre, and is reachable by minibus when trains are due.

From here you can access South Luangwa via the rarely used Chifungwe Gate. The turn off is 40km south of Mpika along the Great North Rd. As it passes over the escarpment road it's a challenging route only to be attempted by experienced drivers in a 4WD.

★ **Bayama's Lodge, Pub & Grill** LODGE $
(☎0977 316143, 0977 410839; www.bayama.de; r US$20-35, meals from US$5; ❄📶) Bayama's Lodge is a real gem for a backwater like Mpika. Under German-Zambian ownership, it is just off the Great North Rd and offers budget rooms or larger chalets. The best feature is a lively restaurant-bar serving mains such as T-bone steaks and homemade pizzas. The bar has cold beer, tunes and a popular pool table.

Shiwa Ng'andu

Deep in the northern Zambian wilderness sits Shiwa Ng'andu, a grand country estate and labour of love of eccentric British aristocrat Sir Stewart Gore-Brown. The estate's crowning glory is Shiwa Ng'andu manor house, which is a magnificent English-style mansion. Driving up to the house through farm buildings, settlements and workers' houses it almost feels like an old feudal domain: there's a whole community built around it, including a school and a hospital, and many of the people now working at Shiwa Ng'andu are the children and grandchildren of Sir Stewart's original staff. Today Gore-Brown's grandchildren live on and manage the estate, which is a working farm.

Shiwa House HISTORIC SITE
(www.shiwangandu.com; tours US$20; ⏲tour 9-11am Mon-Sat, closed to nonguests Sun) The main draw to the area is the surreal sight of Shiwa House, a massive English-style manor materialising seemingly out of nowhere in the middle of rural Zambia. Built in the 1920s, the decaying grand mansion built on a stately lawn is full of old family heirlooms, photographs and stories. There are guided tours of the estate (or there's a self-guided option with booklet), which include a wildlife drive to spot the property's 24 mammal species including puku, kudu, zebra and wildebeest.

Kapishya Hot Springs HOT SPRINGS
(nonguests/guests of Kapishya Lodge US$8/free; ⏲6am-6pm) Located on the premises of Kapishya Hot Springs Lodge, the setting here makes it a marvellous place to take a soak in its blue-green steaming lagoon of bath-hot water surrounded by thick palms. If staying at Kapishya Lodge, then you can use the springs for free. It's about 20km west of Shiwa House.

Sleeping & Eating

★ **Kapishya Hot Springs Lodge** LODGE $$
(☎0211-229261, 0976 970444; www.shiwasafaris.com; camping US$15, d from US$75, per person all-inclusive US$165; 📶🏊) Featuring a scenic river location, with nearby hot springs and

lush rainforest, this lodge is popular for good reason. The chalets are light and spacious, with wooden decks complete with fireplaces and views and there's a lovely campsite with hot showers and barbecue areas. The pool and hot springs are wonderful spots to unwind. Excellent meals are also available.

Shiwa House HISTORIC HOTEL **$$$**
(☎0211-229261; www.shiwasafaris.com; per person with full board from US$470) This old place is suitably attired for a grand old English manor, with fireplaces, four-poster beds, oil paintings and big old roll-top baths. There's a glorious guest sitting-room looking out onto the front lawn, which is even more atmospheric at night when lit by candles and a crackling fire. Tasty dinners are taken in the rather splendid dining room.

Getting There & Away

To reach Shiwa House, head north along the Great North Rd by bus (or car) from Mpika for about 90km towards Chisoso. Look for the signpost to the west, from where a 20km dirt road leads to the house. Kapishya Hot Springs and the lodge are a further 20km along this track.

You can also get to Shiwa from the Mpika to Kasama road – this time look for the signpost pointing east and it's then 42km down the dirt track to Kapishya. There is no public transport along this last section, but vehicle transfers are available from the Great North Rd turnoff for US$35 per vehicle.

Kasama

Kasama is the capital of the Northern Province and the cultural centre of the Bemba people. With its wide, leafy streets and handsome, old, tin-roofed colonial houses, it is the most appealing of the northern towns. Kasama's environs are home to ancient rock art and a beautiful waterfall, as well as to the **Kusefya Pangwena festival** (www.zambiatourism.com).

Buses and minibuses leave for Lusaka (ZMW130, 12 hours) daily. Buses go via Mpika (ZMW80, two hours) and Serenje (ZMW95, four hours). Northbound buses go to Mbala (ZMW35, two hours) and Mpulungu (ZMW50, three hours). Cheaper local minibuses run to Mpulungu, Mbala and Mpika.

The Tazara train station is 6km south of the town centre. The express train to Nakonde (for the Tanzanian and Malawian border) and Dar Es Salaam (1st class ZMW205) leaves in the small hours of Friday night/Saturday morning. Trains to Mpika (ZMW35) and Kapiri Mposhi (ZMW87) pass through on Tuesday night.

Kasama Rock Art HISTORIC SITE
(adult/child US$15/7, camping US$10; ⏲6am-6pm) Archaeologists rate the Kasama rock art as one of the largest and most significant collections of ancient art in Southern Africa, though their quality is outdone in Zimbabwe and Namibia. The works are attributed to Stone Age hunter-gatherers (sometimes known as Twa) and are up to 2000 years old. Many are abstract designs, but some of the finest pictographs show human figures and animals, often capturing a remarkable sense of fluidity and movement, despite being stylised with huge bodies and minute limbs.

★ **Thorn Tree Guesthouse** GUESTHOUSE **$**
(☎0214-221615; kansato@iconnect.zm; 612 Zambia Rd; s/d from ZMW210/270, f from ZMW350;) The Thorn Tree is family-run, homey and very popular, so book ahead to avoid disappointment. Rooms are either in the main house sharing spick-and-span facilities or in larger family rooms, including a three-room cottage. There's a bar and a restaurant serving fresh farm produce; they also roast their own coffee beans on site, so you'll get a decent brew here.

Mbala

Once the colonial centre of Abercorn, this sleepy town sits on the periphery of the Great Rift Valley. From here the road drops about 1000m from the highest settlement in Zambia down to Lake Tanganyika and Mpulungu, the lowest town in the country. Today the only reason to visit is its museum, or as a stop-off point for Kalambo Falls. In practical terms, there's some decent spots for lunch, an ATM, fuel station and some general stores.

Buses run daily to Mpulungu (ZMW15, 50 minutes), Kasama (ZMW45, two hours), Mpika (ZMW110, four to five hours), Serenje (ZMW135, seven hours) and Lusaka (ZMW180, 13 to 15 hours).

Moto Moto Museum MUSEUM
(adult/child ZMW30/15; ⏲9am-4.45pm) This museum in a 1970s modernist building is well worth a visit if you're in the area. It has a large and diverse collection, much of which details the cultural life and history of

the Bemba people. Items on display include old drums, traditional musical instruments and an array of smoking paraphernalia. Particularly noteworthy is an exhibition detailing how young Bemba women were traditionally initiated into adulthood. It includes a life-size, walk-in example of an initiation hut, with background info.

Lake Chila Lodge LODGE $

(☎0977 795241; lakechilalodge@yahoo.com; Lake Chila; camping ZMW150, r incl breakfast ZMW250-500) The most atmospheric place to stay in Mbala is this welcoming lodge located on the shores of Lake Chila, about 2km from town. Rooms are set in spacious chalets with satellite TV and hot showers; the cheaper rondavels offer the best value. The lodge includes a lively little bar-restaurant (mains ZMW20 to ZMW40), which makes for a good road-trip pit stop.

Lake Tanganyika

Spreading over a massive 34,000 sq km, and reaching almost 1500m deep, cavernous Lake Tanganyika is the second-deepest lake in the world and contains about 15% of the earth's fresh water. Believed to be up to 15 million years old and lying in the Great Rift Valley, the shores of the lake reach Tanzania, Burundi, the Democratic Republic of the Congo and Zambia. The climate here is always very hot, especially at the end of the dry season.

Of most interest to visitors are its white sandy beaches that, along with palm trees and snorkelling in crystal clear waters with multicoloured tropical fish, can make it feel more like Thailand than Zambia.

All of the lodges can arrange boat transfers. Most boat transfers are included in the rates with the exception of Mishembe Bay and campers at Isanga Bay Lodge, in which case return transfers are US$100 to US$150. Otherwise you can try the water taxi service (ZMW25), which departs Monday, Wednesday and Friday – leaving Mpulungu at 3pm, and making the return journey about 5am or 6am. However, be warned: it gets very full.

Travel by road is possible, but only with a 4WD as the road is in very poor condition, with plenty of deep sandy stretches. Some taxis may be willing to tackle the road and will charge about ZMW400.

★Mishembe Bay (Luke's Beach) BUNGALOW, CAMPGROUND $

(☎0976 664999; www.facebook.com/mishembebayzambia; camping per person US$10, lodge US$25) With its stunning white sands, palm trees and thatched bungalows, Luke's Beach resembles some secluded Southeast Asian beach paradise. The stilted thatched bungalows are luxurious on the outside, yet remain bare bones within to suit the budget traveller, and feature magnificent views of the water. You'll need to bring along all your own food, but there's a kitchen where you can cook.

Staying here gives you the advantage of being a 1½-hour walk to Kalambo Falls. To get here the boat transfer is around ZMW500 return. The owner Luke is the son of the owners from Thorn Tree in Kasama.

Kalambo Falls Lodge LODGE $$

(☎0973 248476, 0977 430894; www.kalambolodge.com; all-inclusive per person US$70) While it doesn't have a white sandy beach, Kalambo Falls Lodge's waterfront location remains equally spectacular – whether enjoyed from the rooms or lazing on a sunbed. Run by a friendly Zambian-Danish couple, Victoria and Peter, rates include accommodation, activities, food and transfers, making it excellent value. The honeymoon suite in a stone chalet with clawfoot bath is a great option for couples.

Isanga Bay Lodge RESORT, CAMPGROUND $$

(☎0973 472317; www.isangabay.com; camping US$15, r incl breakfast US$80-100) Lake Tanganyika's most popular all-round choice is this South African–managed resort fronted by a pure white sandy beach. Undoubtedly the best pick here are the beach-facing bungalows in magnificent thatched structures; however, it's also a popular spot to pitch a tent; campers can access the same facilities including its lovely restaurant.

Mpulungu

Resting at the foot of mighty Lake Tanganyika, Mpulungu is a crossroads between Eastern, Central and Southern Africa. As Zambia's only international port, it's the terminal for the ferry across the lake to Tanzania. It's also a busy commercial fishing port and several fisheries are based here, some of them exporting tropical fish to aquariums around the world. The streets are fairly lively and busy, especially at night, but there is no real reason to come here unless travelling to Nsumbu National Park, Ndole Bay, the lodges along Lake Tanganyika or northeast to Tanzania. Although it's always very hot, don't be tempted to swim in the lake in this area because there are a few crocs.

Long-distance buses link Mpulungu with Lusaka (ZMW180, 16 hours) via Kasama (ZMW50, three hours) and Mpika (ZMW110, six hours). Minibuses also depart from near the BP petrol station in Mpulungu for Mbala (ZMW15, 40 minutes).

The MV *Liemba,* a hulking ex-German warship, leaves from Mpulungu harbour every second Friday, arriving in Kigoma (Tanzania) on Sunday. Fares for foreigners travelling in 1st, 2nd and economy class are US$100, US$90 and US$70, respectively. Visas can be issued on the ferry and cost US$50 single-entry.

Nkupi Lodge LODGE $
(☎0977 455166; camping/dm ZMW60/75, rondavels with shared/private bathroom from ZMW150/300) The best place for independent travellers is this shady campsite and lodge, a short walk out of town near the lake. It has plenty of space for tents as well as a number of spacious rondavels. There's also a self-catering kitchen and a bar, or otherwise meals are available with plenty of notice. The friendly owners Charity and Dinesh can assist with onward transport to Tanzania.

Nsumbu National Park

Hugging the southern shores of Lake Tanganyika, little-visited **Nsumbu National Park** (Sumbu National Park; adult US$10; ⏲6am-6pm) is a beautiful 2020 sq km of hilly grassland and escarpment, interrupted by rivers and wetlands. Back in the 1970s, this was one of the leading national parks in Africa with the largest density of rhino on the continent, and Kasaba Bay was like the St Tropez of Zambia, with the jet set flying in from South Africa and beyond. Like other remote parks in Zambia, Nsumbu was virtually abandoned in the 1980s and 1990s and poaching seriously depleted wildlife stocks here; however, conditions have improved over the past decade. Poaching has come under control, and animal numbers have increased, in part thanks to a buffer zone created by two Game Management Areas that adjoin the park.

A government ferry chugs up and down the lake ($US5, seven hours), heading north to Nsumbu at 7.30am Monday to Friday. For more comfort, boat charters to Ndole Bay Lodge are US$350 to US$750 (two hours).

Driving here is also an option with a 4WD. The most direct route is along the paved Great North Rd passing Mpika and Kasama before reaching Mporokoso, from where it's rough dirt road for the remaining 135km to the beginning of the park at Mutundu Gate.

★**Ndole Bay Lodge** LODGE, CAMPGROUND $$
(☎088-2165 2077; www.ndolebaylodge.com; camping US$15, chalets with full board from US$100;) Set on a pretty beach just outside Nsumbu National Park, this family-owned lodge has several spacious chalets dotted around the grounds, all made from natural local materials. The newest rooms are stunning and include beautiful furnishings and a huge attached bathroom with Balinese-style outdoor showers. There is also a campsite right under the trees on the sandy beach.

Kalambo Falls

At 221m in height **Kalambo Falls** (adult/child/car US$15/7/15, camping US$15) is twice as high as Victoria Falls, and the second-highest single-drop waterfall in Africa (the highest being Tugela Falls in South Africa). From spectacular viewpoints near the top of the falls, you can see the Kalambo River plummeting off a steep V-shaped cliff cut into the Rift Valley escarpment down into a deep valley, which then winds towards Lake Tanganyika.

Most people visit as a day trip from one of the lodges along Lake Tanganyika or Mbala, though there's a campsite (US$15 per person; bring food and drinking water) for those who want to stay overnight.

The best way for travellers without a car to get here is from Mpulungu. A thrice-weekly taxi boat service (ZMW25) stops at villages east of Mpulungu. It moves quite slowly and makes plenty of stops so just getting to the base of the falls can take all day. Avoid arriving in the dark as it's two to three hours' walk uphill to the viewpoint near the top of Kalambo Falls (and the campsite). It's also possible to hire a private boat from Mpulungu harbour, which will cost around US$150 for a return trip. Ask around at the market near the lake in Mpulungu.

Another alternative is to stay in one of the lakeshore lodges near the falls, from where you could hike to the falls or get them to arrange a boat trip.

THE COPPERBELT

While the Copperbelt Province is the industrial heartland of Zambia, there are a few interesting spots for tourists too. The most important is the Chimfunshi Wildlife Orphanage, one of the largest chimpanzee sanctuaries in the world. The Copperbelt's major towns – Kitwe, Ndola and Chingola – are nice spots for a break, with museums, comfortable hotels and some good restaurants.

The region is home to the country's lucrative copper-mining industry, which is once again prospering following a slump during the 1970s.

Kapiri Mposhi

This uninspiring transit town, about 200km north of Lusaka, is at the southern end of the Tazara railway from Dar es Salaam (Tanzania) and at the fork in the roads to Lusaka, the Copperbelt and northern Zambia.

There's only basic lodging available here, none of which is really recommendable, so it's not really a great town to hang around for the night.

Buses and minibuses from Lusaka (ZMW60, 2½ hours) leave regularly and are a quicker and more convenient option than the irregular local trains.

If disembarking the international train service (p82) from Dar es Salaam run by Tazara railway company, there's a passport check before exiting the station, then from outside the station there's a mad rush for buses to Lusaka and elsewhere. Thieves and pickpockets thrive in the crowds and confusion, so stay alert.

Ndola

Ndola, the capital of the Copperbelt Province (and third largest in Zambia), is a prosperous, sprawling city that makes a good spot to break up the journey or spend the night en route to the Chimfunshi Wildlife Orphanage (p72). Once you get off its main thoroughfare, and hit its genteel, well-tended residential streets, there is no real evidence of its industrial base. Interestingly it's only 10km from the border with the Democratic Republic of Congo.

Copperbelt Museum MUSEUM
(☎0212-617450; Buteko Ave; adult/child US$5/3; ⏲8am-4.30pm) Definitely worth a visit, this museum starts upstairs with its cultural and ethnography galleries exhibiting artefacts used in witchcraft, personal ornaments, smoking and snuffing paraphernalia, and musical instruments such as talking drums. Downstairs it showcases the local mining industry with displays on its history, gemstones and the processing of copper.

Sleeping & Eating

★**Katuba Guesthouse** GUESTHOUSE $
(☎0212-671341, 0978 450245; www.katubaguesthouse.com; 4 Mwabombeni Rd; d incl breakfast ZMW350-450; ❄📶) Comfortable, clean and relaxed, this friendly guesthouse is within a secure residential compound in a well-heeled neighbourhood with jacaranda-lined streets. Rooms are spacious and come with fast wi-fi, cable TV and reliable hot water. Meals are available in the evening (ZMW50), along with cold beers, and there's a complimentary continental breakfast in the morning.

Savoy Hotel HOTEL $
(☎0212-611097; www.savoyhotel.co.zm; Buteko Ave; s/d incl breakfast ZMW350/400; ❄@🏊) It's a bit of a hulking concrete block from the outside and the 154 rooms add up to the largest hotel in the Copperbelt; however, inside the Savoy is upholding standards well – old-fashioned, true, but not without a certain charm.

Michelangelo ITALIAN $$
(☎0212-620325; 126 Broadway; pizzas from ZMW50, mains ZMW90-150; ⏲7.30am-9.40pm Mon-Fri, 8am-2pm & 7-10pm Sat; ❄📶) Long regarded as one of Ndola's best restaurants, this Italian cafe-terrace under a designer awning does thin-crust pizzas, pastas and Western mains. Coffee, gelato or a homemade pastry round the meal off nicely. There is also a small boutique hotel (room from US$130) attached. On Sundays it is only open to hotel guests and local residents.

Getting There & Away

Ndola is located about 320km north of Lusaka, about a 4½-hour drive along a well-maintained but busy stretch of highway.

One of only three cities in Zambia to have an international airport, Ndola's airport has flights daily between Lusaka, South Africa, Ethiopia and Kenya. The airport is 3.5km south of the public bus station.

Ethiopian Airlines (☎0950 585343, 0211-236401; www.ethiopianairlines.com) Direct flights to Addis Ababa.

Kenya Airways (☑ 0212-620709; www.kenya-airways.com) Daily flights to Nairobi.

Proflight Zambia (☑ 0211-271032; www.proflight-zambia.com) Daily flights to Lusaka.

South African Airlink (☑ 0977 777224; www.saairlink.co.za) Offers daily flights to Johannesburg.

Long-distance buses depart from the stand next to the Broadway–Maina Soko roundabout and run to Lusaka (ZMW85, five hours), Kitwe (ZMW20, two hours) and Chingola (ZMW60, 2½ hours). Joldan is a recommended company. The gritty **public bus station** (Chimwemwe Rd) has frequent local chicken buses and minibuses to Kitwe (ZMW17, 45 minutes).

The **train station** (☑ 0212-617641; off President Ave Nth) is 700m north of the Copperbelt Museum, but trains to Lusaka (ZMW40, 12 hours, Monday and Friday) are infrequent and slow.

There are several international car-hire companies such as **Avis** (☑ 0212-620741) at the airport, as well as **Voyagers** (☑ 0212-621333; www.voyagerszambia.com/ndola.php; Arusha St; ⊙ 8am-1pm & 2-5pm Mon-Fri, 9am-noon Sat) travel agency, which can also help with car rental.

Kitwe

Zambia's second-largest city and the centre of the country's mining industry, Kitwe seems far larger than quiet Ndola. Business travellers (read mining consultants) stop here for the good selection of accommodation and eating places.

Kitwe is about 60km northwest of Ndola. The **public bus station** is situated 500m west of Independence Ave, and the **train station** (☑ 0212-223078) is at the southern end of Independence Ave. Frequent minibuses and buses run to Lusaka (ZMW90, five hours), Ndola (ZMW17, 45 minutes) and Chingola (ZMW17, 30 minutes).

Voyagers (☑ 0212-225056; www.voyagerszambia.com/kitwe.php; Enos Chomba Ave) is very helpful and can organise car hire and other travel arrangements.

Dazi Lodge   LODGE **$$**
(☑ 0977 404132; dazilodge2002@yahoo.com; 17 Pamo Ave; r incl breakfast ZMW500-750; ⊙ restaurant 6am-midnight; ☒) It's a bit overpriced, especially as there's no air-con, but Dazi's en-suite rooms are sparkling clean. There's an appealingly kitsch bamboo bar on the lawn near the swimming pool, and a good restaurant, making it a decent place to hang out.

★**Mukwa Lodge**   LODGE **$$$**
(☑ 0212-224266; www.mukwalodge.co.zm; 26 Mpezeni Ave; s/d incl breakfast ZMW895/1195; ✱ @ ☎ ☒) This lodge has gorgeous stone-floor rooms that are beautifully furnished, and the bathrooms are as good as any in Zambia. It's a delightful place to stay that's well worth the indulgence. There are also suites across the road at its excellent restaurant, the Courtyard Cafe.

★**Courtyard Cafe**   INTERNATIONAL **$$**
(☑ 0212-224266; www.mukwalodge.co.zm; Mukwa Lodge, 26 Mpezeni Ave; mains ZMW55-70; ⊙ noon-2pm & 6-9pm; ☎) A part of the boutique Mukwa Lodge, this attached restaurant is hands down Kitwe's best place to eat. Its menu is split between Portuguese and Indian, and both are authentic and exquisite. Its classy decor comprises flagstone floor, heavy wood furniture, French doors onto the garden, plenty of windows and exposed red brick.

Chingola

As the closest town to the Chimfunshi Wildlife Orphanage, Chingola sees its fair share of travellers stopping over for the night. And given it's essentially a huge mine with a settlement wrapped around it, all up it's a surprisingly pleasant and relaxed town. For sleeping, try **Hibiscus Guest House** (☑ 0967 513448, 0977 513448; www.hibiscusguesthouse.com; 33 Katutwa Rd; s/d incl breakfast ZMW350/400; ✱ @ ☎ ☒) or **Emerald Lodge** (☑ 0963 893542; emeraldlodge.manager@emeraldlodgeconsort.com; cnr Consort Ave & Kabundi Rd; r incl full breakfast ZMW450-900; ✱ ☎).

Chingola's bus station is in the centre of town. Frequent buses and minibuses (ZMW16, 30 minutes) run to the station from Kitwe, 50km to the southeast.

Chimfunshi Wildlife Orphanage

On a farm deep in the African bush, about 65km northwest of Chingola, is this impressive **chimpanzee sanctuary** (www.chimfunshi.de/en; day visit adult/child US$6/3; ⊙ 8am-4pm) that's undoubtedly the standout highlight in the Copperbelt region. Home to around 120 adult and young chimps, most have been rescued from poachers and traders in the neighbouring Democratic Republic of Congo or other parts of Africa. It's one of the largest sanctuaries of its kind in the world. This is not a natural wildlife experience, but it's still a unique and fascinating opportunity to observe the chimps as they feed, play and socialise.

You can overnight at **self-catering cottages** (www.chimfunshi.de/en; adult/child with shared bathroom US$30/15) or **camp** (☎0968 568830, 0212-311293; www.chimfunshi.de/en; camping US$15).

From Chingola, you'll need to make the slow, bumpy and incredibly dusty journey across the unsealed Chingola–Solwezi road (hopefully construction will be completed by 2017) for 50km or so until you see the Chimfunshi Wildlife Orphanage sign. From here it's a further 15km. All up count on a two-hour drive from Chingola.

Although most arrive using a private vehicle, you can catch public transport for most of the way here. Take any Solwezi-bound bus and ask to be dropped off at Muchinshi, near to the turnoff to the chimp orphanage, from where you'll need to have pre-arranged a pick up for the remainder of the 25km journey (ZMW100 per person); it's important to prearrange this as mobile phone coverage at the orphanage is poor.

UNDERSTAND ZAMBIA

Zambia Today

Politically speaking it's been a tumultuous few years for Zambia: since late 2014, it's had three presidents (including one who's died), two elections and an overall tense atmosphere characterised by disputed results, riots and violence.

After ruling for three years, President Sata passed away in late 2014 following a long, undisclosed illness, aged 77. He became the second president to die in office within six years, after Levy Mwanawasa passed away in 2008. His temporary replacement was vice president Guy Scott, a white Zambian, who took over the leadership for three months until scheduled elections in 2015; due to the Constitution, Scott wasn't able to run for presidency on the basis of his British parents not being born in Zambia.

In 2015 the defence minister Edgar Lungu was inaugurated as Zambia's sixth president. He won in a narrow victory with 48.4% of the vote, taking over leadership for the remaining one year of Sata's five-year term. He defeated opposition leader Hakainde Hichilema (better known as HH), who denounced the election as fraudulent.

It was a process to repeat itself all over again a year later in the 2016 elections. This time round was marred by political violence, opposition arrests and alleged voting fraud. Lungu again emerged victorious with 50.35% of the vote to Hichilema's 47.67%. Once again there were widespread claims that the results were rigged, and the matter was taken to Zambia's Constitutional Court. The case was duly thrown out, and Lungu was sworn in for his five-year term on 13 September 2016.

The 59-year-old President Lungu faces challenges rising from a number of ongoing issues, namely tackling corruption, nationwide power cuts that continue to cripple the economy, wildlife poaching and the influence of Chinese investment in the mining, agriculture and manufacturing sectors.

History

The first of the 'modern' (still present today) ethnic groups of Zambia to arrive were the Tonga and Ila peoples (sometimes combined as the Tonga-Ila), who migrated from the Congo area in the late 15th century. By 1550 they had occupied the Zambezi Valley and plateau areas north of where Lake Kariba is now – and which is still their homeland today. Next to arrive were the Chewa. Between the 14th and 16th centuries they followed a long and circuitous route via Lakes Mweru, Tanganyika and Malawi before founding a powerful kingdom covering much of present-day eastern Zambia, as well as parts of Malawi and Mozambique. Today the Chewa are still the largest group in eastern Zambia.

The Bemba (most notably the ruling Ngandu clan) had migrated from Congo by crossing the Luapula River into northern Zambia by around 1700. Meanwhile, the Lamba people migrated to the area of the Copperbelt in about 1650. At around the same time, the related Lala settled in the region around Serenje.

In western Zambia, the Lozi people established a dynasty and the basis of a solid political entity that still exists. The Lozi's ancestors may have migrated from what is now Angola as early as AD 450.

Early 19th Century

In the early 19th century, the fearsome reputation of the newly powerful and highly disciplined warrior army under the command of Shaka Zulu in KawZulu Natal (South Africa) led to a domino effect as groups who lived in his path fled elsewhere and in turn displaced other groups. This included the Ngoni, who fled to Malawi and Zambia, as well as the Makololo who moved into southern Zambia, around the towns of Kalomo and Monze, and who were eventually forced further west into southwest Zambia, where they displaced more Tonga people.

Also around this time, the slave trade, which had existed for many centuries, increased considerably. Swahili-Arabs, who dominated the trade on the east coast of Africa, pushed into the interior; many people from Zambia were captured and taken across Lake Malawi and through Mozambique or Tanzania to be sold in the slave markets of Zanzibar.

The Colonial Era

David Livingstone, the Scottish explorer, journeyed through large swaths of Zambia, including the lower Zambezi, where he came upon a magnificent waterfall never before seen by a European, naming it Victoria Falls in homage to royalty back home. On a subsequent trip, Livingstone died while searching for the source of the Nile in northern Zambia. His heart was buried under a tree near the spot where he died, in Chief Chitambo's village, southeast of Lake Bangweulu.

In 1885 claims over African territory by European powers were settled at the Berlin Conference and the continent was split into colonies and spheres of influence – Britain claimed Rhodesia (Zambia and Zimbabwe) and Malawi.

This 'new' territory did not escape the notice of entrepreneur Cecil John Rhodes, who was already establishing mines and a vast business empire in South Africa. Rhodes' British South Africa Company (BSAC) laid claim to the area in the early 1890s and was backed by the British government in 1895 to help combat slavery and prevent further Portuguese expansion in the region.

Two separate territories were initially created – North-Western Rhodesia and North-Eastern Rhodesia – but these were combined in 1911 to become Northern Rhodesia. In 1907 Livingstone became the capital. At around the same time, vast deposits of copper were discovered in the area now called the Copperbelt.

In 1924 the colony was put under direct British control and in 1935 the capital was moved to Lusaka. To make them less dependent on colonial rule, settlers soon pushed for closer ties with Southern Rhodesia and Nyasaland (Malawi), but various interruptions (such as WWII) meant that the Federation of Rhodesia and Nyasaland did not come about until 1953.

Independence & Kaunda

In Zambia the United National Independence Party (UNIP) was founded in the late 1950s by Dr Kenneth Kaunda, who spoke out against the federation on the grounds that it promoted the rights of white settlers to the detriment of the indigenous African population. As other African countries gained independence, Zambian nationalists opposed colonial forces through civil disobedience and a small but decisive conflict called the Chachacha Rebellion.

Northern Rhodesia became independent a year after the federation was dissolved and changed its name to Zambia. While the British government had profited enormously from Northern Rhodesia, the colonialists chose to spend a large portion of this wealth on the development of Southern Rhodesia (now Zimbabwe).

After gaining independence, Zambia inherited a British-style multiparty political system. Kaunda, as leader of the majority UNIP, became the new republic's first president. The other main party was the African National Congress (ANC), led by Harry Nkumbula. But Kaunda disliked opposition. In one swift move during 1972, he disbanded the Zambian ANC, created the 'second republic', declared UNIP the sole legal party and made himself the only presidential candidate.

Consequently Kaunda remained in power for the next 27 years. His rule was based upon 'humanism' – his own mix of Marxism and traditional African values. The civil service was increased, and nearly all private businesses (including the copper mines) were nationalised. But corruption and mismanagement, exacerbated by a fall in world copper prices, doomed Zambia to become one of the poorest countries in the world by the end of the 1970s. The economy continued to flounder, and Zambia's trade routes to the coast through neighbouring countries (such as Zimbabwe and Mozambique) were closed in retaliation for Kaunda's support for several liberation movements in the region.

By the early 1980s Rhodesia gained independence (to become Zimbabwe), which allowed Kaunda to take his country off a war footing, and the Tazara railway to Dar es Salaam (Tanzania) was completed, giving Zambia unencumbered access to the coast. Yet the economy remained on the brink of collapse: foreign-exchange reserves were almost exhausted, serious shortages of food, fuel and other basic commodities were common, and unemployment and crime rates rose sharply.

In 1986 an attempt was made to diversify the economy and improve the country's balance of payments. Zambia received economic aid from the International Monetary Fund (IMF), but the IMF conditions were severe and included cutting basic food subsidies. Subsequent price rises led to country-wide riots in which many people lost their lives. Kaunda was forced to restore subsidies.

The winds of change blowing through Africa during the late 1980s, coupled with Zambia's disastrous domestic situation, meant that something had to give. Following another round of violent street protests against increased food prices in 1990, which quickly transformed into a general demand for the return of multiparty politics, Kaunda was forced to accede to public opinion.

He announced a snap referendum in late 1990 but, as protests grew more vocal, he was forced to legalise opposition parties and announce full presidential and parliamentary elections for October 1991. Not surprisingly, UNIP (and Kaunda) were resoundingly defeated by the Movement for Multiparty Democracy (MMD), led by Frederick Chiluba, a former trade-union leader. Kaunda stepped down without complaint, which may have saved Zambia from descending into anarchy.

The 1990s

President Chiluba moved quickly to encourage loans and investment from the IMF and World Bank. Exchange controls were liberalised to attract investors, particularly from South Africa, but tough austerity measures were also introduced. Once again food prices soared. The civil service was rationalised, state industries privatised or simply closed, and thousands of people lost their jobs.

By the mid-1990s the government's failure to bring about any perceptible improvements to the economy and the standard of living in Zambia allowed Kaunda to confidently re-enter the political arena. He attracted strong support and soon became the UNIP leader. Leading up to the 1996 elections, the MMD panicked and passed a law forbidding anyone with foreign parents to enter politics (Kaunda's parents were from Malawi). Despite intercessions from Western aid donors and world leaders like Nelson Mandela – not to mention accusations that Chiluba's parents were from the Democratic Republic of the Congo (Zaïre) – the law was not repealed. The UNIP withdrew all its candidates in protest and many voters boycotted the election. Consequently Chiluba and the MMD easily won, and the result was grudgingly accepted by most Zambians.

In the 21st Century

The political shenanigans continued unabated at the start of the new millennium: in mid-2001 vice-president Christon Tembo was expelled from parliament by Chiluba, so he formed an opposition party – the Forum for Democratic Development (FDD). Later, Paul Tembo, a former MMD national secretary, joined the FDD but was assassinated the day before he was due to front a tribunal about alleged MMD corruption.

Chiluba was unable to run for a third presidential term in December 2001 (though he badly wanted to change the Constitution so he could). He anointed his former vice-president, Levy Mwanawasa, as his successor, but Mwanawasa only just beat a coalition of opposition parties known as the United Party for National Development (UPND). Again, allegations from international observers about the MMD rigging the results and buying votes fell on deaf ears. To Chiluba's horror, Mwanawasa stripped his predecessor of immunity from prosecution and proceeded to launch an anti-corruption drive, which targeted the former president. In August 2009, after a long-running trial, Chiluba was cleared of embezzling US$500,000 by Zambia's High Court. His wife, however, was not so lucky, having been given a jail term earlier in the year for receiving stolen funds while her husband was in office. In a separate case in 2007, the High Court in Britain ruled Chiluba and four of his aides conspired to rob Zambia of about US$46 million, but in Zambia he was acquitted of such charges in 2009. Only two years later he passed away from a heart attack, aged 68.

Although Zambia remains a poor country, its economy experienced strong growth in the early part of the 21st century with GDP growing at around 6%. However, the country is still very dependent on the world prices of its principal minerals (copper and cobalt).

As well as combating global markets, natural disasters have played a significant role in the country's fortunes. Although a bumper harvest was recorded in 2007, floods in 2008–09 were declared a national disaster and killed dozens of people – the Zambezi River, which flooded much of western Zambia, was said to be at its highest level in 60 years, and crops were severely affected.

In September 2011, Michael Sata, nicknamed 'King Cobra', and his party the Patriotic Front (PF) won national elections. The populist strain in Sata's policy was apparent by his decision to revalue the country's currency. Motivated more by symbolism than economics, it was a move that indicated a sincere focus on redirecting the country's wealth to the majority of Zambians who remained impoverished. He also announced a significant increase in the minimum wage in September 2012, and his administration encouraged Zambian participation and ownership in the tourism industry. However, his presidency was tainted by heavy-handed tactics to clamp down on political opposition. Sata passed away while still in power on 28 October 2014 after battling a long illness, plunging Zambia into a period of political uncertainty and leaving his successor with numerous political, economic and environmental challenges.

Way of Life

Zambia's population is made up of between 70 and 80 different ethnic groups (the final count varies according to your definition of ethnicity, but the Zambian government officially recognises 73 groups). Despite these numbers there is considerable homogeneity among the tribes of Zambia. This is partly due to a long history of people moving around the country, settling new areas or looking for work, and also because after independence President Kaunda fostered national unity, while still recognising the disparate languages and cultures. Intermarriage among the officially recognised groups is also common. Hence Zambia is justifiably proud of its relative lack of ethnic problems, and its official motto on the coat of arms reads: 'One Zambia, One Nation'.

The vast majority (99%) of Zambians are indigenous Africans. The final 1% are Zambian citizens of Indian or European origin (mostly involved in business, commerce, farming and the tourist industry). Many white and Asian families have lived here for generations – although race relations are still sometimes a little strained.

Environment

Landlocked Zambia is one of Africa's most eccentric legacies of colonialism. Shaped like a mangled butterfly, its borders don't correspond to any tribal or linguistic area. And Zambia is huge. At some 752,000 sq km, it's about the size of France, England and the Republic of Ireland combined.

Zambia is chock full of rivers. The Luangwa, the Kafue and the mighty Zambezi dominate western, southern and eastern Zambia, flowing through a beautiful mix of flood plains, forests and farmland. In the north, the main rivers are the Chambeshi and the Luapula, both sources of the Congo River. Northern Zambia has many smaller rivers, too, and the broken landscape helps create a stunning scenery of lakes, rapids and waterfalls.

Of course, Zambia's most famous waterfall is Victoria Falls, where the Zambezi River plunges over a mile-wide cliff before thundering down the long, zigzagging Batoka Gorge. The Zambezi flows into Lake Kariba, created by a dam but still one of the largest lakes in Africa. In northern Zambia is the even larger Lake Tanganyika – it's 675km long, the second deepest in the world, and holds roughly one-sixth of the earth's fresh water.

In the south and east, Zambia is cut by deep valleys, some of of which are branches of the Great Rift Valley. The Zambezi Valley is the largest, and defines the county's southern border, while the 700km-long Luangwa Valley is lined by the steep and spectacular Muchinga Escarpment.

Even the flats of Zambia can be stunning: the endless grassy Busanga Plains in Kafue National Park attract fantastic wildlife, while the Liuwa Plain – part of the even larger Upper Zambezi flood plain that makes up much of western Zambia – is home to Africa's second-largest wildebeest migration.

Some of Zambia's other geographical highlights include the breathtaking high, rolling grasslands of the Nyika Plateau, the seasonally flooded wetlands of the Kafue Flats, the teak forests of the Upper Zambezi, and the Kariba and Mpata Gorges on the Lower Zambezi.

Wildlife

Because of Zambia's diverse landscape, plentiful water supplies, and position between Eastern, Southern and Central Africa, the diversity of animal species is huge. The rivers, of course, support large populations of hippos (at around 40,000, the Zambezi River has Africa's highest population) and crocs, and the associated grasslands provide plenty of fodder for herds of zebras, impalas and pukus (an antelope common in Zambia, but not elsewhere). Although the tiger fish of the Zambezi are related to the South American piranha, there's no record of a human being attacked (however, they are attracted to blood in the water).

Huge herds of rare black lechwe live near Lake Bangweulu, and endemic Kafue lechwe settle in the area around the Kafue River. Kasanka National Park is one of the best places on the continent to see the rare, water-loving antelopes called sitatungas. South Luangwa and Lower Zambezi National Parks are good places to see tall and stunningly graceful giraffes, and Zambia has its own subspecies – Thornicroft's giraffe. South Luangwa has its very own subspecies of wildebeest, too – the light-coloured Cookson's wildebeest – but the best place to see these creatures is the Liuwa Plain, a remote grassland area in western Zambia where thousands converge every year for Africa's second-largest wildebeest migration.

These animals naturally attract predators, so most parks contain lions, leopards, hyenas (which you'll probably see) and cheetahs (which you probably won't). Wild dogs were once very rare but are now encountered more frequently. Elephants, another big drawcard, are also found in huge herds in South Luangwa, Lower Zambezi and some other national parks. Zambia's herds of black rhino were killed by poachers in the 1970s and '80s, but reintroduction programs have seen rhino transported to North Luangwa National Park.

Bird lovers will love Zambia, where about 750 species have been recorded. Twitchers used to the 'traditional' Southern African species listed in the *Roberts* and *Newman's* field guides will spend a lot of time identifying unusual species – especially in the north and west. Most notable are the endangered shoebill storks (found in the Bangweulu Wetlands); fish eagles (Zambia's national bird); and the endemic Chaplin's barbets (found mostly around Monze).

Here's one time when you might groan at biological diversity: there are 37 different species of tsetse flies in Kafue National Park. Chewing garlic cloves is said to help keep them away, but heavy-duty insect repellent containing DEET is more effective.

Plants

About 65% of Zambia, mainly plateau areas and escarpments, is covered in miombo woodland, which consists mainly of broadleaved deciduous trees, particularly various species of *Brachystegia* (another name for this type of vegetation is Brachystegia woodland). Some areas are thickly wooded, others are more open, but the trees never form a continuous canopy, allowing grass and other plants to grow between them.

In the drier, hotter valleys and best-known national parks like South Luangwa and Lower Zambezi, much of the vegetation is mopane woodland. Dominant trees are the species *Colophospermum mopane,* usually around 10m high. The baobab tree also grows here. Many legends and stories are associated with the striking and simultaneously grand and grotesque tree. One has it that the gods, upset over the baobabs haughty disdain for inferior-looking flora, thrust them back into the ground, roots upward, to teach them a lesson in humility. You'll see this landscape in Zambia's best-known national parks, Lower Zambezi and South Luangwa.

Zambia has some of the most extensive wetlands in Southern Africa. These include the Bangweulu Wetlands, along the southern and eastern shores of Lake Bangweulu; and the vast plains of the Kafue Flats downstream from Kafue National Park, which is dotted with seasonally flooded marshes, lagoons and oxbow lakes.

Most grassland in Zambia is low, flat and flooded for part of the year, with hardly a tree in sight. The largest flood-plain area is west of the Upper Zambezi – including

Liuwa Plain National Park – where thousands of square kilometres are inundated every year. Another is the Busanga Plains in Kafue National Park.

Along many of Zambia's rivers are riverine forests. Tourists will see a lot of this type of landscape as national park camps are often built on riverbanks, under the shade of huge trees such as ebony, winterthorn and the unmistakable 'sausage tree' *(Kigelia africana)*.

Evergreen forest, the 'jungle' of Tarzan films, is found only in isolated pockets in northwest Zambia – a remnant of the larger forests over the border in Angola and the Democratic Republic of the Congo.

National Parks

Zambia boasts 20 national parks and reserves (and 34 Game Management Areas, or GMAs), and some 30% of the land is protected, but after decades of poaching, clearing and general bad management, many are just lines on the map that no longer protect (or even contain) much wildlife. However, some national parks accommodate extremely healthy stocks of wildlife and are among the best in Southern Africa. Privately funded conservation organisations have done much to rehabilitate the condition of some of these.

Admission fees to the parks vary. Each ticket is valid for 24 hours from the time you enter the park.

SURVIVAL GUIDE

Directory A–Z

ACCOMMODATION

Zambia offers an excellent choice of accommodation options to cater for all budgets. National park safari lodges especially provide a memorable stay. During shoulder season prices drop, and offer some good deals.

SLEEPING PRICE RANGES

The following price ranges refer to a double room with bathroom in high season (August to October), based on 'international rates'.

$ less than ZMW500 (US$50)

$$ ZMW500–1000 (US$50–100)

$$$ more than ZMW1000 (US$100)

BOOK YOUR STAY ONLINE

For more accommodation reviews by Lonely Planet authors, check out http://lonelyplanet.com/hotels/. You'll find independent reviews, as well as recommendations on the best places to stay. Best of all, you can book online.

ACTIVITIES

Zambia offers an array of activities for the adventurous traveller. Livingstone (and Victoria Falls town in Zimbabwe) are hubs, with adrenaline-pumping options such as white-water rafting and bungee jumping. At the main national parks you can arrange wildlife drives and walks, though you might prefer to safari on water, canoeing downriver alongside basking hippos.

BUSINESS HOURS

Banks Weekdays from 8am to 3.30pm (or 5pm), and 8am to 11am (or noon) on Saturday.

Government offices From 8am or 9am to 4pm or 5pm weekdays, with a one-hour lunch break between noon and 2pm.

Post offices From 8am or 9am to 4pm or 4.30pm weekdays.

Restaurants Normally open for lunch between 11.30am and 2.30pm and dinner between 6pm and 10.30pm.

Shops Keep the same hours as government offices but also open Saturday.

Supermarkets Normally open from 8am to 8pm weekdays, and 8am to 6pm weekends; some open later at Lusaka's big shopping centres.

CHILDREN

Family-friendly destinations Livingstone, Lusaka, South Luangwa.

High chairs Available at many big-city restaurants.

Nappies Available in major cities, but not elsewhere.

Safaris Wildlife drives are fine, but under 12s aren't allowed on safari walks or canoe trips. Some high-end park lodges do not allow children under 12 years, while others have activities and facilities set up for kids, and offer lower child rates.

ELECTRICITY

Supply is 220V to 240V/50Hz and plugs are of the British three-prong variety.

EMBASSIES & CONSULATES

Most embassies or high commissions are located in Lusaka. The British High Commission looks after the interests of Aussies and Kiwis, as the nearest diplomatic missions for Australia and New Zealand are in Harare (Zimbabwe). Most consulates are open from 8.30am to 5pm Monday to Thursday and from 8.30am to 12.30pm Friday; visas are usually only dealt with in the mornings.

Botswanan High Commission (☎0211-250555; 5201 Pandit Nehru Rd; ⏰8am-1pm & 2-4pm Mon-Fri)

British High Commission (☎0211-423200; www.ukinzambia.fco.gov.uk/en; 5210 Independence Ave; ⏰8am-4.30pm Mon-Fri)

Canadian High Commission (☎0211-250833; 5119 United Nations Ave; ⏰7.45am-5pm Mon-Thu, to 12.15pm Fri)

DRC Embassy (☎0211-235679; 1124 Parirenyetwa Rd; ⏰8.30am-1pm & 2-4pm Mon-Thu, to noon Fri)

Dutch Embassy (☎0211-253819; Swedish Embassy, Haile Selassie Ave; ⏰8am-1pm & 2-4pm Mon-Fri)

Finland Embassy (☎0211-251988; www.finland.org.zm; Haile Selassie Ave; ⏰9am-noon & 2-4pm)

French Embassy (☎0977-110020; www.ambafrance-zm.org; 31F Leopards Hill Close; ⏰8am-12.30pm & 2-6pm Mon-Thu, 8am-12.30pm Fri)

German Embassy (☎0211-250644; www.lusaka.diplo.de; 5219 Haile Selassie Ave; ⏰9-11am Mon-Thu)

Irish Embassy (☎0211-291298; www.dfa.ie/irish-embassy/zambia; 6663 Katima Mulilo Rd; ⏰8am-4.30pm Mon-Thu, to 12.30pm Fri)

Kenyan High Commission (☎0211-250722; 5207 United Nations Ave; ⏰9am-12.30pm Mon-Fri)

Malawian High Commission (5202 Pandit Nehru Rd; ⏰8.30am-noon Mon-Thu, to 11am Fri)

Mozambican Embassy (☎0211-220339; 9592 Kacha Rd, Northmead; ⏰8am-1pm Mon-Fri)

Namibian High Commission (☎0211-260407; 30B Mutende Rd, Woodlands; ⏰8am-1pm & 2-4pm Mon-Fri)

South African High Commission (☎0211-260999; 26D Cheetah Rd, Kabulonga; ⏰8.30am-12.30pm Mon-Thu, to 12.30pm Fri)

Swedish Embassy (☎0211-251711; www.swedenabroad.se/lusaka; Haile Selassie Ave; ⏰9am-noon & 2-4pm Mon-Fri)

Tanzanian High Commission (☎0211-253323; 5200 United Nations Ave; ⏰8am-4pm, consular 9am-1pm Mon-Fri)

US Embassy (☎0211-357000; https://zm.usembassy.gov; Kabulonga Rd, Ibex Hill)

Zimbabwean High Commission (☎0211-254006; 11058 Haile Selassie Ave; ⏰8.30am-noon Mon-Thu, to 11am Fri)

INTERNET ACCESS

Wi-fi is available in many lodges across the country, sometimes for a small fee. You can also get online through inexpensive pre-paid sim card internet data bundles; either MTN or Airtel are recommended. For 1GB expect to pay around US$10, which is valid for 30 days. You'll need to bring along your passport to the store to get it activated. Coverage for the most part is fast, but is poor to non-existent within the national parks.

Otherwise there are internet cafes in most large towns.

MONEY

The country's official currency is the Zambian kwacha (ZMW), but US dollars are also widely accepted. Most sizeable towns have ATMs that accept foreign cards.

Cash & ATMs

You can obtain cash (kwacha) at ATMs accepting Visa or MasterCard such as Barclays Bank, Stanbic and Standard Chartered banks in the cities and larger towns. Be aware, however, that it's not unheard of for them to be down, so it's always wise to carry an emegerency wad of back-up cash.

In the cities and larger towns, you can also easily change cash (no commission; photo ID required) at branches of Barclays Bank, FNB, Standard Chartered Bank and Zanaco. We've received reports that many banks, including at least one at the airport, won't accept US dollars issued before 2006.

As of 1 January 2013 three zeros were removed from every bank note denomination and the unit of currency changed from ZK to ZMW; eg ZK90,000 is now ZMW90. Note the old currency is no longer accepted as legal tender.

Credit Cards

Some shops, restaurants and better hotels/lodges accept major credit cards. Visa is the most readily recognised, Mastercard less so and Amex even less again. A surcharge of 4% to 7% may be added to your bill if you pay with a credit card.

It's also worth noting that payment by credit card requires a PIN to authorise the transaction.

Exchange Rates

Australia	A$1	ZMW7.30
Canada	C$1	ZMW7.52
Euro zone	€1	ZMW10.54
Japan	¥100	ZMW8.60
NZ	NZ$1	ZMW6.98
South African Rand	ZAR10	ZMW 7.3
UK	£1	ZMW12.36
US	US$1	ZMW9.95

EATING PRICE RANGES

The following price ranges refer to a standard main course. Remember that this is a guide only and prices will be considerably more in many lodges and camps in national parks.

$ less than ZMW50 (US$5)

$$ ZMW50–100 (US$5–10)

$$$ more than ZMW100 (US$10)

For current exchange rates, see www.xe.com.

Moneychangers

The best currencies to take to Zambia (in order of preference) are US dollars, UK pounds, South African rand and euros; most neighbouring countries' currencies are worthless in Zambia, except at the relevant borders. The exception is Botswanan pula, which can be exchanged in Lusaka.

Tipping

- **Hotels** The top-end lodges and camps often provide separate envelopes for staff and guides if guests should wish to tip.
- **Restaurants** A 10% tip is hugely appreciated for good service, though if restaurants include a 10% service charge, an additional tip isn't required.
- **Safari Guides & Drivers** Around US$5 to US$10 to the driver and guide per day is appropriate, with a higher amount if you're happy with their service, knowledge and guiding skills.

PUBLIC HOLIDAYS

During public holidays, most businesses and government offices are closed.

New Year's Day 1 January
Youth Day 2nd Monday in March
Easter March/April
Labour/Workers' Day 1 May
Africa (Freedom) Day 25 May
Heroes' Day 1st Monday in July
Unity Day 1st Tuesday in July
Farmers' Day 1st Monday in August
Independence Day 24 October
Christmas Day 25 December

SAFE TRAVEL

Zambia is generally very safe, but in the cities and tourist areas there's always a chance of being targeted by muggers or con artists. As always, you can reduce the risk considerably by being sensible.

- While civil strife continues in the Democratic Republic of the Congo, avoid areas along the Zambia–Congo border, especially around Lake Mweru.
- Due to electricity shortages, load-shedding is now a reality of daily life across the country; however, most tourist lodges will have a back-up generator.
- Tsteste flies are an incessant nuisance when driving in many national parks; where problematic, wind the windows up and apply DEET-containing insect repellent.

TELEPHONE

Every landline in Zambia uses the area code system; you only have to dial it if you are calling outside of your area code.

The international access code for dialling outside of Zambia is ☎00, followed by the relevant country code. If you're calling Zambia from another country, the country code is ☎260, but drop the initial zero of the area code.

Mobile Phones

MTN and Airtel are the most reliable mobile (cell) phone networks. If you own a GSM phone, you can buy a cheap SIM card without a problem (including at the Lusaka or Livingstone Airport). You'll need to bring along your passport to have it activated. You can then purchase credit in whatever denominations you need from the same company as your SIM; scratch cards range from ZMW1 to ZMW100. In Lusaka the best place to buy a cheap mobile phone is around Kalima Towers (corner of Chachacha and Katunjila Rds); a basic model will cost around ZMW80.

Numbers starting with 09 plus another two numbers, eg 0977, are mobile-phone numbers. Mobile-phone reception is getting better all the time; generally, it's very good in urban areas and surprisingly good in some rural parts of the country and patchy or non-existent in others. Don't count on any coverage inside the national parks.

TIME

Zambia is in the Central Africa time zone, which is two hours ahead of Greenwich Mean Time (GMT/UTC). There is no daylight saving.

TOURIST INFORMATION

The regional tourist office in Livingstone is worth visiting for specific enquiries, but the main office in Lusaka is generally of little use.

The official website of Zambia Tourism Agency (www.zambiatourism.com) is pretty useful, though be aware a lot of information is out of date.

VISAS

Visas are generally issued upon arrival.

Tourist visas are available at major borders, airports and ports, but it's important to note that you should have a Zambian visa *before* arrival if travelling by train or boat from Tanzania. A yellow fever certificate is not required, but it is often requested by immigration officials if you've come from a country with yellow fever.

All foreign visitors – other than Southern African Development Community (SADC) passport holders who are issued visas free of charge – pay US$50 for single entry (up to one month) and US$80 for double entry (up to three months; which is good if you plan on venturing into one of the bordering countries). Applications for multiple-entry visas (US$80) must be made in advance at a Zambian embassy or high commission. If staying less than 24 hours, for example if you are visiting Livingstone from Zimbabwe, you pay only US$20.

In December 2016 the KAZA visa was reintroduced, which allows most visitors to acquire a single 30-day visa (US$50) for both Zambia and Zimbabwe. As long as you remain within these two countries, you can cross the border multiple times (day trips to Botswana at Kazungula will not invalidate the visa). These visas are available at Livingstone and Lusaka airports, as well as at the Victoria Falls and Kazungula crossings.

Payment can be made in US dollars, and sometimes UK pounds. Other currencies such as euros, South African rand, Botswanan pula or Namibian dollars may be accepted at borders, but don't count on it.

Business visas can be obtained from Zambian diplomatic missions abroad, and application forms can be downloaded at www.zambiaimmigration.gov.zm.

VOLUNTEERING

There's a number of opportunities for those looking to volunteer in Zambia. While various international agencies offer roles in a number of fields, you can try the following places based in Zambia:

Chimfunshi Wildlife Orphanage (p72) Offers several roles managing day-to-day affairs at this chimpanzee refuge; get in touch with African Impact (www.africanimpact.com) which coordinates affairs here, as well as other volunteering options in Zambia.

Game Rangers International (☎ 0973 086519, 0973 085358; www.wildzambia.org) This wildlife NGO offers a range of different opportunities through its volunteer program; check its website for upcoming placements.

Habitat for Humanity (☎ 0211-251087; www.habitatzambia.org) Helps to build houses for the nation's poor; over 2700 houses have been built since 1984.

Tikondane Community Centre (p46) A wonderful grassroots organisation assisting with local communities; it accepts volunteers to help out with anything from teaching, agriculture and permaculture to health care. There's a minimum of two weeks and it costs ZMW2000 per week, inclusive of meals and accommodation. It's based in Katate in eastern Zambia, located between Lusaka and South Luangwa National Park.

Getting There & Away

AIR

Given there are very few direct flights into Zambia from outside Africa, many international visitors are likely to transfer to connecting flights in either Johannesburg or Nairobi.

Airports & Airlines

Zambia's main international airport is in Lusaka. An increasing number of international airlines also fly to the airport at Livingstone (for Victoria Falls), and a lesser amount to Mfuwe (for South Luangwa National Park) and Ndola.

LAND

Zambia shares borders with eight countries, so there's a huge number of crossing points. Most are open daily from 6am to 6pm; the border closes at 8pm at Victoria Falls and at 7pm at Chirundu. Before you leave the Zambian side, ensure that you have enough currency of whatever country you're travelling to or South African rand to pay for your visa (if you require one).

If you are crossing borders in your own vehicle, you need a free Temporary Export Permit (TEP), which is obtained at the border – make sure to retain a copy of this form after it's stamped. Before crossing be sure to inform your rental car company in order to guarantee you have all the required documents in order. You'll likely need to purchase insurance, sometimes called COMESA. It can be bought either at the Zambian border crossings or just after you've gone through formalities on the other country's side (for Zimbabwe, it'll cost around ZMW150). For Zimbabwe you also need an Interpol Certificate (good for three months), which can be obtained from the police in Zambia, and a typed 'Permission to Drive' document, which basically states that the vehicle's owner knows you're driving the car.

You also need to request and complete a Temporary Import Permit (TIP), and of course pay for it. Retain the document and payment receipt for when re-entering Zambia.

Heading back into Zambia you might get hassled from Zambians trying to sell you insurance – you don't need this if you're in a Zambian-registered vehicle.

Note also that Zambia charges a carbon tax for non-Zambian registered vehicles; it's usually about ZMW200 per vehicle.

Botswana

Zambia and Botswana share what is probably the world's shortest international boundary: 750m across the Zambezi River at Kazungula. The pontoon ferry (ZMW2 for foot passengers and US$30 for vehicles) across the Zambezi is

CLIMATE CHANGE & TRAVEL

Every form of transport that relies on carbon-based fuel generates CO_2, the main cause of human-induced climate change. Modern travel is dependent on aeroplanes, which might use less fuel per kilometre per person than most cars but travel much greater distances. The altitude at which aircraft emit gases (including CO_2) and particles also contributes to their climate change impact. Many websites offer 'carbon calculators' that allow people to estimate the carbon emissions generated by their journey and, for those who wish to do so, to offset the impact of the greenhouse gases emitted with contributions to portfolios of climate-friendly initiatives throughout the world. Lonely Planet offsets the carbon footprint of all staff and author travel.

65km west of Livingstone and 11km south of the main road between Livingstone and Sesheke. A bridge has long been in the plans to replace what is a fairly dodgy crossing. There are minibuses (ZMW35, one hour) here daily from Livingstone, departing from Nakatindi Rd in the morning.

A quicker and more comfortable (but more expensive) way to reach Botswana from Zambia is to cross from Livingstone to Victoria Falls (in Zimbabwe), from where shuttle buses head to Kasane.

Buses to Gaborone, via Kasane and Francistown, leave several days a week from Lusaka.

Democratic Republic of the Congo (DRC, Zaïre)

This border is not for the faint hearted. DRC visas are only available to Zambian residents and this rule is strictly enforced unless you can get a letter of invitation from the Congolese government. The most convenient border to use connects Chingola in the Copperbelt with Lubumbashi in Katanga Province, via the border towns of Chililabombwe (Zambia) and Kasumbalesa (DRC). Crossing into the DRC can take a lot of time or money, so it is wise to hook up with some mining consultants or UN workers rather than venturing alone.

Malawi

Most foreigners use the border at Mchinji, 30km southeast of Chipata, because it's along the road between Lusaka and Lilongwe. One figure to keep in mind – it's only 287km from Mfuwe to Lilongwe. Note that visas into Malawi are free for most nationalities.

Further north is another border crossing at Nakonde. Going either way on public transport is extremely difficult; you really need your own wheels.

Mozambique

The main border is between Mlolo (Zambia) and fairly remote Cassacatiza (Mozambique), but most travellers choose to reach Mozambique through Malawi. There is no public transport between the two countries.

Namibia

The only border is at Sesheke (Zambia), on the northern and southern bank of the Zambezi, while the Namibian border is at Wenela near Katima Mulilo. There are bus services to Sesheke from Lusaka and Livingstone respectively; it's 200km west of the latter.

From the Namibian side, it's a 5km walk to Katima Mulilo, from where minibuses depart for other parts of Namibia. Alternatively, cross from Livingstone to Victoria Falls (in Zimbabwe) and travel onwards from there.

South Africa

There is no border between Zambia and South Africa, but several buses travel daily between Johannesburg and Lusaka via Harare and Masvingo in Zimbabwe. Make sure you have a Zimbabwean visa.

Tanzania

The main border by road, and the only crossing by train, is between Nakonde (Zambia) and Tunduma (Tanzania). Bus services run from Lusaka to Nakonde and on to Mbeya. Alternatively, walk across the border from Nakonde, and take a minibus from Tunduma to Mbeya in Tanzania. There is also a crossing at Kasesya, between Mbala and Sumbawanga (Tanzania). At time of research the road was in decent condition and there was daily public transport on both sides of the border.

Although travelling by bus to the Tanzanian border is quicker, the train is a better alternative.

The Tazara railway company usually runs two international trains per week in each direction between Kapiri Mposhi (207km north of Lusaka) and Dar es Salaam (Tanzania). The 'express train' with sleeping compartments leaves Kapiri Mposhi at approximately 4pm on Tuesdays (ZMW334, 42 hours). Kilimanjaro 'ordinary' service dearts 2pm on Fridays (ZMW278, 48 hours). Delays are frequent. A discount of 50% is possible with a student card.

Tickets are available on the spot at the New Kapiri Mposhi (Tazara) train station in Kapiri Mposhi and up to three days in advance from Tazara House in Lusaka. If there are no more seats left at the Lusaka office, don't despair because we've heard from travellers who easily bought tickets at Kapiri Mposhi, and upgraded from one class to another while on board.

It's prudent to get a Tanzanian visa in Lusaka (or elsewhere) before you board the train; at least contact the Tanzanian High Commission in Lusaka about getting a Tanzanian visa on the train or at the border. You can change money on the train, but take care because these guys are sharks.

SEA & LAKE

There is an international port at Mpulungu where you can get the MV *Liemba* ferry along Lake Tanganyika to/from Tanzania.

Getting Around

AIR

The main domestic airports are at Lusaka, Livingstone, Ndola, Kitwe, Mfuwe, Kasama and Kalabo. Dozens of minor airstrips, most notably those in the Lower Zambezi National Park (Proflight flies here regularly), Kafue National Park and North Luangwa National Park, cater for chartered planes.

The departure tax for domestic flights is US$8. Proflight tickets include this tax in the price, but for other flights it must be paid at the airport.

Proflight is the only domestic airline offering regularly scheduled flights connecting Lusaka to Livingstone (for Victoria Falls), Lower Zambezi (Jeki and Royal airstrips), Mfuwe (for South Luangwa National Park), Ndola, Kasama and Solwezi. From 2017 they will commence a flight to Kalabo for Liuwa Plain National Park. Charter companies include Proflight, **Corporate Air** (☎ 0965 037434; http://corporateairlimited.com; Chrismar Hotel, Los Angeles Blvd), **Ngwazi Air Charters** (☎ 0211-271196; www.ngwaziaircharters.com), **Pro Charter** (☎ 0211-271099, 0974 250110; www.procharter-zambia.com) and **Royal Air Charters** (☎ 0969 783128; www.royalaircharters.com).

BUS & MINIBUS

Distances are long, buses are often slow and some (but not many these days) roads are badly potholed, so travelling around Zambia by bus and minibus can exhaust even the hardiest of travellers.

All main routes are served by ordinary public buses, which either run on a fill-up-and-go basis or have fixed departures (these are called 'time buses'). 'Express buses' are faster – often terrifyingly so – and stop less, but cost about 15% more. In addition, several private companies run comfortable European-style express buses along the major routes, eg between Lusaka and Livingstone, Lusaka and Chipata, and Lusaka and the Copperbelt region. These fares cost about 25% more than the ordinary bus fares and are well worth the extra kwacha. Tickets for these buses can often be bought the day before. There are also express buses zipping around the country.

A few general tips to keep in mind. Even on buses with air-conditioning – and it very often doesn't work – try to sit on the side of the bus opposite to the sun. Also avoid seats near the speakers, which can be turned up to unbearably high volume. Try to find a seat with a working seatbelt, and avoid bus travel at night.

Many routes are also served by minibuses, which only leave when full – so full that you might lose all feeling in one butt cheek. Fares can be more or less the same as ordinary buses. In remote areas the only public transport is often a truck or pickup.

CAR & MOTORCYCLE

If you're driving into Zambia in a rented or privately owned car or motorcycle, you will need a Carnet de Passage en Douane (CPD); if you don't have one, a free Customs Importation Permit will be issued to you at major borders instead. You'll also be charged a carbon tax if it's a non-Zambian registered vehicle, which just means a bit more paperwork and around ZMW200 at the border, depending on the size of your car.

Compulsory third-party insurance for Zambia is available at major borders (or the nearest large towns). It is strongly advised to carry insurance from your own country on top of your Zambian policy.

While it is certainly possible to get around Zambia by car or motorbike, many sealed roads are in bad condition and the dirt roads can range from shocking to impassable, particularly after the rains. If you haven't driven in Africa before, this is not the best place to start; particularly when you throw in a herd of angry elephants into the equation. We strongly recommend that you hire a 4WD if driving anywhere outside Lusaka, and certainly if you're heading to any of the national parks or other wilderness areas. Wearing a seat belt in the front seat is compulsory.

Self-drivers should seriously consider purchasing the in-car GPS navigation system Tracks4Africa (www.tracks4africa.co.za), which even shows petrol stations.

Driving Licence

All tourists planning on driving a vehicle in Zambia can drive on their own country's licence for up to three months, so unless you're here long term, you won't need an international driver's licence.

Fuel & Spare Parts

Diesel costs around ZMW11 per litre and petrol ZMW13. Distances between towns with filling stations are great and fuel is not always available, so fill the tank at every opportunity and carry a filled jerry can or two as back-up.

It is advisable to carry at least one spare wheel. If you need spare parts, the easiest (and cheapest) vehicle parts to find are those of Toyota and Nissan.

Hire

Cars can be hired from international and Zambian-owned companies in Lusaka, Livingstone, Kitwe and Ndola. You'll find all the usual chain hire companies at the airport.

Other companies, such as Voyagers (p45), Benmark (p45), **Hemingways** (☎0213-323097; www.hemingwayszambia.com), **4x4 Hire Africa** (☎in South Africa 021-791 3904; www.4x4hire.co.za) and **Limo Car Hire** (☎0977 743145; www.limohire-zambia.com) rent out Toyota Hiluxes and old-school Land Rover vehicles, unequipped or fully decked out with everything you would need for a trip to the bush (including rooftop tents!); prices vary from US$120 to US$250 per day. The best thing about these companies is that vehicles come with unlimited kilometres and you can take them across borders; though read the fine print first.

Most companies insist that drivers be at least 25 years old and have held a licence for at least five years.

Road Conditions

The last few years have seen the conditions of Zambia's roads improve out of sight, with approximately 80% of the major roads tourists use being smooth, sealed tarmac. That said, when the roads are bad they're horrendous, and can involve slow, dusty crawls avoiding pothole after pothole.

Road Rules

- Speed limits in and around cities are enforced, but on the open road buses and Land Cruisers fly at speeds of 140kph to 160kph (not advisable if you're behind the wheel!).
- If you break down, you must place an orange triangle about 6m in front of and behind the vehicle.
- At police checkposts (which are very common) smile, say good morning/afternoon, be very polite and take off your sunglasses. A little respect makes a huge difference to the way you'll be treated. Mostly you'll be met with a smile, perhaps asked curiously where you're from, and waved through without a problem.

HITCHING

As in any other part of the world, hitching is never entirely safe, and we don't recommend it. Travellers who hitch should understand that they are taking a small but potentially serious risk. Despite this general warning, hitching is a common way to get around Zambia. Some drivers, particularly expats, may offer you free lifts, but you should expect to pay for rides with local drivers (normally about the same as the bus fare, depending on the comfort of the vehicle). In such cases, agree on a price beforehand.

TAXI

Often the most convenient and comfortable way of getting around, especially in the cities. They have no meters, so rates are negotiable; be sure to settle on a price before departure.

TOURS

Tours and safaris around Zambia invariably focus on the national parks. Since many of these parks are hard to visit without a vehicle, joining a tour might be your only option anyway. Budget-priced operators run scheduled trips, or arrange things on the spot (with enough passengers), and can often be booked through a backpackers – try Lusaka Backpackers (p38) in Lusaka or Jollyboys Backpackers (p91) in Livingstone.

African View Safaris (☎0213-327271, 0979 374953; www.africanview.it; 10-day safaris from US$1650) This Livingstone-based Italian-run operator offers well-curated safaris across the country. It's also one of Zambia's best for those looking to attend traditional ceremonies or festivals. Motorbike tours were also soon to be on offer.

Barefoot Safaris (☎in South Africa 073-462 9232; www.barefoot-safaris.com) South African–based operator offering safaris to South Luangwa National Park.

Norman Carr Safaris (☎0216-246025; www.normancarrsafaris.com) Zambia's original safari company covers all of South Luangwa, as well as an exclusive concession at Liuwa Plain National Park.

Remote Africa Safaris (☎0216-246185; www.remoteafrica.com) Offers remote safaris in South Luangwa National Park.

Robin Pope Safaris (☎in Malawi 01-794491; www.robinpopesafaris.net) Specialises in walking safaris in South Luangwa.

TRAIN

The Tazara trains between Kapiri Mposhi and Dar es Salaam in Tanzania can also be used for travelling to and from northern Zambia. While the Lusaka–Kitwe service does stop at Kapiri Mposhi, the Lusaka–Kitwe and Tazara trains are not timed to connect with each other, and the domestic and international train terminals are 2km apart.

Zambia's only other railway services are the 'ordinary trains' between Lusaka and Kitwe, via Kapiri Mposhi and Ndola, and the 'express trains' between Lusaka and Livingstone.

Domestic trains are unreliable and ridiculously slow, so buses are always better. Conditions on domestic trains generally range from slightly dilapidated to ready-for-scrap. Most compartments have no lights or locks, so take a torch (flashlight) and something to secure the door at night.

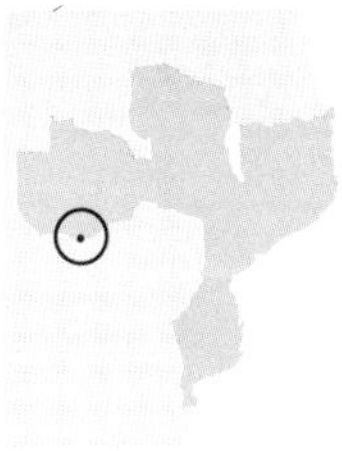

Victoria Falls

Includes ➡

Best Places to Eat

- ➡ Cafe Zambezi (p93)
- ➡ Lola's Tapas & Carnivore Restaurant (p98)
- ➡ Olga's Italian Corner (p93)
- ➡ Lookout Cafe (p97)
- ➡ Boma (p98)

Best Places to Sleep

- ➡ Victoria Falls Hotel (p97)
- ➡ Jollyboys Backpackers (p91)
- ➡ Stanley Safari Lodge (p93)
- ➡ Victoria Falls Backpackers (p97)

Why Go?

Taking its place alongside the Pyramids and the Serengeti, Victoria Falls (*Mosi-oa-Tunya* – the 'smoke that thunders') is one of Africa's original blockbusters. And although Zimbabwe and Zambia share it, Victoria Falls is a place all of its own.

As a magnet for tourists of all descriptions – backpackers, tour groups, thrill seekers, families, honeymooners – Victoria Falls is one of Earth's great spectacles. View it directly as a raging mile-long curtain of water, in all its glory, from a helicopter ride or peek precariously over its edge from Devil's Pools; the sheer power and force of the falls is something that simply does not disappoint.

Whether you're here purely to take in the sight of a natural wonder of the world, or for a serious hit of adrenalin via rafting or bungee jumping into the Zambezi, Victoria Falls is a place where you're sure to tick off numerous items from that bucket list.

When to Go

There are two main reasons to go to Victoria Falls – to view the falls, and to experience the outdoor activities – and each has its season.

July to December is the season for white-water rafting, especially August for hard-core rapids.

From February to June you'll experience the falls at their full force, so don't forget your raincoat.

From July to September you'll get the best views of the falls, combined with lovely weather and all activities to keep you busy.

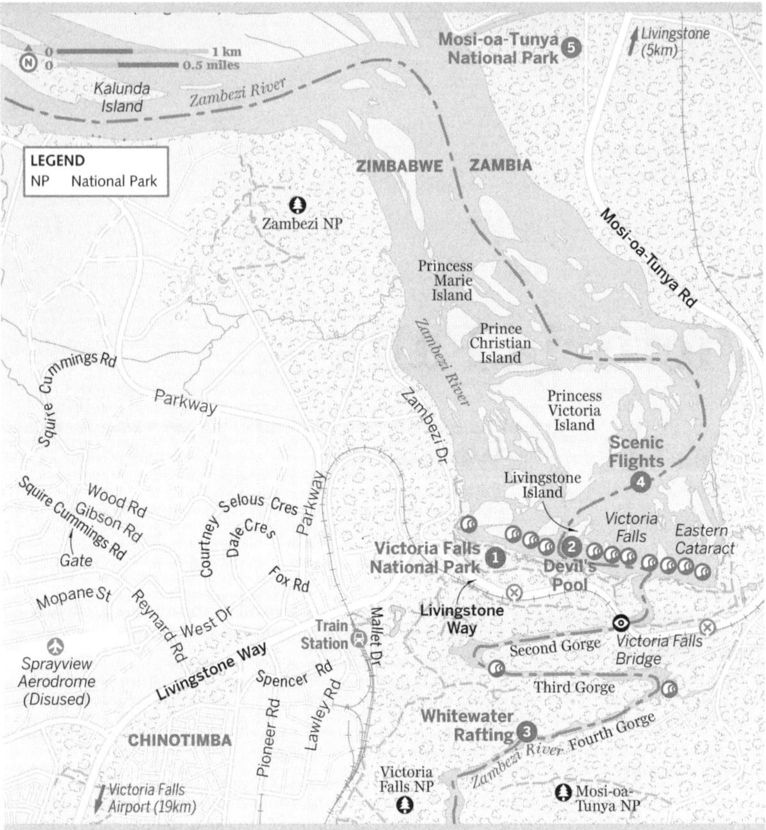

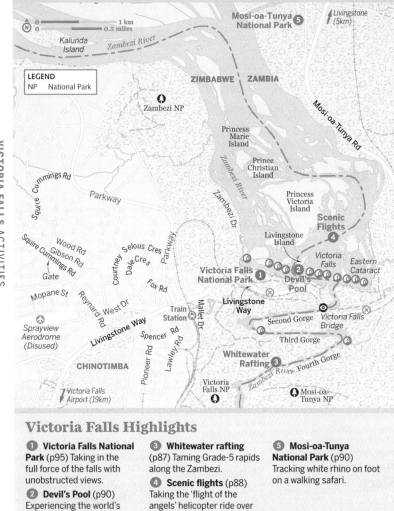

Victoria Falls Highlights

❶ **Victoria Falls National Park** (p95) Taking in the full force of the falls with unobstructed views.

❷ **Devil's Pool** (p90) Experiencing the world's most extreme infinity pool.

❸ **Whitewater rafting** (p87) Taming Grade-5 rapids along the Zambezi.

❹ **Scenic flights** (p88) Taking the 'flight of the angels' helicopter ride over Victoria Falls.

❺ **Mosi-oa-Tunya National Park** (p90) Tracking white rhino on foot on a walking safari.

SEVENTH NATURAL WONDER OF THE WORLD

Victoria Falls is the largest, most beautiful and most majestic waterfall on the planet, and is the Seventh Natural Wonder of the World as well as a Unesco World Heritage Site. A trip to Southern Africa would not be complete without visiting this unforgettable place.

Up to one million litres of water fall – per second – down a 108m drop along a 1.7km wide strip in the Zambezi Gorge; it's an awesome sight. Victoria Falls can be seen, heard, tasted and touched; it is a treat that few other places in the world can offer, a 'must see before you die' spot.

Victoria Falls is spectacular at any time of year, yet varies in the experiences it offers.

Activities

While it's the falls that lures travellers to the region, its awesome outdoor adventure scene is what makes them hang around. From world-class whitewater rafting, bungee jumping and high-adrenalin activities, to scenic flights and walking with rhinos, Victoria Falls is undoubtedly one of the world's premier adventure destinations.

Abseiling

Strap on a helmet, grab a rope and spend the day rappelling down the 54m sheer drop cliff face of Batoka Gorge from US$55.

Birdwatching

Twitchers will want to bring binoculars to check out 470 species of bird that inhabit the region, including Schalow's turaco, Taita falcon, African finfoot and half-collared kingfisher. Spot them on foot in the parks or on a canoe trip along the Zambezi.

Bridge Walk

For those not interested in bungee jumping off the bridge, walking along it is a good alternative. Strapped in with a harness, the guided tours take the walkways running just beneath the Victoria Falls Bridge, and offer a good way to learn about this engineering marvel, as well as fantastic photo ops. It's US$65 per person. Don't forget your passport.

Bungee Jumping & Bridge Swinging

One of the most famous bungee jumps in the world, the leap here is from atop of the iconic Victoria Falls bridge, plunging 111m into the Zambezi River. It's a long way down, but man it's a lot of fun. It costs US$160 per person.

Otherwise there's the bridge swing where you jump feet first, and free fall for four seconds; you'll end up swinging, but not upside down. There are two main spots: one right off the Victoria Falls Bridge, and the other a bit further along the Batoka Gorge. Costs for single/tandem are US$160/240.

Combine bungee with a bridge swing and bridge slide, and it'll cost US$210.

Canoeing & Kayaking

If whitewater rafting isn't for you, there's more relaxed guided canoe trips along the Upper Zambezi River on two-person inflatable canoes. Options include half (US$110) or whole day (US$125 to US$155) trips, and overnight jaunts (US$250 to US$285) and longer trips are available.

There's even more relaxed three-hour guided sunset river float trips where you can kick back and let someone else do the paddling for US$100, including refreshments.

On the Zambian side, take on the Zambezi's raging rapids in an inflatable kayak on a full-day trip (US$155).

Crocodile Cage Diving

On the Zimbabwe side of the falls, bring along your bathers for a close encounter with a Nile croc, where you plunge within the safety of a cage into a croc-filled enclosure wearing a mask and breathing apparatus. It costs US$70

Cultural Activities

Spend an hour in the evening by a campfire drumming under the African sky, which includes a traditional meal, for US$25. On the Zimbabwe side you can visit a local's home for lunch (US$23) or dinner (US$25)

Hiking

There's a good choice of guided walks in the area. One of the most popular treks is the trek down Batoka Gorge to the Boiling Pot (US$48) where you can get up close and personal with Victoria Falls. You can only do this from late August to December.

Horse Riding

Indulge in a bit of wildlife spotting from horseback along the Zambezi. Rides for 2½ hours cost US$100, and full-day trips for experienced riders are US$155.

Jet Boating

This hair-raising trip costs US$120, and is combined with a cable-car ride down into the Batoka Gorge.

Quadbiking

Discover the spectacular landscape surrounding Livingstone, Zambia, and the Batoka Gorge, spotting wildlife as you go on all-terrain quad bikes. Trips vary from ecotrail riding at Batoka Land to longer-range cultural trips in the African bush. Trips are one hour (US$95) or 2½ hours (US$165).

Rafting

This is one of the best white-water rafting destinations in the world, both for experienced rafters and newbies. Rafting can be done on either side of the Zambezi River, so it doesn't matter what side of the border you're on – you'll find Grade 5 rapids. Expect very long rides with huge drops and big kicks; it's not for the faint-hearted.

The best time for rafting is between July and mid-February (low water season); peak season is around August to October. Day trips run between rapids 1 and 21 (to rapid 25 on the Zambian side), covering a distance of around 25km.

The river fills up between mid-February and July (high water season), when day trips move downstream from rapids 11 to 25, covering a distance of around 18km. Only half-day trips are offered during this time. The river will usually close for its 'off season' around April or May, depending on the rain pattern for the year.

Trips are cheaper on the Zimbabwe side, costing about US$120 (versus US$160 in Zambia), but Zambia has the benefit of the cable car (and a few additional rapids) as opposed to the steep climb out on the Zimbabwe side.

Overnight and multiday jaunts can also be arranged.

An add-on activity to rafting is **river-boarding**, which is basically lying on a boogie board and careering down the rapids. A package including rafting for a half/full day is US$170/190. Otherwise get in touch with **Bundu Adventures** (☎0213-324406, 0978-203988; www.bunduadventures.com; 1364 Kabompo Rd, Gemstone Restaurant) about its **hydrospeed surfing** trips, where you can ride rapid number 2 on an Anvil board for US$70 for three hours.

River Cruises

River cruises along the Zambezi range from breakfast cruises to civilised jaunts on the grand *African Queen* and all-you-can-drink sunset booze cruises. Prices range from US$48 to US$85, excluding park fees. They're great for spotting wildlife, though some tourists get just as much enjoyment out of the bottomless drinks. Highly recommended.

Scenic Flights

Just when you thought the falls couldn't get any more spectacular, discover the 'flight of angels' helicopter ride that flies you right by the drama for the undisputed best views available. Rides aren't cheap, but they're worth it. **Zambezi Helicopter Company** (☎013-43569; www.zambezihelicopters.com; flights 13-/25-min US$150/284, plus US$12 govt fee) and **Bonisair** (☎0776 497888; www.bonisair.com; 15-/22-/25-mins US$150/235/277) in Zimbabwe, and **United Air Charter** (☎0955 204282, 0213-323095; www.uaczam.com; Baobab Ridge, Livingstone; 15/20/30min US$165/235/330) and **Batoka Sky** (☎0213-323589; www.seasonsinafrica.com; 15-min flights from US$155) in Zambia all offer flights. Flights cost from US$150 for 15 minutes over the falls, with longer trips available to take in the surrounding area.

On the Zambian side you can take a microlight flight with Batoka Sky, which offers another way to get fabulous aerial views.

Steam Train Journeys

To take in the romance of yesteryear, book yourself a ride on a historical steam train on the **Bushtracks Express** (☎013-45176; www.gotothevictoriafalls.com; 205 Courtney Selous Cr),

THE FALLS VIEWING SEASONS

Though spectacular at any time of year, the falls has a wet and dry season and each brings a distinct experience.

When the river is higher and the falls fuller it's the Wet, and when the river is lower and the falls aren't smothered in spray it's the Dry. Broadly speaking, you can expect the following conditions during the year:

January to April The beginning of the rainy season sees the falls begin their transitional period from low to high water, which should give you decent views, combined with experiencing its famous spray.

May to June Don't forget your raincoat, as you're gonna get drenched! While the falls will be hard to see through the mist, it'll give you a true sense of its power as 500 million litres of water plummets over the edge. The mist during this time can be seen from 50km away. If you want views, don't despair, this is the best time for aerial views with a chopper flight taking you up and over this incredible sight.

July to October The most popular time to visit, as the mist dissipates to unveil the best views and photography options from directly across the falls, while the volume maintains its rage to give you an idea of its sheer force – but only from the Zimbabwe side. However, those on the Zambian side will be able to experience Devil's Pool, which is accessible from August.

November to January The least popular time to visit, as temperatures rise and the falls are at their lowest flow. But they're impressive nevertheless, as the curtain of water divides into sections. The advantage of this time of year is you're able to swim right up to the edge of Devil's Pool on the Zambian side.

a 1953 class 14A Garratt steam train that will take you over the iconic Victoria Falls bridge at sunset with gourmet canapés and unlimited drinks. It's US$125 (including transfers, alcohol and snacks), with departures on Tuesday and Friday either at 5pm or 5.30pm; check the website for the latest schedule. Even if you're not booked on a trip it's worth getting along to the station to watch the drama of its departure.

In Zambia the **Royal Livingstone Express** (☎0213-4699300; www.royal-livingstone-express.com; Mosi-oa-Tunya Rd; US$180 incl dinner, drinks & transfers; ⏲4.30pm Wed & Sat) takes you on a 3½-hour ride including five-course dinner and drinks on a 1924 10th-class or 12th-class steam engine. The journey takes you to through Mosi-oa-Tunya National Park on plush leather couches, en route to the Victoria Falls Bridge for a sundowner. It's priced at $180 per person, including return transfers within Livingstone.

Wildlife Safaris

There are plenty of options for wildlife watching in the area, both in the national park in the immediate area and further afield, as well as private game reserves.

In Zambia the game reserve section of Mosi-oa-Tunya National Park is home to white rhino, and hence a popular spot to tick off that last member from the big five in the wild. You're able to track them on foot for US$80 per person (including park fees), but you can only do this as part of a walking tour. Get in touch with Livingstone Rhino Walks (p91) or Savannah Southern Safaris (p90) for bookings; note that you need to be over 12 years of age.

The Zambezi National Park in Zimbabwe is much bigger in scale and has a greater diversity of wildlife (including a few cats) and some wonderful lodges and campsites along the Zambezi.

On both sides of the border river cruises (from US$48) along the Zambezi River are another popular way to see various wildlife including elephants, hippos and plenty of birdlife.

Another convenient option, only 15km from Victoria Falls town, is the Stanley and Livingstone Private Game Reserve. Set on a 4000-hectare private reserve here you can track the Big Five, including black rhino that have been translocated from Hwange National Park. A standard three-hour game drive costs US$100, or you can do a night drive and a bush dinner (US$137).

Hwange National Park (www.zimparks.org; national parks accommodation per day guests/nonguests US$10/20; ⏲main gate 6am-6pm) in Zimbabwe is the other option, with one of the largest number of elephants in the world, as well as good sightings of predators. A day trip will cost around US$220 (minimum four people), or otherwise it's a two-hour bus ride away.

You can travel further afield, with operators arranging day trips to Chobe National Park in Botswana for US$160 (excluding visas). It's only a one-hour drive from Victoria Falls, and includes a breakfast boat cruise, a game drive in Chobe National Park, lunch and transfer back to Victoria Falls by 5pm. Wildlife viewing is excellent: lions, elephants, wild dogs, cheetahs, buffaloes and plenty of antelopes.

Zipline, Flying Fox & Gorge Swings

Glide at 106km/h along a zipline (single/tandem US$69/111), or soar like a superhero from one country to another (from Zim to Zam) on the 'bridge slide' as you whiz over Batoka Gorge (single/tandem US$45/70). Other similar options are flying-fox rides (US$42).

A *slightly* less terrifying variation of the bungee jump is the gorge swing (US$95), where you take the plunge foot first before swinging across the gorge like a human pendulum.

ℹ Information

Hands down the best independent advice is from **Backpackers Bazaar** (☎013-45828, 013-44511, 013-42208; www.backpackersbazaarvicfalls.com; off Parkway, Shop 5, Bata Bldg; ⏲8am-5pm Mon-Fri, 9am-4pm Sat & Sun) in the town of Victoria Falls, run by the passionate owner, Joy, who has a wealth of all info and advice for Victoria Falls and beyond. In Livingstone, the folks at Jollyboys Backpackers (p91) are also extremely knowledgeable on all the latest happenings. Both are good places to book activities and onward travel.

ZAMBIA

☎260

As Zambia continues to ride the wave of tourism generated by the falls, it manages to keep itself grounded, offering a wonderfully low-key destination. The waterfront straddling the falls continues its rapid development and is fast becoming one of the most exclusive destinations in Southern Africa.

Livingstone

POP 136,897 / ☎0213

The relaxed and friendly town of Livingstone, set just 11km from Victoria Falls, is a fantastic base for visiting the Zambian side of the natural world wonder. It attracts travellers not only to experience the falls but also to tackle the thrilling adventure scene, and has taken on the role of a backpacking mecca. Its main thoroughfare, Mosi-oa-Tunya Rd, leads south to a wonderful stretch of the Zambezi River around 7km from town.

Sights

★Victoria Falls World Heritage National Monument Site WATERFALL

(Mosi-au-Tunya National Park; adult/child/guide US$20/10/10; 6am-6pm) This is what you're here for. The mighty Victoria Falls is part of the Mosi-oa-Tunya National Park, located 11km outside town before the Zambia border. From the centre, a network of paths leads through thick vegetation to various viewpoints.

For close-up views of the **Eastern Cataract**, nothing beats the hair-raising (and hair-wetting) walk across the footbridge, through swirling clouds of mist, to a sheer buttress called the **Knife Edge**.

★Devil's Pool VIEWPOINT

(www.devilspool.net; Livingstone Island; from US$90) One of the most thrilling experiences – not only at the falls but in all of Africa – is the hair-raising journey to **Livingstone Island**. Here you will bathe in Devil's Pool – nature's ultimate infinity pool, set directly on the edge of Victoria Falls. You can leap into the pool and then poke your head over the edge to get an extraordinary view of the 100m drop. Here also you'll see the plaque marking the spot where David Livingstone first sighted the falls.

Mosi-oa-Tunya National Park NATIONAL PARK

(adult/child US$15/7.50; 6am-6pm) This park is divided into two sections: the Victoria Falls area and the wildlife sector. The latter is only 3km southwest of Livingstone, and most famous for its population of white rhino, which you can track on foot. For their protection, the rhino are accompanied by anti-poaching rangers round-the-clock. You can only see them as part of a pre-booked tour (US$80 per person, inclusive of park fees and hotel transfer), booked through Livingstone Rhino Walks or Savannah Southern Safaris.

Livingstone Museum MUSEUM

(☎0213-324429; www.museumszambia.org; Mosi-oa-Tunya Rd; adult/child US$ 5/3; 9am-4.30pm) The excellent Livingstone Museum is the oldest, largest and best museum in the country. It's divided into sections covering archaeology, history, ethnography and natural history. Highlights include its collection of original David Livingstone memorabilia (including signed letters), tribal artefacts (from bark cloth to witchcraft exhibits), a life-sized model of an African village, taxidermy displays and coverage of modern-day Zambian history.

Tours

Savannah Southern Safaris WILDLIFE, WALKING

(☎0973 471486; www.savannah-southern-safaris.com) Offers a range of nature tours, but it's best known for its walks to see white rhino in Mosi-au-Tunya National Park. For two or more people it's US$70, or US$80 for individuals, inclusive of transport and park fees. Note you need to be over 12 years of age.

VISAS

You will need a visa to cross between Zimbabwe and Zambia. These are available at the border, open from around 6am to 10pm.

You can't get multi-entry visas at the Victoria Falls crossings; you'll usually need to apply at your home country embassy before travelling.

- **Crossing into Zambia** A day visit costs US$20 for 24 hours (but you'll need a Zimbabwean double-entry to return), a single-entry visa costs US$50 and double entry is US$80.
- **Crossing into Zimbabwe** A single-entry visa costs US$30 for most nationalities (US$55 for British/Irish and US$75 for Canadian). Double entry is US$45 for most nationalities (US$75 for British/Irish and unavailable for Canadians).

Note that the KAZA Uni-Visa (which formerly allowed travel between the two countries) was suspended in 2016. It's worth checking, though, before you leave to see if it's back in effect.

There are also tours to visit local communities, as well as Livingstone walking tours.

Livingstone Rhino Walks SAFARI
(☑ 0213-322267; www.livingstonerhinosafaris.com; per person US$80) This Livingstone-based tour operator specialises in walking safaris to see white rhino in Mosi-au-Tunya National Park. Visitors must be over 12 years of age. The price is inclusive of park entry fees and transfers in the Livingstone area.

🛏 Sleeping

★ **Jollyboys**
Backpackers HOSTEL, CAMPGROUND $
(☑ 0213-324229; www.backpackzambia.com; 34 Kanyanta Rd; campsite per person US$9, dm US$12-15, d from US$65, d/tr/q with shared bathroom US$45/50/80; ❄@🛜🏊) 🏄 The clued-in owner knows exactly what backpackers want, making Jollyboys popular for good reason. From its friendly staff, social bar and restaurant to the sunken reading lounge and sparkling pool, it's a great place to hang out. Dorms and bathrooms are spotless (with a flashpacker option, too), while the private rooms comprise A-frame garden cottages or very comfortable rooms with air-con and attached bathroom.

Rose Rabbit
Zambezi River Bushcamp TENTED CAMP $
(☑ in Zimbabwe 0784 007283, 0773 368608; www.facebook.com/theroserabbit; Rapid 21, Lower Zambezi River; per person campsite/dm/tented camping/treehouse US$10/15/20/40) This riverside beach camp is one for independent travellers looking for a different scene. Right on rapid 21 of the Lower Zambezi, it will suit not only rafting enthusiasts but also a more free-spirited crowd who are into bonfire jamborees, swimming and hanging out by the beach. As well as campsites, there are dorms, tented camps and A-frame treehouse digs.

Livingstone
Backpackers HOSTEL, CAMPGROUND $
(☑ 0213-324730; www.livingstonebackpackers.com; 559 Mokambo Rd; campsite US$7, dm from US$12, d US$45, with shared bathroom US$65; 🛜🏊) Resembling the *Big Brother* household, this place can be a bit 'party central', particularly when the Gen Y volunteer brigade is on holiday. You'll find them lounging by the pool, in the hot tub, at the bar, or in the sandy outdoor cabana, swinging in hammocks, cooking barbecues or tackling the rock-climbing wall. There is also an open-air kitchen and living room. Very friendly staff.

Fawlty Towers BACKPACKERS, LODGE $
(☑ 0213-323432; www.adventure-africa.com; 216 Mosi-oa-Tunya Rd; dm US$12; r from US$50, with shared bathroom US$45; ❄@🛜🏊) As well as some of the nicest and most spacious dorms we've seen, things have been spruced up here into a guesthouse full of upmarket touches – no longer catering exclusively to backpackers. There's free wi-fi, large well-maintained lawns, a great pool, a bar, a homely lounge, free pancakes for afternoon tea, a self-catering kitchen, and no Basil or Manuel in sight.

Olga's Guesthouse GUESTHOUSE $$
(☑ 0213-324160; www.olgasproject.com; cnr Mosi-oa-Tunya & Nakatindi Rds; s/d/f incl breakfast US$40/60/80; ❄🛜) 🏄 With a good location

VICTORIA FALLS LIVINGSTONE

ZIM OR ZAM?

Victoria Falls straddles the border between Zimbabwe and Zambia, and is easily accessible from both countries. However, the big question for most travellers is: do I visit the falls from the town of Victoria Falls, Zimbabwe, or from Livingstone, Zambia? The answer is simple: visit the falls from both sides and, if possible, stay in both towns. You'll need to pay for extra visas, but you've come this far so it's worth it.

From the Zimbabwean side, you're further from the falls, though the overall views are much, much better. From the Zambian side, for daring souls you can literally stand on top of the falls from Devil's Pool, though from here your perspective is narrowed.

The town of Victoria Falls was built for tourists, so it's easily walkable and located right next to the entrance to the Falls. It has a natural African bush beauty. As for whether it's safe given Zimbabwe's ongoing political issues, the answer is a resolute 'yes'.

Livingstone is an attractive town with a relaxed ambience and a proud, historic air. Since the town of Victoria Falls was the main tourist centre for so many years, Livingstone feels more authentic, perhaps because locals earn their livelihood through means other than tourism. Livingstone is bustling with travellers year-round, though the town is fairly spread out, and is located 11km from the falls.

Livingstone

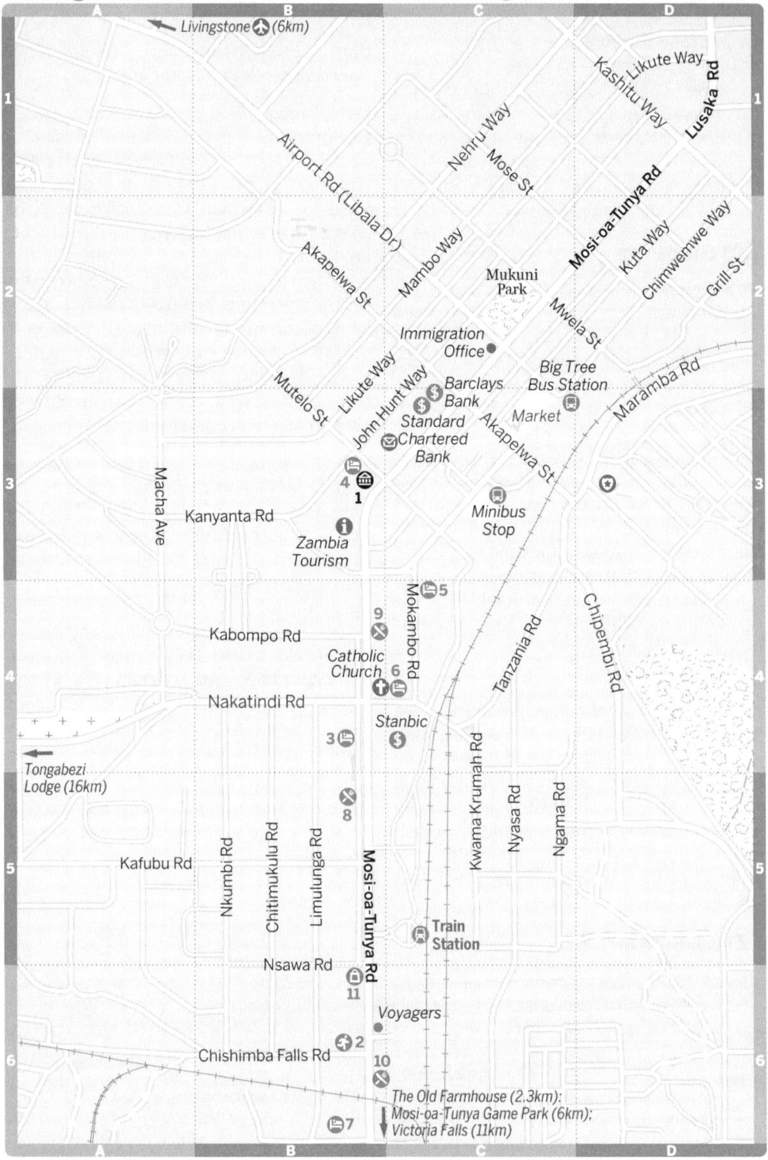

in the centre of town, Olga's offers clean, spacious rooms with cool tiled floors, teak furniture and slick bathrooms just a few feet away. Profits go towards helping an organisation supporting local youth. Another bonus is its on-site Italian restaurant, Olga's Italian Corner.

ZigZag GUESTHOUSE **$$**

(☎0213-322814; www.zigzagzambia.com; 693 Linda Rd, off Mosi-oa-Tunya Rd; s/d/tr incl breakfast

Livingstone

US$50/70/90; P ❄ @ 🛜 🏊) Don't be deceived by the motel-meets-caravan-park exterior: the rooms here are more boutique B&B with loving touches throughout. Rooms are spotless, and set on a sprawling garden property with an assortment of fruit trees, picnic tables, a plush pool and a playground for kids. Its great restaurant is another drawcard, too.

Victoria Falls Waterfront LODGE, CAMPGROUND $$
(☎0213-320606; www.thevictoriafallswaterfront.com; Sichango Dr; campsite per person US$13, s/d tented camping US$36/48, s/d incl breakfast chalet from US$165/215; ❄ 🛜 🏊) Sharing space with the luxury resorts along the banks of the Zambezi, this is the only waterfront lodge that caters to budget travellers. For this reason it's a popular place, with a wilderness charm (crocs inhabit a small creek on the property), and a choice of camping, domed tents or alluring riverside chalets. Its pool with decking and bar overlooking the river is unsurprisingly popular at sunset.

★ **Stanley Safari Lodge** LODGE $$$
(☎in Malawi 0265-1794491; www.stanleysafaris.com; Stanley Rd; per person with full board & activities from US$510; @ 🛜 🏊) Intimate and indulgent, Stanley is a 10km drive from the falls in a peaceful spot surrounded by mopane (woodland). Rooms scattered among the landscaped bush garden are as plush as can be expected at these prices; the standouts are the rustic open-air suites where you can soak up nature from your own private plunge pool. When you tire of that, curl up by the fire in the open-air lounge. Rates are all-inclusive.

Tongabezi Lodge LODGE $$$
(☎0979 312766, 0213-327468; www.tongabezi.com; cottage/house per person incl full board & activities from US$775/875; ❄ 🛜 🏊) Has sumptuous, spacious cottages, open-faced 'treehouses' and private dining decks. The houses are good for families and have private plunge pools. Guests are invited to spend an evening on nearby Sindabezi Island (from US$595 per person), a luxurious, rustic getaway.

Eating

★ **Da Canton** GELATERIA $
(Mosi-Oa-Tunya Rd; gelato small/large cup ZMW8/24, pizza from ZMW19; ⏰9am-11pm) While all the Italian food here is tasty and authentic, it's the homemade gelato that has locals raving. The Italian owner makes all 18 flavours, including all the classics and some original concoctions.

★ **Cafe Zambezi** AFRICAN $$
(☎0978 978578; www.facebook.com/cafezambezi; 217 Mosi-oa-Tunya Rd; mains US$6-10; ⏰7.15am-midnight; 🛜 🌱) Head straight through to the courtyard, sunny by day and candlelit by night. Bursting with local flavour, the broad menu covers local favourites of goat meat, smoky crocodile tail and mopane (woodland) caterpillars. Authentic wood-fired pizzas are a winner or sink your teeth into impala or eggplant-and-haloumi burgers.

★ **Olga's Italian Corner** ITALIAN $$
(www.olgasproject.con; cnr Mosi-oa-Tunya & Nakatindi Rds; pizza & pasta ZMW35-88; ⏰7am-10pm; 🛜 🌱) Olga's does authentic wood-fired thin-crust pizzas, as well as delicious homemade pasta classics all served under a large thatched roof. Great options for vegetarians include the lasagne with its crispy blackened edge served in the dish. All profits go to a community centre to help disadvantaged youth.

Golden Leaf INDIAN $$
(☎0213-321266; 1174 Mosi-Oa-Tunya Rd; mains ZMW54-95; ⏰12.30-10pm) As soon as those aromas hit you upon arrival you'll realise Golden Leaf is the real deal when it comes to authentic

Indian food. It's a good option for vegetarians with a lot of choices including house-made paneer dishes, creamy North Indian curries and tandoori dishes in the evenings.

ZigZag CAFE **$$**
(Mango Tree Cafe; www.zigzagzambia.com/the-mango-tree-cafe; 693 Linda Rd, off Mosi-oa-Tunya Rd; mains from ZMW25-62; ⌚7am-9pm; 📶) ZigZag does drool-inducing homemade muffins, excellent Zambian coffee and smoothies using fresh fruit from the garden. Its changing menu of comfort food is all made from scratch, and you can expect anything from drop scones (pikelets) with bacon and maple syrup to thin-crust pizzas and burgers.

Drinking & Nightlife

The Sundeck BAR
(http://royal-livingstone.anantara.com/the-sun decks; Mosi-au-Tunya Rd; cocktail from ZMW40; ⌚10.30am-7pm; 📶) Just the spot for a sundowner, this open-air bar within the Royal Livingstone Hotel overlooks a dramatic stretch of the Zambezi. As well as the usual bar drinks there's a choice of old-fashioned cocktails such as the Manhattan, Americano and champagne cocktail. There's also decent burgers, mezze platters and salads. From here it's a 15-minute walk to the falls.

Shopping

Wayawaya FASHION & ACCESSORIES
(www.wayawaya.no; Mosi-oa-Tunya Rd; ⌚9am-5pm) A social enterprise founded by two Norwegian girls, Wayawaya sells quality, contemporary handmade bags put together by local women. Its principles are based on the slow fashion movement, and you can meet all the ladies when visiting. Get in touch if you want to volunteer.

Information

DANGERS & ANNOYANCES

Don't walk from town to the falls as there have been a number of muggings along this stretch of road – even tourists on bicycles have been targeted. It's a long and not terribly interesting walk anyway, and simply not worth the risk (especially given there are elephants around). Take a taxi or free shuttle from your guesthouse. While Livingstone is generally a very safe town, avoid walking around town once it becomes dark.

IMMIGRATION

Immigration Office (☎0213-3320648; www.zambiaimmigration.gov.zm; Mosi-oa-Tunya Rd; ⌚8am-1pm & 2-5pm Mon-Fri)

MEDICAL SERVICES

SES-Zambia (www.ses-zambia.com; Mosi-au-Tunya Rd, AVANI Victoria Falls Resort; ⌚8am-5pm) The best medical facility in the area, both for emergency services and general medicine. It's within the **AVANI resort** (☎0978 777044; www.minorhotels.com/en/avani; Mosi-oa-Tunya Rd).

MONEY

The following banks accept MasterCard and Visa, but can occasionally go offline during power outages.

Barclays in town (cnr Mosi-oa-Tunya Rd & Akapelwa St) and at the AVANI resort.

Standard Chartered Bank (Mosi-oa-Tunya Rd) In town.

Stanbic (Mosi-oa-Tunya Rd) In town.

POLICE

Police (☎0213-320116, 0213-323575; Maramba Rd)

POST

Post Office (Mosi-oa-Tunya Rd) Has a poste restante service.

TOURIST INFORMATION

Tourist Centre (☎0213-321404; www.zambiatourism.com; Mosi-oa-Tunya Rd; ⌚8am-5pm Mon-Fri, 8am-noon Sat) Mildly useful and can help with booking tours and accommodation, but Jollyboys and Fawlty Towers have all the information you need.

Getting There & Away

AIR

Livingstone's newly renovated airport – officially known as Harry Mwanga Nkumbula International Airport – is located 6km northwest of town. It has an ATM and free wi-fi. It's around a US$5 taxi ride into town, or US$8 to the waterfront hotels.

South African Airways (☎0213-323031; www.flysaa.com) and **British Airways** (Comair; ☎in South Africa +27 10-3440130; www.britishairways.com) have daily flights to and from Johannesburg (1¾ hours); the cheapest economy fare starts at around US$270 return.

Proflight Zambia (☎0977 335563, in Lusaka 0211-252452; www.proflight-zambia.com) flies daily from Livingstone to Lusaka for around US$210 one way (1¼ hours).

BUS & MINIBUS

Plenty of minibuses and shared taxis ply the route from the Big Tree Bus Station at Livingstone's town market along Senanga Rd in Livingstone. Note that plans are in place to relocate the bus terminal to Nakatindi Rd. As muggings have been reported, it is best to take a taxi if you arrive at night.

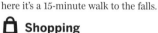

CAR & MOTORCYCLE

If you're driving a rented car or motorcycle, be sure to carefully check all info regarding insurance, and that you have all the necessary papers for checks and border crossings such as 'owners' and 'permission to drive' documents, insurance papers and a copy of the carbon tax receipt. Expect to pay around US$100 in various fees when crossing the border into Zimbabwe.

TRAIN

While the bus is a much quicker way to get around, the train to Lusaka is for lovers of slow travel or trains. The operative word here is *slow*, taking anywhere from 15 to 20 hours for the trip to Lusaka (economy/business/1st-class sleeper ZMW 70/90/135), via Choma, departing 8pm on Monday and Friday. Bring your own food. Reservations are available at the **train station** (☎0961 195353), which is signed off Mosi-oa-Tunya Rd.

Getting Around

CAR & MOTORCYCLE

Hemingways (☎0213-323097; www.hemingwayszambia.com) in Livingstone has new 4WD Toyota Hiluxes for around US$225 per day. Vehicles are fully kitted out with everything you need, including cooking and camping equipment. Drivers must be over 25.

Voyagers (☎0213-320517, 0213-323259; www.voyagerszambia.com; 163 Mosi-oa-Tunya Rd) Zambian operator affiliated with Europcar has reasonably priced 4WDs for around US$100 per day.

TAXIS

Minibuses run regularly along Mosi-oa-Tunya Rd to Victoria Falls and the Zambian border (ZMW5,15 minutes). Blue taxis cost ZMW60 to ZMW80 from the border to Livingstone. Coming from the border, shared taxis are parked just over from the waiting taxis, and depart when full. The going rate for one day's taxi hire around Livingstone and the falls is about US$25.

ZIMBABWE

☎263

There may still be a long way to go, but finally things seem to be looking up for Zimbabwe. All the bad news that has kept it in the glare of the spotlight – rampant land reform, hyperinflation and food shortages – fortunately now seem to be a thing of the past. In reality, safety has never been a concern for travellers here and, even during the worst of it, tourists were never targets for political violence. Word of this seems to have spread, as tourists stream back to the Zim side of the falls.

Victoria Falls

POP 33,360 / ☎013

A genuine bucket-list destination, Victoria Falls remains one of Africa's most famous tourist towns. Not only does it offer the best views of the iconic falls, but it also has a world-class adventure-tourism scene and wildlife safaris.

It's home to the country's tourism industry, and despite Zimbabwe's political issues, it's always been a safe spot for tourists; locals are exceptionally friendly. While for a few years it felt like a resort in off-season, there's no mistake about it now – it's officially reopened for business.

Though built specifically for tourism, it retains a relaxed local feel, and has neat, walkable streets (though not at dark, because of the wild animals) lined with hotels, bars and some of the best crafts you'll find anywhere in Southern Africa.

Sights

★**Victoria Falls National Park** WATERFALL
(US$30; 6am-6pm) Here on the Zimbabwe side of the falls you're in for a real treat. Some two-thirds of Victoria Falls are located here, including the main falls themselves, which flow spectacularly year-round. The walk is along the top of the gorge, following a path with various viewing points that open up to extraordinary front-on panoramas of these world-famous waterfalls.

★**Jafuta Heritage Centre** CULTURAL CENTRE
(www.elephantswalk.com/heritage.htm; Adam Stander Dr, Elephant's Walk; admission by donation; 8am-5pm) FREE This impressive little museum details the cultural heritage of Zimbabwe's indigenous ethnic groups. There's good background information on the Shona, Ndebele, Tonga and Lozi people, as well as fascinating artefacts, jewellery and costumes.

Zambezi National Park NATIONAL PARK
(☎013-42294; www.zimparks.org; day/overnight US$15/23; 6am-6pm) Just 5km from the town centre is this vastly underrated national park, comprising 40km of Zambezi River frontage and a spread of wildlife-rich mopane (woodland) and savannah. It's best known for its herds of sable, elephant, giraffe, zebra and buffalo, plus the occasional (rarely spotted) lion, leopard and cheetah. It's easily accessible by 2WD vehicle.

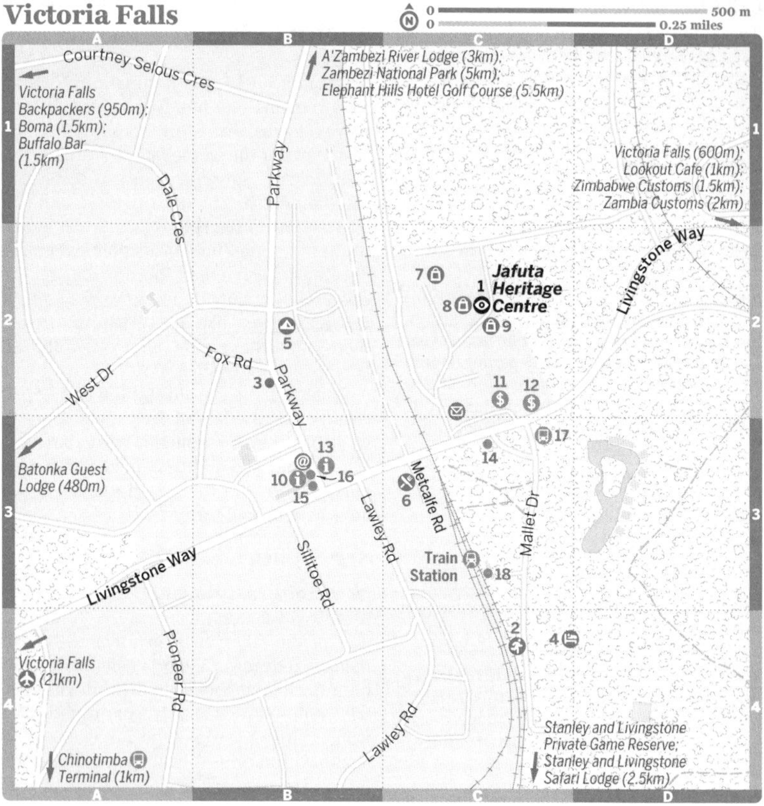

Victoria Falls

Top Sights
1 Jafuta Heritage Centre C2

Activities, Courses & Tours
2 Bushtracks Express C4
3 Wild Horizons B2

Sleeping
4 Victoria Falls Hotel C4
5 Victoria Falls Restcamp & Lodges B2

Eating
Africa Café .... (see 8)
In Da Belly Restaurant .... (see 5)
6 Lola's Tapas & Carnivore Restaurant C3

Drinking & Nightlife
Stanley's Terrace .... (see 4)

Shopping
7 Big Curio Open Market C2
8 Elephant's Walk Shopping & Artist Village C2
Matsimela .... (see 8)
Ndau Collection .... (see 8)
Prime Art Gallery .... (see 8)
9 Tshaka's Den Complex C2

Information
10 Backpackers Bazaar B3
11 Barclays Bank C2
12 Standard Chartered Bank C2
13 Zimbabwe Tourism Authority B3

Transport
14 Avis C3
15 FastJet B3
16 Hertz B3
17 Intercape Pathfinder C3
18 Train Ticket Office C3

Stanley and Livingstone Private Game Reserve WILDLIFE RESERVE

(Victoria Falls Private Game Reserve; ☎013-44571; www.stanleyandlivingstone.com/activities) This private 4000-hectare game reserve 12km from town has the Big Five, including the critically endangered black rhino, which you're almost guaranteed to see. Game drives are US$100, US$135 for a night drive with a bush dinner.

Sleeping

★Victoria Falls Backpackers HOSTEL, CAMPGROUND $

(☎013-42209; www.victoriafallsbackpackers.com; 357 Gibson Rd; camping/dm per person US$10/18, d US$60, with shared bathroom US$50; @ 📶 🏊) One of the best budget choices in town, this long-standing backpackers received a much-needed revamp when the original owners returned. The eclectic mix of rooms are scattered among the well-tended garden property full of quirky touches. Other notable features are its bar, small inviting pool, games room and TV lounge, plus self-catering kitchen, massage and fish spa.

Victoria Falls Restcamp & Lodges CAMPGROUND, LODGE $

(☎013-40509; www.vicfallsrestcamp.com; cnr Parkway & West Dr; camping/dm US$16/20, s/d dome tents from US$29/40, s/d chalets without bathroom US$35/46, cottages from US$127; ❄ 📶 🏊) A great alternative for independent travellers, it has a relaxed holiday-camp feel, within secure grassy grounds, with a choice of no-frills dorms, lodge-style rooms (or pricier air-con rooms with bathroom) and safari tents. There's a lovely pool and fantastic open-air restaurant, In Da Belly. Wi-fi available (for a fee).

Zambezi National Park Lodge CHALETS, CAMPGROUND $$

(☎013-42294; www.zimparks.org; camping $17, cottage $138; ❄) These wonderful two-bedroom cottages are right on the Zambezi river. You'll need to bring your own food, but all come with fridges, full kitchen, couches, TV, bathtubs and even air-con. There's an outdoor barbecue area too. Further into the park are basic bush campsites (firewood US$5), but with no water or ablutions.

★Victoria Falls Hotel LUXURY HOTEL $$$

(☎0772 132175, 013-44751; www.victoriafallshotel.com; 1 Mallet Dr; s/d incl breakfast from US$423/455; ❄ 📶 🏊) Built in 1904, this historic hotel (the oldest in Zimbabwe) oozes elegance and sophistication. It occupies an impossibly scenic location, looking across manicured lawns (with roaming warthogs) to the gorge and bridge. You can't see the falls as such, but you do see the spray from some rooms. Taking high tea here at Stanley's Terrace is an institution.

Stanley and Livingstone Safari Lodge LODGE $$$

(☎013-44571; www.stanleyandlivingstone.com; Stanley & Livingstone Private Game Reserve; r per person incl full board & activities US$436; ❄ 📶 🏊) Set on a private game reserve 15km from Victoria Falls, this luxury lodge will suit visitors without the time to visit a national park but who want to be surrounded by wildlife. Rooms on the luxurious grounds feature all the modern comforts combined with Victorian-style bathrooms featuring claw-foot tubs, lounge suite and patio.

Batonka Guest Lodge GUESTHOUSE $$$

(☎013-47189/90; www.batonkaguestlodge.com; Reynard Rd; s/d incl breakfast US$195/300; ❄ 📶 🏊) 🍃 Mixing modern comforts with colonial charm, Batonka is an excellent choice for those not wanting a large-scale resort. It has a relaxed ambience, with rooms overlooking a landscaped lawn and inviting pool. Rooms have stylish bathrooms, cable TV and filter coffee. The reception/bar/restaurant is in a homestead-style building with wrap-around veranda and a boutique interior design with original artwork throughout.

Elephant Camp LODGE $$$

(☎013-44571; www.theelephantcamp.com; s/d incl full board US$838/1118; @ 📶 🏊) One of the best spots to splash out; the luxurious 'tents' have a classic lodge feel and are set on a private concession within the Victoria Falls National Park. Each room has its own outdoor private plunge pool and balcony decking to spot grazing animals or the spray of the falls. You might get to meet Sylvester, the resident cheetah.

Eating

★Lookout Cafe CAFE $$

(☎0782 745112; www.wildhorizons.co.za/the-lookout-cafe; Batoka Gorge; mains US$12-15; ⏰8am-7pm; 📶) A stunning location overlooking Batoka Gorge. Enjoy views of the bridge and the Zambezi river while tucking into a burger or crocodile kebab, or a cold drink on its open-air deck or grassy lawn terrace. It's operated by **Wild Horizons** (☎013-44571, 0712 213721; www.wildhorizons.co.za; 310 Parkway Dr), so you'll get the added

Victoria Falls & Mosi-oa-Tunya National Parks

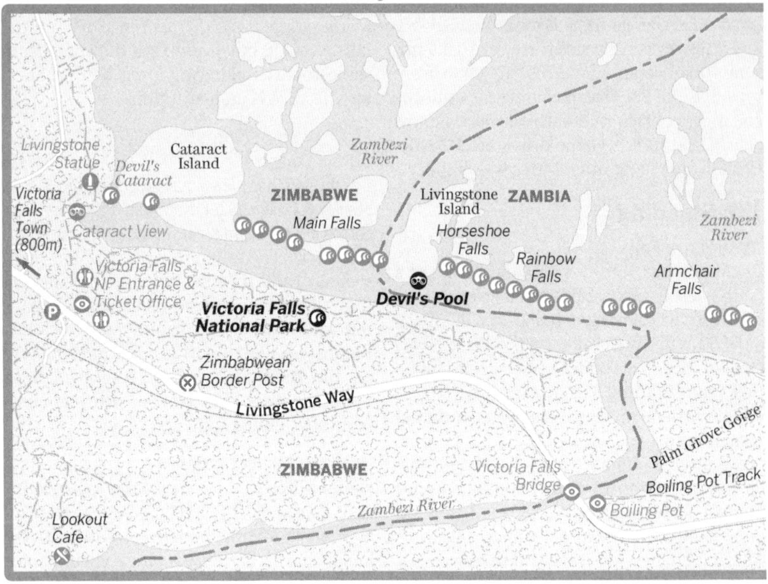

entertainment of watching daredevils take the plunge or soar across the gorge.

Africa Café CAFE $$
(www.elephantswalk.com/africa_cafe.htm; Adam Stander Dr, Elephant's Walk; breakfast/burgers US$7/11; 8am-5pm;) This appealing outdoor cafe does the best coffee in Victoria Falls, made by expert baristas using beans sourced from Zimbabwe's eastern highlands. There's plenty of seating scattered about to enjoy big breakfasts, burgers, vegetarian dishes and desserts such as its signature baobab-powder cheese cake. There's a bar, too.

★ **Lola's Tapas & Carnivore Restaurant** SPANISH, AFRICAN $$
(013-42994; 8B Landela Complex; dishes US$8-20; 8am-10pm;) Run by welcoming host Lola from Barcelona, this popular eatery combines a menu of Mediterranean cuisine with local game meats, with anything from crocodile ravioli to paella with kudu. Other items include zebra burgers, impala meatballs, and more traditional tapas dishes. There's also a full spread of all-you-can-eat game meat for US$30.

★ **Boma** AFRICAN $$
(013-43211; www.victoria-falls-safari-lodge.com; Squire Cummings Rd, Victoria Falls Safari Lodge; buffet US$40; dinner 7pm, cafe from 7am) Enjoy a taste of Africa at this buffet restaurant set under a massive thatched roof. Here you can dine on smoked crocodile tail, BBQ warthog, guinea fowl stew and wood-fired spit roasts; and the more adventurous can try a mopane worm (you'll get a certificate from the chef for your efforts). There's also traditional dancing (8pm), interactive drumming (8.45pm) and fortune telling by a witch doctor. Bookings essential.

In Da Belly Restaurant AFRICAN, INTERNATIONAL $$
(013-332077; Parkway, Victoria Falls Restcamp & Lodges; meals US$5-15; 7am-9.30pm) Under a large thatched hut, looking out to a sparkling pool, this relaxed open-air eatery has a menu of warthog schnitzel, crocodile curry and impala burgers, as well as one of the best breakfast menus in town. The name is a play on Ndebele, one of the two major population tribes in Zimbabwe.

Drinking & Nightlife

★ **Stanley's Terrace** HIGH TEA
(013-44751; www.victoriafallshotel.com/stanleys-terrace; Mallet Dr, Victoria Falls Hotel; high tea for 1-/2-people US$15/30; high tea 3-6pm;) The Terrace at the stately Victoria Falls Hotel just

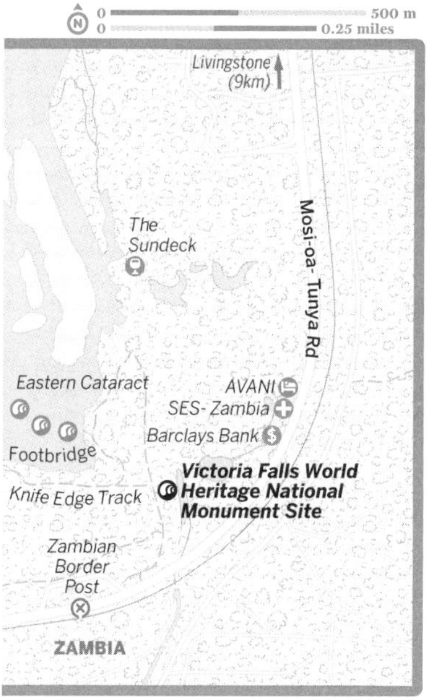

brims with English colonial ambience. High tea is served to a postcard-perfect backdrop of the gardens and Victoria Falls Bridge, with polished silverware, decadent cakes and three-tiered trays of finger sandwiches. (Cucumber? Why yes, of course.) A jug of Pimms makes perfect sense on summer day at US$24. The only thing missing is croquet.

Buffalo Bar BAR
(www.victoria-falls-safari-lodge.com; Squire Cummings Rd, Victoria Falls Safari Lodge; 7am-10pm) Unquestionably the best sundowner spot in town; enjoy a gin-and-tonic on its outdoor terrace overlooking distant animals on the plains of Zambezi National Park. Part of the Victoria Falls Safari Lodge, it's a good pre-dinner spot if you've got a booking at the hotel's Boma restaurant. Otherwise come during the day for the 1pm vulture feeding.

Shopping

★Elephant's Walk Shopping & Artist Village SHOPPING CENTRE
(0772 254552; www.elephantswalk.com; Adam Stander Dr; 9am-5pm) A must for those in the market for quality Zimbabwean and African craft, this shopping village is home to boutique stores and galleries owned by a collective that aims to promote and set up local artists.

At the back of Elephant's Walk Village you'll find local vendors at **Big Curio Open Market** (Adam Stander Dr), and the **Tshaka's Den Complex** (7.30am-6pm), both of which sell locally made handicraft and Shona sculpture.

Matsimela COSMETICS
(www.matsimela.co.za; Adam Stander Dr, Elephant's Walk; 8am-5pm) South African body-care brand Matsimela has set up shop here with an enticing aroma of natural scented soaps, body scrubs and bath bombs (anything from rose and lychee to baobab-seed oil). They also offer massage treatments (from US$30), manicures and pedicures.

Prime Art Gallery ART
(0772 239805; www.primeart-gallery.com; Adam Stander Dr, Elephant's Walk; 8am-5pm) This quality gallery, run by two friendly brothers, represents more than 40 local artists, most notably it has original pieces by Dominic Benhura, Zimbabwe's pre-eminent current-day Shona sculptor whose worked has been exhibited around the world.

Ndau Collection JEWELLERY
(013-386221; www.ndaucollectionstore.com; Adam Stander Dr, Elephant's Walk; 8am-6pm) This upmarket showroom stocks handmade individual pieces, including silver bracelets, rings and necklaces, made at its on-site studio. They also sell exquisite antique African trade beads to be incorporated into custom-made jewellery. Its range of organic fragrances made using local ingredients is also popular, as are its croc-skin purses and briefcases.

Information

DANGERS & ANNOYANCES

Mugging is not such a problem any more, but at dawn and dusk wild animals such as elephants and warthogs do roam the streets away from the town centre, so take taxis at these times. Although it's perfectly safe to walk to and from the falls, it's advisable to stick to the more touristed areas.

INTERNET ACCESS

Most lodges and restaurants offer wi-fi; otherwise there are a few internet cafes about town, including **Econet** (Park Way; per 30min/1hr US$1/2; 8am-5pm Mon-Fri, to 1pm Sat & Sun).

MONEY

Barclays Bank (off Livingstone Way)

Standard Chartered Bank (off Livingstone Way)

POST

Post Office (off Livingstone Way)

TOURIST INFORMATION

Backpackers Bazaar (p89) Definitive place for all tourist info and bookings.

Zimbabwe Tourism Authority (☎0772 225427, 013-44202; zta@vicfalls.ztazim.co.zw; Park Way; ⏲8am-6pm) A few brochures, but not very useful.

Getting There & Away

AIR

Victoria Falls Airport is located 18km southeast of town. Its new international terminal opened in late 2015.

While nothing compared to the heydays of the 1980s and '90s, there's still no shortage of flights arriving at Victoria Falls. Most come from Johannesburg (US$150 to US$500 return). There are also regular flights from Harare with FastJet and Air Zimbabwe for as little as US$20.

Check out www.flightsite.co.za or www.travelstart.co.za, where you can search all the airlines including low-cost carriers (and car-hire companies) for the cheapest flights and then book yourself.

Air Namibia (☎0774 011320, 0771 401918; www.airnamibia.com)

Air Zimbabwe (☎0712 212121, 013-443168, 013-44665; www.airzimbabwe.aero)

British Airways (☎013-2053; www.britishairways.com)

FastJet (☎86 7700 6060; www.fastjet.com/zw; cnr Livingstone Way and Parkway Dr; ⏲9am-4pm Mon-Fri, to 1pm Sat)

South African Airways (☎04-702702; www.flysaa.com)

BUS & SHARED TAXI

Though its standards have dropped in recent years, **Intercape Pathfinder** (☎0778 888880; www.intercapepathfinder.com) easily remains the safest and most comfortable bus company in Zimbabwe.

To Bulawayo & Harare

Intercape Pathfinder has departures for Hwange National Park (US$10, two hours), Bulawayo (US$15, six hours) and Harare (US$35, 12 hours) on Wednesday, Friday and Sunday at 7.30am from outside the Kingdom Hotel. You can book tickets online. If you're heading to Hwange National Park, you'll need to tell the driver beforehand as it only stops there on request. There's no direct bus to Harare, so you'll have to transfer to an awaiting bus at Bulawayo.

From Chinotimba Bus Terminal, Bravo Tours and Extra City have departures throughout the day to Bulawayo (US$13) and Harare (US$25). Buy tickets at the bus station. They can also drop you on the main road outside Hwange National Park, but you'll need to pre-arrange transport from there.

Note that, due to the prevalence of elephants and donkeys on the road, it's best to avoid this journey at night.

To Johannesburg

These days it's almost quicker to fly, but you can take the Intercape Pathfinder from Vic Falls to Bulawayo, then connect with Intercaper Greyhound to Johannesburg.

CAR & MOTORCYCLE

If you're driving a rented car into Zambia, you need to make sure you have insurance and carbon tax papers, as well original owner documents. When you enter Zambia you are issued with a Temporary Import Permit, valid for while you are in the country. This must be returned to immigration for them to acquit the vehicle.

TRAIN

A popular way of getting to/from Victoria Falls is by the overnight *Mosi-oa-Tunya* train that leaves Victoria Falls daily at 7pm for Bulawayo (economy/2nd/1st class US$8/10/12, 12 hours). First class (comprising two-berth compartments) is the only way to go. Be aware that delays of several hours aren't uncommon, and you'll need to bring your own food. Make reservations at the **ticket office** (⏲7am-noon & 2-7pm) inside the train station.

The luxurious **Rovos Rail** (☎in South Africa 012-315 8242; www.rovos.com; from US$1650) to Pretoria also departs from here.

Getting Around

CAR & MOTORCYCLE

Zimbabwe Car Hire (☎0783 496253, 09-230306; www.zimbabwecarhire.com; Victoria Falls Airport) gets positive reviews for its good rates, and is a good place for 4WDs. All the big name companies, such as **Hertz** (☎013-47012; www.hertz.co.za; 1 Bata Bldg, Parkway; ⏲8am-5pm Mon-Fri), **Avis** (☎091 2511128; www.avis.com; 251 Livingstone Way) and **Europcar** (☎013-43466; Victoria Falls Airport), have offices in town and at the airport.

TAXI

A taxi around town costs about US$10, or slightly more after dark.

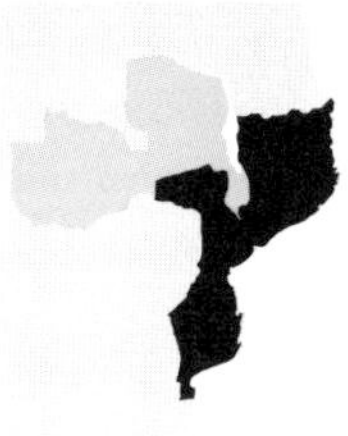

Mozambique

POP 25.3 MILLION

Includes ➡

Best Places to Sleep

- ➡ Coral Lodge 15.41 (p147)
- ➡ Nkwichi Lodge (p151)
- ➡ Ibo Island Lodge (p157)
- ➡ &Beyond Benguerra (p127)
- ➡ Montebelo Gorongosa Lodge & Safari (p131)

Best Places to Eat

- ➡ Cinco Portas (p157)
- ➡ Rickshaws Cafe (p145)
- ➡ Café del Río (p134)
- ➡ Restaurante Maúa (p132)
- ➡ Green Turtle Restaurant & Beach Bar (p122)

Why Go?

Mozambique beckons with its coastline and swaying palms, its traditions, its cultures, its vibe and its opportunities for adventure. This enigmatic southeast African country is well off most travellers' maps, but it has much to offer those who venture here: long, dune-fringed beaches, turquoise waters abounding in shoals of colourful fish, well-preserved corals, remote archipelagos in the north, pounding surf in the south and graceful dhows with billowing sails. Add to this colonial-style architecture, pulsating nightlife, a fascinating cultural mix and vast tracts of bush. Discovering these attractions is not always easy, but it is unfailingly rewarding. Bring along patience, a tolerance for long bus rides, some travel savvy and a sense of adventure, and jump in for the journey of a lifetime.

When to Go

Maputo

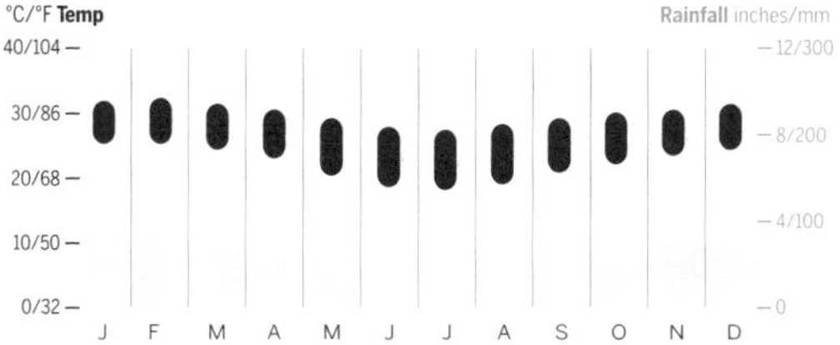

May–Nov Cooler, dry weather makes this the ideal time to visit.

Dec–Apr Rainy season can bring washed-out roads and occasional flooding in the south and centre.

Holidays Southern resorts fill up during Christmas, Easter and August; advance bookings advised.

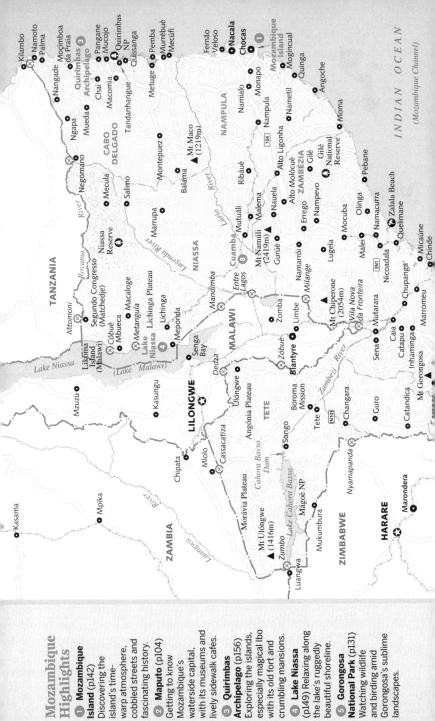

Mozambique Highlights

1. **Mozambique Island** (p142) Discovering the island's time-warp atmosphere, cobbled streets and fascinating history.

2. **Maputo** (p104) Getting to know Mozambique's waterside capital, with its museums and lively sidewalk cafes.

3. **Quirimbas Archipelago** (p156) Exploring the islands, especially magical Ibo with its old fort and crumbling mansions.

4. **Lake Niassa** (p149) Relaxing along the lake's ruggedly beautiful shoreline.

5. **Gorongosa National Park** (p131) Watching wildlife and birding amid Gorongosa's sublime landscapes.

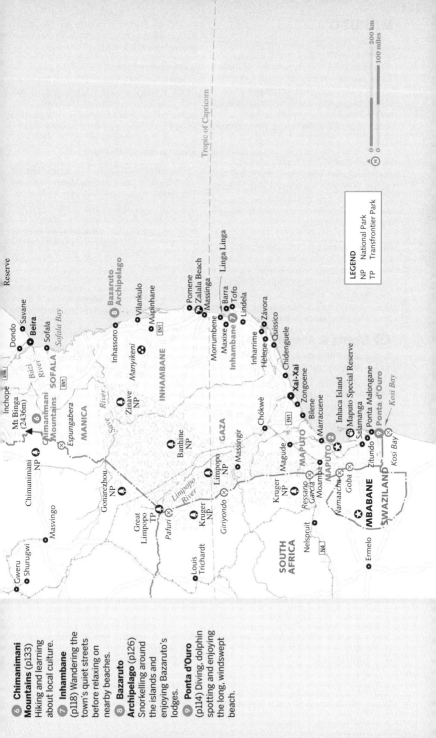

6 Chimanimani Mountains (p133) Hiking and learning about local culture.

7 Inhambane (p118) Wandering the town's quiet streets before relaxing on nearby beaches.

8 Bazaruto Archipelago (p126) Snorkelling around the islands and enjoying Bazaruto's lodges.

9 Ponta d'Ouro (p114) Diving, dolphin spotting and enjoying the long, windswept beach.

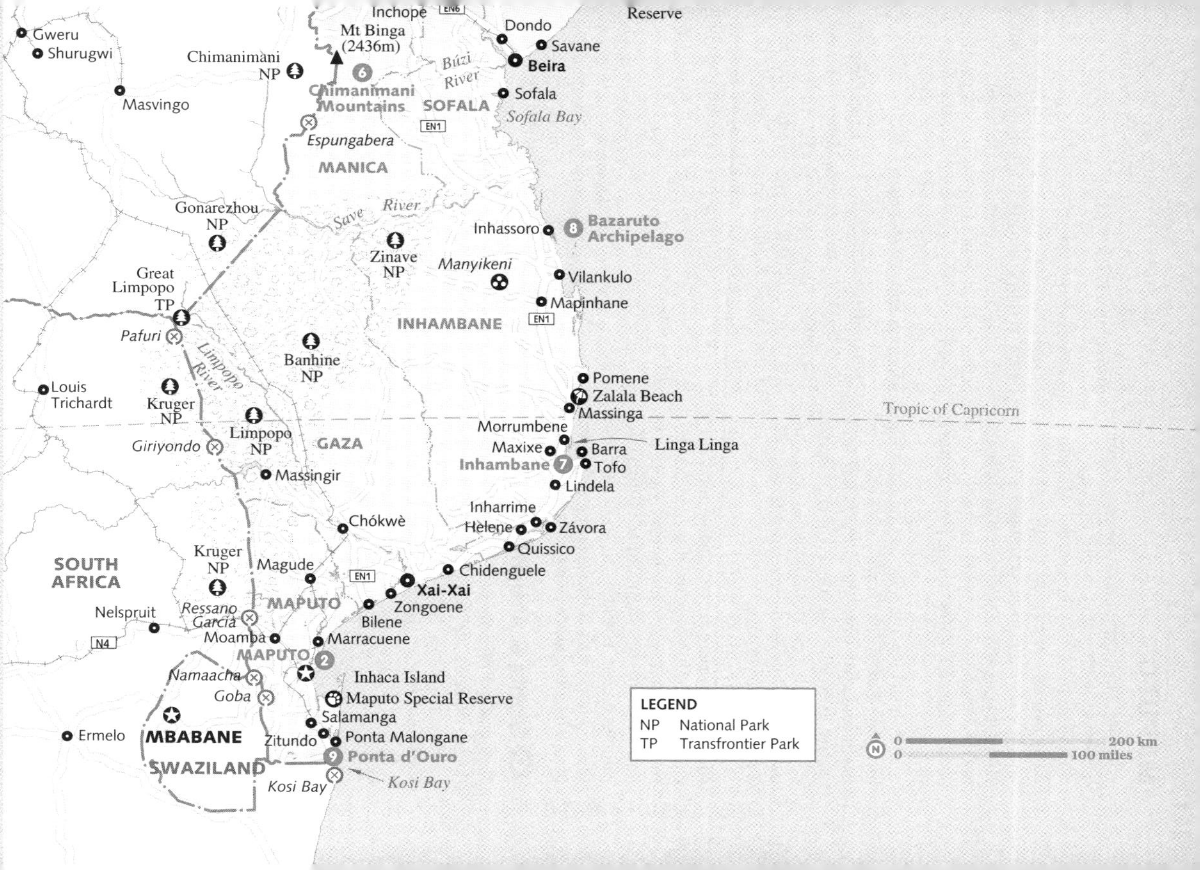

MAPUTO

With its Mediterranean-style architecture, waterside setting and wide avenues lined with jacaranda and flame trees, Maputo is easily one of Africa's most attractive capitals. It's also the most developed place in Mozambique, with a wide selection of hotels and restaurants, well-stocked supermarkets, shady sidewalk cafes and a lively cultural scene.

The heart of the city is the bustling, low-lying *baixa* (old town), spreading out north and east from the port. A few kilometres away, the seaside Avenida Marginal is lined with new developments on its inland side, while on the sea side life moves at a more leisurely pace.

Maputo is pricier than elsewhere in the country. Yet prices are reasonable and there's enough selection to make it a good destination no matter what your budget. Getting to know the city is a highlight of visiting Mozambique and essential to understanding the country. Don't miss spending time here before heading north.

Sights & Activities

National Art Museum MUSEUM

(Museu Nacional de Arte; ☎21-320264; artemus@tvcabo.co.mz; 1233 Avenida Ho Chi Minh; Mtc20, Sun free; 11am-6pm Tue-Fri, 2-6pm Sat & Sun) Half a block west of Avenida Karl Marx, the National Art Museum has an excellent collection of paintings and sculptures by Mozambique's finest contemporary artists, including Malangatana and Alberto Chissano.

Fort FORTRESS

(Fortaleza; Praça 25 de Junho; Mtc20; 9.30am-4pm) The old fort was built by the Portuguese in the mid-19th century near the site of an earlier fort. Inside is a garden and a small museum with remnants from the era of early Portuguese forays to the area. The sealed, carved wooden coffin of Ngungunhane – final ruler of the famed kingdom of Gaza – is on display in one of the side rooms.

Praça da Independência PLAZA

This wide and imposing plaza is the gateway from the upper part of town to the *baixa*. It's rimmed by several notable buildings and well worth a stroll.

Iron House HISTORIC BUILDING

(Casa de Ferro; Praça da Independência) This house was designed by Eiffel (or an associate) in the late 19th century as the governor's residence, but its metal-plated exterior proved unsuitable for tropical conditions.

Cathedral of Nossa Senhora da Conceição CATHEDRAL

(Praça da Independência) With its simple but imposing lines and soaring, white spire, this cathedral is one of Maputo's most attractive buildings. It was completed in 1944. Inside, don't miss the altar work, the stained-glass windows and the paintings.

City Hall NOTABLE BUILDING

(Conselho Municipal; Avenida Samora Machel) The hulking, neoclassical City Hall looks down over the *baixa* area from a low hill at the top of Avenida Samora Machel. The building, which was completed in 1947, is still in active use today, so it cannot usually be visited unless you have business in one of the offices inside.

Train Station HISTORIC BUILDING

(Caminho dos Ferros de Moçambique, CFM; Praça dos Trabalhadores) Maputo's landmark train station is one of the city's most imposing buildings. The dome was designed by an associate of Alexandre Gustav Eiffel (of Eiffel Tower fame), although Eiffel himself never set foot in Mozambique. Also impressive are the wrought-iron latticework, pillars and verandas gracing the dark-green exterior. Inside is the **Kulungwana Espaço Artístico** (☎21-333048; www.kulungwana.org.mz; Praça dos Trabalhadores; 10am-5pm Tue-Fri, to 3pm Sat & Sun), with a small exhibition of works by local and visiting artists, and sculptures and paintings for sale.

Municipal Market MARKET

(Mercado Municipal; Avenida 25 de Setembro; 8am-6pm Mon-Sat, 9am-2pm Sun) With its long rows of vendors, tables piled high with produce, fresh fish and colourful spices, and stalls overflowing with everything from brooms to plastic buckets, the Municipal Market is Maputo's main market and well worth a stroll. Get here early, when everything is still fresh, and before the crowds.

National Money Museum MUSEUM

(Museu da Moeda; Praça 25 de Junho; Mtc20; 11am-5pm Tue-Fri, 9am-3.30pm Sat, 2-5pm Sun) Housed in a restored yellow building on the corner of Rua Consiglieri Pedroso, the National Money Museum dates from 1860. Inside are exhibits of local currency, ranging from early barter tokens to modern-day bills.

Natural History Museum MUSEUM

(Museu de História Natural; ☎21-490879; Praça Travessa de Zambezi; Mtc50, Sun free; ⏲9am-3.30pm Tue-Fri, 10am-5pm Sat & Sun) The Natural History Museum, near Hotel Cardoso, is worth a stop simply to see its stately Manueline architecture and its garden with a mural by Malangatana. Inside are some taxidermy specimens accompanied by interactive computer terminals, a small ethnography exhibit and a fascinating display of what is probably the region's only collection of elephant foetuses.

Clube Marítimo de Desportos SWIMMING

(☎21-491373; clubemaritimo@tdm.co.mz; Avenida Marginal; per day Mtc400; ⏲5am-8pm Mon-Fri) For lap swimming, try the 25m pool at Clube Marítimo de Desportos. At weekends, the pool is open for members only.

Tours

★Bairro Mafalala Walking Tour CULTURAL

(☎82 418 0314, 82 415 1580; www.iverca.org; ⏲3hr tour per person Mtc1000-1500) This excellent walking tour through Mafalala *bairro* focuses on exploring the area's rich historical and cultural roots. It includes a stop at a local *curandeiro* (healer) and a traditional dance performance. The per-person price varies depending on group size; tours depart off Avenida Marien N'gouabi. Highly recommended.

Maputo a Pé WALKING

(☎82 419 0574; www.facebook.com/Maputo.a.Pe/; tour per person about Mtc2000) These informative and recommended walking tours of Maputo focus on the city's rich historical, architectural and artistic legacies. They're a great way to get an overview of the city and an introduction to its major sights and rich traditions.

Festivals & Events

There's almost always an art or music festival happening in Maputo. For upcoming events check with the Centro Cultural Franco-Moçambicano (p111).

Festival Azgo CULTURAL

(www.azgofestival.com; ⏲May) This Maputo-based extravaganza has become Mozambique's largest arts and culture festival, featuring artists from Mozambique as well as elsewhere in the region.

Marrabenta Festival CULTURAL

(http://ccfmoz.com; ⏲Feb) To hear *marrabenta* – Mozambique's national music – at its best, don't miss the annual Marrabenta Festival. It's held mostly in Maputo but also takes place in Beira, Inhambane and several other locations. The timing is set to coincide with Marracuene's Gwaza Muthini (p19) commemorations.

Sleeping

If you want to be in the thick of things, choose somewhere in or near the *baixa* (best for budgets too). For sea breezes and tranquillity, head to the upper part of town, around Sommerschield and Polana, or to Avenida Marginal and Costa do Sol.

Baixa

Base Backpackers HOSTEL $

(☎82 452 6860, 21-302723; thebasebackpackers@gmail.com; 545 Avenida Patrice Lumumba; dm/d Mtc500/1500; @) This scruffy but friendly backpackers is small, but justifiably popular and often full, with a convenient, quiet location on the edge of the *baixa*. It has a kitchen, backyard bar, terrace and braai (barbecue) area with views to the port. Via public transport from Junta, take a 'Museu' *chapa* to the final Museu stop, from where it's a short walk.

Hotel Monte Carlo HOTEL $$

(☎82 300 2006, 21-304048; www.montecarlo.co.mz; 620 Avenida Patrice Lumumba; r Mtc4000-6800; ❄@📶🏊) A convenient central location, efficient staff, tidy rooms (some of the higher-priced ones are quite spacious) and a restaurant make this business hotel overall good value.

Residencial Palmeiras BOUTIQUE HOTEL $$

(☎82 306 9200, 21-300199; www.palmeiras-guesthouse.com; 948 Avenida Patrice Lumumba; s/tw/d Mtc3950/4850/4850; ❄📶) This popular place has bright decor, comfortable, good-value rooms (all but one with private bathroom) and a tiny garden. It's near the British High Commission on a quiet but central street, and just a short walk from the *baixa*.

Hotel Cardoso HOTEL $$$

(☎21-491071; www.cardoso-hotel.com; 707 Avenida Mártires de Mueda; s/d from US$290/315;

Central Maputo

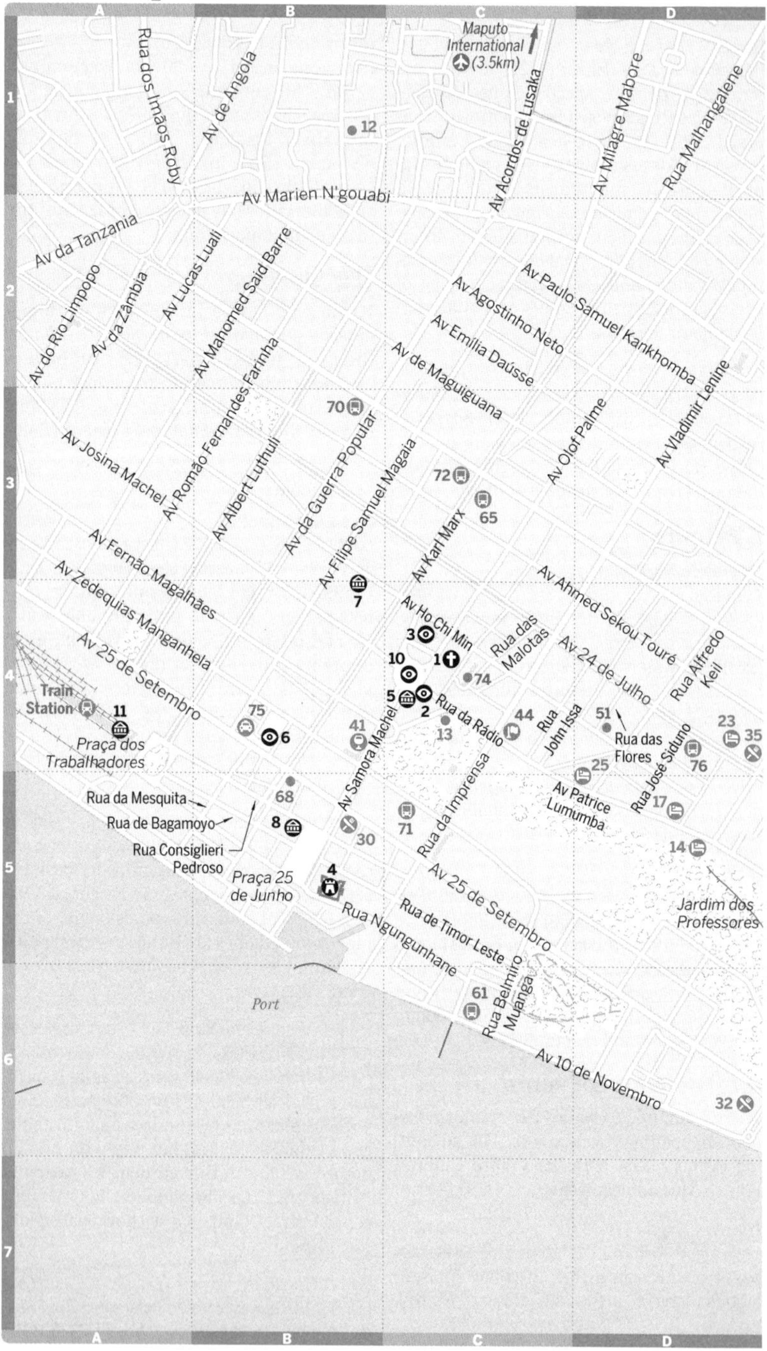

Maputo International (3.5km)
Rua dos Imãos Roby
Av de Angola
Av Acordos de Lusaka
Av Milagre Mabore
Rua Malhangalene
Av Marien N'gouabi
Av da Tanzania
Av do Rio Limpopo
Av da Zâmbia
Av Lucas Luali
Av Mahomed Said Barre
Av Romão Fernandes Farinha
Av Paulo Samuel Kankhomba
Av Agostinho Neto
Av Emília Daússe
Av de Maguiguana
Av Vladimir Lenine
Av Olof Palme
Av Josina Machel
Av Albert Luthuli
Av da Guerra Popular
Av Filipe Samuel Magaia
Av Karl Marx
Av Fernão Magalhães
Av Zedequias Manganhela
Av Ho Chi Min
Rua das Malotas
Av Ahmed Sekou Touré
Av 24 de Julho
Rua Alfredo Keil
Av 25 de Setembro
Train Station
Praça dos Trabalhadores
Av Samora Machel
Rua da Rádio
Rua John Issa
Rua das Flores
Rua José Siduno
Av Patrice Lumumba
Rua da Imprensa
Rua da Mesquita
Rua de Bagamoyo
Rua Consiglieri Pedroso
Praça 25 de Junho
Rua Ngungunhane
Rua de Timor Leste
Rua Belmiro Muanga
Jardim dos Professores
Port
Av 10 de Novembro

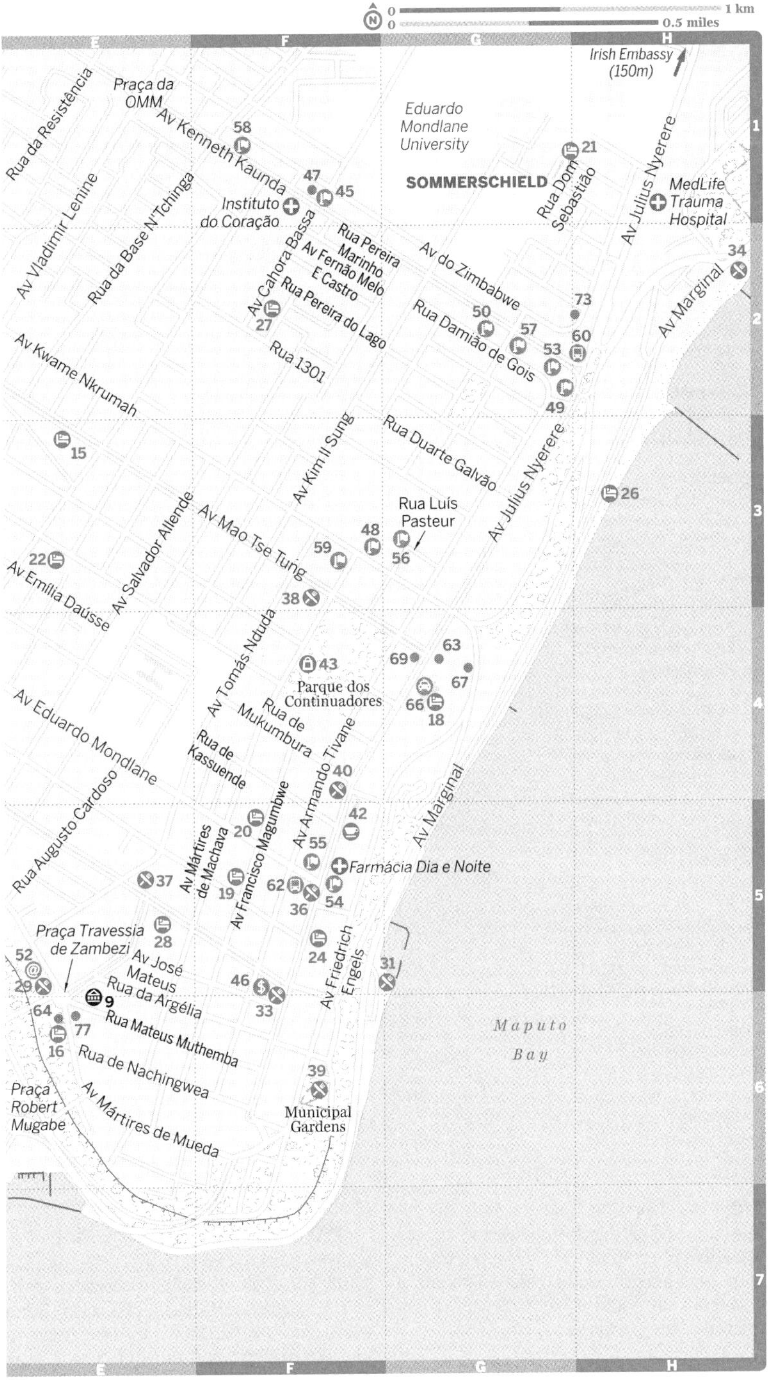
0 1 km
0 0.5 miles
Irish Embassy (150m)
Praça da OMM
Rua da Resistência
Av Kenneth Kaunda
Eduardo Mondlane University
SOMMERSCHIELD
Rua Dom Sebastião
Av Julius Nyerere
MedLife Trauma Hospital
Av Vladimir Lenine
Rua da Base N'Tchinga
Instituto do Coração
Av Cahora Bassa
Rua Pereira Marinho
Av Fernão Melo E Castro
Rua Pereira do Lago
Av do Zimbabwe
Av Marginal
Rua Damião de Gois
Av Kwame Nkrumah
Rua 1301
Av Kim Il Sung
Rua Duarte Galvão
Av Julius Nyerere
Rua Luís Pasteur
Av Salvador Allende
Av Mao Tse Tung
Av Emília Daússe
Av Tomás Nduda
Parque dos Continuadores
Rua de Mukumbura
Av Eduardo Mondlane
Rua de Kassuende
Av Armando Tivane
Av Marginal
Rua Augusto Cardoso
Av Mártires de Machava
Av Francisco Magumbwe
Farmácia Dia e Noite
Praça Travessia de Zambezi
Av José Mateus
Rua da Argélia
Av Friedrich Engels
Rua Mateus Muthemba
Rua de Nachingwea
Maputo Bay
Praça Robert Mugabe
Av Mártires de Mueda
Municipal Gardens
MOZAMBIQUE MAPUTO

Central Maputo

Sights

1 Cathedral of Nossa Senhora da Conceição C4
2 Centro Cultural Franco-Moçambicano C4
3 City Hall C4
4 Fort B5
5 Iron House C4
Kulungwana Espaço Artístico .... (see 11)
6 Municipal Market B4
7 National Art Museum B4
8 National Money Museum B5
9 Natural History Museum E6
10 Praça da Independência C4
11 Train Station A4

Activities, Courses & Tours

12 Bairro Mafalala Walking Tour B1
13 Maputo a Pé C4

Sleeping

14 Base Backpackers D5
15 Fatima's Place E3
16 Hotel Cardoso E6
17 Hotel Monte Carlo D5
18 Hotel Polana G4
19 Hotel Terminus F5
20 Hoyo-Hoyo Residencial F5
21 Montebelo Indy Congress Hotel G1
22 Mozaika E3
23 Pensão Martins D4
24 Residencial Duqueza de Connaught F5
25 Residencial Palmeiras D5
26 Southern Sun H3
27 Sundown Guesthouse F2
28 Villa das Mangas E5

Eating

29 Café Acacia E5
30 Café Continental B5
31 Cais 66 .... G5
32 Feira Popular D6
33 Gianni Sorvetaria F6
34 Marisqueira Sagres H2
35 Mimmo's D4
36 Mundo's F5
O Escorpião .... (see 32)
37 Pastelaria & Restaurante Cristál E5
38 Pizza House F3
39 Surf F6
40 Taverna F4

Drinking & Nightlife

41 Café-Bar Gil Vicente B4
Cais 66 .... (see 31)
42 La Dolce Vita Café-Bar F5

Shopping

43 Feira de Artesanato, Flôres e Gastronomia de Maputo F4

Information

44 British High Commission C4
45 Canadian High Commission F1
46 Cotacambios F5
47 Dana Agency F1
Dana Tours .... (see 47)
48 Dutch Embassy F3
49 French Embassy G2
50 German Embassy G2
51 Immigration Department D4
52 Livro Aberto E5
53 Malawian High Commission G2
Pizza House Internet Café .... (see 38)
54 Portuguese Embassy F5
55 South African High Commission F5
56 Swazi High Commission G3
Tanzanian High Commission .... (see 27)
57 US Embassy G2
58 Zambian High Commission F1
59 Zimbabwean High Commission F3

Transport

60 Chapas to Costa do Sol H2
61 Chapas to Ponta d'Ouro C6
62 Cheetah Express F5
63 Europcar G4
64 Expresso Rent-A-Car E6
65 Greyhound C3
66 Hotel Polana Taxi Rank G4
67 Kenya Airways G4
68 LAM Central Reservations B5
69 LAM Sales Office G4
Luciano Luxury Coach .... (see 71)
Museu .... (see 9)
70 Ponto Final B3
71 Post Bus Ticketing Office C5
72 Ronil C3
73 South African Airways H2
74 TAP Air Portugal C4
Taxi Rank .... (see 36)
75 Taxi Rank B4
76 Translux D4
77 Tuk-Tuk Stand E6

✱@🛜≋) Opposite the Natural History Museum, and on the clifftop overlooking the bay, this 130-room hotel is a Maputo classic, with good service, well-appointed rooms, a business centre and a bar with views over the water and port area.

Avenida Marginal & Costa do Sol

Maputo Backpackers HOSTEL $

(☎82 467 2230, 21-451213; maputobp@gmail.com; 95 Quarta Avenida (Rua das Palmeiras), Bairro Triunfo; dm/d Mtc750/3200, s/d without bathroom Mtc2100/2500) A small, quiet place well away from the centre and near Costa do Sol, with a handful of rooms (including eight- and 10-bed dorms) with fans but no nets. *Chapas* to/from town (Mtc7) stop nearby: ask the driver to let you off at 'Escola', which is on Quinta Avenida; walk back one block to Maputo Backpackers. Taxis charge from Mtc300.

Southern Sun HOTEL $$$
(☑ 21-495050, in South Africa 011-461 9744; www.tsogosun.com/southern-sun-maputo; Avenida Marginal; s/d from US$220/250; ❈ @ 🗗 ≋) Set attractively directly on the water (although there's no beach swimming), Southern Sun has comfortable rooms, attentive service, a small gym and a waterside restaurant. The overall ambience is amenable, and the combination of a waterside location and full facilities makes it very good value in its class.

Sommerschield & Polana

Hoyo-Hoyo Residencial HOTEL $
(☑ 82 300 9950, 21-490701; www.residencialhoyo-hoyo.co.mz; 837 Avenida Francisco Magumbwe; s/d from Mtc2960/3330; ❈ 🗗) This solid, no-frills hotel lacks pizzazz, but its 36 small rooms are serviceable and reasonably comfortable, and the ambience is familial.

Pensão Martins PENSION $
(☑ 21-301429; pensaomartins@gmail.com; 1098 Avenida 24 de Julho; s/d/tr/ste Mtc2500/3000/3500/4000; ❈ ❈) This peach-coloured establishment has a sleepy reception area and bland but mostly spacious rooms in a convenient central location.

Fatima's Place HOSTEL $
(☑ 21-302994, 82 185 1577; www.mozambiquebackpackers.com; 1321 Avenida Mao Tse Tung; dm/s/d US$12/40/55, s/d/tr/q with shared bathroom US$35/45/60/75; 🗗) In the upper part of town, the long-standing Fatima's has an outdoor kitchen-bar, a small courtyard garden, a mix of rooms and lots of travel info.

Hotel Terminus HOTEL $$
(☑ 21-491333; www.terminus.co.mz; cnr Avenidas Francisco Magumbwe & Ahmed Sekou Touré; s/d from Mtc3850/6150; ❈ @ 🗗 ≋) This three-star establishment in the upper part of town has small but well-appointed rooms with TV, plus good service and facilities, a business centre, a small garden, a tiny pool and a restaurant. It's popular with business travellers and often fully booked.

Sundown Guesthouse HOTEL $$
(☑ 84 313 7202, 21-497543; www.hotelmaputo.com; 107 Rua 1301, Sommerschield; r US$115; ❈ @ 🗗) This popular place offers good-value, well-appointed double-bedded rooms in a small apartment block on a quiet street in the Sommerschield residential area.

Mozaika BOUTIQUE HOTEL $$
(☑ 84 367 4650, 21-303939; www.mozaika.co.mz; 769 Avenida Agostinho Neto; s/d incl breakfast from Mtc3680/4610, apt Mtc7900; ❈ @ 🗗 ≋) This boutique hotel – in a convenient central location – is justifiably popular, with eight small rooms, each decorated with its own theme and set around a small garden courtyard with a tiny pool. There's also a self-catering apartment and a bar.

Residencial Duqueza de Connaught BOUTIQUE HOTEL $$
(☑ 21-492190, 21-302155; www.duquezadeconnaught.com; 290 Avenida Julius Nyerere; s/d Mtc3850/4950; ❈ 🗗 ≋) This lovely, quiet, eight-room boutique hotel is in a restored home with polished wood, linen bedding and spotless rooms. Meals can be arranged with notice.

Villa das Mangas HOTEL $$
(☑ 21-497078; www.villadasmangas.com; 401 Avenida 24 de Julho; s/d from Mtc4982/5680; ❈ 🗗 ≋) The pluses at this tidy, whitewashed establishment are its aesthetics and its convenient central location. Rooms – most clustered around the pool in a tiny garden area – are small, with TV and mosquitoes.

Montebelo Indy Congress Hotel HOTEL $$$
(☑ 21-498765, 21-480505; www.montebelohotels.com; 99 Rua Dom Sebastião, Sommerschield; s/d/chalets from Mtc7670/8330/15,665; ❈ @ 🗗 ≋) This place, in a quiet corner of Sommerschield, has well-appointed rooms and apartments ('chalets') set in expansive, manicured, enclosed gardens. There's a pool with an adjoining children's play area, plus a gym and a good restaurant.

Hotel Polana HOTEL $$$
(☑ 21-241700, 21-491001; www.serenahotels.com; 1380 Avenida Julius Nyerere; r from US$270; ❈ @ 🗗 ≋) In a prime location on the clifftop with uninterrupted views over the sea, the Polana is Maputo's classiest hotel. Rooms are in the elegant main building or in the 'Polana Mar' section closer to the water. There's a large pool set amid lush gardens, a

business centre, and a restaurant with daily breakfast and dinner buffets.

Eating

Baixa

Café Continental CAFE $

(cnr Avenidas 25 de & Samora Machel; light meals from Mtc200; 6am-10pm) This faded but classic place in the *baixa* is a Maputo landmark, with a large selection of well-prepared pastries, plus light meals, a large seating area, a small street-side terrace and lots of ambience.

Café Acacia CAFE $$

(Jardim dos Professores, Avenida Patrice Lumumba; light meals from Mtc350; 7am-9pm;) A tranquil garden setting with a children's play area and bay views, plus tasty pastries and coffees.

Avenida Marginal & Costa do Sol

Fish Market MARKET $

(Mercado de Peixe; Avenida Marginal; dishes Mtc250-400; 9am-9pm Mon-Fri, 8am-11pm Fri-Sun) The lively Fish Market is in a large white building en route to Costa do Sol. Peruse the many creatures that inhabit the nearby waters, or go all the way and choose what you'd like from the main hall and get it grilled at one of the small adjoining restaurants. Cooking prices average about Mtc160 per kilo.

Stalls also offer rice, chips or other accompaniments on order. Waits can be long on weekends. The best time to visit is late afternoon.

Supermarés SUPERMARKET $

(Avenida Marginal, Costa do Sol; 9am-7pm Mon-Sat, to 1pm Sun) A large mall with a supermarket, as well as ATMs and many shops.

Restaurante Costa do Sol SEAFOOD $$

(21-451662; costadosol1908@hotmail.com; Avenida Marginal, Costa do Sol; mains from Mtc400-900; noon-11pm Tue-Sun; P) A Maputo classic dating from 1938, this beachside place – now under new management – draws the crowds on weekend afternoons. There's seating on the large sea-facing porch or indoors, and an array of seafood dishes and grills, with prawns the speciality. It's about 5km from the centre at the northern end of Avenida Marginal.

Cais 66 SEAFOOD $$

(84 547 5906; Avenida Marginal, at Clube Naval; mains from Mtc400; 10am-midnight) Enjoy sushi and snacks on the upstairs deck or seafood grills in the breezy waterside dining area downstairs. It's located at Clube Naval, Maputo's long-standing yacht club.

O Escorpião PORTUGUESE $$

(21-302180; meals from Mtc400; 11.30am-3pm & 6.30-10.30pm Tue-Sun) O Escorpião, in the **Feira Popular** (cnr Avenida 25 de Setembro & Rua Belmiro Muanga; admission Mtc20; 11.30am-midnight; P), close to the entrance, is a classic Portuguese family-style restaurant offering a wide selection of well-prepared Portuguese and Mozambican dishes.

Marisqueira Sagres SEAFOOD $$$

(21-495201; 4272 Avenida Marginal; seafood mains Mtc500-950; 9am-midnight Tue-Sun) This waterside place is popular for dinner and Sunday lunch, with a large menu of well-prepared seafood platters, plus meat grills and continental fare, and a small pool.

Sommerschield & Polana

Pizza House CAFE $

(21-485257; 601/607 Avenida Mao Tse Tung; pizzas & light meals Mtc80-400, daily menu Mtc300; 6.30am-10.30pm;) Popular with locals and expats, this place has sidewalk seating, plus reasonably priced Portuguese-style pastries, sandwiches, burgers, grilled chicken and a good-value daily menu.

Surf CAFE $

(Jardim dos Namorados, Avenida Friedrich Engels; snacks & light meals from Mtc150; 7.30am-9pm;) This large, amenable place has indoor and garden seating, views from the escarpment over the bay, a children's play area, reasonably priced snacks and light meals, and fast service.

Gianni Sorvetaria GELATERIA $

(www.gianni.co.mz; ground fl, Polana Shopping Centre, cnr Avenidas Julius Nyerere & 24 de Julho; gelato from Mtc90; 7am-9pm) Delicious Italian gelato, plus sandwiches and light meals.

Mimmo's PIZZA $

(21-309491; cnr Avenidas 24 de Julho & Salvador Allende; meals Mtc250-450; 11am-11pm) This bustling street-side pizzeria also has pastas, and seafood and meat grills. Service is usually prompt. Check your bill and your change carefully.

Pastelaria & Restaurante Cristál — CAFE $$

(☎84 302 3560, 82 281 5180; restaurantecristal@hotmail.com; 554 Avenida 24 de Julho; snacks/mains from Mtc100/400; ⏲6.30am-11pm) This long-standing place has delicious pastries and breads, light meals, indoor and street-side seating, and a popular, reasonably priced restaurant serving well-prepared local and continental dishes.

Taverna — EUROPEAN $$

(☎84 444 5550, 84 444 5551; 995 Avenida Julius Nyerere; meals Mtc450-700; ⏲noon-3pm & 6-10pm Mon-Fri, noon-3.30pm Sun) Tasty Portuguese cuisine with *fado* music in the background and a large wine selection; it's just up from Avenida Eduardo Mondlane.

Mundo's — BURGERS, PUB $$

(☎84 468 6367, 21-494080; cnr Avenidas Julius Nyerere & Eduardo Mondlane; mains Mtc200-500; ⏲8.30am-10pm; 📶 👪) Burritos, burgers, pizzas and other hearty fare are served up in large portions on wooden tables set around a street-side veranda and cooled by a misting system in the summer months.

Drinking & Nightlife

Thursday to Saturday are the main nights; things only get going after 11pm. Cover charges range from Mtc50 to Mtc200.

Cais 66 — BAR

(☎21-493204; Clube Naval, Avenida Marginal; ⏲10am-2am) The late-night waterside bar at the yacht club is especially popular with old-timers on Thursday and Friday.

La Dolce Vita Café-Bar — CAFE

(822 Avenida Julius Nyerere; ⏲10am-late Tue-Sun; 📶) This sleek tapas and late-night place has live music on Thursday evening. By day, try the juices and smoothies.

Café-Bar Gil Vicente — BAR

(43 Avenida Samora Machel; ⏲8pm-late) A popular place with a constantly changing array of groups. Most performances start about 10pm or later.

Entertainment

Centro Cultural Franco-Moçambicano — CULTURAL CENTRE

(☎21-314590; www.ccfmoz.com; Praça da Independência) An excellent place, with art exhibitions, music and dance performances, films, theatre, a craft shop, a cafe and more.

Shopping

Feira de Artesanato, Flôres e Gastronomia de Maputo — ARTS & CRAFTS

(Parque dos Continuadores, Avenida Mártires de Machava; ⏲9am-5pm) Batiks, woodcarvings and other crafts at stalls spread throughout the Parque dos Continuadores.

Information

IMMIGRATION

Immigration Department (Serviço Nacional de Migração (Senami); 316 Avenida Ho Chi Minh; ⏲for visa matters 7.30am-2pm Mon-Fri) Just downhill from Avenida Amilcar Cabral. Allow five to seven days for processing visa extensions.

INTERNET ACCESS

Livro Aberto (Maputo Community Library; www.livroaberto.org; Avenida Patrice Lumumba; ⏲8am-4pm Mon-Fri, 9am-4pm Sat; 📶) There's wi-fi access and places to sit, plus the chance for Portuguese lessons or volunteering at this local community library in Jardim dos Professores.

Pizza House Internet Café (Avenida Mao Tse Tung; per hr Mtc60; ⏲7.30am-10pm Mon-Fri, 9am-5pm Sat; 📶) Upstairs at Pizza House.

MEDICAL SERVICES

Farmácia Dia e Noite (☎84 505 8238; 764 Avenida Julius Nyerere; ⏲24hr) Opposite the South African High Commission.

Instituto do Coração (☎82 305 3097, 82 327 4800, 21-416347; 1111 Avenida Kenneth Kaunda; ⏲24hr) Western standards and facilities for all ailments (not just cardiac issues); meticals, US dollars and Visa cards accepted.

MedLife Trauma Hospital (☎84 302 0999; 2986 Avenida Julius Nyerere; ⏲24hr) Western standards and facilities; meticals, US dollars and Visa cards accepted.

MONEY

There are 24-hour ATMs all over town, including at the airport. Changing cash is easy. Travellers cheques are not accepted anywhere.

Cotacambios (ground fl, Polana Shopping Centre, cnr Avenida Julius Nyerere & Mao Tse Tung; ⏲9am-9pm Mon-Sat, 10am-8pm Sun) Useful for changing cash out of hours.

SAFE TRAVEL

Although most tourists visit Maputo without mishap, be vigilant and take precautions.

- Avoid carrying a bag (thieves may think you have something valuable).
- Avoid situations in which you are isolated.
- At night, always take a taxi.

➡ Avoid the stretches of Avenida Marginal between Praça Robert Mugabe and the Southern Sun hotel; the access roads leading down to the Marginal from Avenida Friedrich Engels; and the area below the escarpment south of Avenida Patrice Lumumba.

➡ Areas off-limits to pedestrians (no photos) include the eastern footpath on Avenida Julius Nyerere in front of the president's residence and the Ponta Vermelha zone in Maputo's southeastern corner.

TRAVEL AGENCIES

Dana Agency (☎ 21-484300; eduarda@dana.co.mz; ground fl, 1170 Avenida Kenneth Kaunda) Domestic and international flight bookings.

Dana Tours (☎ 21-497483; www.danatours.com; 1st fl, 1170 Avenida Kenneth Kaunda) Specialises in travel to the coast, and can also sort you out for destinations throughout Mozambique, plus Swaziland and South Africa. Midrange and up.

Mozaic Travel (☎ 84 333 2111, 21-451379; www.mozaictravel.com; 1072 Rua Acordo de Nkomati) Excursions around the country, including to Limpopo National Park and Bazaruto Archipelago. Located in Bairro Triunfo, off Avenida Marginal.

ℹ Getting There & Away

AIR

Kenya Airways, LAM, South African Airways and TAP Air Portugal have regular flights to Maputo.

Kenya Airways (☎ 21-495483; www.kenya-airways.com; 333/659 Avenida Barnabé Thawé) On the hill side going down to Avenida Marginal.

LAM Central Reservations (☎ 82 147, 84 147, 21-468800, 21-326001; www.lam.co.mz; cnr Avenidas 25 de Setembro & Karl Marx) In the *baixa*.

LAM Sales Office (☎ 21-496101, 21-490590; www.lam.co.mz; cnr Avs Julius Nyerere & Mao Tse Tung)

South African Airways (☎ 21-488970, 84-488 9700; www.flysaa.com; 520 Avenida do Zimbabwe) In Sommerschield.

TAP Air Portugal (☎ 21-303927, 21-303928; www.flytap.com; Hotel Pestana Rovuma, 114 Rua da Sé)

BUS

Maputo's main long-distance bus depot for up-country arrivals and departures is **'Junta'** (Terminal Rodovia'ria Interprovincial da Junta; cnr Avenida de Moçambique & Rua Gago Coutinho), about 7km (Mtc300 in a taxi) from the city centre. Time your travels to avoid arriving at night. *Chapas* to Swaziland, South Africa and Namaacha in southern Mozambique also depart from Junta. **Benfica** (Avenida de Moçambique) is useful for *chapas* to Marracuene. Chapas to Ponta d'Ouro depart from Catembe.

Correios de Moçambique (the postal service) runs buses from Maputo to Beira, Chimoio, Tete, Quelimane and Nampula, departing from its **ticketing office** (☎ 82 332 5812, 82 312 3103; postbusmoz@correios.co.mz; Avenida Zedequias Manganhela) behind the main post office on Avenida Zedequias Manganhela. In late 2016 the service was suspended due to the political skirmishes in the centre of the country.

Sample prices and travel times for daily routes from Maputo include Inhambane (Mtc600, seven hours), Tofo (Mtc750, 7½ hours), Vilankulo (Mtc900, nine hours) and Beira (Mtc1700, 17 hours). There is twice-weekly service from Junta to Nampula (Mtc3100, 36 hours) and Pemba (Mtc3600), with overnight stops en route, although it's better to do these journeys in stages.

Johannesburg

Departure and ticketing points for express buses to Johannesburg:

Greyhound (☎ 21-302771, in South Africa 011-611 8000; www.greyhound.co.za; Avenida Karl Marx; ⏲ 6.30am-7pm Mon-Fri, 6.30am-noon & 6-7pm Sat, 6.30am-7am & 6-7pm Sun) Avenida Karl Marx, just south of Avenida Eduardo Mondlane.

Luciano Luxury Coach (☎ 84 661 5713, in South Africa 072-278 1921, 083 993 4897; Avenida Zedequías Manganhela) Behind the main post office.

Translux (☎ 21-303829, 21-303825, in South Africa 086 158 9282; www.translux.co.za; Simara Travel & Tours, 1249 Avenida 24 de Julho; ⏲ ticket sales only 7am-5pm Mon-Fri, to 10am Sat & Sun) At Simara Travel & Tours.

Nelspruit

Cheetah Express (☎ 84-244 2103, in South Africa 013-755 1988; cheetahexpressmaputo@gmail.com; cnr Avenidas Eduardo Mondlane & Julius Nyerere) Daily between Maputo and Nelspruit (Mtc1300 return, no one-way option), departing Maputo at 6am from Avenida Eduardo Mondlane next to Mundo's.

Tofo

Fatima's Place (p109) has a daily shuttle between Maputo and Tofo (Mtc800). With notice, it does pick-ups from other Maputo hotels. If seats are still remaining, it will also stop at Junta to take on additional passengers.

ℹ Getting Around

TO/FROM THE AIRPORT

Maputo International Airport (☎ 21-465827/8; www.aeroportos.co.mz) is 6km northwest of the city centre (Mtc400 to Mtc600 in a taxi).

BUS & CHAPA

Buses have name boards with their destination. City rides cost about Mtc5.

Chapas go everywhere, with the average price for town trips Mtc5 to Mtc7. Most are marked with route start and end points, but you should also listen for the destination called out by the conductor. To get to Junta, look for a *chapa* going to Zimpeto, Zona Verde or Jardim; coming from Junta into town, look for a *chapa* heading to 'Museu'.

Chapas to Costa do Sol (cnr Avenidas Kenneth Kaunda & Julius Nyerere)

Chapas to Ponta d'Ouro (Catembe Ferry Pier, Avenida 10 de Novembro)

Museu *Chapas* to the airport and Junta (Mtc7 from Museu to Junta). *Chapas* marked 'Museu-Benfica' go along Avenida Eduardo Mondlane.

Ponto Final (cnr Avenidas Eduardo Mondlane & Guerra Popular) Terminus for *chapas* running along Avenida Eduardo Mondlane.

Ronil (cnr Avenidas Eduardo Mondlane & Karl Marx) *Chapas* to Junta, Benfica and Matola.

CAR

Park in guarded lots when possible, or tip the young boys on the street to watch your vehicle. There are several options for renting vehicles.

Avis (☎21-321243; www.avis.co.za; Maputo International Airport) At the airport, with offices also in Beira, Nampula and Tete; good deals often available.

Europcar (☎84 302 8330, 21-497338; www.europcar.co.mz; 1418 Avenida Julius Nyerere) Next to Hotel Polana and at the airport. Offices also in Beira, Nampula and Tete.

Expresso Rent-A-Car (☎21-493619; timisay@tropical.co.mz; Avenida Mártires de Mueda) At Hotel Cardoso; 2WD vehicles only.

Sixt (☎82 302 3555, 21-465250; www.sixt.co.mz; Maputo International Airport) Offices also in Beira, Tete, Nampula and Pemba.

TAXI & TUK-TUK

➡ Taxi ranks include the **Hotel Polana taxi rank** (Avenida Julius Nyerere) and those in front of most other top-end hotels. Taxis also park at the **Municipal Market** (Avenida 25 de Setembro) and in front of **Mundo's restaurant** (Avenida Julius Nyerere). Town trips start at Mtc150. From central Maputo to Costa do Sol costs Mtc300 to Mtc400. From Junta to anywhere in the city centre costs Mtc350 to Mtc400.

➡ Tuk-tuks are less expensive than taxis (town trips from Mtc100), although they can be hard to find. Look for them opposite **Hotel Cardoso** (Rua Mateus Muthemba), and on Avenida Julius Nyerere, just up from the South African High Commission.

AROUND MAPUTO

Inhaca Island

Just 7000 years ago – almost yesterday in geological terms – Inhaca Island (Ilha de Inhaca) was part of the Mozambican mainland. Today this wayward chunk of Mozambican coastline lies about 40km offshore from Maputo, and is an enjoyable weekend getaway. It's also an important marine research centre, known in particular for its coral reefs. The reefs are among the most southerly in the world, and since 1976 parts of the island and surrounding waters have been designated a **marine reserve** (Reservas Florestais e Marinhas da Inhaca; ☎21-901090; www.ebmi.uem.mz; adult Mtc200). Over 300 species of bird have also been recorded on the island.

The **Fernando Nhaca Lodge** (☎82 718 8549; d Mtc2000, with shared bathroom Mtc1000) is a good budget place with simple rooms with nets in a private home in Inhaca village. You can arrange meals with the owner or cook your own food. It's about a 15-minute walk from the ferry pier, or Sr Fernando will meet you with his vehicle at the ferry with advance notice (no charge).

The long-standing **Restaurante Lucas** (☎87 611 3006; rlucas.inhaca@gmail.com; mains Mtc400-700; ⏲from 7am) is a local-style restaurant and the main place to eat. It's pricey, but the seafood grills are delicious, and the ambience is laid-back. Order in advance if you're in a rush or if you fancy a particular dish. It's about a five-minute walk from the ferry dock.

ℹ Getting There & Away

The government ferry *Nyaleti* departs from Maputo's Catembe pier at 7.30am on Tuesday, Thursday, Saturday and Sunday (Mtc400, three hours). Departures from Inhaca are at 3pm. Dana Tours also organises Inhaca excursions.

Marracuene & Macaneta Beach

Macaneta is the closest open-ocean beach to Maputo, with stiff sea breezes and long stretches of dune-fringed coast. It's on a narrow peninsula divided from the mainland by the Nkomati River, and is reached via Marracuene, 35km north of Maputo along the EN1. For sleeping, try **Jay's**

Beach Lodge (☎84 863 0714; www.jaysbeachlodge.co.za; per vehicle for day visitors US$3, camping US$8, chalet d/q US$45/85). About 20km north, and a possible stopping point for self-drivers, is Blue Anchor Inn (☎21-900559, 82 325 3050; www.blueanchorinn.com; adult/child Mtc1120/560).

Take any northbound *chapa* (minibus) from Benfica (Mtc50, one hour) to Marracuene, from where it's a 10-minute walk through town to the Nkomati River, crossed by a new bridge. Once over the bridge on the other side, follow the rutted road for about 5km to a junction of sorts, from where you'll find most of the Macaneta places about 5km to 8km further, and signposted. There are unofficial 'shuttle' vehicles that charge Mtc150 return between the river and the beach lodges. Otherwise, there is no public transport; hitching is slow except at weekends. For drivers, a 4WD is essential.

SOUTHERN MOZAMBIQUE

Long, dune-fringed stretches of white sand, heaping plates of prawns, diving and snorkelling, an established tourism infrastructure, and straightforward road and air access from South Africa make Mozambique's southern coast an ideal destination if you're seeking a beach holiday or an easy introduction to the country.

Ponta d'Ouro & Ponta Malongane

The colonial-era town of Ponta d'Ouro has boomed in popularity in recent years and is the first Mozambique stop on many Southern Africa overland itineraries. Its best asset is its excellent beach: long, wide and surf-pounded. Offshore waters host abundant life, including dolphins, whale sharks and – from July to October – whales. Thanks to Ponta d'Ouro's proximity to South Africa, it fills up on holiday weekends. South African rand are accepted almost everywhere.

About 5km north is the quieter and even more beautiful Ponta Malongane, with an expanse of windswept coastline fringed by high, vegetated dunes and patches of coastal forest.

Activities

Diving

The Tandje Beach Resort compound is the base for several dive operators, and more are in town. Instruction and equipment rental are available at all. Ask about low-season and midweek discounts.

Diving is possible year-round; the best months are November to February and May to September.

Blue Reef Divers DIVING
(☎082 453 8694; www.brdivers.co.za; Parque de Malongane, Ponta Malongane) This dive operator based at Parque de Malongane offers various packages, with discounts available for advance bookings.

Devocean Diving DIVING
(☎84 418 2252; www.devoceandiving.com; Ponta d'Ouro) This long-established PADI five-star resort is in the town centre next to the police station. In addition to a range of diving instruction and excursions, it also offers budget accommodation at its popular divers' camp within its large, walled compound.

Dolphin Tours

Dolphins frequent the waters off Ponta d'Ouro, and many visitors come hoping to catch a glimpse of these beautiful creatures. However, remember that they're wild, which means sightings can't be guaranteed. And as studies have shown that human interaction with dolphins can be detrimental to their health, it's best to stick to ethical guidelines such as those produced by National Oceanic and Atmospheric Administration (NOAA) program Dolphin SMART. Advice includes staying at least 45m from dolphins, and never chasing, touching or swimming in close quarters with them.

Prices are about Mtc1350 per person for a two-hour excursion, generally also involving snorkelling near Ponta Malongane and sailing down towards the lighthouse on the Mozambique–South Africa border.

Dolphins can be spotted year-round (although there are no refunds if you don't spot any). Whale sharks are best seen between July and November. Between June and August it's chilly in the boats, so bring a windbreaker. If conditions are stormy or too windy, the boats don't go out. From October/November to February the sea tends to be calmest.

Dolphin Centre WILDLIFE WATCHING
(Somente Aqua Dolphin Centre; ☎21-901189, 84 242 9864; www.thedolphincentre.com; Ponta d'Ouro; dolphin tours adult/child Mtc1350/1200) This place, at the southernmost end of town, is worth visiting, if only to read its information about dolphins. Tours take about two hours, and are preceded by a presentation on these lovely mammals and their environment. The centre also has rooms to rent.

Dolphin Encountours WILDLIFE WATCHING
(☎84 330 3859; www.dolphin-encountours.co.za; Ponta d'Ouro) Dolphin Encountours is based in the main square in the town centre, just next to the BCI ATM. It offers a variety of excursions, some for dolphin spotting and some for diving.

Sleeping

Ponta d'Ouro

Tandje Beach Resort CAMPGROUND $
(Ponta do Ouro Camp; ☎84 597 2660, in South Africa 011-465 3427; reservations@tandjebeachresort.com; Ponta d'Ouro; camping from Mtc500, 2-/4-person bungalows from Mtc2800/5000) In addition to the facilities and budget accommodation of **Scuba Adventures** (☎21-900430; www.scubaadventures.co.za; Ponta d'Ouro) dive camp, located on its grounds, Tandje has a shaded, seaside camping area with shared ablutions and basic bungalows, including a few beach-facing ones. It's at the southern end of town.

Coco Rico BUNGALOW $
(☎84 875 8029, in South Africa 034-413 2515; www.cocorico.co.za; Ponta d'Ouro; 8-person chalets from Mtc6600;) About 200m north of the town centre, past the Catholic church, Coco Rico has large, well-equipped, eight-person wooden self-catering chalets just back from the beach.

Motel do Mar Beach Resort HOTEL $$
(☎82 764 0380, 21-650000; www.pontadoouro.co.za; Ponta d'Ouro; 4-person chalets with/without sea view US$125/105;) In a fine seaside location (though not all rooms manage to have full sea views), this motel is a throwback to colonial days. It has a restaurant that does seafood grills, a 1960s ambience and blocks of faded but nevertheless quite pleasant two-storey self-catering chalets.

Ponta Malongane

Ponta Malongane CAMPGROUND $
(☎076 418 2523, in South Africa 082 453 8694; http://brdivers.co.za/malongane-accomodation/; Parque de Malongane, Ponta Malongane; camping adult/child US$10/5, dive-camp tents US$30, 4-person self-catering chalets US$120) This long-running, laid-back place is based in the sprawling, shaded Parque de Malongane. It has various accommodation options, including camping, four-person rondavels (round, traditional-style huts) and chalets, and small, rustic twin-bedded log huts.

Tartaruga Marítima Luxury Camp TENTED CAMP $$
(☎84 373 0067, in South Africa 035-340 7013; www.tartaruga.co.za; Ponta Malongane; s/d US$66/100;) About 2km north of the main Ponta Malongane 'junction', and well signposted, this lovely and tranquil retreat has spacious, comfortable safari-style tents tucked into coastal forest behind the dunes and is just a few minutes' walk from a wonderful stretch of beach. There's no restaurant, but there is a raised lounge-bar and self-catering braai (barbecue) area with ocean views.

Eating

Café Love CAFE $$
(Ponta d'Ouro; meals Mtc300-500; 7am-10pm) Tasty pizzas, pastas, salads and desserts and a changing daily special. Also has a small children's adventure playground. It's along the main road uphill from the market.

Ponta Beach Bar & Fishmonga SEAFOOD $$
(fishmonga@pontainfo.com; Main Sq, Ponta d'Ouro; snacks/mains from Mtc100/250; 8am-7pm;) Directly overlooking the main Ponta d'Ouro beach, this place has a chilled vibe, and a large menu featuring tasty and generously portioned waffles, burgers, seafood grills and more.

Mango Tropical Cafe CAFE $$
(☎84 780 6593; mangoshack@hotmail.co.za; Ponta d'Ouro; mains Mtc480; 8am-5pm Fri-Wed) This quiet rooftop cafe serves up good smoothies, fresh juices, mezze platters and light seafood meals. It's located on the main road, above the Dolphin Centre.

Information

There's a BCI ATM in the small square at the entrance to town.

Getting There & Away

PONTA D'OURO

Car

Ponta d'Ouro is 120km south of Maputo. The road is potholed but in decent shape for the first 60km. Thereafter, parts are under renovation, while other sections are soft, deep sand. Allow about three hours in a private vehicle (4WD only), although this time will be reduced once the planned paving between the Kosi Bay border post and Maputo is completed (estimated to be December 2017).

Chapa

Direct *chapas* (minibuses) depart Maputo's Catembe ferry pier by about 6am or earlier on Tuesday and Friday (Mtc200, five hours). Departures from Ponta d'Ouro are on Wednesday and Saturday from in front of the market. Otherwise take the ferry to Catembe, where there are several direct *chapas* daily. From Ponta d'Ouro back to Catembe, there is a *chapa* most weekdays departing at 4am. Arrange with the driver the evening before to pick you up at your hotel.

A bridge is being constructed across Maputo Bay – the estimated completion date is December 2017. Together with the rehabilitation of the road between Maputo and the Kosi Bay border post, it will change all of this information, so ask around before setting off.

From South Africa

The Kosi Bay border crossing is 11km south of Ponta d'Ouro. If the ongoing paving work hasn't reached this section by the time you do, you'll need a 4WD for the sandy track. Most *chapas* from Catembe pass here first, before stopping at Ponta d'Ouro (Mtc50 from the border to Ponta d'Ouro). Coming from South Africa, there's a guarded lot just over the border where you can leave your vehicle in the shade for R40 per day. All the hotels do pick-ups from the border for about US$10 to US$15 per person (minimum two people). Allow about five hours for the drive to/from Durban (South Africa).

PONTA MALONGANE

There's no public transport to Ponta Malongane, though *chapas* between Maputo and Ponta d'Ouro stop at the signposted turnoff, about 5km before Ponta Malongane. To get between Ponta d'Ouro and Ponta Malongane, you can walk along the beach at low tide (7km) or go via the sandy road.

Bilene

This small resort town sits on the large Uembje Lagoon, which is separated from the open sea by a narrow, sandy spit and dunes. If you're based in Maputo with a car at your disposal, it makes an enjoyable getaway, but if you're touring and want some sand, head further north to the beaches around Inhambane or south to Ponta d'Ouro.

Bilene is 140km north of Maputo and 35km off the main road. A direct bus departs Maputo's Praça dos Combatentes ('Xikelene') at about 6am (Mtc200, five hours). Otherwise go to Maputo's Junta station and have any northbound transport drop you at the Macia junction, from where pickups run throughout the day to/from Bilene (Mtc30, 30 minutes).

Leaving Bilene, there are direct departures daily at 6am to Xipamanine in Maputo, and again at about 11.30am to Maputo's Xikelene. All Bilene departures are from the main junction at the market – at the base of the hill just before the beach. Some transport also departs just uphill from the market, from the BCI roundabout.

Complexo Palmeiras (☎82 304 3720, 282-59019; http://complexopalmeiras.blogspot.com; campsites Mtc180, plus per person Mtc240, 2-/4-person chalets Mtc2800/3000) has camping, basic and poorly ventilated concrete chalets, and dark two-person rondavels. What it lacks in appealing accommodation is compensated for by the beautiful, large, white-sand beach out the front. Bring your own towels. Follow the main road into town to the final T-junction, then go left for about 1km.

The tidy, long-standing **Café O Bilas** (light meals & snacks Mtc140-250; ⏲8am-7pm) next to the petrol station is good for pizzas, hamburgers and other light meals. There's also a rooftop terrace.

Limpopo National Park

Together with South Africa's Kruger National Park and Zimbabwe's Gonarezhou National Park, Limpopo National Park forms part of the Great Limpopo Transfrontier Park, with Kruger and Limpopo linked via two fully functioning border crossings. Most visitors use Limpopo as a transit corridor between Kruger and the coast. There are also several 4WD eco-trails, as well as light hiking and canoeing. All activities can be booked through www.dolimpopo.com.

Poaching is a problem in Limpopo. Wildlife on the Mozambique side can't compare with that in South Africa's Kruger, and it's

WORTH A TRIP

MAPUTO SPECIAL RESERVE

This pristine 1040-sq-km wilderness area, about two hours from the capital and formerly known as the Maputo Elephant Reserve, is at the centre of efforts by the Peace Parks Foundation (www.peaceparks.org) to protect the wildlife and ecosystems of the surrounding Maputaland area. Thanks to wildlife-translocation efforts by the Mozambican and South African governments and the Peace Parks Foundation, numbers of animals in the reserve have increased. The reserve's elephant population is currently estimated at about 450, although these are threatened by ongoing poaching. Other species include hippos, giraffes, zebras and impalas.

The main attraction at Maputo Special Reserve is its pristine wilderness feel – it offers a real bush adventure close to the capital. The stunning terrain is another draw, mixing woodland, grassland, dune forest and open beach. It is wild and impenetrable in parts. Due to this, and to the skittishness of some of the wildlife, it's quite possible to visit without seeing many animals.

More of a certainty are the birds: over 300 types have been identified, including fish eagles and many wetland species. The coastline is also an important nesting area for loggerhead and leatherback turtles; peak breeding season is November to January.

Accommodation in the reserve is limited to a rustic, sea-facing **campsite** (camping adult/child Mtc200/100) and a luxury **beach lodge** (☎84 247 6322; www.anvilbay.com; Ponta Chemucane, Maputo Special Reserve; per person with full board US$434; wifi).

Maputo travel agencies operate day and overnight trips to the reserve. Otherwise you'll need your own (4WD) transport. The main entrance (also known as 'Futi Gate' or 'West Gate') is 65km from Catembe along the Ponta d'Ouro road. From here it's 3km to the park gate, and then 35km (about 1½ hours) further along a rough road to the coast and the campground. Further along the Ponta d'Ouro road there's a second, signposted entrance ('Gala Gate' or 'South Gate'), from where it's 22km into the reserve.

The road leading to the park entrances was under rehabilitation in late 2016, and will ultimately be paved from Maputo Special Reserve north to Maputo and south to the Kosi Bay border post. For now a 4WD is necessary both to reach the reserve, and to travel inside the reserve, where some tracks are deep sand.

quite possible to spend time in the park without seeing large animals.

Sleeping & Eating

Campismo Aguia Pesqueira CAMPGROUND $
(☎84 301 1719; www.limpopopn.gov.mz; camping Mtc210, d chalets Mtc1500) This good park-run campground is set on the edge of the escarpment overlooking Massingir Dam, about 55km from Giriyondo border crossing and about 25km from Massingir. All sites have lovely views over the dam, plus braai facilities. There's a communal kitchen and ablutions, plus several rustic two-bed self-catering chalets, also with views.

Covane Community Lodge LODGE, CAMPGROUND $$
(☎28-951055, 86 958 7864; www.covanecommunitylodge.com; camping Mtc330, hut s/d Mtc925/1850, chalet d Mtc2400) This community-owned and commercially run place is about 13km outside Limpopo's Massingir gate on a rise overlooking the dam. It offers lovely, good-value lakeside chalets, plus camping and rustic twin-bedded bush huts.

Machampane Wilderness Camp TENTED CAMP $$$
(☎in South Africa 021-701 7860; www.dolimpopo.com; s/d all-inclusive US$260/350) The upmarket Machampane has five spacious, well-appointed safari tents in a tranquil setting directly overlooking a section of the Machampane River, where you're likely to see hippos plus a variety of smaller wildlife and many birds. Morning and evening guided walks are included.

Getting There & Away

The main park entrance on the Mozambique side is **Massingir Gate** (6am-6pm), about 5km from Massingir town (which has an ATM). It's reached via a signposted turnoff from the EN1 at Macia junction that continues through Chokwé town (where there's also an ATM) on to Massingir. While daily *chapas* go between Maputo's Junta and Massingir (Mtc220), there is no possibility for onward transport within the park, so Limpopo remains primarily a self-drive destination.

To enter Limpopo from South Africa's Kruger park, you'll also need to pay Kruger park-entry fees, and Kruger's gate quota system applies (see www.sanparks.org for information).

The closest petrol stations on the Mozambique side are in Xai-Xai, Chókwè and Massingir. Travelling via Mapai, there is no fuel until Mapinhane.

Xai-Xai

Xai-Xai (pronounced 'shy-shy', and known during colonial times as João Belo) is a long town, stretching for several kilometres along the EN1. It's of little interest to travellers, but the nearby **Xai-Xai Beach** (Praia do Xai-Xai), about 10km from the town centre, has invigorating sea breezes, and it's an agreeable overnight stop if you're driving to or from points further north. Nearby are other lovely beaches, including stunning **Chidenguele**, about 70km north of Xai-Xai and about 5km off the EN1.

The busy 'praça' transport stand is near the old Pôr do Sol complex on the main road at the southern end of town. Buses to Maputo depart from here daily at about 6am (Mtc350, four hours). It's marginally faster to take one of the north–south through buses, although getting a seat can be a challenge. Wait by the Pôr do Sol complex or, better, walk or take a *chapa* (minibus) to the *pontinha* (bridge control post), where all traffic needs to stop. Some through buses also stop at the old Oliveiras depot along the main road at the northern end of town, diagonally opposite the Catholic church.

To Xai-Xai Beach (Mtc5), chapas depart from the praça transport stand, or you can catch them anywhere along the main road. They run at least to the roundabout, about 700m uphill from the beach, and sometimes further.

Complexo Halley HOTEL **$**
(☎82 312 5900, 282-35003; complexohalley1@yahoo.com.br; Xai-Xai Beach; d Mtc2500-3000; ❄) This long-standing beachfront hotel is the first place you reach after coming down the beach-access road from town, and it's an appealing choice. It has stiff sea breezes, a seaside esplanade, a good restaurant and pleasant, homey rooms (ask for one that' faces the sea). All rooms have hot-water bathroom and some have air-con and TV.

On Friday evening there's an all-night disco at the hotel; on Saturday it's across the road at the beachside esplanade.

Reef Resort BUNGALOW **$$**
(☎82 972 9867, in South Africa 083 305 1588; www.reefresort.co.za; Xai-Xai Beach; 4-/8-person houses from Mtc6600/11,400) This midsize, low-key self-catering place has chalets of varying sizes, all with lovely decks overlooking the sea. The owners have made efforts to provide access for travellers with disabilities, and several of the chalets are wheelchair friendly. Follow the road from town down to the beach, then go north along the waterside track for about 2km.

Inhambane

With its serene waterside setting, tree-lined avenues, faded colonial-style architecture and mixture of Arabic, Indian and African influences, Inhambane is one of Mozambique's most charming towns and well worth a visit. It has a history that reaches back at least a millennium, making it one of the oldest settlements along the coast. Today Inhambane is the capital of Inhambane province, although it's completely lacking in any sort of bustle or pretence. It is also the gateway to a fine collection of beaches, including Tofo and Barra.

Sights

Museum MUSEUM
(☎293-20756; cnr Avenida da Vigilância & Rua 1 de Maio; donations welcome; ⏲9am-5pm Tue-Fri, 2-5pm Sat & Sun) FREE This tiny museum near the unmissable new mosque is well worth a stop. Its displays include collections of traditional musical instruments, clothing and household items from the surrounding area. Some of them have captions in English.

Cathedral of Nossa Senhora de Conceição CATHEDRAL
The beautiful old Cathedral of Nossa Senhora de Conceição, dating from the late 18th century, is just northwest of the jetty. It is no longer used for services, and it is not possible to go inside, although the exterior is well worth a look.

Inhambane

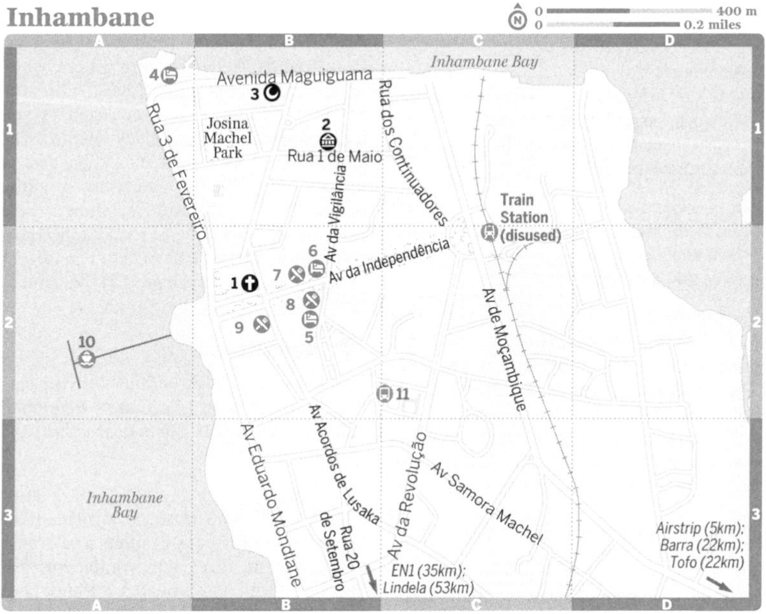

Inhambane

Sights

1 Cathedral of Nossa Senhora de Conceição B2
2 Museum B1
3 Old Mosque B1

Sleeping

4 Casa do Capitão A1
5 Hotel África Tropical B2
6 Hotel Inhambane B2

Eating

7 Buena Vista Café B2
8 TakeAway Sazaria B2
9 Verdinho's B2

Transport

10 Boats & Dhows to Maxixe A2
11 Bus Station C2

Old Mosque MOSQUE
Along the northern end of the waterfront road is Inhambane's attractive 'Old Mosque', dating to 1840.

Sleeping & Eating

Hotel África Tropical PENSION $
(Sensasol; ☎84 641 7312; Rua da Liberdade; r Mtc1500; ❄) África Tropical has a row of small, tidy rooms facing a tiny garden. Some rooms have a double bed, others a double plus a single; all have fan, net and hot water. Breakfast is extra, and there's a small restaurant. The hotel's just off Avenida da Independência.

Hotel Inhambane HOTEL $
(☎293-30375; hotelinhambane@sirmotors.com; Avenida da Independência; s/d/tr Mtc3414/3414/4160; ❄) This centrally located hotel has simple, mostly clean and mostly spacious rooms with TV and hot water. There's no food on site, but several eateries are within easy walking distance.

Casa do Capitão HOTEL $$$
(☎84 026 2302, 293-21408/9; www.hotelcasadocapitao.com; Avenida Maguiguana; r from Mtc9750; ❄📶🏊) This low-key hotel is in a fantastic location, overlooking Inhambane Bay on two sides. Views are wonderful and rooms are well appointed. It's the most upmarket choice in town – a nice treat if you're in

Inhambane on a honeymoon or if you just want pampering.

TakeAway Sazaria CAFE $
(Avenida da Independência; mains from Mtc100; ⊙8am-5pm Mon-Fri) Tasty, inexpensive soups, *pregos* (steak rolls) and sandwiches to eat there or take away.

Buena Vista Café AFRICAN $
(Avenida da Independência; meals Mtc200-350; ⊙8am-10pm Tue-Sun) Inexpensive, tasty daily menus and local dishes.

Verdinho's EUROPEAN $$
(☎84 563 1260; 70 Avenida Acordos de Lusaka; mains Mtc250-450; ⊙8am-10pm Mon-Sat;) The popular Verdinho's features a large menu including tasty salads, burgers, pizzas, pasta and continental dishes, and seating indoors or at shaded tables outside on the patio, where you can watch the passing scene.

Getting There & Away

AIR

LAM has five flights weekly connecting Inhambane with Maputo, Vilankulo and Johannesburg (from about US$100 one way). Inhambane's airstrip is 5km southeast of town.

BOAT

Small motorised passenger boats operate from sunrise to sundown between Inhambane and Maxixe (Mtc10, 25 minutes). The pier on the Maxixe side is just across the EN1 from the main bus stand. Sailing dhows do the trip more slowly for Mtc5, and one of Inhambane's great morning sights is sitting on the jetty and watching them load up. It's also possible to charter a motorboat (from about Mtc200, 10 minutes).

BUS & CAR

The bus station is behind the market. *Chapas* (minibuses) to Tofo run throughout the day (Mtc15 to Mtc18, one hour). There is a daily direct bus to Maputo, departing at 5.30am (Mtc600, seven hours, 450km). Fatima's Nest in Tofo has a daily shuttle to Maputo (Mtc800) that stops at Inhambane. There's also at least one bus daily in the morning from Inhambane to Vilankulo (Mtc300). For all other southbound and northbound transport, you'll need to head to Maxixe.

Coming from Maputo, a direct bus departs Junta station between 5am and 6am, or take any northbound bus to Maxixe.

There's at least one daily *chapa* to Maxixe (Mtc50) via the shortcut road; the turnoff from the EN1 is at the Agostinho Neto area, 20km south of Maxixe.

Tofo

Thanks to its sheltered azure waters, white sands, easy access and fine diving, the beach at Tofo has long been legendary on the Southern Africa holiday circuit. The magnificent beach runs in a long arc, at the centre of which is a small town with a perpetual party atmosphere. Many people come to Tofo expecting to spend a few days, and instead stay several weeks or more. For something quieter, head around the point to Barra, or further north or south.

Activities

Tofo is Mozambique's unofficial diving capital. There's a good selection of dive operators, all of which offer instruction and equipment rental.

Tofo Scuba DIVING
(☎82 826 0140; www.tofoscuba.com) This PADI five-star Gold Palm resort offers a full range of instruction, dives and equipment, and also has nitrox and a heated training pool. It's at the northern end of the beach, with a surf shop and a good cafe adjoining.

Liquid Dive Adventures DIVING
(☎0846 512 737, 0846 130 316; www.liquiddiveadventures.com) This PADI Green Star outfit offers Open Water courses and other instruction plus a full range of diving. It's at the entrance to town: go left at the first Y-intersection, and Liquid Dive Adventures is about 150m up on the left. There's also a small vegetarian restaurant on the premises.

Diversity Scuba DIVING
(☎82 932 9042, 293-29002; www.diversityscuba.com) In the town centre near the market, this PADI five-star Gold Palm Instructor Development Centre offers the usual array of instruction and dives, and also has Nitrox. Upstairs is a small cafe.

Peri-Peri Divers DIVING
(☎82 550 5661; www.peri-peridivers.com) A full range of dives and PADI diving instruction, with a focus on personalised, small-group dives. It's next to Albatroz Lodge, just south of the town centre on the small bluff above the beach.

Sleeping

Wuyani Pariango HOSTEL $
(☎84 712 8963; www.pariangobeach.com; camping Mtc300, dm Mtc500, r Mtc2500, with shared

bathroom Mtc1500-1800;) This good budget place is in the centre of Tofo, just north of the market and just back from the beach. It has various simple reed-and-thatch rooms in the backyard walled garden plus space to pitch a tent.

Nordin's Lodge BUNGALOW $
(84 520 4777, 293-29009; 2-/4-person chalets Mtc2000/4000) The unassuming Nordin's is at the northern edge of town in a good, shaded location directly on the beach. It has four rustic, dark and rather faded thatched chalets that come with hot water, fridge and self-catering facilities.

Albatroz Lodge LODGE $
(293-29005, 82 255 8450; www.albatrozlodge.com; 2-/4-/6-person chalets Mtc1500/3000/3500;) Albatroz has large, rustic thatched self-catering cottages in a quiet setting on the bluff overlooking the beach. There's a restaurant and a dive operator next door.

Fatima's Nest HOSTEL $
(82 185 1575; www.mozambiquebackpackers.com; camping Mtc400, dm Mtc500, s/d/tr Mtc1600/2200/3200, without bathroom Mtc1000/2000/2600) The long-standing Fatima's, ever popular and now considerably expanded, has camping, dorm beds and a mix of very basic bungalows and rooms, all on low dunes overlooking the beach just north of the town centre. There's also kitchen, bar, pool table and evening beach bonfires.

Casa Na Praia GUESTHOUSE $$
(82 821 5921; www.casanapraiatofo.com; d Mtc5500-8800, tr Mtc4500-10,000) This place in the centre of Tofo beach has accommodation in three buildings: the more luxurious Casa Amarela, with lovely, attached beach-facing rooms with verandas; the cosy Bungalow Africa; and Casa Azul, a cheery white-with-blue trim, colonial-era house. There are semi-open-air bathrooms, each one different, and a very nice, beachside cafe–breakfast area.

Casa do Mar B&B $$
(in South Africa 082 455 7481; www.casa-do-mar.co.za; r US$140;) This luxury B&B overlooking the main section of Tofo beach has bright, spotless rooms – some with sea views – in a large private home, and a chef who prepares gourmet meals. Breakfast is extra.

Hotel Tofo Mar HOTEL $$$
(82 393 2545; www.hoteltofomar.com; s/d Mtc4080/6300, with sea view from Mtc5640/8700) Situated in a prime location directly on the beach in the town centre, the recently renovated Hotel Tofo Mar has clean, bright rooms and good service. The restaurant-bar area is usually a hive of activity in the evenings.

Eating & Drinking

Beach Baraca BREAKFAST $
(mains Mtc180-250; 7.30am-8pm) In the central market area, Beach Baraca serves tasty smoothies, good, healthy breakfasts, wraps and sandwiches.

Branko's Bar PIZZA $
(pizza Mtc190-350) This tiny, unassuming place in the central market area has tasty pizzas, plus seafood and beef cooked on 'hot rocks' at your table. It's usually packed.

Café Happi CAFE $
(snacks & light meals from Mtc100; 7am-5pm;) This good veg-only cafe at Liquid Dive Adventures has tasty breakfasts, salads, sandwiches, smoothies and more. It's near the entrance to town: go left at the Y-junction, and it's about 100m further on the left.

What U Want ITALIAN $$
(mains Mtc300-500) Tasty Italian and Mozambican cuisine, good pizzas and starters like focaccia and bruschetta. It's in the centre of town, just northwest of the market area.

Mr Fresh SUPERMARKET
(8.30am-6.30pm Mon-Fri, 8am-6pm Sat, 8.30am-5pm Sun) This small place is Tofo's main supermarket. It's near the town entrance: go left at the Y-junction when coming into town, and it's just ahead on the right.

Information

Tofo On-Line (per minute Mtc3; 9am-6pm;) In the town centre, just northeast of the market. It also sells tasty apple crumble as well as other snacks.

Getting There & Away

Chapas (minibuses) run throughout the day along the 22km sealed road between Tofo and Inhambane, departing Tofo from about 5am (Mtc15 to Mtc18 for a large bus, one hour). To Maputo's Junta, there's usually one direct bus daily, departing Tofo by about 5am (Mtc750, 7½ hours). Fatima's Nest also has a daily shuttle to Maputo (Mtc800). Otherwise you'll need to go via Inhambane or Maxixe. If you do this and want to catch an early north/southbound bus, it's possible in theory to sleep in Tofo, but for a more sure connection, stay in Inhambane the night before.

If you leave early from Maputo, it's possible to get to Inhambane in time to continue straight on to Tofo that day, with time to spare.

Tofinho

Perched high up on an escarpment running between a dramatic rocky outcrop and a green point of land is Tofinho, Mozambique's unofficial surfing capital. Its topography and the prevailing winds ensure high-quality surfing from March to September, with the best months being June and July. It's also a chilled beach destination in its own right, and works well in combination with the lively beach town of Tofo, just to the north.

Self-drivers can reach Tofinho by following the road from Inhambane to Tofo, and then taking a sharp right uphill just before the entrance to Tofo. There is no public transport.

Turtle Cove BUNGALOW, CAMPGROUND **$**
(☎82 719 4848; www.turtlecovetofo.com; camping US$10, dm US$15, chalet d US$50; ❄) This is the spot to go if you're interested in chilling out, with Moorish-style stone houses with bathrooms, a few very basic grass huts, camping and a slow restaurant.

Mozambeat Motel BUNGALOW, CAMPGROUND **$**
(☎84 422 3515; www.mozambeat.com; camping US$5, dm US$15, cabin d/tr US$55/70; 📶 🏊) Partiers will likely enjoy this place. It offers a mix of accommodation, including camping (your tent or theirs), dorm beds, small and simple wooden cabins and larger stone-and-thatch suites, all set around a garden.

Casa John GUESTHOUSE **$$**
(☎in South Africa 082 451 7498; www.casajohn.co.za; 2-/3-bedroom houses US$150/225; 🏊) Just back from the cliff near the monument, this place has lovely, well-appointed two- and three-bedroom self-catering houses ('Casa John' and 'Casa Amarela') in a breezy setting overlooking the sea.

Barra

Barra sits at the tip of the Barra Peninsula, where the waters of Inhambane Bay mix with those of the Indian Ocean. Many self-drivers prefer Barra's quieter scene and its range of midrange accommodation options, but Tofo is a better bet if you're backpacking or relying on public transport.

Daily *chapas* (minivans) go between Inhambane and Conguiana village along the Barra road. From here, you'll need to sort out a pick-up or walk (it's about 4km to the main hotel area).

The self-catering **Bayview Lodge** (☎84 743 3334; www.bayviewlodgemoz.com; 2-/4-/16-person houses from US$95/190/260; ❄) is just back from lovely Barra Beach. There's one large 16-person house (minimum booking for seven people), and several smaller one- and two-bedroom brick cabins. The beach is just a short walk away, and there's a good in-house restaurant on the sand. Turn left at the main junction coming into Barra, from where it's signposted.

Green Turtle Restaurant & Beach Bar (☎82 026 0580; mains Mtc450-550) is the closest to gourmet dining that you'll find in the area, with tasty French cuisine – the seafood dishes and desserts are particularly notable – and lovely views. It's on the beach about 2km to the left of Barra junction at Bayview Lodge, and well signposted.

Maxixe

Maxixe (pronounced ma-*sheesh*) is about 450km northeast of Maputo on the EN1 and is convenient as a stopping point for traffic up and down the coast. It's also the place to get off the bus and onto the boat if you're heading to Inhambane, across the bay.

Buses to Maputo (Mtc550, 6½ hours, 450km) depart from the bus stand by the Tribunal (court) from 6am. There are no buses to Beira originating in Maxixe; you'll need to try to get space on one of those coming from Maputo that stop at Maxixe's main bus stand (Mtc1200 from Maxixe to Beira). Thirty-seater buses to Vilankulo originating in Maputo depart Maxixe from about 10am from the main bus stand. Otherwise, *chapas* (minibuses) to Vilankulo (Mtc200, 3½ hours) depart throughout the day from Praça 25 de Setembro (Praça de Vilankulo), a couple of blocks north of the bus stand in front of the Conselho Municipal.

If you're driving to Inhambane, take the shortcut road signposted to the east about 20km south of Maxixe in the Agostinho Neto area.

Stop Residencial MOTEL $

(☎82 125 2010, 293-30025; stopmaxixe96@hotmail.com; d/tw/ste Mtc1800/1800/2000; ❄) Tidy, functional rooms with hot-water bathrooms. Most of the rooms are in a low multistorey building just off the EN1 next to Barclays Bank. For bookings, directions and check-in, go to Restaurante Stop next to the ferry.

Restaurante Stop PORTUGUESE $

(☎293-30025; EN1; mains Mtc200-300; ⏲6am-10pm) Restaurante Stop, on the northern side of the jetty, has prompt service, clean toilets, tasty meals and a shaded dining terrace. It makes a good rest point on the journey north or south.

Massinga & Morrungulo

The bustling district capital of Massinga is a convenient stocking-up point if you're heading to the beach, with numerous shops, a petrol station and a garage. Nearby is beautiful Morrungulo beach. Its long, wide, white sands – stretching seemingly endlessly in both directions – are fringed by a low escarpment topped with dense stands of coconut palms.

Morrungulo is 13km from the main road down a good dirt track that's negotiable with a 2WD. Sporadic *chapas* (minibuses; Mtc25) run from the Massinga transport stand (on the EN1) to Morrungulo village, close to Morrungulo Beach Lodge , and within about 3km of Sylvia Shoal.

About 1.5km north of the junction where the road from the EN1 joins the sandy coastal track is the unassuming **Sylvia Shoal** (☎in South Africa 083 270 7582, in South Africa 071-604 8918; www.sylviashoal.co.za; camping/barracas US$10/12, chalet d/q US$58/82), with shaded campsites, a handful of self-catering chalets set behind low dunes and a restaurant (during low season open with advance bookings only).

Morrungulo Beach Lodge (☎84 246 7533, 293-70101; www.morrungulo.com; camping adult/child US$10/5, 4-person garden/seafront chalets US$95/115) has rustic, thatched beachfront and garden self-catering bungalows and campsites on a large, manicured bougainvillea- and palm-studded lawn running down to the beach. The setting – with magnificent views of Morrungulo Bay from the escarpment – is outstanding, although the colonial-era ambience may be a turnoff for some. It's 13km off the EN1, and signposted about 8km north of Massinga.

Pomene

Pomene, the site of a colonial-era beach resort, is known for its fishing and birding, for its striking estuarine setting and especially for its magnificent open-ocean coastline. The area is part of the **Pomene Reserve** (adult/vehicle Mtc400/400), which protects coastal and marine life. The beach here is beautiful, especially up near the point by the lighthouse and the now-derelict Pomene Hotel.

Pomene is on the coast about halfway between Inhambane and Vilankulo, off the EN1. The turnoff is about 11km north of Massinga (which is the best place to stock up) and is signposted immediately after the Morrungulo turnoff. From the turnoff, which is also the end of the tarmac, it's about 55km (1½ to two hours) further along an unpaved road to Pomene village and the main accommodation options, both of which are signposted.

Pomene View LODGE $

(☎84 465 4572; www.pomeneview.co.za; 5-/6-person chalets US$90/110; 🏊) Pomene View, on a rise amid the mangroves and coastal vegetation on the mainland side of the estuary, is small and tranquil, with its own special appeal and wide views. Accommodation is in self-catering brick-and-thatch chalets, and there's a bar and restaurant. From the signposted turnoff north of Massinga, it's about 54km to get here (follow the Pomene View signs).

Pomene Lodge LODGE, CAMPGROUND $$

(☎in South Africa 076-583 1662, in South Africa 011-023 9901; www.barraresorts.com; camping US$15, water chalet s/d US$100/165; 🏊) Pomene Lodge, in a fine setting on a spit of land between the estuary and the sea, has no-frills self-catering reed bungalows just back from the beach, plus a row of faded but spacious and nicer 'water chalets' directly over the estuary. The lodge is a few kilometres from Pomene village. Self-drivers will need a 4WD.

Vilankulo

Vilankulo is the finishing (or starting) point of Mozambique's southern tourism circuit. It's also the gateway for visiting the nearby Bazaruto Archipelago, separated from the mainland by a narrow channel of turquoise sea. During South African holidays, Vilankulo is overrun with pickups and 4WDs, but otherwise it's a quiet, slow-paced town with some lovely nearby beaches.

Activities

Diving

Diving here is rewarding, and it's possible year-round. The best months are April to September and the worst are December and January, although conditions can vary markedly within these periods. The main sites are well offshore around the Bazaruto Archipelago (about a 45-minute boat ride away).

Odyssea Dive DIVING
(☎82 781 7130; www.odysseadive.com) This reliable outfit is the main dive outfitter in Vilankulo, offering a range of dives and PADI instruction. It's at the southern end of town, about 500m south of the Old Market on the beach.

Dhow Safaris

Several outfits offer day or overnight dhow safaris around the Bazaruto Archipelago. Besides the recommended Sailaway, Marimba Secret Gardens also organises good day trips to Bazaruto (from US$60 per person) as well as to lovely Santa Carolina Island (from US$70 per person) – all including park fees, lunch and snorkelling equipment. There is officially no camping on the islands in the park; operators running overnight tours camp along the mainland coast.

There are also many independent dhow operators in Vilankulo. If you go with a freelancer, remember that while some are reliable, others may quote tempting prices, and then ask you to 'renegotiate' things once you're well away from shore. Check with the **tourist information office** (Rua da OMM; ⏰8am-3.30pm Mon-Fri, 9am-1pm Sat) or with your hotel for recommendations and don't pay until you're safely back on land. For non-motorised dhows, allow plenty of extra time to account for wind and water conditions; it can take two to three hours

Vilankulo

Activities, Courses & Tours
1 Kite Surfing Centre A1
Odyssea Dive .... (see 3)
2 Sailaway B2

Sleeping
3 Casa Babi B4
4 Casa Jules & Zombie Cucumber Backpackers B3
5 Hotel Dona Ana B1

Eating
6 Café Moçambicano A3
7 Café Zambeziana B4
8 Kilimanjaro Café B2
9 Taurus Supermarket B2

Transport
10 Buses to Maputo A4
11 New Market Transport Stand B2

(sometimes longer) under sail from Vilankulo to Magaruque, and much longer to the other islands. For motorised dhows, plan on about five hours' return travel time between Vilankulo and Bazaruto.

Sailaway DHOW SAFARIS
(☎293-82385, 82 387 6350; www.sailaway.co.za; per person snorkelling excursion/overnight safari from US$75/260) The recommended Sailaway offers day and overnight island dhow safaris. Check out its website for a sampling of the possibilities. All boats have extra motors, safety and first-aid equipment and communication gear on board. Sailaway's Vilankulo base is on the road paralleling the beach road, about 400m south of the Hotel Dona Ana.

Horse Riding

Mozambique Horse Safari HORSE RIDING
(☎84 251 2910; www.mozambiquehorsesafari.com) Mozambique Horse Safari, based in Chibuene, offers rides on the beach, including a fishing-village tour, for riders of all levels. A wonderful experience.

Kite Surfing

Kite Surfing Centre KITESURFING
(www.kitesurfingcentre.com) Lessons, rentals and – best of all – kite surfing safaris to the islands. It's north of town, next to the signposted Casbah Beach Bar.

Sleeping

Baobab Beach Backpackers HOSTEL, CAMPGROUND $
(☎82 731 5420, 84 413 3057; www.baobabbeach.net; Rua do Palacio, Bairro Desse; camping US$7, dm US$10, bungalow d from US$34, with shared bathroom from US$26) With its waterside setting, chilled vibe and straightforward, good-value bungalows, Baobab Beach is a favourite with the party set. It has a popular, reasonably priced restaurant, and an area for self-catering. It's about 500m south of the Old Market. Walking here from town is fine by day; at night, it's best to take a taxi.

Casa Jules & Zombie Cucumber Backpackers HOSTEL $
(☎84 421 2565, 84 686 9870; www.casajules.com; dm Mtc500, s/d from Mtc2500/3000;) This place just back from the beach road offers a quiet vibe, hammocks, bar, restaurant, tranquil gardens and helpful staff. Accommodation is in dorms or simple, tidy, thatched garden huts (as part of the original Zombie Cucumber Backpackers), or more spacious double and triple rooms up on the hillside at the newer 'Casa Jules'.

Marimba Secret Gardens BUNGALOW $$
(☎82 005 3015, 84 048 9098; www.marimba.ch; dm/d/tw US$18/104/110; @) This appealing place is set slightly back from the beach about 25km north of Vilankulo along a bush track. Accommodation is in beautifully designed octagonal bungalows on stilts, and there's a restaurant and evening bonfires. It's a good bet if you're looking for a quiet spot to relax away from Vilankulo's bustle and seeking a chance to get acquainted with local life.

Aguia Negra LODGE $$
(☎293-82387, in South Africa 083 289 0036; www.aguianegrahotel.com; s/d/tr/q Mtc2500/4500/5400/7200;) This is a lovely place, with thatched A-frame chalets set around a spacious, green, grassy compound directly overlooking the sea. Each chalet has an open loft area, and there's a sparkling blue pool and a restaurant. It's about 2km north of the Hotel Dona Ana junction.

Archipelago Resort RESORT $$
(☎84 775 8433, 293-84022; www.archipelago-resort.com; 6-person garden/sea-view bungalows from US$170/190;) This wonderful resort has 18 spacious, well-appointed Indonesian-style self-catering bungalows set in expansive green grounds overlooking the sea. All have large verandas, two bedrooms and two bathrooms downstairs, and a two-bed loft.

Casa Babi B&B $$$
(☎84 412 6478, 82 781 7130; www.casababi.com; s/d US$125/170;) This cosy place has four beach-facing rooms, plus a five-person self-catering chalet in the small garden behind. All rooms are attractively decorated, and each has its own terrace and swing.

Hotel Dona Ana HISTORIC HOTEL $$$
(☎293-83200; www.thehoteldonaana.com; Rua da Marginal; s/d from US$170/280;) The Dona Ana is a throwback to Vilanculo's earlier days, with pastel-pink-and-grey art deco design and a waterside location. Its 52 rooms are bright and pleasant – most are in the main hotel building, and some are in the greener, more tranquil 'Beach Wing' annex.

Eating

Café Moçambicano CAFE $
(Avenida Eduardo Mondlane; pastries from Mtc25) A good budget bet, with tasty pastries, bread, yoghurt, juice and a small, tidy indoor eating area plus a bakery next door. It's opposite Barclays Bank.

Café Zambeziana CAFE $
(light meals from Mtc250) Immediately to your right when exiting the old market, this local place has tasty but inexpensive grilled chicken and barbecue sandwiches.

Kilimanjaro Café CAFE $
(breakfast Mtc150-200, sandwiches & light meals Mtc250-300; 8am-5pm Mon-Sat;) Salads, sandwiches, pizza, pasta and a changing daily menu plus smoothies and gourmet coffees. It's in the Lexus shopping mall.

Taurus Supermarket SUPERMARKET
(Avenida Eduardo Mondlane; 7am-6pm Mon-Sat) Well stocked for self-catering. It's near the end of the tarmac road, diagonally opposite Millennium BIM.

Shopping

Machilla Magic ARTS & CRAFTS
(82 393 3428; www.machillamagic.com; 8am-4pm Mon-Fri, to 2pm Sat) This place sells an appealing selection of reasonably priced handicrafts, 95% of which are made from reclaimed or recycled materials. It's on the beach road, about 2.5km north of Hotel Dona Ana.

Information

SOS Netcare 911 (Nhamacunda Medical Centre; 84 378 1911; 24hr) This new, well-equipped medical clinic has pharmacy, dentist, laboratory and modern facilities. It can handle minor surgeries and can also assist with arrangements for medical evacuation to South Africa or elsewhere. It's in the Nhamacunda area, about 6km north of town past the beach hotels. It also has an ambulance.

Getting There & Away

AIR

Offices for all airlines are at the airport, which also has an ATM. The airport turnoff is along the road running to Pambara junction, 1.5km from the main roundabout at the entrance to town. From the turnoff, it is 2km further.

LAM has daily flights to/from Maputo (from about US$150 one way) and **SAAirlink** (in South Africa 011-451 7300; www.flyairlink.com) has daily flights from Johannesburg (about US$150 one way).

BUS

Vilankulo is 20km east of the EN1, down a tarmac access road, with the turnoff at Pambara junction. *Chapas* (minibuses) run between the two throughout the day (Mtc20). Except for large buses to Maputo and *chapas* to Chibuene, all transport departs from the transport stand at the **new market** (Mercado Novo; Avenida Eduardo Mondlane).

- **Beira** (Mtc550 to Mtc600, 10 hours) Buses depart Vilankulo between 4.30am and 6am at least every second day; book the afternoon before.
- **Chimoio** There's no direct bus to Chimoio. You'll need to take a Beira bus as far as Inchope junction (Mtc550 to Mtc600 from Vilankulo), and then get a minibus from there.
- **Inhassoro** (Mtc85, 1½ hours, several daily)
- **Maputo** (Mtc950, nine to 10 hours, usually two daily, departing from 3.30am) Book your ticket with the drivers the afternoon before and verify the time. Departures are from a stop in front of the small red shop one block up from the old market, opposite the tribunal and west of the main road. Coming from Maputo, departures from Junta are at about 5am.
- **Maxixe** (Mtc200, three to four hours) Several minibuses depart each morning to Maxixe (for Inhambane and Tofo). Allow six to seven hours for the entire journey from Vilankulo to Tofo.

Bazaruto Archipelago

The Bazaruto Archipelago has clear, turquoise waters filled with colourful fish, and offers diving, snorkelling and birding. It makes a fine upmarket holiday if you're looking for the quintessential Indian Ocean getaway.

The archipelago consists of five main islands: Bazaruto, Benguera (also spelled Benguerra, and formerly known as Santo António), Magaruque (Santa Isabel), Santa Carolina (Paradise Island or Ilha do Paraíso) and tiny Bangué.

Since 1971 much of the archipelago has been protected as **Bazaruto National Park** (Parque Nacional de Bazaruto; adult Mtc400). You'll see dozens of bird species, including fish eagles and pink flamingos. There are also red duikers, bushbucks and, especially on Benguera, Nile crocodiles. Dolphins swim through the clear waters, along with 2000 types of fish, plus loggerhead, leatherback and green turtles. Most intriguing are the elusive dugongs.

If you have limited funds, try visiting the archipelago on a dhow cruise from Vilankulo, or come in low season, when some lodges offer special deals.

Activities

Diving

Diving is generally best from about May to September, although it's possible year-round, and visibility can vary greatly even from day to day. Dives, equipment rental and dive-certification courses can be organised at any of the island lodges, or in Vilankulo.

Snorkelling at Santa Carolina island is considered among the best in the archipelago and is possible just offshore. Magaruque is also noted for its fine snorkelling in the crystal-clear shallows just off the beach on the island's southwestern corner.

Sleeping & Eating

★ &Beyond Benguerra LODGE **$$$**
(☎ in South Africa 011-809 4300; www.andbeyond.com/benguerra-island/; r per person all-inclusive from US$765;) This is perhaps the most intimate of the archipelago lodges, with lovely, well-spaced beach chalets ('cabanas') and villas ('*casinhas*'), fine beachside dining under the stars and a good selection of activities. The entire lodge is open design, with open-air showers, luxury bathtubs with views, and private infinity plunge pools. It's well worth the splurge, if your budget allows.

Azura Benguerra RESORT **$$$**
(☎ 84 731 0871, in South Africa 011-467 0907; www.azura-retreats.com; r per person all-inclusive from US$655;) This lovely place is one of the archipelago's most luxurious retreats. Accommodation is in secluded beach villas nestled amid tropical vegetation, with private plunge pools, wonderful cuisine, outdoor showers under the stars, fine views and a selection of activities.

Anantara Bazaruto Island Resort & Spa RESORT **$$$**
(☎ 84 304 6670, in South Africa 010-003 8979; bazaruto.anantara.com/; r with full board from US$800;) This is the largest and most outfitted lodge in the archipelago. It offers a mix of private villas and beachfront chalets, and a range of activities. While it lacks the laid-back island touch of many of the other places, for some visitors this will be compensated for by the high level of comfort and amenities.

Getting There & Away

SAAirlink flies five times weekly between Johannesburg and Vilankulo, from where you can arrange island helicopter or boat transfers with the lodges. **CR Aviation** (☎ 84 490 9734; www.craviation.co.mz; Vilankulo Airport) has flights connecting Vilankulo with Bazaruto (about US$335 return). **Archipelago Charters** (☎ 84 839 5204, in South Africa 083 378 4242; www.archipelago.co.za) has a helicopter service connecting Vilankulo with Bazaruto, Benguera and Magaruque, and also offers scenic-flight charters.

There are airports on Benguerra Island and Bazaruto Island.

All the top-end lodges arrange speedboat transfers for their guests. Most day visitors reach the islands by dhow from Vilankulo, where there are a number of dhow safari (p124) operators.

CENTRAL MOZAMBIQUE

Central Mozambique – Sofala, Manica, Tete and Zambézia provinces – doesn't draw the tourist crowds, although it's a convenient transit zone. However, ignore it and you'll miss out on some of the country's most intriguing secrets: Mozambique's most accessible national park (Gorongosa), its finest hiking area (Gurúè), its most abundant birdlife (Caia and Marromeu) and its best fishing lake (Cahora Bassa).

Beira

Faded, withered and decidedly rough around the edges, Mozambique's second-largest city seems like a place that's been left behind. Yet even seedy Beira has its highlights. There's **Macuti Beach** (Praia de Macuti; Avenida das FPLM), an unkempt but broad swath of sand commandeered by weekend footballers and haunted by shipwrecks, some glorious if grimy examples of colonial architecture and a few eating surprises if you know where to look.

The heart of the city is the area around the Praça do Município and Praça do Metical. To the north is the old commercial area of the *baixa*, while about 1km east is Praça do Maquinino, the main transport hub. From Praça do Município, tree-lined streets lead south and east through shady Ponta Gêa and on to Macuti Beach.

Beira

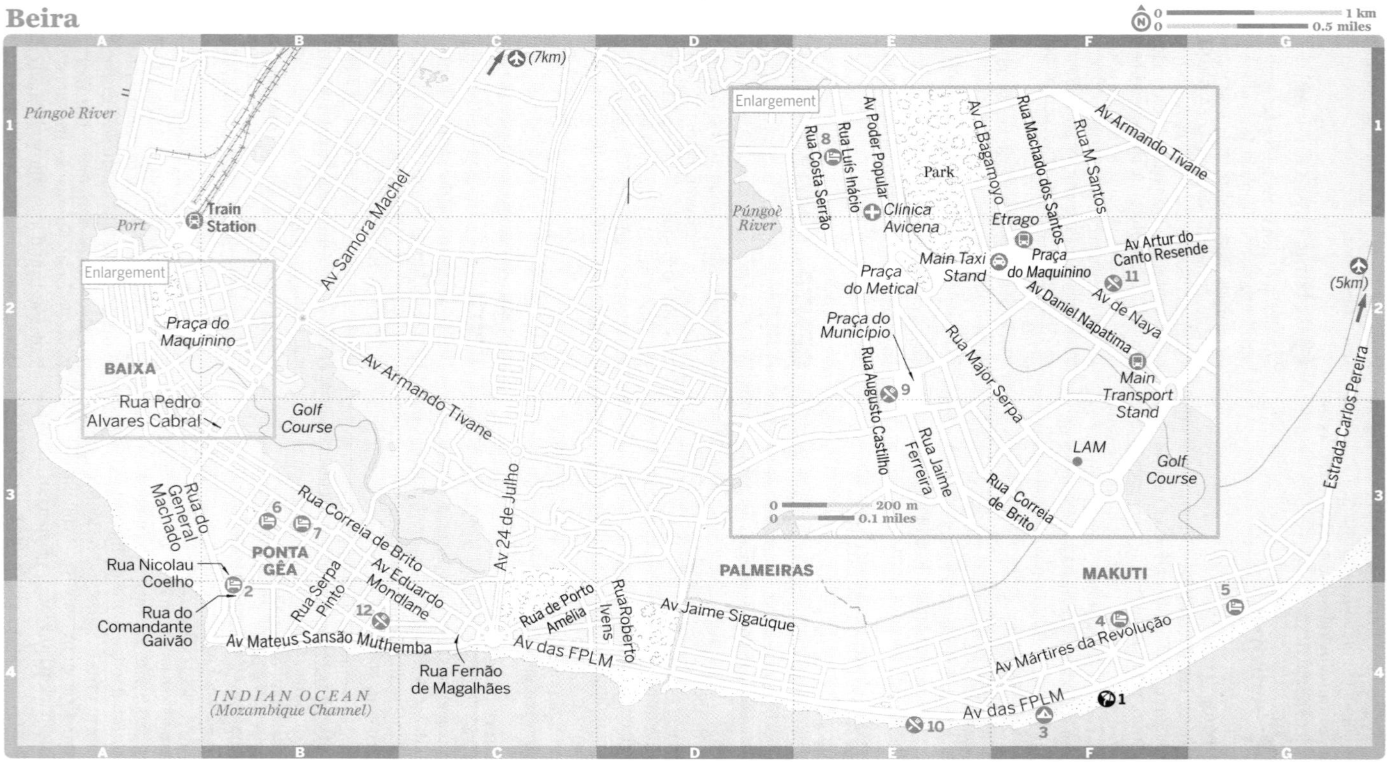
0 — 1 km
0 — 0.5 miles
A B C D E F G
1 2 3 4
Púngoè River
Port
Train Station
(7km)
Enlargement
Praça do Maquinino
BAIXA
Rua Pedro Alvares Cabral
Golf Course
Av Samora Machel
Av Armando Tivane
Av 24 de Julho
Rua do General Machado
Rua Nicolau Coelho
Rua do Comandante Gaivão
PONTA GÊA
Rua Correia de Brito
Av Eduardo Mondlane
Rua Serpa Pinto
Av Mateus Sansão Muthemba
Rua Fernão de Magalhães
INDIAN OCEAN
(Mozambique Channel)
Rua de Porto Amélia
RuaRoberto Ivens
Av das FPLM
Av Jaime Sigaúque
PALMEIRAS
MAKUTI
Av Mártires da Revolução
Av das FPLM
Estrada Carlos Pereira
(5km)
Enlargement
Púngoè River
Rua Costa Serrão
Rua Luís Inácio
Av Poder Popular
Clínica Avicena
Park
Av d Bagamoyo
Rua Machado dos Santos
Rua M Santos
Av Armando Tivane
Etrago
Praça do Maquinino
Main Taxi Stand
Praça do Metical
Av Artur do Canto Resende
Av de Naya
Av Daniel Napatima
Praça do Município
Rua Major Serpa
Main Transport Stand
Rua Augusto Castilho
Rua Jaime Ferreira
LAM
Golf Course
Rua Correia de Brito
0 — 200 m
0 — 0.1 miles
1 2 3 4 5 6 7 8 9 10 11 12

Beira

Sights

1 Macuti Beach.......F4

Sleeping

2 Beira Guest House.......B4
3 Biques.......F4
4 Hotel Sena.......F4
5 Jardim das Velas.......G4
6 Pensão Moderna.......B3
7 Royal Guest House.......B3
8 VIP Inn Beira.......E1

Eating

Biques.......(see 3)
9 Café Riviera.......E2
10 Clube Náutico.......E4
11 Restaurante 2 + 1.......F2
12 Tutto D'Italy.......B4

Sleeping

Royal Guest House GUESTHOUSE $

(☎23-324030; 1311 Avenida Eduardo Mondlane; r incl breakfast Mtc3000; ❄📶🏊) This intimate residential-style B&B in the shady Ponta Gêa area has large, characterful rooms with mini fridge, TV and laundry service. No meals (apart from breakfast) are available. There's a pleasant garden and small pool out the back.

Biques CAMPGROUND $

(☎84 597 7130, 23-313051; Macuti Beach; camping Mtc200; P) Although it acts primarily as a beach bar and restaurant, ever-popular Biques, set on a breezy rise overlooking Macuti Beach, also offers limited camping space. It's the only camping spot in town and a good place for watching the sunset.

Pensão Moderna PENSION $

(☎23-329901; Rua Marques Sá da Bandeira; d/tr Mtc1755/2750) The inaptly named Moderna isn't exactly a bastion of shining modernity these days, but it still serves as a good budget bet, with adequate rooms, most with fan and shared bathroom. It's two blocks south of the cathedral.

Beira Guest House GUESTHOUSE $$

(☎82 315 0460; woodgateangola@yahoo.co.uk; Rua Nicolau Coelho; r incl breakfast Mtc3500; ❄📶🏊) A B&B in an old private home in the residential Ponta Gêa, just off Rua do Comandante Gaivão. The clean rooms come with mosquito nets and swatters. It's good value and friendly, and there's a small garden and pool.

VIP Inn Beira HOTEL $$

(☎23-340100; www.viphotels.com; 172 Rua Luís Inácio; s/d incl breakfast from Mtc4100/4400; ❄📶) All things considered, the VIP is probably your best accommodation bet in Beira's *baixa*, a little oasis of light in an otherwise dark and dingy quarter. The clean, spacious lobby opens a theme that continues upstairs in rooms that are comfortable, if lacking in wow factor. Bank on a substantial buffet breakfast, a relaxing bar and very helpful staff.

★ **Jardim das Velas** HOTEL $$$

(☎23-312209; www.jardimdasvelas.wixsite.com; 282 Avenida das FPLM, Makuti Beach; d/q US$105/120; P❄📶) For a fantastic alternative to the business hotels of Macuti, check into this quiet Mediterranean-style place near the lighthouse. Upstairs are six spotless, modern doubles with views of the sea, and there are six equally well-equipped four-person family rooms with bunks downstairs. A lush walled garden hosts breakfast and an all-day cafe and snack bar that makes excellent waffles.

Hotel Sena BUSINESS HOTEL $$$

(☎23-311070; www.senahotel.net; 189 Avenida Mátires da Revolução; s/d Mtc6500/7800; P❄📶) A few blocks back from Macuti Beach, the Sena styles itself as a business hotel, though there's a boutique edge to its slick lobby and super-modern rooms. The hotel opened in 2010, but a new wing complete with gym

TRAVEL & SECURITY IN CENTRAL MOZAMBIQUE

Following attacks by Renamo opposition forces on buses in the provinces of Sofala, Manica, Tete and Zambézia in 2016, the public-transport system has been in a state of flux. Some services are suspended, several routes are subject to military convoys (p167) and a couple of bus companies are not operating at all. As a result, transport information for the region is particularly liable to change. Check ahead before travelling in central Mozambique and always review the current security situation before setting out.

and restaurant was added in 2016. Service is – as you'd expect – businesslike and it offers cheaper deals at weekends.

Eating

Café Riviera CAFE $
(Praça do Município; mains from Mtc150; 7.30am-9pm Mon-Sat, to 7pm Sun) Head to this old-world street-side cafe for caffeine Portuguese style and a *bolo* (cake) as you watch the passing Beira scene – both the pretty and the gritty. It offers all the usual snacks, including chicken and samosas, in an African colonial atmosphere that'll make you feel as though you've slipped into a Graham Greene novel.

★ **Biques** INTERNATIONAL $$
(23-313051, 84 597 7130; Macuti Beach; mains from Mtc400; 10am-10pm) Biques (pronounced *beaks*) is a sight for sore eyes if you've just emerged bleary-eyed from the bush. Perched on a rise overlooking a windswept scoop of Macuti Beach, it's long been revered by overlanders for its pizza oven, triple-decker club sandwiches and sweet chocolate brownies. Wash your meal down with a frosty beer (served in a *real* beer glass).

Clube Náutico SEAFOOD $$
(23-311720; www.restaurantnautico.com; Avenida das FPLM, Macuti Beach; mains Mtc400-750, plus admission per person Mtc20; 8am-10pm;) This colonial-era swimming and social club is a popular waterside hang-out. Average food and slow service are redeemed by the relaxing beachside setting.

★ **Tutto D'Italy** ITALIAN $$$
(87 427 4569; Rua Vasco Fernando Homen; pasta Mtc400-600, mains Mtc650-850; 11am-10pm;) Top of the list of 'weird epiphanies in Beira' is this fabulous Italian restaurant hidden (there's no sign) in a children's park on the cusp of the Ponta Gêa neighbourhood. All the Italian favourites – antipasti, veal, octopus and pasta dishes – are served here, and all taste as though they've been teleported from Rome or Naples.

Restaurante 2 + 1 AFRICAN $$$
(23-323434; 100 Rua 7; mains Mtc500-1200; 10am-11pm) Get past the cheap 2+1 Takeaway outside and dive into the air-conditioned heaven of this lovely restaurant, a plush, inviting culinary star in the otherwise dilapidated Maquinino neighbourhood. The helpful waiters dress up for work and.the food is (and tastes) equally smart. This being Beira, the fish is king, though it's often doused with Portuguese flavours.

Information

Clínica Avicena (23-327990; Avenida Poder Popular; 24hr) Just north of Praça do Metical.

Getting There & Away

AIR

Beira Airport is 7km northwest of town. There are flights on **LAM** (23-324142, 23-303112; www.lam.co.mz; 85 Rua Major Serpa Pinto) twice weekly to/from Johannesburg, daily to/from Maputo, and several times weekly to/from Tete, Nampula, Pemba and Lichinga. **SAAirlink** (23-301569, 23-301570; www.flyairlink.com; Beira Airport) flies several times weekly between Beira and Jo'burg.

BUS & CHAPA

Beira has several transport hubs depending on what bus company you're using, but the main one is in the Praça do Maquinino area, bounded by Avenidas Daniel Napatima and Samora Machel. There's no real order to things; ask locals where to go for buses to your destination.

Because Beira is off the main north–south EN1, an option for northbound or southbound passengers is to go to Inchope, a scruffy junction 130km west of Beira (Mtc130, three hours), where the EN6 joins the EN1, and try your luck with passing Maputo–Nampula buses there. Warning: they are often full and waits can be long.

Chimoio

To Chimoio (Mtc200, three hours), *chapas* (minivans) go throughout the day from the main transport stand in the city centre. For Gorongosa National Park you'll need to change at Inchope.

Maputo

Numerous companies serve Maputo (Mtc1700, 17 hours), including **Etrago** (82 320 3600; www.etrago.co.mz), departing Tuesday and Thursday at 3pm and Saturday at 3am from Praça do Maquinino in the city centre.

Quelimane

For Quelimane (Mtc700, 10 hours), direct Nagi Investimentos and Maning Nice buses leave daily by 5.30am. Alternatively, some through buses en route to Nampula stop at Nicoadala, from where you can get a *chapa* the remaining 40km.

Vilankulo

To Vilankulo (Mtc550 to Mtc600, 10 hours, daily), there's a direct bus departing by about 4.30am.

Getting Around

Chapas to Makuti (Mtc10) depart from the main transport stand.

The **main taxi stand** is at the western edge of Praça do Maquinino. Taxis don't cruise for business, and companies come and go, so ask your hotel for the updated numbers.

A taxi to the airport should cost between Mtc450 and Mtc500.

Car rental can be arranged at Beira Airport with **Sixt** (☎23-302651; www.sixt.com; Beira Airport) and **Europcar** (☎23-303090; Beira Airport).

Gorongosa National Park

About 170km northwest of Beira is **Gorongosa National Park** (Parque Nacional de Gorongosa; ☎82 308 2252; www.gorongosa.org; adult/child per day US$20/10; ⏲6am-6pm Apr-Dec), which was gazetted in 1960 and soon made headlines as one of Southern Africa's premier wildlife parks. It was once renowned for its large prides of lions, as well as for its elephants, hippos, buffaloes and rhinos, but the civil war during the 1980s and early 1990s destroyed its infrastructure. Rehabilitation work began in 1995, and in 1998 Gorongosa reopened to visitors.

In recent years the park has received a major boost thanks to assistance from the US-based Carr Foundation, which has joined with the government of Mozambique to fund Gorongosa's long-term restoration and ecotourism development.

The Montebelo lodge is the only option in the park itself, though it should be joined by **Muzimu Tented Camp** (www.gorongosacollection.com) in late 2017.

Gorongosa Adventures Campsite CAMPGROUND $
(☎82 957 1436; gorongosainfo@gmail.com) About 9km outside the main gate, and 500m off the park access road, is this unsignposted, unnamed campsite, which works as an option if you arrive after the park closes (6pm). It has twin-bed permanent tents under bamboo roofs; clean, hot showers; and well-equipped cooking facilities. Make contact in advance to check it's open and to confirm prices.

★ **Montebelo Gorongosa Lodge & Safari** LODGE $$
(☎82 308 2252; www.gorongosa.org; s/d Mtc3300/4300, bungalow s/d Mtc4125/5125; P ❄ 📶 ≈) Located at Chitengo park headquarters, Montebelo has lovely comfortable rooms in rondavels or standard blocks. Count on hot water, soap, mosquito nets and night-time coffee. It also offers the opportunity to organise 'fly camps', depositing you deep in the bush with your own tent and guide (US$500 per person for two nights including flight, meals and guide).

Getting There & Away

The park turnoff is at Inchope, about 130km west of Beira, from where it's 43km north along reasonable tarmac to Nota village and then 11km east along an all-weather gravel road to the park gate. From the gate it's another 18km to Montebelo Gorongosa Lodge and park HQ.

The park entrance is reachable with a 2WD. *Chapas* (minibuses) heading north from Inchope to Gorongosa town (Vila Gorongosa), about 25km beyond the park turnoff, will drop you at the turnoff, from where you can arrange a pickup with park staff (bookings essential). Pickups are also possible from Beira, Chimoio and Inchope; see www.gorongosa.net for prices.

Chimoio

Chimoio is a gateway city, not just for travellers heading into and out of Zimbabwe (located 100km west) but also for the dual lures of Chimanimani and Penha Longa, the rugged mountainous frontiers that are loaded with DIY, back-to-nature experiences.

Sleeping

Pink Papaya HOSTEL $
(☎82 555 7310; http://pinkpapaya.atspace.com; cnr Ruas Pigivide & 3 de Fevereiro; dm/s/d/q Mtc500/1000/1300/2000) Pink Papaya is one of the few genuine backpacker hostels in central Mozambique and an excellent orientation point if you've just arrived from Zimbabwe. Located in a salubrious part of town near the governor's mansion, it has helpful management, clean dorm beds and doubles, and a well-equipped kitchen and braai area. Breakfast is available on request.

Residencial Dabhad PENSION $
(☎251-23264; http://dabhad.com; cnr Ruas do Bárue & dos Agricultores; r incl breakfast from Mtc1750; P ❄ 📶) The Dabhad offers good value: friendly, basic twin or double rooms have TV, hot water and even mini toothbrushes. No meals apart from breakfast.

★**Residencial Chinfura** B&B $$
(251-22640; Avenida Liberdade; r Mtc2200-3300; P) In terms of value for money, this is probably the best accommodation option in Chimoio. Located on the edge of the main town behind a guarded entrance, the large rooms are separated from the main house and have their own pleasant terrace and breakfast room. Beds are large, towels are thick, there are coffee-making facilities and the wi-fi is strong.

Hotel Castelo Branco HOTEL $$$
(82 522 5960, 251-23934; Rua Sussundenga; s/d incl breakfast Mtc7200/8200; P) Castelo Branco looks alluring from the outside, but inside it's beige, bare and, frankly, overpriced. Not that you'll be uncomfortable: the hotel's clean and spacious, and the service is good. The place just lacks sparkle. Making up for the lack of character are a small garden, a pleasant pool and a hearty breakfast buffet.

Eating

Banana Split BURGERS, SNACKS $
(cnr Ruas Pigivide & Dr Araujo de la Cerda; snacks Mtc150-400; 7am-9pm) This new locally run place offers a Mozambican take on fast food, with burgers, wraps, samosas and desserts served in a small, bright four-table cafe or available for takeaway. The daily cakes are delightful.

Restaurante-Bar Jumbo EUROPEAN $
(Rua do Bárue; mains about Mtc300; 10am-9pm) The basic but reliable Jumbo has grilled chicken and continental dishes. Seating is downstairs in a dark bar or in a cosy wood-panelled room upstairs.

Ponto do Encontro CAFE $$
(Avenida 25 de Setembro; mains Mtc350-650; 7am-9pm) The aptly named 'meeting point' is one of the town's best meeting and eating places, both as a Portuguese-style cafe (the coffee and pastries are excellent) and as a restaurant. The house special is chicken in mushroom sauce, served with rice and chips. It also has a buffet-style counter at lunchtime.

★**Restaurante Maúa** AFRICAN $$$
(Feria Popular, EN6; mains Mtc500-800; 11am-10pm Tue-Sun) Tap any local with taste buds and they'll probably tell you that this place – one of several restaurants in the **Feira Popular** (EN6) complex – serves the best food in Chimoio, possibly even central Mozambique. The menu leans heavily towards Mozambican flavours, with excellent tiger prawns, piri-piri chicken, steak and *matapa* (cassava leaves sauteed with cashews and coconut milk).

Information

Eco-Micaia Office (82 303 4285; www.micaia.org) The office of local foundation Eco-Micaia can offer info on Ndzou Camp and the Chimanimani Reserve in general. It's behind the Shoprite supermarket just off the main EN1 highway.

Getting There & Away

There are three flights weekly on **LAM** (251-24715; Hotel Inter, Av 25 de Setembro; 8.30am-4.30pm Mon-Fri, 8am-noon Sat) to Maputo, with some flights also stopping in Beira. The tiny airport is 10km from town, and signposted about 5km west of Chimoio along the Manica road.

Most transport leaves from the main bus station, near the train station. Several bus companies operate out of Chimoio, including national stalwarts Maning Nice and Nagi Investimentos. The Nagi office is next to **Shoprite** (EN6; 9am-8pm Mon-Sat, to 3pm Sun) supermarket.

Manica

Little Manica, 70km west of Chimoio, is situated in what was once the heart of the kingdom of Manica and an important gold-trading area. The surrounding region makes good hiking terrain.

All transport departs from the market, diagonally opposite Millennium BIM. *Chapas* (minibuses) run frequently to/from Chimoio (Mtc65, one hour) and to the Zimbabwean border (Mtc25, 30 minutes).

Chinamapere Rock Paintings ARCHAEOLOGICAL SITE
Depicting animal and human figures, these rock paintings are thousands of years old (exact dates vary) and are thought to have been left by the San people. Locals consider the site sacred. The paintings are located about 5km from town and are signposted ('*pinturas rupestres*').

Geology Museum MUSEUM
(Museu de Geologia; 251-24433; 7am-3.30pm Mon-Fri) FREE This collection of rocks highlighting the local geology is probably less interesting than the handsome colonial building in which it's housed – it dates from 1883.

The museum is enlivened by a few recently added explanation boards (in Portuguese).

Sleeping

Manica Lodge LODGE $

(☎251-62452; Bairro Josina Machel; small/large rondavel d Mtc1700/2200; P ❄ 📶) At the western end of town, about 400m off the main road (the signposted turnoff's just after the immigration office), this agreeable establishment has stone rondavels scattered like hobbit houses around tranquil, manicured gardens. The larger ones are reasonably spacious and have a TV. There's also a good restaurant (mains Mtc300 to Mtc600) and friendly, helpful staff.

Pensão Flamingo PENSION $

(☎251-62385; EN6; r Mtc1500; ❄) On the main road a few blocks west of Millennium BIM, this small-town resthouse-style place is a cut above your average African roadside digs. Simple, clean rooms come with bathroom, towels and air-con units, plus there's a reasonable restaurant (mains Mtc150 to Mtc350) downstairs.

Chimanimani Mountains

Silhouetted against the horizon on the Zimbabwean border southwest of Chimoio are the surprisingly green and wooded Chimanimani Mountains, with **Mt Binga** (2436m), Mozambique's highest peak, rising up on their eastern edge. Much of the range is encompassed by the **Chimanimani National Reserve** (Reserva Nacional de Chimanimani; adult/vehicle/camping Mtc400/400/200), which is part of the larger Chimanimani Transfrontier Conservation Area (ACTF), together with Chimanimani National Park in Zimbabwe.

It's possible to hike throughout the mountains, but facilities are scant and public transport practically nonexistent. Consequently most visitors come in their own 4WDs, armed with tents and plenty of supplies. Those who come generally make a beeline for Mt Binga, which can be climbed in two days, with one night spent on the mountain – the best starting point is Chikukwa, where guides (essential) and porters can be arranged. Travellers lucky enough to climb Binga often list it as one of their Mozambique highlights.

To reach the main reserve entrance *(portão)* on the Mussapa Pequeno River via public transport, take a *chapa* (minibus) from Chimoio to Sussundenga (one hour, Mtc45). Once in Sussundenga, you'll need to wait for another vehicle going towards Rotanda. After passing Munhinga, watch for the signposted Chimanimani turnoff. Ask the bus driver to drop you at 'container', from where you'll have to walk 4km along a track through lovely miombo (woodland) to the reserve entrance. From there, it's another 26km to Chikukwa Camp, starting point for the Mt Binga climb.

Drivers should head 15km south of Sussundenga to Munhinga and then branch west towards Rotunda. At 'container' turn south again into the reserve.

Ndzou Camp CAMPGROUND, HUT $

(☎82 303 4285, 86 779 1665; camping per tent Mtc500, dm Mtc750, rondavel d Mtc2500) Ndzou Camp, a joint venture between Eco-Micaia (p132) and the local community, is a basic back-to-nature place in the middle of Moribane Forest Reserve with admirable eco-credentials (solar-powered lighting and recycled rainwater). It offers camping, rondavels and a small family lodge; for the time being, it's the only real non-camping place to stay in the Chimanimani area.

Tete

There are two Tetes: the hot, dusty, frenetic city that greets you with all the subtlety of a microwave oven during the day, and the cool, sedate, infinitely more inviting place that seduces you at sunset.

Straddling the mighty Zambezi, Tete has been an important trade centre and river crossing for centuries. There was a Swahili settlement here long before the Portuguese arrived in the 1530s, and the Europeans quickly established it as a base for ivory and gold marketing. These days the river is forded by two bridges, the impressive Samora Machel suspension bridge, dating from 1973, and a second, more functional road bridge that opened in 2014.

For travellers, Tete is primarily a journey breaker on the way to Malawi or Zambia, or a base to visit the Cahora Bassa dam area.

Sleeping

Guesthouse Milano GUESTHOUSE $

(☎84 843 9547; Avenida Independencia No 1727; d Mtc2500; ❄ 📶 🏊) This attractive guesthouse is a dark horse on the accommodation scene, tucked away on a side street in the city centre. Quiet rooms out the back are large, fresh and well tended, and a small plunge pool decorates an appealing courtyard.

Motel Tete MOTEL $
(☎252-22345, 82 588 2040; N103; r from Mtc2500; P❄📶🏊) If you can handle the slightly out-of-town setting (which has its advantages in hot, hectic Tete), this Tete institution is an excellent option, set off by its location overlooking the river. The 'motel' moniker doesn't do the place justice. Rooms are large and light-filled with all amenities, and there's a handy on-site restaurant and swimming pool.

It's about 15 minutes on foot from Tete town centre along the main road to Changara.

Hotel Inter Tete BUSINESS HOTEL $$
(☎251-24200; www.interhotels.co.mz; 18B Avenida 25 de Setembro; r from Mtc6500; P❄📶🏊) Tete's newest hotel is a large, business-like affair with modern, functional rooms, well-manicured grounds and a few bells and whistles – the gym and spa area are particularly pleasant. The main sticking point is the location, which is a little out in the sticks and fails to capitalise on the city's prime riverside setting.

Villa Habsburg GUESTHOUSE $$$
(☎252-20323; www.villahabsburg.com; s/d US$120/200; ❄📶) Possibly the most un-Tete-like of all Tete's accommodation is this lovely B&B in a renovated mansion on the north bank of the river about 1km downriver from the suspension bridge. It has four well-appointed rooms, arty common areas, a cricket-pitch-quality lawn and impressive river views.

Eating

VIP Café INTERNATIONAL, CAFE $$
(cnr Avenidas da Liberdade & Julius Nyerere; mains Mtc180-450; ⏲7am-9pm) This clean, air-conditioned restaurant might lack your typical Mozambican feel, but it's the best place to grab a coffee, ice cream, pastry or salad while cooling off.

★ **Café del Río** INTERNATIONAL $$$
(☎84 746 3740; www.cafedelrio.co.za; mains Mtc500-1000; ⏲8am-10.30pm Tue-Thu, to midnight Fri & Sat, to 9.30pm Sun) When Tete's heat has melted you to a runny pulp, revive your spirits at Cafe del Rio, a beautiful thatched restaurant furnished like an upmarket African safari lodge that catches gorgeous sunsets over the Zambezi. You can easily while away a whole evening here playing chess, smoking cigars, knocking back cocktails and enjoying steak and the local speciality, *pende* fish.

Getting There & Away

AIR

LAM (☎252-22056; Avenida 24 de Julho; ⏲8.30am-4.30pm Mon-Fri) flies several times weekly to/from Maputo, Beira, Lichinga, Nampula, Quelimane and Johannesburg. There are also international flights to Harare (Zimbabwe) and Lilongwe (Malawi). Tete's **Chingozi Airport** is 6km from town on the Moatize road (Mtc500 in a taxi); take any *chapa* (minibus) heading to Moatize.

BUS & CHAPA

Due to political unrest in late 2016, transport in and out of Tete is in a state of flux. Check on arrival for updates and proceed with caution.

Most long-distance buses to places such as Maputo, Beira and Chimoio depart from the Interprovincial Transport Terminal at Retiro, about 8km south of Tete (Mtc300 in a taxi).

Beira

To/from Beira, services are handled by Nagi Investimentos and Acai; they depart Tete at 6am most days (Mtc700, seven to eight hours), political unrest permitting.

Chimoio

To/from Chimoio (Mtc500, six to seven hours), the first departures in each direction are between 4.30am and 5am, which means that, theoretically, if you're travelling from Chimoio to Blantyre (Malawi) via Tete, you'll be able to make the journey in one long day without overnighting in Tete, after walking across the bridge to catch transport to Zóbuè.

Moatize

For Moatize (Mtc15), *chapas* depart throughout the day from the Moatize bus stand on Rua do Qua in the city centre.

Songo

To Songo (for Cahora Bassa Dam), several pickups daily depart from the old *correios* (post office) building in the lower part of town near the cathedral (Mtc190).

Ulóngwe

To Ulóngwe, there is at least one direct *chapa* departing daily from Mercado da OUA. Otherwise, take any car heading to Zóbuè, get out at the Angónia junction about 15km before Zóbuè and get onward transport from there.

Cahora Bassa Dam & Songo

Songo (150km northwest of Tete) is a purpose-built Mozambican town constructed specifically for builders raising massive Cahora Bassa dam, the fifth-largest dam in the world. The dam is set at the head of a magnificent gorge in the mountains and makes a good day or overnight trip from Tete. It's also a wonderful destination for anglers, and is renowned for its tiger fish.

Chapas (minibuses) run several times daily between Tete and Songo (Mtc150, three to four hours), departing Tete from the old *correios* (post office) building. Once in Songo, it's another 7km down to the dam – you'll have to walk or hitch. Ugezi Tiger Lodge does pick-ups from Tete (US$180 for a car fitting six people).

Hidroeléctrica de Cahora Bassa DAM
(HCB; ☎252-82157, 252-82224, 252-82221) The dam, including the impressive underground turbine rooms, can be visited by advance arrangement only. Contact Hidroeléctrica de Cahora Bassa in Songo – look for the HCB office in the *substação* (substation) and ask for Relações Públicas (Public Relations), or ask at one of the hotels. There's no charge for a visit, and permits are no longer necessary to enter Songo. However, you'll need to get a letter of approval from HCB; allow at least 24 hours.

Sleeping & Eating

Centro Social do HCB BUNGALOW $
(☎252-82666; r Mtc2500;) This pleasant place in the town centre has clean, comfortable twin-bed rooms set in large, manicured grounds. All rooms have fridge, window screens and private bathroom with hot water. Breakfast is extra.

Songo Hotel by Montebelo HOTEL $$
(☎252-8270407; www.montebelohotels.com; Barrio Norte; s/d/ste Mtc6000/7000/8000; P) If you're feeling isolated in Songo, head to one of the Montebelo group's newer acquisitions (formerly Hotel Girassol), a small but select place with pleasant gardens, a pool with sunloungers and modern rooms with flat-screen TV and (usually) wi-fi. The restaurant – all white tablecloths and polished glasses – is equally recommendable.

Ugezi Tiger Lodge LODGE $$
(☎84 599 8410; www.ugezitigerlodge.co.za; camping Mtc600, s/d Mtc2750/5150; P) Anglers, or anyone wanting an escape to nature, will love this rustic fishing camp perched on a hill overlooking Lake Cahora Bassa. Choose between camping; basic, somewhat faded chalets on the densely vegetated hillside; and a self-catering houseboat. It's all very no-frills, but the morning scenery on the lake at the base of the property (there's no beachfront) is beautiful.

Caia

This village is the main north–south crossing point over the Zambezi River – the 2376m-long Armando Emílio Guebuza Bridge opened in 2009. It's mainly used as a pit stop on the journey between Beira and Quelimane, but there's a forest reserve with overnight accommodation 30km to the south that's one of the best places in Mozambique for birdwatching.

M'phingwe Lodge LODGE $
(☎82 301 6436; www.mphingwe.com; EN1; cabins Mtc900-1250, without bathroom Mtc600-850, cottages Mtc1550-2950) Located in **Catapu Forest Reserve** (www.dalmann.com; EN1), M'phingwe has six rustic but spotless double cabins (two with shared bathroom) and two family cottages. There's an on-site restaurant with simple, meat-heavy meals plus a network of trails in the adjacent forest offering excellent birdwatching. The complex is 32km south of Caia on the main EN1 road. No camping.

Quelimane

Quelimane is a small city with a scruffy sensibility that acts as a convenient waystation for travellers jockeying between northern and southern Mozambique, or overlanders heading for the border with Malawi. The mainstay of the local economy is the coconut, best enjoyed in a sauce atop your chicken known as *frango à zambeziana*.

Sleeping & Eating

Hotel Chuabo HOTEL $
(☎24-213182, 24-213181; 232 Avenida Samora Machel; s/d Mtc2975/3150;) The Chuabo is a Quelimane institution, one of the few hotels anywhere in Mozambique that managed to stay running throughout the war

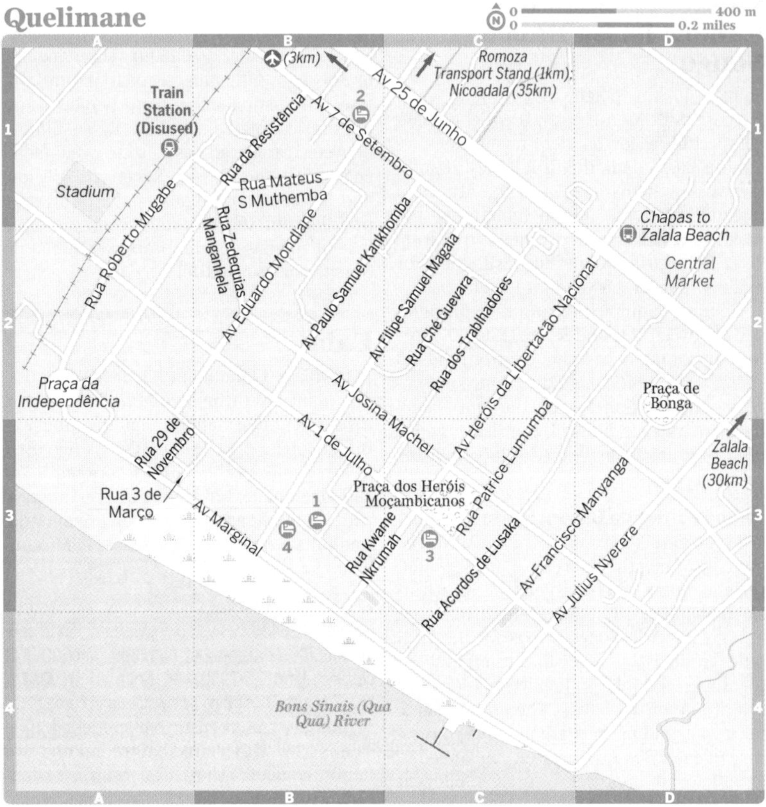

Quelimane

Sleeping

1 Hotel Chuabo B3
2 Hotel Elite B1
3 Hotel Flamingo C3
4 Pensão 1 de Julho B3

years. These days the whole place reeks of another era – if you like (unintentional) retro, this is your bag. Drink in the furry carpets, oversized bedrooms, wood-strip walls and – best of all – curvaceous staircase that spirals down six levels.

Pensão 1 de Julho HOTEL $
(☎24-213067; cnr Avenidas Samora Machel & Filipe Samuel Magaia; tw Mtc2000, without bathroom Mtc1500; ❄) The 1st of July is distinctly old-fashioned, or maybe those dusty wooden animal carvings were never in fashion – who knows? Near the old cathedral, this faded budget choice has reasonable rooms with fan, sink and bucket shower, and a central location near the river. Skip the food.

Hotel Elite HOTEL $$
(☎24-219900; www.elitehotels.com; cnr Avenidas 7 de Setembro & Eduardo Mondlane; r/ste Mtc3900/5600; ❄ 📶 🏊) Look out, Quelimane: the accommodation bar has been raised! Seeming small and relatively modest, the new Hotel Elite is something of a palace behind its outer skin and not as small as the exterior suggests. The 23 deluxe rooms come with all mod-cons, and a number are equipped with king-sized beds and sofas.

Hotel Flamingo HOTEL $$
(☎82 552 7810, 24-215602; www.hotelflamingoquelimane.com; cnr Rua Kwame Nkrumah & Avenida 1 de Julho; incl breakfast s Mtc2000-3200, d Mtc2500-3800; P ❄ 📶 🏊) This pop-

ular hotel opposite Praça dos Heróis has two levels of motel-style rooms arranged around a central pool and restaurant. It's nothing to look at from the outside but far more salubrious within. The substantial breakfasts come with eggs, chips and baked beans.

Getting There & Away

The transport stand (known locally as 'Romoza') is at the northern end of Avenida Eduardo Mondlane. *Chapas* (minibuses) run frequently to/from **Nicoadala** at the junction with the main road (Mtc50, 45 minutes). Routes south towards Beira were in flux in late 2016 due to political unrest.

BEIRA

To Beira (Mtc700, 10 hours) there's a daily bus leaving between 4am and 5am.

CHIMOIO

To Chimoio (Mtc750, eight hours), a Maning Nice bus departs daily at 3am from its office on Avenida Eduardo Mondlane, about 1km past the Romoza transport stand and on the opposite side of the road.

GURÚÈ

To Gurúè (Mtc350, six hours) there's a bus daily at 4.30am; buy your ticket the day before. Even with a ticket, it's best to show up early at the bus stand to be sure of a seat.

NAMPULA

To Nampula, Nagi Investimentos and Maning Nice buses depart daily at around 4.30am (Mtc700, 10 hours). Several vehicles also run daily to **Mocuba** (Mtc200, two to three hours), from where you can get onward transport to Nampula via Alto Molócuè, or to the Malawi border at Milange.

ZALALA

Chapas to Zalala (Mtc50, one hour) depart Quelimane from next to the central market, at the corner of Avenidas Heróis da Libertação Nacional and 25 de Junho.

OFF THE BEATEN TRACK

ZALALA BEACH

The closest beach to Quelimane is Zalala Beach, about 30km northeast of town. Long and wide, with a row of fringing palms and a large village nearby, it's an ideal day excursion for getting a taste of local Zambézian life. The drive out from Quelimane is bumpy and scenic, through extensive coconut plantations formerly owned by Companhia da Zambézia. For overnighting, try the lovely **Zalala Beach Lodge** (☎24-217055, 84 390 1630; www.zbls.org; s/d US$100/150, with half board US$115/180, with full board US$125/200; P ❄ ≋) . *Chapas* (minibuses) to Zalala Beach (Mtc50, one hour) depart Quelimane from next to the central market.

Mocuba

The large, lively town of Mocuba is the junction for travel between Quelimane and Nampula or Malawi. It's home to a large market and an impressive 300m-long bridge over the wide, gently flowing Licungo River. Travellers stop here to cool off, fuel up, grab a snack and use the ATM.

Transport to Quelimane (Mtc200, two to three hours) leaves from the market throughout the day. For Nampula (Mtc500), the best bet is to try to get a seat on the Nagi bus from Quelimane, which passes Mocuba from about 7am. There are several vehicles daily in the morning between Mocuba and Milange (Mtc300, four hours), departing from Mocuba's market, though you'll maximise your chances of a lift by walking west past the airstrip to the Milange road junction. Mocuba to Gurúè costs around Mtc250.

Pensão Cruzeiro PENSION $
(☎24-810184; Avenida Eduardo Mondlane; tw/d Mtc1000/1200; P ❄) Bog-standard African resthouse with dark, grubby-looking rooms that do, at least, have running water, air-con and soap.

Padaria e Pasteleria Africa BAKERY $
(Avenida Eduardo Mondlane; snacks from Mtc50; ⏲7am-6pm) Don't judge a book by its cover: this rather bare-looking bakery knocks out super-fresh, melt-in-your-mouth pastries.

Gurúè

Floating like a hazy apparition amid sloping tea plantations, with the solid mass of Mt Namúli (2419m), Mozambique's second-highest peak, standing sentinel in the background, Gurúè is a joy to behold, especially after the long and bumpy journey to get here. Rest assured: every bump is worth it. This is one of Mozambique's primary hiking areas, where you can stroll through tea plantations at sunset, take a picnic to a local waterfall or address the steep (and sacred) slopes of Mt Namúli.

Pensão Gurúè PENSION $
(☎82 579 4512; pensao.gurue@gmail.com; Avenida Eduardo Mondlane; r Mtc2500; ❄) On the main street in the lower part of town, this pension is *the* place in Gurúè, not just for its simple, comfortable rooms but also for its affiliated restaurant downstairs and the fact that it acts as an information portal for the area. Austrian owner Peter has been here for 20 years and knows the area intimately.

Getting There & Away

Transport in Gurúè departs from near the market at the lower end of town.

There's at least one daily bus to Nampula (Mtc350, six hours); otherwise you'll have to do the journey in stages, changing in Nampevo and possibly also Alto Molócuè. Buses leave at 5am or earlier – essential if you're trying to make a connection in Nampevo.

For connections to/from Quelimane, there's a daily direct *chapa* (minibus) departing at 4.30am (Mtc350, six hours); buy tickets the day before. Otherwise there are several vehicles daily to Mocuba (Mtc250, 3½ to four hours), from where you can continue to Quelimane.

There's usually one vehicle daily between Cuamba and Gurúè (Mtc250 to Mtc300, five hours).

NORTHERN MOZAMBIQUE

With tranquil Lake Niassa to the west, wild Niassa Reserve in the centre and the palm-fringed islands of the Quirimbas Archipelago off the east coast, northern Mozambique is the country's last frontier, a potpourri of mystery, intrigue and adventure. While poor roads and remoteness can make travel here a challenge, it's never boring. However, with natural gas recently discovered in the area, the north may change quickly. Visit soon, before the magic disappears.

Nampula

Anchored by its white cathedral and embellished with a museum, Nampula is worth a brief stopover if you're in the area. Indeed, many travellers find themselves resting up here before pitching north to Pemba or east to Mozambique Island.

Sights & Activities

Cathedral of Nossa Senhora de Fátima CATHEDRAL
(Avenida Eduardo Mondlane) Easily Nampula's most handsome and attention-drawing sight, the creamy white city cathedral dates from the late colonial period: the Portuguese finished building it in 1956. After admiring its twin towers and elegant dome, head inside to see the colourful stained glass and – if you're lucky – catch the choir in full song.

WORTH A TRIP

HIKES FROM GURÚÈ

Mt Namúli Rising up from the hills about 15km northeast of Gurúè are the mist-shrouded slopes of **Mt Namúli** (2419m), from which flow the Licungo (Lugela) and Malema Rivers. If you find yourself in the area with time to spare, it makes a scenic but challenging climb for which you'll need a good level of fitness and lack of a fear of heights (as there are several near-vertical spots where you'll need to clamber on all fours).

Cascata Don't worry if you haven't the time or energy to summit Mt Namúli. Equally memorable is the 8km (one way) hike to the *cascata* (waterfall) in the hills north of town. Take a picnic, carry plenty of water and allow an easy day for the excursion. A guide isn't required, as you'll encounter plenty of local villagers and tea pickers along the route.

To get there, head first to the UP4 tea factory (also known as Chá Sambique), which you can see in the distance to the north; ask locals to point out the way and allow about 45 minutes on foot. From UP4 it's approximately another two hours on foot along a winding track through the tea plantations to the falls, which will be to your right. Swimming is possible in the pools above the cascades.

Museu Nacional de Etnografia MUSEUM
(National Ethnography Museum; Avenida Eduardo Mondlane; Mtc100; ⌚9am-5pm Tue-Fri, 2-5pm Sat & Sun) This museum makes a gallant effort to showcase the life and culture of Mozambique's complicated tribes and ethnic groups, although the end product is a little dusty and lacking in resources. Most interesting are the exhibits dedicated to Makonde culture around the town of Mueda in Cabo Delgado province. Even better, there's a Makonde Collective (p140) selling handmade artefacts out the back.

Complexo Bamboo Swimming Pool SWIMMING
(Ribáuè Rd; adult/child Mtc250/150) This leafy complex 7km northwest of Nampula's city centre has a pool and makes a good spot to cool off.

Sleeping

Ruby Nampula HOSTEL $
(☎84 206 7756; rubybackpackers@outlook.com; Rua Daniel Napatima; dm/d Mtc750/1850; 📶) Ruby's has clean dormitories and a couple of private doubles. There's hot water, a self-catering kitchen and a small bar selling snacks and cakes. (There's another Ruby's on Mozambique Island (p144). Once jointly owned, they've recently separated. However, there's still some reciprocity between the two.) The staff are very helpful with onward-travel information – this is a good jumping-off point for Mozambique Island.

Complexo Bamboo CHALET $
(☎26-216595, 26-217838; bamboo@teledata.mz; Ribáuè Rd; s/d/ste Mtc2350/2750/3750; P ❄ 🏊) Well-maintained rooms (the twins are nicer than the doubles) in expansive grounds with a playground make this a good choice for families. All rooms have TV and mini fridge, and there's a popular restaurant. It's about 7km out of town; follow Avenida de Trabalho west from the train station, then right onto Ribáuè Rd; Bamboo is 1.5km down on the left.

Quality Residencial HOTEL $
(☎26-217872, 26-216871; www.residencialquality.com; 953 Avenida de Trabalho; s/d/ste from Mtc2200/2500/2950; P ❄ 📶) Over a decade old and showing it, the Quality is about 1km from the city centre along the Quelimane road, meaning it's handy for most bus departures (the station's a 10-minute walk with bags). Rooms are a little dark and worn but have various amenities, including kettle and hot water. Service is friendly.

★**Hotel Milénio** HOTEL $$
(☎26-218877; 842 Avenida 25 de Setembro; d/ste Mtc3900/4500; ❄ @ 📶 🏊) What might look like a standard business hotel has raised the game in Nampula with some useful bonuses, most notably a gym (with proper working machines), a sizeable outdoor pool, well-equipped, surgically clean rooms and, arguably, the best restaurant in town. For what you get, the price is a veritable bargain.

Residencial Primavera HOTEL $$
(☎26-214600; www.residprimavera.blogspot.ca; Rua 1024; r incl breakfast Mtc3500; ❄ 📶 🏊) Hidden behind the museum, this thoroughly decent new option offers a lot more than its ordinary exterior suggests. Rooms are furnished to a high standard and well stocked with complimentary water, bathroom ablutions, coffee-making equipment and fluffy towels. There's a small, modern breakfast room and a patio hosting a pool and a huddle of gym equipment. Service is professionally friendly.

Nampula Hotel by Montebelo HOTEL $$
(☎26-216000; www.montebelohotels.com; 326 Avenida Eduardo Mondlane; s/d Mtc3785/4435; P ❄ 📶) The former Girassol hotel, now rebranded, isn't really one of the Montebelo chain's most inspiring options and is overrated with four stars. The ugly high-rise building (in which the hotel occupies the 4th floor) doesn't help. Rooms are business bland, with TV, mini fridge and beige decor. The restaurant is three floors down on the 1st floor.

Eating

★**Hotel Milénio Restaurant** INDIAN $$
(842 Avenida 25 de Setembro; mains Mtc450-700; ⌚12.30-3pm & 6.30-10pm) Equipped with a chef from Mumbai, this sleek restaurant at Hotel Milénio knocks out the best Indian food in northern Mozambique, with excellent meat and vegetarian dishes. Recommended is the lamb biriyani, the *bhuna* and the chicken tikka. All come with lashings of rice and/or naan. Equally spicy are some finely seasoned Mozambican standards. No alcohol served.

Nampula

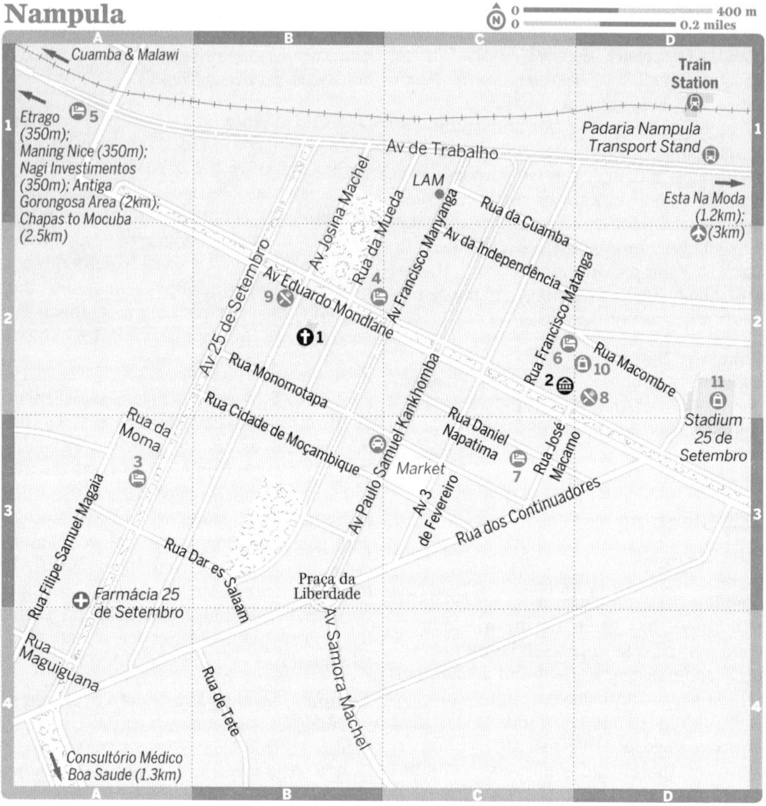

VIP Cafe INTERNATIONAL **$$**
(cnr Avenidas Eduardo Mondlane & Josina Machel; snacks from Mtc100, mains Mtc400-600; ⏲7am-10pm) This clean, new, impossibly inviting nook in a glassy shopping centre draws you in with its shiny espresso machine and display case replete with fresh pastries. Cakes aside, there's a full laminated menu of sandwiches, burgers and fuller dishes, some with Lebanese inflections.

Sporting Clube de Nampula EUROPEAN **$$**
(Avenida Eduardo Mondlane; mains Mtc300-600; ⏲8am-10pm; ☑) You're practically guaranteed to meet a fellow traveller or expat at this shady post-colonial watering hole next to the ethnography museum. Some just come for beers and conversation at the outdoor bar. Others gravitate to the indoor dining area for *bife a portuguesa* (steak and eggs), grilled fish, *feijoada* (beans and sausages) and a couple of Chinese-influenced plates.

Shopping

Makonde Collective ARTS & CRAFTS
(Avenida Eduardo Mondlane; ⏲9am-5pm Tue-Fri, 2-5pm Sat & Sun) *The* place to buy Makonde crafts – primarily the legendary woodcarvings – plus you can see the craftspeople at work. It's located in an open compound behind the ethnology museum.

Sunday Morning Craft Market ARTS & CRAFTS
(stadium; ⏲dawn-noon Sun) Held in the town's large stadium, this market is a good place for crafts. Go early, before things get hot and crowded.

Information

Consultório Médico Boa Saude (☎84 460 5170, 84 601 5600; Rua dos Viveiros, Bairro Muahivire) One of the better bets if you're ill. Just off Avenida das FPLM.

Nampula

Sights

1 Cathedral of Nossa Senhora de Fátima B2
2 Museu Nacional de Etnografia C2

Sleeping

3 Hotel Milénio A3
4 Nampula Hotel by Montebelo B2
5 Quality Residencial A1
6 Residencial Primavera C2
7 Ruby Nampula C3

Eating

Hotel Milénio Restaurant .... (see 3)
8 Sporting Clube de Nampula D2
9 VIP Cafe B2

Shopping

10 Makonde Collective D2
11 Sunday Morning Craft Market D2

Farmácia 25 de Setembro (Avenida 25 de Setembro; 8am-6pm Mon-Sat, 9am-1pm Sun) Just down from Hotel Milénio.

Getting There & Away

AIR

Nampula Airport is very handily positioned just 4km northeast of the city centre (Mtc200 in a taxi).

There are flights on **LAM** (26-213322, 26-212801; Avenida Francisco Manyanga; 8am-4pm Mon-Fri, 9.30am-11.30am Sat) to Maputo daily, and to Beira, Lichinga, Quelimane, Tete and Pemba several times weekly. There are also flights to Johannesburg (South Africa), Nairobi (Kenya) and Lilongwe (Malawi).

BUS & CHAPA

Most long-distance buses depart from next to the Petromac petrol station in the Antiga Gorongosa area (from the train station, follow Avenida de Trabalho west for around 2km). Companies with ticket offices here include **Maning Nice** (82 706 2820; Avenida de Trabalho), **Nagi Investimentos** (84 955 1669, 84 265 7082; Avenida de Trabalho) and Etrago. Note that Nagi Investimentos services to Pemba and other destinations in Cabo Delgado province leave from another location near the airport roundabout in the east of town. Esta Na Moda ticketing and departures are at a roundabout 1.5km east of the train station. Most services leave at the crack of dawn.

Beira

Nagi Investimentos and Maning Nice both service Beira (Mtc1500 to Mtc1700, 16 hours) daily, departing at 3am.

Cuamba

Nagi Investimentos serves Cuamba (Mtc400, seven hours) daily, leaving at 5am.

Lichinga

Nagi Investimentos serves Lichinga (Mtc1000, 15 hours), leaving Thursday and Saturday at 4am.

Moçimboa da Praia & Mueda

Maning Nice services Moçimboa da Praia (Mtc600, 13 hours, daily), Mueda (Mtc700, daily) and Montepuez (Mtc500, nine hours, daily).

Mocuba

Maning Nice buses run to Mocuba (Mtc500) or you can opt for a cheaper but slower and less comfortable *chapa*.

Mozambique Island

To Mozambique Island (Mtc200, three to four hours) *chapas* depart between 5am and 11am from the transport stand along Avenida do Trabalho just outside the train station. Look for one that's going direct; many go only to Monapo, where you'll need to stand on the roadside and wait for another vehicle. The best connections are found on one of the *tanzaniano chapas*, which depart Nampula between about 7am and 10am, depending on how early they arrive from Mozambique Island, and which continue more or less nonstop to the island. This transport stand is also the place to find *chapas* to Mossuril, Namapa and other points north and east.

Pemba

To Pemba (Mtc500, six to seven hours) your best bet is Nagi Investimentos (daily from between 3am and 5am) or Esta Na Moda, with a daily service leaving at noon.

Quelimane

To Quelimane (Mtc600 to Mtc700, 10 hours), Maning Nice and Nagi Investimentos buses leave daily at 3am and 4am respectively.

TRAIN

A passenger train connects Nampula and Cuamba. It traditionally ran daily (except Monday) in either direction. However, since 2015, due to line rehabilitation and preference being given to freight (mainly coal), it has been reduced to a twice-weekly passenger service leaving Nampula on Saturday and Tuesday at 5am. Hopefully it will revert to its full schedule soon. The spectacular but typically African journey takes 10 to 12 hours. There are theoretically three classes of carriage (executive/1st/2nd Mtc600/400/170), although they might not function on all trips. It's well worth investing in executive if you can.

Tickets can be purchased between 2pm and 5pm on the day before travel (but not earlier).

Boarding starts at 4am. Arrive early and bring plenty of snacks. As with all Mozambican transport, be sure to check ahead for current schedules at the **train station** (☎21-344800; www.cdn.co.mz; 1000 Avenida de Trabalho).

Getting Around

The main **taxi rank** (Avenida Paulo Samuel Kankhomba) is near the market. For car hire, **Sixt** (☎82 300 5170, 26-216312; www.sixt.com), **Europcar** (☎84 322 3473; www.europcar.com) and several others are at the airport.

Mozambique Island

Dhows shifting silently through shallow seas, bruised colonial buildings withering elegantly in the tropical heat, and the voices of a church choir competing with the muezzin's call to prayer. You'll encounter all this and more within the crowded confines of Mozambique Island, one of the historical highlights of Africa, a fragrant melange of African, Portuguese, Swahili, French and Goan flavours left to mellow in the iridescent waters of the Indian Ocean for centuries.

Half-forgotten until it was recognised as a World Heritage Site in 1991 and still bizarrely overlooked by the average African safari enthusiast, the diminutive island (500m wide by 3km long) protects a romantic cluster of semi-ruined, semi-restored edifices known as Stone Town in its northern half. Further south lies Makuti Town, a crowded collection of dishevelled reed houses that's home to 15,000 Mozambicans.

Sights

While wandering through Stone Town, watch for the restored, ochre-toned **BIM building** (Avenida Amilcar Cabral) and the ornate **colonial administration offices** overlooking the gardens east of the **hospital**, itself an impressive neoclassical building. A few blocks north of the market is the recently restored **Hindu temple** and, on the island's western edge, a fairly modern **mosque** (Rua da Solidariedade) painted an unmissable shade of green.

Mozambique Island

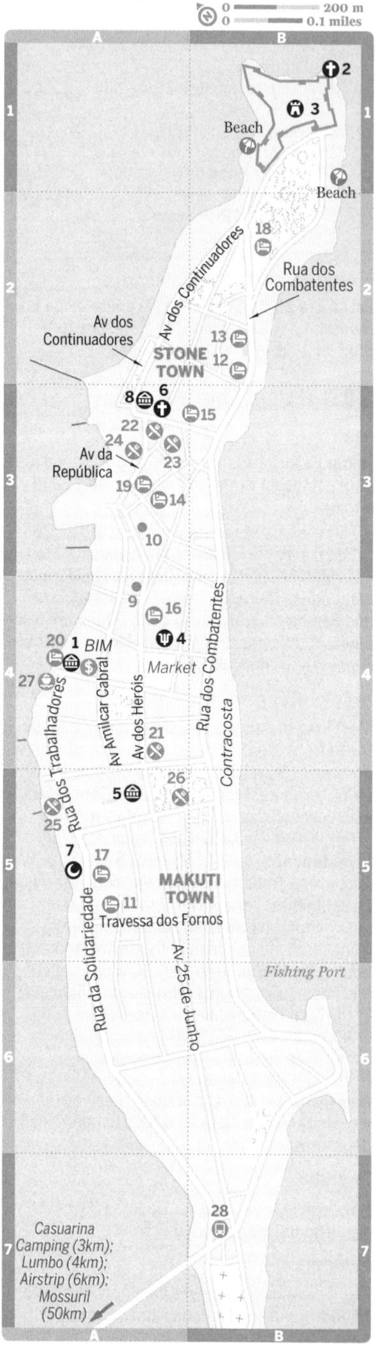

Mozambique Island

Palace & Chapel of São Paulo MUSEUM
(Palácio de São Paulo; ☎26-610081; adult/child Mtc100/50; ⊙8am-4.30pm) This imposing terracotta edifice – the former governor's residence and now a museum – dates from 1610. The interior hosts the recently refurbished **Museu de Artes Decorativas**, which gives a remarkable glimpse of what upper-class life must have been like during the island's 18th-century heyday. In addition to household items from Portugal, Arabia, India and China, there are many pieces of original furniture, including an important collection of beautifully ornamented Indo-Portuguese pieces carved by Goan craftsmen.

In the chapel, don't miss the altar and the pulpit, the latter of which was made in the 17th century by Chinese artists in Goa (India). On the ground floor is the small but fascinating **Maritime Museum**, with gold coins, ship compasses, Chinese porcelain and other items recovered from local shipwrecks.

One ticket covers both museums as well as the Museu de Arte Sacra next door. Tours are guided and available in several languages, including Portuguese and English.

Fort of São Sebastião FORTRESS
(adult/child Mtc100/50; ⊙8am-4.30pm) The island's northern end is dominated by the massive Fort of São Sebastião – the oldest complete fort still standing in sub-Saharan Africa and, arguably, the finest military building on the continent. Construction began in 1558 and took 62 years. The fort has withstood numerous Dutch, British and Omani bids to diminish it. While the structure remains in a pretty unkempt state, with little explanatory information, it size and aura, along with the views from its battlements, are awe-inspiring.

Just beyond the fort, at the island's tip and accessed via the fort entrance, is the tiny **Chapel of Nossa Senhora de Baluarte**, built in 1522 and the oldest European building in the southern hemisphere.

Igreja da Misericórdia CHURCH
(Church of Mercy) With a distinctive white facade, this church is best viewed while sitting at a table in the Café-Bar Áncora d'Ouro opposite. The original church was destroyed during a Dutch raid in 1607; the current structure dates from the 17th century.

Museu de Arte Sacra MUSEUM
(Museum of Sacred Art) Containing religious ornaments, paintings and carvings, this museum is housed in the former hospital of the Holy House of Mercy, a religious guild that assisted the poor and sick in several Portuguese colonies from the early 1500s onwards. Entry is included in your São Paulo palace (p143) ticket and you'll get the same multilingual guide.

Activities

Strong tidal flows make it dangerous to swim around Mozambique Island's northern and southern ends. The cleanest of the island's patches of sand is Nancaramo Beach, next to the fort. For beautiful, clean sand, head across Mossuril Bay to Chocas and Cabaceira Pequena (p146), or to the beach on Goa Island.

Ilha Blue   TOURS
(☑ 84 396 9438; www.ilhablue.com; Avenida dos Heróis) ✈ Run by an expat British-Australian couple, this professional, community-involved tour company offers cycling, snorkelling, kayaking and dhow safaris, all led by local guides. It shares digs with a clothes shop called Orera Orera in Stone Town.

Genito Magic Tour   TOURS
(☑ 84 546 4817; www.genitomagictour.com; Avenida dos Heróis) ✈ Under the tutelage of Unesco-recognised guide Genito, aka 'Harry Potter', you can arrange tours of Makuti Town (US$8) and/or Stone Town and the fort (US$8). Also available are fishing with local fisherfolk and dhow excursions to local islands (with snorkelling). Genito's based at Magic Internet Cafe in Stone Town.

🛏 Sleeping

Ruby Backpacker   HOSTEL $
(☑ 84 866 0200; ruby.backpackers@gmail.com; Travessa da Sé; dm/d Mtc650/1550; @ 🛜) Located in a renovated 400-year-old house, the island's only backpackers is a good one. It has dorm beds upstairs and downstairs, twin and double rooms, a self-catering kitchen, hot showers, a bar, a fantastic rooftop terrace, bicycle rental, laundry service, a travellers' noticeboard and lots of information about onward travel.

Mooxeleliya   GUESTHOUSE $
(☑ 82 454 3290, 26-610076; flora204@hotmail.com; d incl breakfast with/without air-con Mtc2500/2000) Mooxeleliya (the Makua name translates roughly as, 'Did you rest well?') has five simple but spacious, high-ceilinged rooms upstairs and two darker, three- to four-person, family-style rooms downstairs. There's a small cooking area with fridge and a communal TV/sitting area. It's just down from the Misericórdia church.

Casa das Ondas   GUESTHOUSE $
(☑ 82 569 2888, 82 438 6400; Rua dos Combatentes; incl breakfast r Mtc2300, with shared bathroom Mtc1700; ✳ 🛜) A Dutch-Mozambican-run guesthouse with three very characterful rooms that reflect the hybrid personality of Mozambique Island. Rooms are spacious

and recently renovated; only one has a private bathroom. It's just to the left of the cinema.

Casuarina Camping   CAMPGROUND $
(☑ 84 616 8764; casuarina.camping@gmail.com; camping Mtc250, d from Mtc2000, with shared bathroom from Mtc1000; 🛜) On the mainland opposite Mozambique Island, a two-minute walk from the bridge (to your right, coming from the island), Casuarina has a well-maintained campground on a small, clean beach, plus simple bungalow-style rooms and ablution blocks with bucket showers. The seemingly basic restaurant is lauded by those in the know, especially for its pizza (made in a real oven).

Casa de Yasmin   GUESTHOUSE $
(☑ 82 676 8850, 26-610073; Rua dos Combatentes; r/ste Mtc1500/2500; ✳) This family house at the island's northern end has a quintet of clean but view-less downstairs rooms (each with bathroom and air-con) and a larger upstairs suite with a glimpse of the sea. It's the white house to the right of the cinema. There's no sign.

Pousada Ilha de Moçambique   HOTEL $
(☑ 26-610101; Rua dos Combatentes; s/d incl breakfast from Mtc2600/2800; ✳) In a good setting at the island's northern tip in the shadow of the fort and opposite a beach, this place has a governmental, utilitarian feel despite a recent renovation. The 22 boring rooms hold no surprises, except perhaps the large windows and sea views. There's a restaurant.

Amakuthini   GUESTHOUSE $
(Casa de Luís; ☑ 82 436 7570, 82 540 7622; dm Mtc500, d incl breakfast Mtc1200) For total cultural immersion, head to this authentic but rough-around-the edges place in Makuti Town, the scruffy neighbourhood of reed houses where the locals live. It has an eight-bed dorm and several small, dark rooms with fan in a tiny garden behind the family house. All beds have nets.

★ O Escondidinho   HOTEL $$
(☑ 26-610078; www.oescondidinho.net; Avenida dos Heróis; s/d Mtc3900/4400, with outside bathroom Mtc2500/3300; ✳ 🛜) In a sturdy but genteel old trading house in Stone Town, you can recline like a colonial lord in atmospheric high-ceilinged rooms furnished with four-poster beds draped with mosquito nets. Seven of the 10 rooms have large bathrooms

and there are more refinements downstairs, with a flower-embellished garden and small pool overlooked by one of the town's best restaurants.

Villa Sands BOUTIQUE HOTEL **$$**
(82 744 7178; www.villasands.com; Rua dos Trabalhadores; d from Mtc7000;) Imagine a cross between Swedish and Mozambican design (if you can) and you've imagined Villa Sands, which mixes sleek, minimalist Scandinavian lines with more elaborate African accents: think gilded mirrors and wood-beamed roofs. Bright boutique-style rooms overlook the water; the upstairs ones have views and their own pool, and there's also a restaurant (meals from Mtc600) and rooftop terrace.

Excursions, including diving trips, can be organised.

Patio dos Quintalinhos GUESTHOUSE **$$**
(Casa de Gabriele; 26-610090, 82 419 7610; www.patiodosquintalinhos.com; Rua do Celeiro; incl breakfast d US$73, with shared bathroom US$45, ste/q from US$78/90;) Opposite the green mosque, Quintalinhos has a handful of comfortable, creatively designed rooms set around a small courtyard, including one with a loft, and a suite with skylight and private rooftop balcony with views to the water. There's also a rooftop terrace, a pool and secure parking. Staff can help with bicycle rental and excursions.

★ **Jardim dos Aloés** B&B **$$$**
(87 827 4645; www.jardim-dos-aloes.com; Rua Presidente Kaunda; r incl breakfast Mtc10,500-11,200;) These three exquisite suites are relatively new on the island scene and have upped the ante, mixing retro decor (record players, antique phones) and interesting books with elements of the island's past and present. It's a beautiful melange of hammocks, terraces and alcoves hidden behind high walls in the heart of Stone Town.

Eating

Sara's Place AFRICAN **$**
(Avenida 25 de Junho; mains Mtc150-300; 8am-10pm) Inhabiting a reed house in the square opposite the hospital, Sara's is a confirmed local favourite – small and scruffy, but salt-of-the-earth – where you can taste chicken and fish served with the unique island speciality *matapa de siri siri* (seaweed with coconut milk).

LOCAL KNOWLEDGE

MATAPA DE SIRI SIRI

Word on the street says you haven't really been to Mozambique Island until you've tasted *matapa de siri siri*. This local take on a popular Mozambican dish takes the standard *matapa* recipe – ground cassava leaves slow-cooked with garlic, onion, coconut milk and cashews – and substitutes the cassava leaves with a local seaweed. For good measure, prawns are sometimes added to the mix. *Matapa de siri siri* has a soft, stew-like consistency not unlike sautéed spinach and works well as a starter served with bread, but it can also be used as a side dish. It's not only fragrant but also highly nutritious, and it's only available in its classic homemade form on Mozambique Island.

Café-Bar Âncora d'Ouro CAFE **$**
(26-610006; Barrio do Museu; snacks from Mtc200; 8am-9pm Thu-Tue) This lovely cafe evokes the faded charm of colonial Mozambique, with old black-and-white prints adorning the walls and hefty tomes on the tables. There's no better place to relax with coffee and a muffin (or waffles) as you listen to the choir across the square and watch kids chase tyres. It's opposite the Misericórdia church.

★ **Rickshaws Cafe** INTERNATIONAL **$$**
(82 678 0098; Rua dos Trabalhadores; mains Mtc495-610; 7am-11pm) The new kids on the block have nabbed a beautiful sunset location on the island's western side where you can sit alfresco and relish food from a menu that mixes Mozambican favourites with fish tacos, pizza, brownies and burgers. It's American run, and the name harks back to a method of transport once popular on the island.

★ **Karibu** SEAFOOD **$$**
(84 380 2518; Barrio do Museu; mains Mtc400-800; 11am-3pm & 6-9.15pm Tue-Sun) This excellent new restaurant in Stone Town specialises in the island's seafood bounty. Tuna, prawns, marlin and lobster are all done to perfection here, overseen by the hands-on Portuguese owner. Choose from the chalkboard menu and sit alfresco in front of artfully arranged antiques in the window.

Relíquias FUSION $$

(☎82 525 2318; Avenida da República; mains Mtc190-600; ⏲10am-10pm Tue-Sun) This popular if unexciting spot does all the local standards, including seafood, hot chicken, prawn or goat curries, and *matapa* (cooked cassava leaves with peanut sauce) and coconut rice. Seating is indoors or out the back overlooking the water. There's a *menu ecónomico* for Mtc190.

Bar Flôr de Rosa ITALIAN $$

(☎82 745 7380; Avenida dos Heróis; mains Mtc400-550; ⏲5pm-midnight Mon-Sat) This small, chic, Italian-run place has espresso, a selection of pasta, pizza, soups and sandwiches, and a rooftop terrace for sundowners, plus live music on Friday and Saturday in season. It's near the hospital.

Information

BIM (Avenida Amilcar Cabral; ⏲8am-3pm Mon-Fri) Has an ATM (Visa and MasterCard), and changes cash (US dollars, euros and rand).

Getting There & Away

BOAT

There's at least one dhow daily connecting Mozambique Island with Cabaceira Grande and Mossuril, departing the island between about noon and 1pm from the beach down from BIM bank next to Villa Sands hotel, and departing Mossuril about 6am (Mtc25). For Sunset Boulevard, ask to be dropped off at 'São João', from where the *pensão* is just a five- to 10-minute walk up from the beach. From Mossuril village, it's about 1½ hours on foot to Cabaceira Grande.

However, most travellers charter a motorised dhow (about Mtc1500 if you haggle) to the Cabaceiras so they can come back the same day. Hotels on Mozambique Island can also organise Chocas/Cabaceira excursions. For all travel to/from the Cabaceiras, be prepared for lots of wading and walking.

BUS & CHAPA

Mozambique Island is joined by a one-lane, 3.5km bridge (built in 1967) to the mainland (there are half-a-dozen passing places). Most *chapas* (minibuses) stop about 1km before the bridge in Lumbo, where you'll need to get into a smaller pickup to cross over Mossuril Bay, due to vehicle weight restrictions on the bridge. (Thanks to lack of traffic, it's perfectly pleasant to walk the 3.5km across the bridge.)

Leaving Mozambique Island, all transport departs from the bridge.

Lumbo

Chapas to Lumbo cost Mtc10.

Nampula

The only direct cars to Nampula (Mtc200, three hours) are the *tanzaniano* minibuses, with one or two departing daily between 3am and 5am. The best thing to do is to ask at your hotel for help to get a message to the driver to collect you at your hotel pre-dawn. For all later departures, you will need to change vehicles at Monapo and sometimes also at Namialo. Chartering a vehicle from Nampula to Mozambique Island costs from about Mtc3000 one way.

Pemba

For travel direct to Pemba, take the 4am *tanzaniano* from the island to the main junction in Namialo (Mtc100, one hour). Large buses from Nampula start passing the Namialo junction from about 6am and usually have space (about Mtc300, six hours from Namialo to Pemba). If you miss these, there are always smaller vehicles going north.

CAR

Maximum weight is 1.5 tonnes. There's a Mtc10 toll per vehicle, payable on the mainland side.

Around Mozambique Island

Chocas, Cabaceira Pequena & Cabaceira Grande

North of Mozambique Island and across Mossuril Bay is the old Portuguese holiday town of Chocas. The town itself is of minimal interest, but just south along a sandy track roughly paralleling the beach is the traditional fishing village of **Cabaceira Pequena**, with a long, beautiful white-sand beach and views across the bay to Mozambique Island. Minutes inland are the ruins of an old Swahili-style **mosque** and the remains of a **cistern** used as a watering spot by Portuguese sailors.

Further along (northwest) from Cabaceira Pequena is semi-abandoned **Cabaceira Grande**, with a small treasure trove of ruins.

Flocks of pink flamingos stalk the mangroves and tidal pools on the adjacent beach.

Igreja de Nossa Senhora dos Remedios CHURCH

(Cabaceira Grande) This isolated church, tucked behind the mangroves close to the shore, retains a rare beauty enhanced by both its age and its setting. Built on the orders of Portuguese governor Pedro de Castro in 1579 for the Dominicans who maintained a convent on nearby Mozambique Island, it was later taken over by the Jesuits. Surviving details include the huge wooden doors, a gold-leaf altarpiece carved in India and an alfresco cistern once used by mariners.

🛏 Sleeping

Carrusca Mar & Sol BUNGALOW **$**
(☑82 516 0173, 26-213302; 4-/7-person bungalows Mtc1750/3500) At Carrusca Mar & Sol it's all about the beach, which has a wild, windswept, desert-island feel, at least during the week (weekends can be unpleasantly crowded). Accommodation wise you're talking fairly rustic. The handful of spacious bungalows have hammocks and terraces, and are set on a rise between the mangroves and one of the best stretches of sand.

★ Coral Lodge 15.41 LODGE **$$$**
(☑82 902 3612; www.corallodge1541.com; Cabaceira Pequena; s/d all-inclusive US$400/800; ❄@🛜☲) 🏊 If they gave out six stars for hotels, Coral Lodge might just qualify. Everything gets top marks, from the setting (an idyllic beach with its own natural diving lagoon) and the rooms (the beds have built-in air-con) to the service (akin to having your own butler) and the business ethics (most staff hail from the local village of Cabaceira Pequena).

ℹ Getting There & Away

It's easy to charter a boat from Mozambique Island to the beaches at Cabaceira Grande and Pequena. Start haggling at around Mtc2000 for the return trip with a wait.

There's one daily direct *chapa* (minibus) between Nampula and Chocas, departing Nampula between 10am and noon, and departing Chocas about 4am (Mtc200, five hours). Otherwise take any transport between Nampula or Monapo and Mozambique Island to the signposted Mossuril turnoff, 25km southeast of Monapo (Mtc150 from Nampula to the Mossuril turnoff). Sporadic *chapas* go from here to Mossuril (20km), and on to Chocas (12km further), with no vehicles after about 3pm. From Chocas, it's a 30-minute walk at low tide to Cabaceira Pequena, and one to 1½ hours to Cabaceira Grande.

Cuamba

This lively if unexciting rail and road junction was formerly known as Novo Freixo. With its dusty streets, flowering trees and large student population, it's the economic centre of Niassa province and a convenient stop-off if you're travelling to/from Malawi, especially if you're catching the train. The area is known for its garnet gemstones and for its scenic panoramas, especially to the east around Mt Mitucué (Serra Mitucué).

Quinta Timbwa CHALET **$**
(☑82 300 0752, 82 692 0250; quintatimbwa@yahoo.com.br; Cruze dos Chiapas; rondavels Mtc2500; ❄) This place is set on a large estate about 2.5km from town, and signposted. It's tranquil and good value, with spotless, pleasant rooms – some in attached rows, some in small rondavels – surrounded by expansive grounds featuring a small lake. It's ideal for families or for anyone with their own transport. There's also a restaurant (mains Mtc350 to Mtc600).

Pensão São Miguel PENSION **$**
(☑271-62701; Avenida 3 de Fevereiro; incl breakfast r with fan/air-con Mtc1000/1200; ❄) This long-standing, local-style guesthouse has small, clean rooms crowded behind the restaurant-bar area. Each room has one small double bed. While it's not the most luxurious of establishments, it's the best value-for-price option in the town centre, and located an easy 10-minute walk from the train station and bus stand.

ℹ Getting There & Away

BUS & CHAPA
Most transport leaves from Maçaniqueira market, at the southern edge of town and just south of the railway tracks. *Chapas* (minibuses) also come to meet arriving trains. The best time to find transport is between 5am and 6am, and at the station on Tuesday and Saturday afternoons, when the train from Nampula arrives.

TRAIN
A passenger train connects Cuamba and Nampula. It traditionally ran daily (except Monday) in either direction. However, since 2015 it has been reduced to a twice-weekly passenger service leaving Cuamba on Sunday and Thursday at 5am. Hopefully it will revert to its full schedule soon. The journey takes 10 to 12 hours. There are theoretically three classes of carriage (executive/1st/2nd Mtc600/400/170), although they

might not function on all trips. It's well worth investing in executive if you can.

Tickets can be purchased between 2pm and 5pm on the day before travel (but not earlier).

Boarding starts at 4am. Arrive early and bring plenty of snacks. As with all Mozambican transport, always check ahead at the station for current schedules.

Lichinga

In Mozambique's remote northwestern corner, Lichinga is what passes for the bright lights. With its dusty unpaved roads, vivid purple jacarandas and vaguely soporific air, you could be excused for thinking you've arrived in a small town as opposed to a provincial capital. Things to enjoy in Lichinga include the cool climate and the equally cool ambience. Most visitors use it as a springboard for Lake Niassa, an hour to the west, but there's a smattering of low-key restaurants and hotels for lingerers.

Sleeping & Eating

Residencial 2+1 HOTEL $
(☎82 381 1070; Avenida Samora Machel; s/d Mtc2000/2500; ❄) Clean, efficient, central and within easy walking distance of the bus stand, this otherwise journeyman hotel is augmented by its excellent **restaurant** (Avenida Samora Machel; mains Mtc500-700; ⏲noon-10pm).

Ponto Final HOTEL $
(☎82 304 3632, 271-20912; Rua Filipe Samuel Magaia; d Mtc2000, s with shared bathroom Mtc1300; ❄) At the northeastern edge of town, this above-average resthouse has clean, low-ceilinged rooms with flat-screen TVs and mosquito nets. Staff are friendly and a local artist has recently produced some lovely African murals in the courtyard.

Massenger Villa HOTEL $$
(☎82 345 4988; www.massengervilla.com; Rua No 3, Bairro de Massenger; s/d Mtc2720/3360; P❄🛜🏊) This new place a couple of kilometres north of the airport has clean, minimalist rooms, a restaurant and the largest and best swimming pool in town.

Lichinga Hotel by Montebelo HOTEL $$
(☎271-21280; www.montebelohotels.com; Rua Filipe Samuel Magaia; s/d Mtc4850/5460; ❄🛜🏊) The former Girassol hotel (the company recently rebranded as 'Montebelo'), this place remains Lichinga's most upmarket option and one of the few places in the province catering to business travellers. Despite being a bit of an oasis in an otherwise isolated town (laptop users hog the lobby for wi-fi), it lacks the pizzazz of Montebelos elsewhere.

Getting There & Away

AIR

LAM (☎271-20434, 271-20847; Praça do Liberados; ⏲8.30am-4.30pm Mon-Fri), just off the airport road, operates several flights weekly to/from Maputo, going via Tete (weekly) or Nampula (three times weekly) and sometimes Beira. Flights out of Lichinga tend to be heavily booked, so reconfirm your reservation and show up early at the airport.

BUS & TRUCK

Most transport – bar some buses to Tanzania – departs from beside the market, with vehicles to most destinations leaving by around 6am.

Cuamba via Mandimba

To Cuamba (Mtc500 to Mtc600, eight hours), Sckelane runs buses on Tuesday, Thursday and Saturday leaving at 3am. The same route is also covered by Nagi Investimentos. Most buses pass through the border town of Mandimba (Mtc300).

Marrupa

There's a daily bus to Marrupa (Mtc500, five hours), from where you may be able to get onward travel to Montepuez.

Metangula

To Metangula (Mtc200, 2½ hours) *chapas* (minibuses) leave mostly in the early morning.

Segundo Congresso (Matchedje) & Rovuma River

To Segundo Congresso (Matchedje) and the Rovuma River (Mtc650, six hours), at least one pickup truck goes daily, leaving anywhere between 7am and noon from the dusty street just before the transport stand. Trucks also stop on Avenida Julius Nyerere on the road north out of town (before the airport turnoff). Once over the border bridge, you can get transport to Songea for about Tsh12,000. In both directions, you'll need to have your visa in advance if using this crossing.

Getting Around

Lúrio Empreendimentos (☎87 161 9022; lurioempreendimentos@teledata.mz; Rua No 3, Bairro de Massenger) has a variety of 4WD vehicles for rent, with or without driver, at very fair rates. A taxi usually waits near Lichinga Hotel by Montebelo. Otherwise, Lúrio Empreendimentos can help with booking taxis.

Lake Niassa

Most people think of Lake Malawi as – well – Malawian, but 25% of its waters lie within Mozambique. Guarding the quieter, less developed side of the lake (which is called Lago Niassa in these parts), the Mozambican shoreline sees a small but steady stream of adventure travellers who quickly realise they've stumbled upon a wild and wonderful African paradise that few others know about.

A small sprinkling of ecolodges and budget bamboo cabins nestles among the sandy coves and giant baobabs that punctuate the shore between Meponda and Cóbuè, offering water activities, barefoot beach fun and integration with local communities.

Within Niassa's deep blue waters are over 500 species of fish, including more than 350 that are unique to the lake. The lake is also home to about a third of the planet's known cichlid (freshwater fish) species, including the brightly coloured mbuna.

Metangula

Metangula is the largest Mozambican lakeshore town – which isn't saying much. About 8km north is the tiny village of **Chuwanga**, which is on an attractive beach and is a popular weekend getaway from Lichinga.

N'Tendele Lodge CABIN **$$**
(☎87 407 4732; www.ntendele.com; dm/d US$20/80;) Continuing the tradition of sustainable, community-involved lakeside lodges, N'Tendele is a tranquil and beautifully simple place set in 4 hectares of miombo (woodland). It offers unadorned dorm or double rooms as well cottage tents, but, with the wilderness on your veranda, you won't be spending much time in them.

Mbuna Bay CHALET **$$$**
(☎82 536 7781; www.mbunabay.ch; s/d with full board in bush bungalow US$150/240, in beach chalet US$210/340) About 15km south of Metangula, ecofriendly Mbuna Bay has four wooden beachfront cottages, four brick cottages set back in the bush, and one wattle-and-daub cottage. All have creatively designed bathrooms (some open-air), and all are comfortable in a rustic way. Snorkelling, dhow sails, kayaking and yoga can be arranged, as can transfers from Lichinga. Food (included) is entirely vegetarian.

Getting There & Away

BOAT

Brought into service in 2013, the MV *Chambo* links Metangula with various ports around Lake Niassa in both Malawi and Mozambique. There's a twice-weekly northern route from Metangula via Cóbuè to Likoma Island (Malawi) and Nkata Bay (Malawi), and a once-weekly southern route linking Metangula with Meponda (Mozambique) and Chipoka (Malawi).

The northern run leaves Metangula at 2am on Saturday and Wednesday. The southern route leaves at 2am on Monday. The fare from Metangula to Likoma is US$14.

Departures in Metangula are from the small dhow port just down from Bar Triângulo and below the Catholic church.

CHAPA

Daily *chapas* (minibuses) connect Metangula and Lichinga (Mtc200, two to 2½ hours), most departing Lichinga early. There's also at least one *chapa* (usually an open-backed truck) daily between Metangula and Cóbuè (Mtc250, four hours). Departures in Metangula are from the fork in the road just up from the market at Bar Triângulo; look for the yellow Mcel wall. The final 20km or so of the tarmac road from Lichinga to Metangula is very scenic as the road winds down to the lakeshore.

There are occasional *chapas* between Metangula and Chuwanga, and hitching is easy on the weekend. Otherwise get a Cóbuè *chapa* to drop you at the Chuwanga turnoff, though it's probably just as fast to walk from Metangula. To get to Messumba, you'll need your own 4WD.

Cóbuè

Tiny Cóbuè is the gateway to Mozambique if you're travelling from Malawi via Likoma Island, 7km offshore. The island is surrounded by Mozambican waters but belongs to Malawi.

In addition to being one of the only places in Mozambique where you can procure an on-the-spot visa, Cóbuè's attractions include a lakeside setting dotted with mango trees, the remains of a school once used as a wartime base by Frelimo, and an oversized church, formerly a ruin but recently fixed with a new roof.

House of Chambo CABIN **$**
(www.houseofchambo.com; Mala Village; cabins per person incl breakfast US$25) Newly opened in 2016, the Chambo hosts three simple but beautifully sited bamboo bungalows right on the beach beside Lake Niassa. On offer are meals, a bar and a raft of activities including

guided safari walks. It's 8km southwest of Cóbuè; you can take a boat or walk.

Rest House Mira Lago PENSION $
(Pensão Layla; r with shared bathroom Mtc750; P) Directly in the village centre, this place has solar-powered lighting and a row of no-frills, clean rooms. Each has a small double bed. Meals can sometimes be organised with notice.

Getting There & Away

BOAT

The MV *Chambo* stops at Cóbuè twice a week on its run between Metangula and Likoma Island and on to Nkata Bay in Malawi. There are departures north to Likoma Island (US$2, one hour) on Saturday and Wednesday at 8am, and departures south to Metangula (US$12, five hours) on Thursday at 2pm and Sunday at 11am.

Meanwhile, fishing boats depart daily (in the morning) between Cóbuè and Likoma Island (about US$7 one way). Mozambique visas are issued in Cóbuè (US$30) but *not* Metangula. If you're travelling to/from Malawi, you'll need to go to Immigration (on the hill near the large antenna) to get your passport stamped.

BUS & CAR

Chapas (minibuses), usually in the form of open-back trucks, run between Metangula and Cóbuè, usually departing Metangula about 7am and Cóbuè about 8am (Mtc250, four hours).

The road between Cóbuè and Metangula (75km) is in reasonable condition, and there's secure parking at Khango Beach and Rest House Mira Lago in Cóbuè. (Walking between Cóbuè and Metangula takes about two days, going along the river via the villages of Ngoo and Chia.)

Niassa Reserve

The **Niassa Reserve** (Reserva do Niassa; ☎21-329807; http://www.facebook.com/NiassaReserve; adult/child/vehicle per day Mtc200/50/200) is a vast tract of miombo (woodland) and grass savannah dotted with inselbergs (steep, abrupt hills) that supports Mozambique's largest wildlife populations.

Hard to get to, and with park management currently focused on tackling poaching rather than promoting tourism, Niassa gets only a handful of annual visitors. For the time being, aspiring adventurers will need to come equipped with their own transport, food and tents.

The reserve covers 42,000 sq km, an area roughly the size of Denmark.

The reserve's one luxury safari camp, **Lugenda Bush Camp**, closed for major refurbishment in early 2016; check with Kaskazini (p155) for updates. At present, the only accommodation is at several scattered hunting camps (used mainly by trophy hunters on organised excursions) or the rudimentary ranger camp near Mbatamila headquarters, where you can pitch a tent (US$10). To visit, you'll need to bring all your own gear, or arrive on an organised trip.

Information

Reserve headquarters are about 40km southwest of Mecula at Mbatamila.

Wildlife in Niassa is spread relatively thinly over a vast area, with dense foliage and only a skeleton network of bush tracks. As a result, most tourism to date has been exclusively for the well heeled (either photography or hunting oriented), with the most feasible way to visit by charter plane from Pemba. With the gradual upgrading of road connections linking Cabo Delgado and Niassa provinces, this is beginning to change, although the reserve's main market is likely to remain top end for the foreseeable future.

For self-drivers it's possible in theory to do drive-in visits. However, given the lack of a developed network of tracks, this is only recommended for the adventure and the wilderness rather than for the safari or 'Big Four' aspects (there are no rhinos in Niassa). Note that the reserve's tsetse flies are very aggressive and very numerous. Any activity in a vehicle will need to be done with windows up.

Getting There & Away

There are two approaches to the Niassa Reserve, both of which converge on the small town of Marrupa. By far the easiest route is from Lichinga in the west on a good paved road (about five hours). From the east, the road is good through Montepuez to Balama. The Balama–Marrupa section is in poorer condition, but it's passable in the dry season (April to November). Allow a full day from Pemba. There's cheap accommodation available in Montepuez.

At Marrupa there's fuel, camping and basic accommodation. From Marrupa, the remaining 100km stretch up to the Lugenda River and on into the reserve is dirt but in reasonable shape.

The unpaved road from Cuamba to Marrupa is another doable option, especially during the dry season. Petrol is generally available on the roadside in Mecula, although this should not be relied upon, and on the whole, driving itineraries in the reserve will be limited by how much extra fuel you can carry.

WORTH A TRIP

NKWICHI LODGE

Apart from its convenient location, the main reason to come to Cóbuè is to get to **Nkwichi Lodge** (www.nkwichi.com; s/d with full board in chalet US$450/690, in private house US$495/760), one of the most appealing and genuinely community-integrated lodges in the region and worth all of the many dollars it costs to stay there.

For setting, service, romance, proximity to nature and integration with the local community, Nkwichi Lodge can rival anywhere in Africa. Gracing the shores of Lake Niassa, its seven hand-crafted bungalows seem to spring naturally from the rocks and foliage, and come equipped with private outdoor baths and showers built into the bush. Several look out onto their own white-sand coves.

There are also two private houses, each with lake views, private chef, and lots of space and privacy.

The lodge lays on activities aplenty, including canoeing, multinight wilderness walking safaris, and visits to the lodge's demonstration farm. It is linked with the Manda Wilderness Community Conservation Area, a privately initiated conservation area along the lakeshore that also promotes community development and responsible tourism. The surrounding bush is full of ospreys, palm-nut vultures, Pel's fishing owls, fish eagles and 200-year-old baobab trees.

Nkwichi is only accessible by boat from Cóbuè or Likoma Island (Malawi). Transfers (45 minutes) can be arranged with reservations.

Once across the Lugenda, you'll need to sign in at the reserve before continuing on towards Mecula and Mbatamila park headquarters – about 45km from the gate, and set in the shadow of the 1441m-high Mt Mecula – where you can arrange a guide.

Montepuez

Montepuez, a busy district capital, previously rivalled Pemba as the largest town in Cabo Delgado province. Today it's known for its marble quarries and as the start of the wild 'road' west across Niassa province towards Lichinga. The main road in Montepuez is Avenida Eduardo Mondlane; most places are either on or just off it.

The transport stand is about two blocks south of Avenida Eduardo Mondlane; turn down the street with Millennium BIM. Several *chapas* (minibuses) daily go between Pemba and Montepuez (Mtc250, three hours). Heading west, there's regular transport to Balama (Mtc180), but from there to Marrupa (for Niassa Reserve) there's no option other than hitching a lift with a tractor or a truck. If you're driving, the Balama-Marrupa stretch is only navigable in the dry season.

VS Lanchonete FAST FOOD $
(☎272-51051; Avenida Eduardo Mondlane; snacks Mtc250-400; ⏲8am-9pm) This chicken-and-chips place with plastic picnic tables should sate your appetite if you're heading towards the wilds of Niassa. Also rents a few clean rooms (from around Mtc1800).

Pemba

The gateway to the north, Pemba sprawls across a small peninsula that juts into the enormous and magnificent Pemba Bay, one of the world's largest natural harbours. Established in 1904 as administrative headquarters for the Niassa Company, Pemba was known for much of its early life as Porto Amelia. Today it's the capital of Cabo Delgado province and a city of three distinct parts. The mildewed *baixa* area is home to the low-lying port, the old town and the lively township of **Paquitequete**. Steeply uphill from here, the busier and less atmospheric town centre is the place to get things done, with banks and offices, a few restaurants and the main bus stand. About 5km east of the town centre is **Wimbi** (also spelled Wimbe) **Beach**, the hub of tourist activity and the favoured destination of most visitors.

Activities

There's a small swimming pool at Clube Naval (p154).

CI Divers DIVING
(☎272-20102; www.cidivers.co.za; Pieter's Place, Avenida Marginal, Wimbi Beach) The only

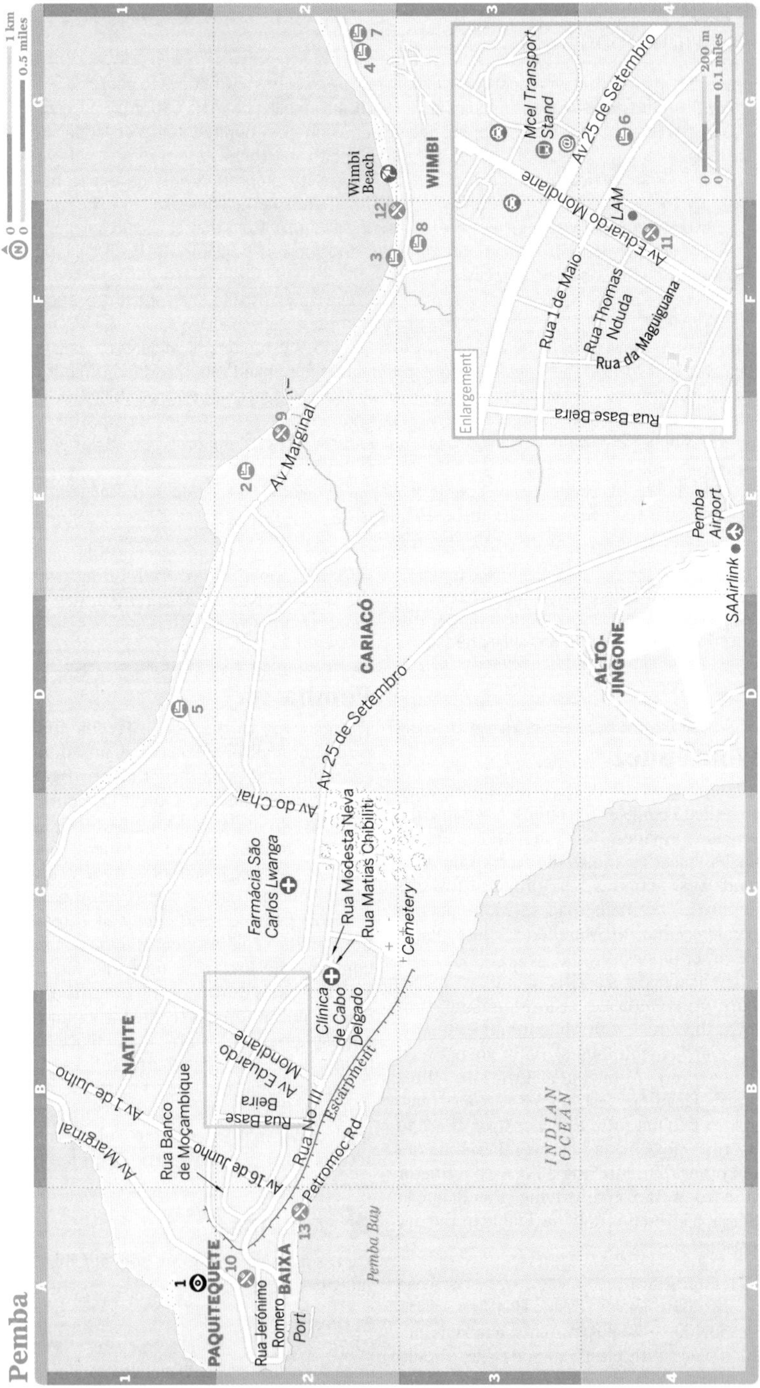
Pemba
0.5 miles
1 km
PAQUITEQUETE
BAIXA
NATITE
CARIACÓ
WIMBI
ALTO-JINGONE
Rua Jerónimo Romero
Port
Pemba Bay
Av Marginal
Av 1 de Julho
Rua Banco de Moçambique
Av 16 de Junho
Rua Base Beira
Av Eduardo Mondlane
Rua No III
Petromoc Rd
Escarpment
Clínica de Cabo Delgado
Rua Modesta Neva
Rua Matias Chibiliti
Cemetery
Farmácia São Carlos Lwanga
Av do Chai
Av 25 de Setembro
INDIAN OCEAN
Wimbi Beach
Pemba Airport
SAAirlink
Enlargement
200 m
0.1 miles
Mcel Transport Stand
LAM
Rua 1 de Maio
Rua Thomas Nduda
Rua da Maguiguana

Pemba

Sights

1 Paquitequete A1

Activities, Courses & Tours

CI Divers .... (see 7)

Sleeping

2 Avani Pemba Beach Hotel E2
3 Náutilus Hotel F2
4 Pieter's Place G2
5 Raphael's Hotel D1
6 Residencial Lys G4
7 Residencial Reggio Emilia G2
8 Wimbi Sun Residencial F3

Eating

9 Clube Naval E2
10 Locanda Italiana A2
11 Pastelaria Flor d'Avenida F4
12 Pemba Dolphin F3
Procongel .... (see 13)
13 Wilson's Wharf A2

Shopping

Artes Maconde .... (see 2)

Information

Kaskazini .... (see 2)

independent dive operator in Pemba, CI Divers is based at South African–run Pieter's Place (p153). It offers PADI open-water certification (US$560 for a four-day course) and guided dive immersions (US$70). Boats launch from the Náutilus Hotel and sail out to a 12m to 30m wall replete with coral and marine life roughly 1km out to sea.

Sleeping

In & Near Town Centre

Residencial Lys HOTEL $
(☎ 272-20951; Rua 1 de Maio; s/d Mtc1500/2000; ❄) Your only overnight option in central Pemba won't win any hotel beauty pageants, though rooms are better than the dark reception area suggests. Bank on air-con and hot and cold water, but not wi-fi.

Raphael's Hotel HOTEL $$
(☎ 272-25555; www.raphaelshotel.com; Praça 25 de Setembro; r from US$85; P ❄ 📶 🏊) A new waterfront, Chinese-owned hotel, Raphael's is handily located halfway between central Pemba and Wimbi Beach. The architecture's hardly photo-worthy, but the rooms are large and well stocked (with coffee, water and shampoo), and there's a downstairs bar featuring a lovely terrace equipped with wicker sofas. Other bonuses include pool, gym, restaurant and strong wi-fi.

Wimbi Beach

Pemba Magic Lodge CAMPGROUND, BUNGALOW $
('Russel's Place'; ☎ 272-21429; www.pembamagiclodge.com; Avenida Marginal; camping per site Mtc700, tent hire Mtc1000, dm/s/d Mtc1000/3500/5200; 📶) In business since 1998, Russel's Place is Pemba's nominal backpackers, located on the eastern extension of Wimbi Beach (called Nanhimbe) about 3.5km beyond Complexo Náutilus. It offers the full gamut of budget accommodation: campsites, rent-a-tents, a five-bed dorm and private bungalows made out of local materials (one of which sleeps six).

Residencial Reggio Emilia GUESTHOUSE $$
(☎ 82 888 0800, 272-21297; www.wix.com/ake elz/Residencial-Reggio-Emilia; 8696 Avenida Marginal; r/apt from Mtc3500/7500; P ❄ 📶) This tranquil spot along the extension of the Wimbi Beach road has 10 clean, spacious rooms – with hot water, air-con, satellite TV, mini fridge and quality mattresses – and a two-bedroom self-catering apartment in quiet grounds. All are appealingly decorated with locally sourced materials such as Palma mats, and all have mosquito screens on the windows. Breakfast (extra) is served on request.

Wimbi Sun Residencial GUESTHOUSE $$
(☎ 82 318 1300; bookings@wimbisun.co.mz; 7472 Avenida Marginal; r/d Mtc4000/4500; ❄ 📶) Clean, modern rooms (the best are the spacious 'suites'), none with nets and all with bathroom and TV, are on offer here. It's at the start of the Wimbi Beach strip, diagonally opposite Complexo Náutilus on the inland side of the road.

Pieter's Place GUESTHOUSE $$
(☎ 82 682 2700; www.pietersdiversplace.co.za; Avenida Marginal; r US$60-100; ❄ 📶) Built around a huge, ancient baobab tree (into which you can climb and have breakfast in an improvised treehouse), Pieter's Place has an amiable African-backpackers feel to it. It's also diving central, thanks to the on-site CI Divers (p151). Building work was being completed on some new rooms in late 2016;

all will have private bathroom, mosquito nets and coffee-making tray.

Náutilus Hotel HOTEL $$
(☎86 610 6652; www.thenautiluspemba.com; Avenida Marginal; s/d Mtc5000/7310;) Affiliated with a longstanding restaurant on Wimbi Beach and under new management, these new rondavels built on raised boardwalks on the sand are shaded by palm trees and situated well away from the restaurant bustle. The circular rooms have glass doors opening onto private decks and sitting areas. There's also a beautiful infinity pool to frame the mandarin-orange sunsets.

★ **Avani Pemba Beach Hotel** HOTEL $$$
(☎272-21770; www.pembabeachresort.com; 5470 Avenida Marginal; s US$264-366, d US$310-430; P@) If you're a romantic with a penchant for luxurious beachside hotels that have an Arabian bent, then this five-star establishment is the business. Sitting like a mini-Alhambra in expansive grounds north of Wimbi Beach, it has well-equipped rooms, a dreamy restaurant, gym, spa and infinity pool, a handy travel agent, and staff who touch their heart when they say 'good morning'.

Eating

In & Near Town Centre

Pastelaria Flor d'Avenida CAFE $
(☎272-20514; Avenida Eduardo Mondlane; mains Mtc300-350; 6am-10pm Mon-Sat) It doesn't look much from the outside, but this long-standing, informal eatery with mainly outdoor tables delivers the goods when it comes to coffee and pastries.

Procongel DELI $
(Petromoc Rd; 9am-1pm & 2-5pm Mon-Fri, 9am-1pm Sat) The pricey but well-stocked Procongel is attached to **Wilson's Wharf** (☎84 742 2909; Petromoc Rd; mains Mtc450-850; 8am-late Mon-Sat;) in the *baixa*, with produce, imported cheeses and gourmet items.

★ **Locanda Italiana** ITALIAN $$
(☎82 688 9050, 272-20672; 487 Rua Jerónimo Romero; pizza & pasta Mtc300-400, mains Mtc500-600; 10am-10pm) Something of a vision in the quiet, well-worn streets of the *baixa*, this Italian-run restaurant serves up al dente pasta (the *ragú* is excellent) and wood-fired-oven pizzas in the flower-embellished courtyard of a restored building. If you're looking for a day off root vegetables and chicken piri-piri, this is the place to go.

Wimbi Beach

Pemba Dolphin SEAFOOD $$
(☎272-20937; Avenida Marginal; mains Mtc500; 7am-late) Directly on Wimbi Beach, the very relaxed Dolphin has a beach-bar ambience, seafood grills and pizzas, and live music from 6.30pm to 9.30pm.

Kauri INTERNATIONAL $$
(Avenida Marginal; mains Mtc400-800; 11am-10pm Tue-Sun) The restaurant at Kauri Resort overlooks the Indian Ocean in more ways than one. Parts of the menu also look to India for inspiration and there are Chinese dishes too. It's the local seafood, however, that tops the bill, particularly the lobster.

Clube Naval SEAFOOD, CONTINENTAL $$$
(☎82 304 4887, 272-21770; Avenida Marginal; mains Mtc450-1600; 11am-10pm;) The default expat hang-out, the good ole naval club enjoys a prime waterside setting just off the western curve of Wimbi Beach. Sundowners are practically obligatory here, but the restaurant also has a large menu featuring salads, seafood, chicken, ribs, pizzas and desserts. There's a volleyball area on the sand, a swimming pool and a small children's playground.

Shopping

Artes Maconde ARTS & CRAFTS
(Avenida Marginal; 8am-3pm Mon-Fri, 9am-noon Sat) Even if you don't think you want to buy crafts, it's worth stopping in at the excellent Artes Maconde at Avani Pemba Beach Hotel (p154). It sells a wide range of quality carvings, crafts and textiles sourced from throughout Mozambique as well as elsewhere in the region.

As far as quality of the artistry and uniqueness of the art are concerned, it's one of the best craft shops in the country, and craftspeople come from outlying villages throughout Cabo Delgado province and as far away as the Democratic Republic of Congo (Zaïre) to deliver their wares. It does international air and sea shipping and also takes orders.

Information

INTERNET

Sycamore Services (☎272-21999; 1282 Avenida 25 de Setembro; per hr Mtc200;

⌚7.30am-8pm Mon-Sat, 8am-noon Sun) Internet connection; it's just after Mcel.

MEDICAL

Clínica de Cabo Delgado (☎272-21462; Rua Modesta Neva 10) For basic medical treatment, although quality is erratic.

Farmácia São Carlos Lwanga (⌚7am-6.30pm Mon-Fri, 8am-5pm Sat) One block back from Avenida 25 de Setembro opposite the church.

TOURIST INFORMATION

Kaskazini (☎272-20371, 82 309 6990; www.kaskazini.com; Pemba Beach Hotel, Avenida Marginal; ⌚8am-3pm Mon-Fri, 9am-noon Sat) Efficient, knowledgeable and a good first stop. It gives free information on Pemba and elsewhere in northern Mozambique, helps with accommodation and flight bookings, and can organise everything from dhow safaris to sunset cruises.

Getting There & Away

AIR

Pemba Airport is 4km southwest of the city centre. **LAM** (☎272-21251; Avenida Eduardo Mondlane; ⌚7am-4.30pm Mon-Fri, 9.30-11.30am Sat) flies daily to/from Maputo (via Nampula and/or Beira) and twice weekly to/from Dar es Salaam (Tanzania) and Nairobi (Kenya). **SAAirlink** (☎272-21700; www.flyairlink.com; Airport) flies twice weekly to Johannesburg.

For charter flights to the Quirimbas Archipelago, book direct with **CR Aviation** (☎84 490 9734; www.craviation.co.mz) or go through travel agency Kaskazini.

Expect to pay from Mtc400 to Mtc500 for a taxi from the airport to town.

BUS & CHAPA

Nearly all transport passes along Avenida 25 de Setembro, Pemba's main drag.

Ibo & Quirimbas Islands

For the Quirimbas get a *chapa* (minibus) from the Mcel Transport Stand to the boat dock at Tandanhangue (Mtc300 to Mtc400, four to eight hours) via Quissanga. *Chapas* leave daily between 4am and 5am.

Moçimboa & Mueda

Maning Nice buses go to Moçimboa da Praia (Mtc300, five to six hours) and on to Mueda (Mtc400, eight hours).

Mozambique Island

For Mozambique Island the best bet is to go to Nampula and then get onward transport from there the next day. You can also try your luck getting out at Namialo junction and looking for onward transport from there, but the timing often doesn't work out, and Namialo is unappealing as an overnight spot.

Nampula & Maputo

The Etrago bus to Maputo (Mtc3500, two days) stops in Nampula (Mtc500, six to seven hours) on its way south. It leaves from the Mcel Transport Stand at 3am Tuesday, Thursday and Saturday. Other companies covering the route include Nagi Investimentos and Esta Na Moda.

Getting Around

BUS & TAXI

There are taxi ranks on Avenida Eduardo Mondlane just down from Mcel and at the same junction along Avenida 25 de Setembro. Town to Wimbi Beach costs Mtc150 to Mtc200. There's also a public bus that runs between 6am and 7pm from town to Wimbi Beach and beyond (Mtc10), and the occasional *chapa* from the Mcel Transport Stand to the Complexo Náutilus roundabout (Mtc10).

CAR

Safi Rentals (☎82 380 8630; www.pembarentacar.com) comes highly recommended, offering reliable car rentals at very reasonable prices (with a trusted driver if required). Rates include unlimited kilometres, opening the door to many attractions in the north that would otherwise be inaccessible for budget and midrange travellers. It's also possible to arrange car rentals through Kaskazini.

Murrébuè

Murrébuè is a lovely long stretch of white sand fringed by turquoise Indian Ocean waters that has recently started to gain attention for its optimal kitesurfing conditions. Although it's slowly being developed (two new resorts have opened in the last couple of years), it remains a pleasantly quiet alternative to Pemba's Wimbi Beach. The strip lies 12km south of Pemba.

Most of the Murrébuè lodges can organise airport pick-ups (check when booking). Otherwise regular *chapas* (minibuses) run between Pemba and the beach.

Sleeping

Ulala Lodge BUNGALOW **$$**

(☎82 741 5104; www.ulala-lodge.com; s/d in bungalow US$81/92, in stilt bungalow US$150/162; 📶) 🍃 Small is beautiful at Ulala, right on Murrébuè Beach, with six wind- and solar-powered bamboo bungalows and a separate large dining/relaxing area. A couple of the bungalows are raised on stilts just back from the beach; two others cater for families. All have hot water, nets and covered decks and are visited by the sea breeze.

nZuwa Lodge BUNGALOW, CAMPGROUND **$$**
(☎82 730 6365; www.nzuwa.com; camping per site US$15, tent rental US$20, bungalows US$100-120; 📶) At the far northern end of the beach, nZuwa offers a rustic, undone Mozambique beach paradise where comfort doesn't have to be compromised. It's all palm-frond-roofed bungalows, hammocks on the beach, epic breakfasts and raspberry-ripple sunsets. Kayaks and snorkelling gear can be borrowed.

Chuiba Bay Lodge B&B **$$$**
(☎82 305 0836; www.chuibabaylodge.com; s/d US$200/300; ❄📶🏊) You'll feel like a Swahili sultan as you recline in the tropical luxury of the Chuiba Bay. Six stone bungalows with individual, ethnic-chic decor are arranged around a romantically lit pool. The bathrooms are particularly notable, with deep tubs and statuettes holding up the sinks, not to mention the lobby-lounge with its piano and mini library. And...ah...the beach.

Il Pirata BUNGALOW **$$$**
(☎82 380 5790; www.murrebue.com; s/d with full board US$110/175) At the northern end of the beach, this Italian-run place is a hub of activity, particularly with regard to kitesurfing. Lessons can be arranged at the on-site Pirate Kites. Accommodation comes in three lovely reed-bamboo bungalows, and there's a lauded Italian restaurant too (open to nonguests at weekends). Airport transfers can be arranged.

Quirimbas Archipelago

Hidden like pirate treasure off Mozambique's north coast, the islands of the Quirimbas archipelago conceal a multitude of secrets, from the brilliant coral reefs of Medjumbe to the ancient baobab trees of Quilaluia. But none of the 31 islands can equal mysterious Ibo, the archipelago's de facto capital. Haunted by a tumultuous history, and now a bubbling blend of Portuguese, Swahili, Indian and African cultures, Ibo feels as though it fell into a stupor in the 1850s and has yet to awaken.

Elsewhere the Quirimbas are as much about natural beauty as history. Their soft white beaches, dotted with low-key, high-end resorts, are rightly legendary, while the bird and marine life, which can be seen on tranquil diving or walking excursions, is immense.

Today many of the southern islands, including Ibo and Matemo, are part of **Quirimbas National Park** (Quirimbas National Park; entry fee US$12), which also includes large inland areas on the fringing coastline.

Ibo Island

Ibo, the best known of the Quirimbas islands, is a one-of-a-kind place that rivals Mozambique Island as one of the nation's historical highlights. Its quiet streets are lined with dilapidated villas and crumbling, moss-covered buildings, and they echo with the footsteps of bygone centuries. Architecturally Ibo is relatively open, with wide streets rather than narrow medieval lanes, although its ambience is strangely insulated; the population of around 3000 is concentrated on the island's northern tip. The best time to visit is during a clear, moonlit night, when the old colonial houses take on a haunting, almost surreal aspect.

Ibo doesn't have many beaches, but as compensation there are magical sunset views over the mudflats just north of the tiny port. With some time, you can also take day excursions to a nearby sandbank or to a lovely patch of beach on the other side of the island.

Sights & Activities

Fort of São João Baptista FORT
(Mtc50; ⏲7am-noon & 2-5pm) At the island's northern end is the star-shaped Fort of São João Baptista, built in 1791 and designed to accommodate up to 300 people. When Ibo was linked to the slave trade, the fort's dark, cramped lower chambers were used as slave holding points. Today the fort is known for the silver artisans who have set up shop near the entrance. Much of the silver they use comes from melted-down coins and is often of inferior quality, but the distinctive, refined Swahili artisanship is among the best in the region.

Inside the fort is the small, slightly unkempt **Museu Marítimo** (Maritime Museum), focusing on local Mwani culture. Explanations are in Portuguese, but an English translation is available.

You can climb on to to the ramparts to enjoy perfect ocean views.

Raúl Pereira WALKING
(☎86 208 6046; per person Mtc1200) Raúl is Ibo's history guide, and his relaxed but engaging walking tour of Ibo's wonderful, semi-abandoned Stone Town is practically compulsory if you want to absorb the island's flavour. Raúl can be contacted independently or through Cinco Portas.

Sleeping

Pensão Café do Ibo PENSION $
(Ibo Coffee Guesthouse; ☎82 551 7501; Airfield Rd; r Mtc2000-2500) Clean, quiet, slightly cramped rooms are available in this small private home opposite a coffee plantation. It's about a 10-minute walk from the dhow port, following the road towards the airfield with the water to your right.

Karibuni CABIN, CAMPGROUND $
(☎82 703 2200; camping Mtc120, r Mtc400-700) Karibuni is Ibo on a budget, with very basic rooms in local-style thatched huts and space in a small garden to pitch your tent. Meals can be prepared, but you'll need to bring your own food.

★**Cinco Portas** GUESTHOUSE $$
(☎86 926 2399; www.cincoportas.com; Avenida República; s US$50-80, d US$85-140, apt US$160-195;) Ibo is an idyll wherever you stay, but Cinco Portas could well offer the best deal when you factor in price, friendly ambience and flawless, nothing-is-too-much-trouble service. Housed in a spruced-up old warehouse with a brilliant waterside setting, its small but comfortable rooms are complemented by lovely communal areas embellished with mahogany carvings and the best restaurant on the island.

Miti Miwiri BOUTIQUE HOTEL $$
(☎82 543 8564, 26-960530; www.mitimiwiri.com; d/tr/f US$65/80/90; @) One of Ibo's stalwarts, Miwiri reflects the island's magical atmosphere. Its lush walled garden is a popular place for people to hang for drinks, food, sheesha pipes and general info under the mango trees. The hotel occupies one of Ibo's finest old houses, and its large rooms have high ceilings and grand, if not opulent, decor.

Baobibo – Casa de Hospedes GUESTHOUSE $$
(☎82 815 2892; www.baobibo.com; d US$60-75, ste US$90-110) Just up from the dhow port, Baobibo offers several light-filled bungalows made from traditional materials. The clean, well-made bucket showers use recycled rainwater. One bungalow is designed for families. There's a garden, a lovely sitting area and activities – including bike and kayak rental – on tap. Baobibo also runs a campsite on Matemo Island.

★**Ibo Island Lodge** LODGE $$$
(www.iboisland.com; s/d with full board US$460/720;) This nine-room luxury boutique hotel – the most upmarket accommodation on Ibo – is housed in three restored 19th-century mansions in a prime setting overlooking the water near the dhow port. Furnishings throughout reflect the nuances of Ibo's past (Swahili, Indian, Portuguese and African), with mahogany chests, four-poster beds, and indoor and open-to-the-stars showers.

Ulani Lodge LODGE $$$
(☎87 595 8114; www.ulanilodge.com; Rua António de Almeida; s/d US$80/100;) This new Portuguese-owned place in one of Ibo's finest and most lovingly restored mansions opened in late 2016. It offers large, high-ceilinged rooms, a shady garden and pool, and plenty of colonial atmosphere.

Eating

Kumawe SEAFOOD $
(☎82 741 4616; Rituto; mains Mtc300) A couple of homes in the *bairro* known as Rituto offer meals if organised in advance (enquire at Cinco Portas (p157)). A local will pick you up and take you to their small house, where you'll likely dine on the catch of the day, along with *matapa* (cassava leaves sauteed with cashews and coconut milk) and rice.

Medjumbe & Matemo

Idyllic Medjumbe is a narrow sliver of island draped with white coral sand. There are no permanent residents. Instead Medjumbe hosts an airstrip, an old lighthouse and the paradisaical **Anantara Medjumbe Island Resort** (www.medjumbe.anantara.com; per person with full board from US$595;). It's located approximately 70km due north of Ibo.

The much larger island of Matemo lies 20km north of Ibo and has been inhabited for generations – it was an important cloth-manufacturing centre into the 17th century. Today villages dot much of the north and interior of the island. There's no resort, but camping is available through Baobibo on Ibo, and Ibo's Miti Miwiri can help arrange day trips.

Quilaluia

Until recently, tiny Quilaluia, just south of Quirimba Island, was inhabited only by seasonal fishing communities. Now it's a protected marine sanctuary and home to **Azura Quilálea Private Island** (www.azura-retreats.com/azura-quilalea; r per person with full board US$675-945; ❄) , a low-key, high-quality small resort with nine sea-facing villas. The surrounding waters offer prime diving and snorkelling immediately offshore, while the island itself protects some ancient baobab trees.

Quirimba Island

Just south of Ibo, Quirimba is the most economically active island of the archipelago, with large coconut plantations, a sizeable sisal factory and an airstrip. It's not particularly scenic, though it does have some lovely stretches of sand. You can walk (with a guide) between Quirimba and Ibo at low tide, a beautiful excursion incorporating dense mangroves, expansive beaches and warm tidal pools.

Quirimba was an important Muslim trading centre well before the arrival of the Portuguese. In 1522 it was raided by the Portuguese and the town was destroyed, but it was later rebuilt. In the 16th century Quirimba served as a centre for missionary work.

Quirimba Guesthouse GUESTHOUSE **$$**
(☎82 308 3930, 86 144 3964; quirimba.island@gmail.com; r US$60) On the grounds of an old coconut estate, this German-run place has six clean rooms and offers food (US$30 for two meals). Bookings are essential.

Vamizi, Rongui & Macalóè

These three islands are part of a privately funded, community-based conservation project. For now, only Vamizi has **accommodation** (www.andbeyond.com/vamizi-island; d all-inclusive from US$1970; ❄) , with lodges on Rongui and Macalóè a possibility in the future.

Historically, the most important of the three islands was Vamizi, a narrow, paradisiacal crescent about midway between Moçimboa da Praia and Palma at the northernmost end of the archipelago. It was long a Portuguese and Arabic trading post – there are the ruins of an old Portuguese fort at its western end. A large village and several marvellous beaches lie to the north and east. All three islands are important seasonal fishing bases.

Moçimboa da Praia

This coastal outpost is the last major town before the Rovuma River and the Tanzanian border. Like Palma, further north, it has become a focus for the lucrative natural-gas industry. Most local residents are Mwani ('People of the Sea') – a Swahili, and hence Muslim, people known for their textiles and silver craftsmanship, as well as for their rich song and dance traditions. Moçimboa da Praia does a brisk trade with Tanzania, both legal and illegal, and from here northwards a few words of Swahili will often get you further than Portuguese.

The town itself is long, stretching over several kilometres between the main road and the sea. In the upper section are a small market, several *pensões* (cheap pensions), a petrol station and the transport stand.

IBO ISLAND COFFEE

One of Ibo's many peculiarities is a rare coffee plant known as *coffea racemose loureiro* that grows wild on the island and is cultivated by the locals for domestic consumption. Unlike Arabica coffee, which requires shade, altitude and sufficient moisture for successful cultivation, Ibo's coffee thrives at sea level and is highly resistant to drought. The plant yields a green fruit that, when harvested, dried and roasted, produces a light, pleasant herbal coffee that is low in caffeine. For a taster cup, head to the **Casa das Conchas** (⌚6am-5pm) in the old town.

Thought to have been brought to Ibo by Arabic traders, *racemosa loureiro* coffee was feted by the Portuguese during the colonial period, but it never saw large-scale commercial success. Today a nascent project sponsored by the World Wildlife Fund in tandem with the Slow Food Foundation is aiming to revive production and promote Ibo's coffee as a commercially viable alternative to the island's struggling fishing industry.

About 2km east, near the water, are a few more places to stay, plus police and immigration, a lively fish market and the dhow port.

Hotel Chez Natalie CHALET, CAMPGROUND $
(82 439 6080, 272-81092; natalie.bockel@gmail.com; camping Mtc500, d with shared bathroom Mtc1000, 4-person chalets Mtc2800; P) By far the best bet in town if you have your own transport, Natalie's has large grounds overlooking the estuary, camping and a handful of rustic but elegant family-style four-person chalets with mosquito nets, coffee maker and grill. It's very tranquil. Breakfast and other meals are available by advance arrangement only.

Complexo Vumba BUNGALOW $$
(87 609 7554; Avenida Marginal; r from Mtc4600;) This place has clean, air-conditioned rooms and is currently favoured by Moçimboa's growing contingent of natural-gas workers. It also has Moçimboa's best **restaurant** (mains from Mtc250; 8am-9pm). It's along the road paralleling the beach.

Getting There & Away

The transport stand is near the market at the entrance to town, and close to the large tree. Several pickups go daily to/from the Rovuma River ('Namoto') via Palma (Mtc250, two hours). The road to Palma is paved and in good shape. To Pemba (Mtc300, five to six hours), Maning Nice buses depart daily by 3am. Several pickups also do the journey, departing by 7am from the main road in front of the market. Maning Nice goes daily to/from Nampula (Mtc500, 13 hours), and several vehicles go daily to/from Mueda (Mtc150, two hours).

Mueda

Mueda is the first (or last) major town on the Mozambique side if you're crossing to/from Tanzania on the Unity Bridge. In 1960 it was the site of the infamous massacre of Mueda (p161). There's a statue commemorating Mueda's role in Mozambican independence and a small museum at the western end of town.

Several bus companies, including Maning Nice, have daily buses to Pemba (Mtc300, nine hours) and Moçimboa da Praia (Mtc150, two hours). They depart at 5am. There's also at least one vehicle (usually a pickup) daily to the Negomano border (Mtc500), including a 7am departure. All transport leaves from the main road opposite the market. After about 10am, it's difficult to find vehicles to any destination.

If you're driving, there are two roads connecting Mueda with the main north–south road. Most traffic uses the good road via Diaca (50km). The alternative route via Muidumbe (about 30km south of Diaca) is scenic, winding through hills and forests, but rougher. (Near Muidumbe is **Nangololo**, a mission station and an important base during the independence struggle, with an old airstrip large enough to take jets.)

Pensão Mtima PENSION $
(86 314 5303; Rua 1 de Maio; r Mtc1250, with shared bathroom Mtc350) Just off the main road through town, the Mtima has two classes of room: the basic variety with shared bucket bathroom, and some newer pews with air-con and private bathroom. Don't be put off by the scruffy restaurant (mains Mtc250 to Mtc450): lashings of chicken and chips emerge from the slightly iffy-looking kitchen.

Palma

Traditionally a fishing community known for its basketry and mat weaving, Palma now rivals Tete as Mozambique's fastest-changing city. The reason: natural gas. Huge offshore gas fields were discovered in 2010 and foreign investors have been piling in with their chequebooks ever since. Several plush new hotels aimed at the gas industry have already opened, with more on the way.

Palma sits on the coast nestled among coconut groves 45km south of the Tanzanian border. A melting pot of languages, with Makwe, Makonde, Mwani, Swahili and Portuguese all spoken, it doesn't hold many sights per se, and is usually used as a staging post on the way to Tanzania.

All transport leaves from the Boa Viagem roundabout at the town entrance. Some drivers continue down to the main market.

Chapas (minibuses) from Moçimboa da Praia en route to the Rovuma River pass Palma from about 6am (Mtc300 from Palma to the border). Transport from the Rovuma south to Moçimboa da Praia passes through Palma from about 10am, and there's at least one vehicle from Palma to Moçimboa

WORTH A TRIP

ISLAND TO ISLAND WALKS

A unique and interesting day trip is to hike from Ibo to neighbouring Quirimba Island immediately to the south – and you don't need to walk on water to do it. At low tide the two islands are effectively joined by a series of sandbars.

Because the timing of the walk depends on the tides and involves navigating along narrow channels through dense mangrove swamps, it's wise to hire a guide – ask at any of Ibo's hotels. With stops, it should take a person of average fitness two to three hours to complete. Once you're on Quirimba Island, your guide can organise a seafood lunch with one of the families who live in the village overlooking the beach. Subsequently you can explore Quirimba's long, untarnished beaches or just watch Mozambican village life as you wait for the tide to come in. A small boat, weaving a curvaceous path through the overhanging mangroves, will ferry you back to Ibo when the water's high enough.

da Praia each morning (Mtc250, one hour) along a good, graded road.

Karibu Palma Hotel HOTEL $$$
(☎87 274 5982; www.karibupalmahotel.com; d incl breakfast from US$107; ❄📶) Built on the back of Palma's gas boom, this well-appointed new hotel is aimed mainly at business people. Twelve spick-and-span rooms are arranged in smart two-storey blocks overlooking well-manicured gardens. There's also a decent on-site restaurant nestled under a thatched shelter and good buffet breakfasts.

UNDERSTAND MOZAMBIQUE

Mozambique Today

In Mozambique's hotly contested 2014 national elections, Frelimo insider Filipe Nyusi won at the national level. However Renamo, which won at the parliamentary level in five central and northern provinces, alleged widespread irregularities and rejected the results.

Since then, ongoing low-level conflict between Frelimo and Renamo – fuelled also by the discovery of major coal and natural-gas deposits in the country's north – has marred Mozambique's once glowing image as a post-war success story. While economic forecasts remain positive overall, other challenges include corruption and lack of free political debate in the public arena.

History

In the Beginning

The first Mozambicans were small, scattered clans of nomads, possibly distant cousins of the San, who were likely trekking through the bush as early as 10,000 years ago. They left few traces and little is known about this era.

About 3000 years ago, Bantu-speaking peoples from the Niger Delta in West Africa began moving through the Congo basin. Over a period of centuries they journeyed into East and southern Africa, reaching present-day Mozambique sometime around the 1st century AD, where they made their living farming, fishing and raising livestock.

Early Kingdoms

Most of these early Mozambicans set themselves up in small chiefdoms, some of which gradually coalesced into larger states or kingdoms. These included the Karanga (Shona) in central Mozambique and the renowned kingdom of Monomotapa, south and west of present-day Tete.

Southern Mozambique, which was settled by the Nguni and various other groups, remained decentralised until the 19th century, when consolidation under the powerful kingdom of Gaza gave it at least nominal political cohesion.

Arrival of the Arabs

From around the 8th century AD, sailors from Arabia began to arrive along the East African coast. Trade flourished and intermarriage with the indigenous Bantu speakers gave birth to the Swahili language and culture. By the 9th century several settlements had been established, including Kilwa island, in present-day Tanzania, which soon became the hub of Arab trade networks throughout southeastern Africa. Another was Sofala, near present-day Beira, which by the 15th century was the main link connecting Kilwa with the old Shona kingdoms and the inland goldfields. Other early coastal ports and settlements included those at Mozambique Island, Angoche, Quelimane and Ibo Island, all ruled by local sultans.

Portuguese Adventurers

In 1498 Vasco da Gama landed at Mozambique Island en route to India. Within a decade of da Gama's arrival, the Portuguese had established themselves on the island and gained control of numerous other Swahili-Arab trading posts – lured in part by their need for supply points on the sea route to the east and in part by their desire to control the gold trade with the interior.

Over the next 200 years the Portuguese set up trading enclaves and forts along the coast, making Mozambique Island the capital of what they called Portuguese East Africa. By the mid-16th century, ivory had replaced gold as the main trading commodity and by the late 18th century, slaves had been added to the list, with close to one million Africans sold into slavery through Mozambique's ports.

Portugal's Power Struggle

In the 17th century the Portuguese attempted to strengthen their control by setting up *prazos* (vast agricultural estates) on land granted by the Portuguese crown or by wresting control of it from local chiefs.

The next major effort by the Portuguese to consolidate their control came in the late 19th century with the establishment of charter companies, operated by private firms who were supposed to develop the land and natural resources within their boundaries. In reality these charter companies operated as independent fiefdoms and did little to consolidate Portuguese control. With the onset of the 'Scramble for Africa' in the 1880s, Portugal was forced to strengthen its claims in the region. In 1891 a British-Portuguese treaty was signed formalising Portuguese control in the area.

Early 20th Century

One of the most significant events in early-20th-century Mozambique was the large-scale migration of labour from the southern provinces to South Africa and Rhodesia (present-day Zimbabwe). This exodus was spurred by expansion of the Witwatersrand gold mines and by the passage of a new labour law in 1899. The new law divided the Mozambican population into non-indigenous *(não indígenas or assimilados)*, who had full Portuguese citizenship rights, and indigenous *(indígenas)*, who were subject to the provisions of colonial laws and forced to work, to pay a poll tax and to adhere to a form of pass laws.

Another major development was the growing economic importance of the southern part of the country. As ties with South Africa strengthened, Lourenço Marques (now Maputo) took on increasing importance as a major port and export channel and in the late 19th century the Portuguese transferred the capital here from Mozambique Island.

In the late 1920s António Salazar came to power in Portugal. He sealed off the colonies from non-Portuguese investment, abolished the remaining *prazos* and consolidated Portuguese control over Mozambique. Overall, conditions for Mozambicans worsened considerably.

Mueda Massacre

Discontent with the situation grew and a nationalist consciousness gradually developed. In June 1960, at Mueda in northern Mozambique, an official meeting was held by villagers protesting peacefully about taxes. Portuguese troops opened fire on the crowd, killing many demonstrators. Resentment at the 'massacre of Mueda' helped politicise the local Makonde people and became one of the sparks kindling the independence struggle. External support came from several sources, including Julius Nyerere's government in neighbouring Tanganyika (now Tanzania). In 1962, following a meeting of various political organisations working in exile for Mozambican independence, the Frente pela Libertação de Moçambique (Mozambique Liberation Front; Frelimo) was formed in Dar es Salaam (Tanzania), led by Eduardo Chivambo Mondlane.

Independence Struggle

Frelimo was plagued by internal divisions from the outset. However, under the leadership of the charismatic Mondlane and operating from bases in Tanzania, it succeeded in giving the liberation movement a structure and in defining a program of political and military action to support its aim of complete independence for Mozambique. On 25 September 1964 Mondlane proclaimed the beginning of the armed struggle for national independence.

In 1969 Mondlane was assassinated by a letter bomb at his office in Dar es Salaam. He was succeeded as president by Frelimo's military commander, Samora Moises Machel. Under Machel, Frelimo sought to extend its area of operations to the south. The Portuguese, meanwhile, attempted to eliminate rural support for Frelimo by implementing a scorched-earth campaign and by resettling people in a series of *aldeamentos* (fortified village complexes).

However, struggles within Portugal's colonial empire and increasing international criticism sapped the government's resources. In 1974, at a ceremony in Lusaka (Zambia), Portugal agreed to hand over power to Frelimo and a transitional government was established. On 25 June 1975 the independent People's Republic of Mozambique was proclaimed with Samora Machel as president and Joaquim Chissano, a founding member of Frelimo's intellectual elite, as prime minister.

Early Years of Independence

The Portuguese pulled out virtually overnight, leaving the country in a state of chaos with few skilled professionals and virtually no infrastructure. Frelimo, which found itself suddenly faced with the task of running the country, threw itself headlong into a policy of radical social change.

Frelimo's socialist program proved unrealistic, however, and by 1983 the country was almost bankrupt. Onto this scene came the Resistência Nacional de Moçambique (Mozambique National Resistance; Renamo), a ragtag group that had been established in the mid-1970s by Rhodesia (now Zimbabwe) as part of its destabilisation policy, and later kept alive with backing from the South African military and certain sectors in the West.

Ravages of War

Renamo had no ideology of its own beyond the wholesale destruction of social and communications infrastructure within Mozambique and the destabilisation of the government. Many commentators have pointed out that the war that went on to ravage the country for the next 17 years was thus not a 'civil' war but one between Mozambique's Frelimo government and Renamo's external backers. Recruitment was sometimes voluntary but frequently by force. Roads, bridges, railways, schools and clinics were destroyed. Atrocities were committed on a massive and horrific scale.

The drought and famine of 1983 crippled the country. Faced with this dire situation, Frelimo opened Mozambique to the West in return for Western aid.

In 1984 South Africa and Mozambique signed the Nkomati Accord, under which South Africa undertook to withdraw its support of Renamo, and Mozambique agreed to expel the African National Congress (ANC) and open the country to South African investment. While Mozambique abided by the agreement, South Africa exploited the situation to the full and Renamo's activity did not diminish.

Samora Machel died in a plane crash in 1986 under questionable circumstances and was succeeded by the more moderate Joaquim Chissano. The war between the Frelimo government and the Renamo rebels continued, but by the late 1980s political change was sweeping through the region. The collapse of the USSR altered the political balance, and the new president of South Africa, FW de Klerk, made it more difficult for right-wing factions to supply Renamo.

Peace

By the early 1990s, Frelimo had disavowed its Marxist ideology. A ceasefire was arranged, followed by a formal peace agreement in October 1992 and a UN-monitored disarmament and demobilisation campaign. Since then, Mozambique has been remarkably successful – at least on the surface – in moving beyond its history of war and transforming military conflict into political competition. Most notable was the relatively smooth leadership transition in 2004, when Armando Guebuza of the ruling Frelimo political party was elected to succeed long-serving former president Joaquim Chissano (also of Frelimo). Any easy re-election for Guebuza followed in 2009.

Cuisine

Mozambique's cuisine blends African, Indian and Portuguese influences, and is especially noted for its seafood as well as its use of coconut milk and piri-piri (chilli pepper).

Where to Eat

Roadside or market *barracas* (food stalls) serve plates of local food such as *xima* (a maize- or cassava-based staple) and sauce for about Mtc400 or less.

Most towns have a cafe, *pastelaria* or *salão de chá* serving coffee, pastries and inexpensive snacks and light meals such as omelettes, *pregos* (thin steak sandwiches) and burgers.

Restaurant prices and menu offerings are remarkably uniform throughout the country, ranging from about Mtc300 to Mtc500 for meals such as grilled fish or chicken served with rice or potatoes. Most restaurants also offer hearty Portuguese-style soups.

Markets in all larger towns sell an abundance of fresh tropical fruit along with a reasonably good selection of vegetables. High-quality meats from nearby South Africa are sold in delis and supermarkets.

The Arts

Dance

On Mozambique Island and along the northern coast, watch for *tufo* (a dance of Arabic origin). It is generally performed by women, wearing matching *capulanas* (sarongs) and scarves, and accompanied by special drums (some more like tambourines) known as *taware*.

In the south, one of the best-known dances, particularly in Maputo, is *marrabenta*, which combines Mozambican rhythms with Portuguese folk-music influences. Its energetic swaying and infectious rhythms embody Mozambique's history of struggle and optimistic determination.

The *casas de cultura* (cultural centres), found in every provincial capital, are good places to get information on traditional dance performances. Another excellent contact is Maputo's Centro Cultural Franco-Moçambicano (p111).

Literature

During the colonial era, local literature generally focused on nationalist themes. Two of the most famous poets of this period were Rui de Noronha and Noémia de Sousa.

In the late 1940s José Craveirinha (1922–2003) began to write poetry focusing on the social reality of the Mozambican people and calling for resistance and rebellion, which eventually led to his arrest. Today he is honoured as Mozambique's greatest poet, and his work, including 'Poem of the Future Citizen', is recognised worldwide.

As the armed independence struggle gained strength, Frelimo freedom fighters began to write poems reflecting their life in the forest, their marches and the ambushes. One of the finest of these guerrilla poets was Marcelino dos Santos.

With Mozambican independence in 1975, writers and poets felt able to produce literature without interference. This newfound freedom was soon shattered by Frelimo's war against the Renamo rebels, but new writers emerged, including the internationally acclaimed Mia Couto, whose works include *Voices Made Night* and *The Last Flight of the Flamingo*. Contemporary female writers include Lilia Momple *(The Eyes of the Green Cobra)* and Paulina Chiziane *(Niketche – A Story of Polygamy)*.

Music

The *timbila* orchestras of the Chopi people in southern Mozambique are one of the country's best-known musical traditions.

Modern music flourishes in the cities and the live-music scene in Maputo is excellent. *Marrabenta* is considered Mozambique's national music. It developed in the 1950s in the suburbs of Maputo (then Lourenço Marques) and has a light, upbeat style and distinctive beat inspired by the traditional rural *majika* rhythms of Gaza and Maputo provinces. It is often accompanied by a dance of the same name.

Sculpture & Painting

Mozambique is known for its woodcarvings, particularly for the sandalwood carvings found in the south and the ebony carvings of the Makonde.

The country's most famous painter is Malangatana Valente Ngwenya – universally known as Malangatana – whose style is characterised by dramatic figures and flamboyant yet restrained use of colour, and by its highly symbolic social and political commentary. Other internationally acclaimed artists include Bertina Lopes and Roberto Chichorro.

Natural Environment

Mozambique has extensive coastal lowlands forming a broad plain 100km to 200km wide in the south and leaving it vulnerable to seasonal flooding. In the north, this plain narrows and the terrain rises to mountains and plateaus on the borders with Zimbabwe, Zambia and Malawi. In central Mozambique, the predominant geographical feature is the Zambezi River valley and its wide delta plains. In many areas of the north, particularly in Nampula and Niassa provinces, towering granite outcrops (inselbergs; literally 'island mountains') dominate the landscape.

Wildlife

ANIMALS

While more than 200 types of mammal wander the interior, challenging access, dense vegetation and skittishness on the part of the animals can make spotting them difficult, and Mozambique shouldn't be viewed as a 'Big Five' destination. Work is proceeding in reviving several parks and reserves, especially Gorongosa National Park, which offers Mozambique's most accessible wildlife watching. However, poaching is taking a heavy toll, especially on the country's elephant population.

BIRDS

Of the approximately 900 bird species that have been identified in the Southern Africa region, close to 600 have been recorded in Mozambique. Among these are numerous aquatic species found primarily in the southern wetlands. On Inhaca Island alone, 300 bird species have been recorded. Rare and unique species (most of which are found in isolated montane habitats such as the Chimanimani Mountains, Mt Gorongosa and Mt Namúli) include the dappled mountain robin, the chirinda apalis, Swynnerton's forest robin, the olive-headed weaver and the green-headed oriole.

MARINE LIFE

Coastal waters host populations of dolphins, including spinner, bottlenose, humpback and striped dolphins, plus loggerhead, leatherback, green, hawksbill and olive ridley marine turtles. The coast also serves as a winter breeding ground for the humpback whale, which is found primarily between Ponta d'Ouro and Inhambane. Between July and October it's also common to see whales in the north, offshore from Pemba.

Dugongs have been sighted around Inhambane Bay, Angoche, Mozambique Island, Nacala and the Quirimbas and Bazaruto Archipelagos.

Plants

Almost 6000 plant species have been recorded, including an estimated 250 that are thought to be found nowhere else in the world. The Maputaland Centre of Plant Diversity, straddling the border with South Africa south of Maputo, is one of the most important areas of the country in terms of plant diversity and has been classified as a site of global botanical significance. The Chimanimani Mountains are also notable for their plant diversity, with at least 45 endemic species. Other important highland areas include the Gorongosa Massif (Sofala province) and Mt Chiperone, Mt Mabu and Mt Namúli (all in Zambézia province).

National Parks & Reserves

Mozambique has seven national parks: Gorongosa, Zinave, Banhine, Limpopo and Mágoè in the interior; Bazaruto National Park offshore; and Quirimbas National Park, encompassing both coastal and inland areas in Cabo Delgado province. Mágoè, Zinave and Banhine have no tourist infrastructure, although restocking of Zinave with elephants and other wildlife from South Africa's Kruger National Park is currently under way.

Wildlife reserves include Niassa, Marromeu, Pomene, Maputo and Gilé. The Chimanimani National Reserve has a network of rustic camps for hikers.

SURVIVAL GUIDE

Directory A–Z

ACCOMMODATION

Accommodation in coastal areas fills during Christmas and New Year's, Easter and other South African school holidays; advance bookings are recommended. Ask about rainy-season and children's discounts.

When quoting prices, many establishments distinguish between a *duplo* (room with two twin beds) and a *casal* (room with double bed). Rates are often quoted in US dollars or South African rand. Payment can almost always be made in meticals, dollars or rand.

ACTIVITIES

Birdwatching

Prime birding areas include:

- Bazaruto Archipelago
- Gorongosa National Park
- Lake Niassa
- Maputo Special Reserve

Useful websites with bird lists and announcements of regional birding activities:

- **African Bird Club** (www.africanbirdclub.org)
- **Fatbirder** (www.fatbirder.com)
- **Indicator Birding** (www.birding.co.za)
- **Southern African Birding** (www.sabirding.co.za)

Diving & Snorkelling

Attractions include the chance to sight dolphins, whale sharks, manta rays and dugongs; opportunities to discover new sites; the natural beauty of the Mozambican coast; seasonal humpback-whale sightings; excellent fish diversity; and a generally untouched array of hard and soft corals, especially in the north. You'll also have most spots almost to yourself.

Equipment, instruction and certification are widely available along the coast, including in Ponta d'Ouro, Tofo, Vilankulo, the Bazaruto Archipelago, Pemba and the Quirimbas Archipelago. Prices are comparable to those elsewhere in East Africa but somewhat higher than in South Africa.

Hiking

The best hiking area is the Chimanimani Mountains, which includes Mt Binga, Mozambique's highest peak. The hills around Gurúè offer good walking.

Surfing & Kitesurfing

The best waves are at Ponta d'Ouro in the far south of the country and at Tofinho. Boards can be rented at both places.

> **SLEEPING PRICE RANGES**
>
> The following price ranges refer to a double room in high season.
>
> **$** less than Mtc3500 (US$50)
>
> **$$** Mtc3500–7000 (US$50–100)
>
> **$$$** more than Mtc7000 (US$100)

Kitesurfing has a small but growing following, especially in the north near Pemba, and around Vilankulo. A good initial contact is **Kite Surfing Centre** (p125).

Wildlife Watching

The main wildlife-watching destination is Gorongosa National Park. Other possibilities include Niassa Reserve, Maputo Special Reserve and Limpopo National Park. Apart from in Gorongosa, the chances of spotting significant wildlife are small, and Mozambique shouldn't be considered a 'Big Five' destination.

BUSINESS HOURS

Banks 8am to 3pm Monday to Friday

Bars 5pm to late

Cafes 7.30am to 9pm

Exchange bureaus (casas de câmbio) 8.30am to 5pm Monday to Friday, to noon Saturday

Government offices 7.30am to 3.30pm Monday to Friday

Restaurants Breakfast 7am to 11am, lunch noon to 3pm, dinner 6.30pm to 10.30pm

Shops 8am to noon and 2pm to 6pm Monday to Friday, 8am to 1pm Saturday

CHILDREN

- **Cots & spare beds** Easily arranged; average cost Mtc500.
- **Child seats for hired cars** Occasionally available; confirm in advance.
- **Restaurant high chairs** Occasionally available.
- **Formula, disposable nappies and wet wipes** Available in pharmacies, large supermarkets and markets in larger towns.
- **Child care** Easy to arrange informally through your hotel.
- **Prams** Impractical; use a Mozambican-style sling carrier instead.

ELECTRICITY

Electricity is 220V to 240V AC, 50Hz, usually accessed with South African-style three-round-pin plugs or two-round-pin plugs.

EATING PRICE RANGES

The following price ranges refer to a standard main course.

$ less than Mtc325 (US$5)

$$ Mtc325–650 (US$5–10)

$$$ more than Mtc650 (US$10)

EMBASSIES & CONSULATES

All of the following embassies are located in Maputo. The closest Australian representation is in South Africa.

British High Commission (82 313 8580; www.gov.uk/government/world/mozambique; 310 Avenida Vladimir Lenine)

Canadian High Commission (21-492623; www.canadainternational.gc.ca/mozambique; 1138 Avenida Kenneth Kaunda)

Dutch Embassy (21-484200; http://mozambique.nlembassy.org; 324 Avenida Kwame Nkrumah)

French Embassy (21-484600; www.ambafrance-mz.org; 2361 Avenida Julius Nyerere)

German Embassy (21-482700; www.maputo.diplo.de; 506 Rua Damião de Gois)

Irish Embassy (21-491440; www.dfa.ie/mozambique; 3630 Avenida Julius Nyerere)

Malawian High Commission (21-492676; 75 Avenida Kenneth Kaunda)

Portuguese Embassy (21-490316; www.maputo.embaixadaportugal.mne.pt/en/; 720 Avenida Julius Nyerere)

South African High Commission (21-243000; www.dfa.gov.za/foreign/sa_abroad/sam.htm; 41 Avenida Eduardo Mondlane)

Swazi High Commission (21-491601, 21-492117; 1271 Rua Luís Pasteur)

Tanzanian High Commission (21-490112, 21-490110; ujamaa@zebra.uem.mz; 115 Rua 301)

US Embassy (21-492797; http://maputo.usembassy.gov; 193 Avenida Kenneth Kaunda)

Zambian High Commission (21-492452; 1286 Avenida Kenneth Kaunda)

Zimbabwean High Commission (21-490404, 21-488877; zimmaputo@zimfa.gov.zw; 1657 Avenida Mártires de Machava)

INTERNET ACCESS

Internet access is easy and fast in Maputo and other major centres, where there are numerous wi-fi spots and internet cafes. Most mid-range and top-end hotels also offer wi-fi.

MONEY

Mozambique's currency is the metical (plural meticais, pronounced 'meticaish') nova família, abbreviated as Mtc. Visa-card withdrawal from ATMs is the best way of accessing money.

ATMs

- All larger and many smaller towns have ATMs for accessing cash meticals. Most accept Visa cards; Millennium BIM and Standard Bank machines also, and less reliably, accept MasterCard.
- Many machines have a limit of Mtc3000 (US$120) per transaction. BCI's limit is Mtc5000 (US$200) and some Standard Bank machines dispense up to Mtc10,000 (US$400) per transaction.

Changing Money

- US dollars are easily exchanged everywhere; together with South African rand, they are the best currency to carry.
- Only new-design US dollar bills will be accepted. Euros are easy to change in major cities, but elsewhere you're likely to get a poor exchange rate.
- *Casas de câmbio* (exchange bureaus) are the most efficient places to change money. They usually give a rate equivalent to or slightly higher than that of the banks and are open longer hours.
- It is also possible to change money at some banks; BCI branches are generally good. Most banks don't charge commission for changing cash. Millennium BIM branches will let you change cash only if you have an account.
- Changing money on the street isn't safe anywhere and is illegal; asking shopkeepers is a better bet.

Cash

- Note denominations include Mtc20, Mtc50, Mtc100, Mtc200, Mtc500 and Mtc1000, and coins include Mtc1, Mtc2, Mtc5 and Mtc10. One metical is equivalent to 100 centavos (Ct); there are Ct1, Ct5, Ct10, Ct20 and Ct50 coins.
- Carry a standby mixture of US dollars (or South African rand, especially in the south) and meticals (including a good supply of small-denomination notes, as nobody ever has change) for times when an ATM is nonexistent or not working.

Credit Cards

- Credit cards are accepted at most (but not all) top-end hotels, at many midrange places, especially in the south, and at some car-hire agencies; otherwise they're of limited use in Mozambique.
- Visa is by far the most useful, and is also the main (often only) card for accessing money from ATMs.

Exchange Rates

Australia	A$1	Mtc60
Canada	C$1	Mtc60
Euro zone	€1	Mtc75
Japan	¥100	Mtc77
New Zealand	NZ$1	Mtc57
South Africa	R1	Mtc5
UK	UK£1	Mtc102
US	US$1	Mtc78

For current exchange rates, see www.xe.com.

Tipping

In low-budget bars and restaurants, tipping is generally not expected, other than perhaps by rounding up the bill. At upmarket and tourist establishments, tipping is customary (from 10% to 20%, assuming service has been good). Tips are also warranted, and always appreciated, if someone has gone out of their way to do something for you.

Travellers Cheques

Travellers cheques are not accepted for exchange or direct payment in Mozambique.

PUBLIC HOLIDAYS

New Year's Day 1 January
Mozambican Heroes' Day 3 February
Women's Day 7 April
International Workers' Day 1 May
Independence Day 25 June
Lusaka Agreement/Victory Day 7 September
Revolution Day 25 September
Peace & Reconciliation Day 4 October
Christmas/Family Day 25 December

For South African school-holiday dates, see the calendar link at www.saschools.co.za.

SAFE TRAVEL

Mozambique is a relatively safe place and most travellers shouldn't have any difficulties. That said, there are a few areas where caution is warranted. Government travel advisories are a good source of updated information.

Petty theft and robbery are the main risks: watch your pockets or bag in markets; don't leave personal belongings unguarded on the beach or elsewhere; and minimise trappings such as jewellery, watches and external money pouches.

If you leave your vehicle unguarded, don't be surprised if windscreen wipers and other accessories are gone when you return. Don't leave anything inside a parked vehicle.

When at stoplights or slowed in traffic, keep your windows up and doors locked, and don't leave anything on the seat next to you where it could be snatched.

In Maputo and southern Mozambique carjackings and more violent robberies do occur, although most incidents can be avoided by taking the usual precautions: avoid driving at night; keep the passenger windows up and the doors locked if you are in a vehicle (including a taxi) at any time during the day or night; avoid walking alone or in a group at dusk or at night, particularly in isolated areas; and avoid isolating situations in general. Don't walk alone along the beach away from hotel areas. If you're driving and your car is hijacked, hand over the keys immediately.

All this said, don't let these warnings deter you; simply be a savvy traveller. The vast majority of visitors enjoy this beautiful country without incident.

GOVERNMENT TRAVEL ADVISORIES

Australia www.smartraveller.gov.au

Canada www.travel.gc.ca

UK www.gov.uk/government/organisations/foreign-commonwealth-office

New Zealand www.safetravel.govt.nz

USA www.travel.state.gov

Hassles & Bribes

More likely than violent crime are simple hassles with underpaid authorities in search of a bribe. The worst offenders here are regular (ie grey-uniformed, non-traffic) police. If you get stopped you shouldn't have any problems as long as your papers are in order. Being friendly, respectful and patient helps (you won't get anywhere otherwise), as does trying to give the impression that you know what you're doing and aren't new in the country. Sometimes the opposite tack is also helpful: feigning complete ignorance if you're told that you've violated some regulation, and apologising profusely. It's also worth remembering that only traffic police are authorised to stop you for traffic infractions. If you're stopped by non-traffic police, you can ask to wait until a traffic-police officer arrives – often this will defuse the bribe attempt.

If you are asked to pay a *multa* (fine) for a trumped-up charge, playing the game a bit (asking to speak to the *chefe* (supervisor) and requesting a receipt) helps to counteract some of the more blatant attempts, as does insisting on going to the nearest *esquadrão* (police station); you should always do these things anyway.

Road Convoys

As of late 2016, timed army convoys were escorting all road traffic on the EN1 between the Save River and Muxungue, as well as on the EN1 between Nhamapadza (Gorongosa area) and Caia, and on the EN7 between Nova Vanduzi and Luenha (en route between Chimoio and Tete). Before you set off, it's highly recommended that you check your country's government travel advisory for updates on the security situation.

TELEPHONE

Land-line area codes must be dialled whenever you're making long-distance calls. As with mobile numbers, there is no initial zero.

Mozambique's country code is +258.

Mobile Phones

Mobile phone numbers are seven digits long, preceded by 82 for Mcel, 84 for Vodafone and 86 for Movitel.

Do not use an initial zero; seven-digit mobile numbers listed with zero at the outset are in South Africa and must be preceded by the South Africa country code (27) when dialling.

All companies have outlets in major towns at which you can buy Sim-card starter packs (from Mtc50), fill out the necessary registration form, and buy top-up cards.

TIME

Mozambique time is GMT/UTC plus two hours. There is no daylight-saving time.

VISAS

Visas are required by all visitors except citizens of South Africa, Swaziland, Zambia, Tanzania, Botswana, Malawi, Mauritius and Zimbabwe.

Travellers residing in a country with Mozambique diplomatic representation are required to obtain visas in advance of arrival in Mozambique or they must pay an additional 25% for visas obtained at the border. However, in an effort to encourage tourism, the government announced in early 2017 that one-month single-entry tourist visas could now be obtained on arrival at 44 land borders (including all major aiports and many major borders, but not the border with Tanzania) for Mtc2000. It is too early to tell how this new announcement will be implemented. Our advice is to try to get your visa in advance, especially if you will be arriving in Maputo via bus from Johannesburg. But failing that, it is well worth trying your luck at the border.

For visas purchased in advance, fees vary according to where you buy your visa and how quickly you need it. The maximum initial length of stay is three months. Express (24-hour to 48-hour) visa service is available at several Mozambican embassies and high commissions, and same-day visa service (within 24 hours) is available at several places, including Johannesburg and Nelspruit (South Africa) and Dar es Salaam (Tanzania), but at a price.

No matter where you get your visa, your passport must be valid for at least six months from the dates of intended travel, and have at least three blank pages.

For citizens of countries not requiring visas, visits are limited to 30 days from the date of entry, after which you'll need to exit Mozambique and re-enter.

The length of each stay for multiple-entry visas is determined when the visa is issued, and varies from embassy to embassy.

Visa Extensions

Visas can be extended at the *migração* (immigration office) in most provincial capitals, provided you haven't exceeded the three-month maximum stay, at a cost of Mtc2000 for one month.

Processing takes two days (with payment of an approximately Mtc200 supplemental express fee) to two weeks.

Don't wait until the visa has expired, as extensions are not granted automatically; hefty fines are levied for overstays.

Getting There & Away

AIR

Airports & Airlines

Airports in Mozambique:

Maputo International Airport (p112) Mozambique's main airport.

Vilankulo Regional flights.

Beira (p130) Regional flights.

Nampula Airport (p141) Regional flights.

Moçimboa da Praia Regional charter flights.

Pemba Airport (p155) Regional flights.

Airlines servicing Mozambique:

Coastal Aviation (safari@coastal.co.tz) Charter flights between Dar es Salaam (Tanzania) and Moçimboa da Praia, with connections to Pemba and the Quirimbas Archipelago.

Kenya Airways (www.kenya-airways.com) Nairobi (Kenya) to Pemba and Maputo.

Linhas Aéreas de Moçambique (LAM; ☎82 147, 84 147, 21-326001, 21-468800; www.lam.co.mz) The national airline. Offers flights connecting Johannesburg (South Africa) with Maputo, Vilankulo and Beira; and Dar es Salaam (Tanzania) with Pemba, Nampula and Maputo.

SAAirlink (p126) Johannesburg (South Africa) to Vilankulo, Beira, Nampula, Tete and Pemba; and Durban (South Africa) to Maputo.

South African Airways (www.flysaa.com) Johannesburg (South Africa) to Maputo and Vilankulo.

TAP Air Portugal (www.flytap.com) Lisbon (Portugal) to Maputo.

LAKE

Malawi

The MV *Chambo* ferry (Mtc300, 6½ hours between Metangula and Likoma Island; Mtc40, 1½ hours between Cóbuè and Likoma Island; and Mtc500, 12 to 13 hours between Metangula and Nkhata Bay) connects Metangula and Cóbuè twice weekly with Likoma Island (Malawi) and weekly with Nkhata Bay (Malawi). A southern route connecting Metangula with Chipoka (Malawi, Mtc550, 11 to 12 hours) via Meponda is also running. Contact the **Malawi Shipping Company** (☎ 01-587411; www.malawitourism.com/pages/content/index.asp?PageID=164) for confirmation of prices and schedules.

The journey between Cóbuè and Likoma Island (Malawi) can also be done by local fishing boats (about US$7 one way), which wait each morning at both destinations for passengers.

There are immigration posts in Metangula and Cóbuè (and on Likoma Island and in Nkhata Bay, for Malawi). At the time of research, it was possible to get a Mozambique visa at Cóbuè (although this may soon change) but not at Metangula.

LAND

Malawi

Border Crossings

- **Cóbuè** On Lake Niassa.
- **Dedza** 85km southwest of Lilongwe.
- **Entre Lagos** Southwest of Cuamba.
- **Mandimba** Northwest of Cuamba.
- **Metangula** On Lake Niassa.
- **Milange** 120km southeast of Blantyre.
- **Vila Nova da Fronteira** At Malawi's southern tip.
- **Zóbuè** On the Tete Corridor route linking Blantyre (Malawi) and Harare (Zimbabwe); this is the busiest crossing.

To & From Blantyre

- Via Zóbuè: vehicles go daily from Blantyre to the border via Mwanza. Once in Mozambique (the border posts are separated by about 5km of no-man's land), chapas (converted passenger trucks or minivans) go daily to Tete (Mtc190, 1½ hours Zóbuè to Tete).
- Via Vila Nova da Fronteira: daily minibuses go from Blantyre to Nsanje and on to the border. Once across, there are chapas to Mutarara, and from there to Sena and on to Caia on the main north–south road.
- Via Melosa (about 2km from Milange town, and convenient for Quelimane and Gurúè): buses go from Blantyre via Mulanje to the border. Once across, several vehicles go daily to Mocuba (Mtc300), from where there is frequent transport south to Quelimane and north to Nampevo junction (for Gurúè) and Nampula.
- Entre Lagos (for Cuamba and northern Mozambique): possible with your own 4WD (allow about 1½ hours to cover the 80km from Entre Lagos to Cuamba), or by *chapa* (about 2½ hours between the border and Cuamba). On the Malawi side, minibuses go from the border to Liwonde. Another option is the weekly Malawi train between the border and Liwonde (currently Thursday morning from Liwonde to Nayuchi on the border, and from Nayuchi back to Liwonde that same afternoon). There is basic accommodation at Entre Lagos if you get stuck. The closest bank is in Mecanhelas (Mozambique), about 25km away.
- Via Mandimba: Malawian transport goes frequently to Mangochi, where you can get minibuses to Namwera, and on to the border at Chiponde. Once in Mozambique (moto-taxis bridge the approximately 1.5km of no-man's land for Mtc50, and then vehicles take you to Mandimba town), several vehicles daily go from Mandimba to both Cuamba (three hours) and Lichinga (Mtc300).

To & From Lilongwe

The Dedza border is linked with the EN103 to/from Tete by a scenic tarmac road. From Tete, there's at least one *chapa* daily to Ulongwé and on to Dedza. Otherwise, go in stages from Tete via Moatize and the junction about 15km southwest of Zóbuè. Once across, it's easy to find transport for the final 85km to Lilongwe.

South Africa

Border Crossings

- **Giriyondo** (8am to 4pm October to March, to 3pm April to September) 75km west of Massingir town, 95km from Kruger National Park's Phalaborwa Gate.
- **Kosi Bay** (8am to 5pm) 11km south of Ponta d'Ouro.
- **Pafuri** (8am to 4pm) 11km east of Pafuri Camp in Kruger National Park.
- **Ressano Garcia–Lebombo** (6am to midnight) Northwest of Maputo; very busy.

To & From Durban

Luciano Luxury Coach (p112) goes between Maputo and Durban via Namaacha and Big Bend in Swaziland (US$28, nine to 10 hours) departing Maputo at 6.30am Tuesday and Friday and Durban (Pavillion Hotel, North Beach) at 6.30am Wednesday and Sunday.

To & From Kruger National Park

Neither the Pafuri nor the Giriyondo crossing is accessible via public transport. Visas should be arranged in advance. Officially you're required to have a 4WD to cross both borders, and a 4WD is essential for the Pafuri border, which crosses the Limpopo River near Mapai (for which there is a makeshift ferry during the rains). Allow two days between Pafuri and Vilankulo. The basic **Nhampfule Campsite** (☎84 301 1719; www.limpopopn.gov.mz; camping Mtc210) at Limpopo National Park's Mapai entry gate has hot-water showers.

Note that if you are entering/leaving South Africa via Giriyondo or Pafuri, you will be required to show proof of payment of one night's lodging within the Great Limpopo Transfrontier Park (ie either in Limpopo National Park or South Africa's Kruger National Park) to fulfil SANParks' requirement for one compulsory overnight within the transfrontier park for all visitors.

To & From Nelspruit & Johannesburg

Large 'luxury' buses do the route daily (US$25 to US$40 one way, nine to 10 hours between Maputo and Johannesburg's Park Station; US$13 to US$15 one way, four hours between Maputo and Nelspruit's Promenade Hotel). All lines also service Pretoria, with a change of buses at Park Station. It's essential to organise your Mozambique visa in advance. Tickets should also be purchased one day in advance of travel.

Cheetah Express (p112) Daily between Maputo and Nelspruit (Mtc1300 return, no one-way tickets), departing Maputo at 6am from Avenida Eduardo Mondlane next to Mundo's (p111), and departing Nelspruit at 4pm from Mediclinic, Crossings and Riverside Mall.

Greyhound (p112) Daily from Johannesburg's Park Station complex at 7.45am, and from Maputo at 7am and 7pm.

Luciano Luxury Coach (p112) Daily Monday to Saturday from Johannesburg (Hotel Oribi, 24 Bezuidenhout Ave, Troyville) at 5pm, and Sunday at 9.30am; and from Maputo daily except Saturday at 8.30pm.

Translux (p112) Operates jointly with City to City; the Translux service is generally the better of the two. Daily from Johannesburg's Park Station at 8.45am (at 7.50am for City to City); and from Maputo at 7.45am (at 7.20am for City to City).

To & From Ponta d'Ouro

The Kosi Bay border crossing is 11km south of Ponta d'Ouro along a sandy track (now 4WD but soon to be paved), and most *chapas* from Catembe (opposite Maputo, on Maputo Bay) pass here, before stopping at Ponta d'Ouro (Mtc50 from the border to Ponta d'Ouro). Coming from South Africa, there's a guarded car park just over the border where you can leave your vehicle in the shade for R40 per day. Most Ponta d'Ouro hotels do pick-ups from the border from about US$10 to US$15 per person (minimum two people). Allow about five hours for the drive to/from Durban.

Swaziland

Border Crossings

Goba–Mhlumeni (open 24 hours) Southwest of Maputo.

Lomahasha–Namaacha (7am-8pm) In Swaziland's extreme northeastern corner.

To & From Manzini

There are at least one or two direct *chapas* daily between Maputo and Manzini (Mtc370). It's about the same price and sometimes faster to take a *chapa* between Maputo and Lomahasha–Namaacha (Mtc70, 1½ hours), walk across the border, and then get Swaziland transport on the other side (about US$5 and three hours from the border to Manzini).

For self-drivers, the Namaacha border is notoriously slow on holiday weekends; the quieter border at Goba (Goba Fronteira), reached via a scenic, winding road from Maputo, is a good alternative. The road from Swaziland's Mananga border (open 7am to 6pm), connecting north to Ressano Garcia–Lebombo, is another option.

Tanzania

Border Crossings

For all Mozambique–Tanzania crossings it is essential to arrange your Mozambique (or Tanzania) visa in advance.

- **Kilambo** 130km north of Moçimboa da Praia, and called Namiranga or Namoto on the Mozambique side.
- **Moçimboa da Praia (Mozambique)** Immigration and customs for those arriving by plane or dhow.
- **Mtomoni** Unity Bridge 2; 120km south of Songea (Tanzania).
- **Negomano** Unity Bridge.
- **Palma (Mozambique)** Immigration and customs for those arriving by dhow or charter flight.

To & From Masasi

The main vehicle crossing over the Rovuma is via the Unity Bridge at Negomano (7.30am to 4pm in Mozambique, 8.30am to 5pm in Tanzania), near the confluence of the Lugenda River. From Masasi, go 35km southwest along the Tunduru road to Nangomba village, from where a good 68km track leads down to Masuguru village. The bridge is 10km further at Mtambaswala. Once over, there is 160km on a bush track with fine, deep, red dust (mud during the rains, and often blocked by trucks). This track continues through low land bordering the Rovuma before climbing up to Ngapa (shown as Moçimboa do Rovuma on some maps), where there is a customs and immigration checkpoint, as well as stunning views down over the Rovuma River basin. From Ngapa to Mueda is 40km further on a reasonable dirt road (four to six hours from the bridge to Mueda, longer during the rains).

Via public transport, there's a daily *chapa* from Masasi to Mtambaswala (Tsh6000) each morning. On the other side, a *chapa* leaves Negomano by about 1pm for Mueda (Mtc500). Going in the other direction, if you arrive at Mtambaswala after the *chapa* for Masasi has left (it doesn't always coordinate with the vehicle arriving from Mueda), there are some basic guesthouses for sleeping.

To & From Mtwara

Vehicles go daily from 6am from Mtwara (Tanzania) to Kilambo (Tsh6000, one hour) and on to the Rovuma River, which is in theory crossed daily by the MV *Kilambo* ferry. The ferry, again in theory, takes half a dozen cars plus passengers (Tsh30,000/500 per vehicle/person). However, its passage depends on tides, rains and mechanical issues. If it is not operating, you'll need to negotiate a ride in a smaller boat or a dugout canoe (about Tsh5000, 10 minutes to over an hour, depending on water levels; dangerous during heavy rains). The border is a rough one, and it's common for touts to demand up to 10 times the 'real' price for the boat crossing. Watch your belongings, especially when getting into and out of the boats, and keep up with the crowd.

Once you're in Mozambique, several pickups go daily to the Mozambique border crossing at Namiranga, 4km further on, and from there to Palma and Moçimboa da Praia (US$13, three hours). The road on the Mozambican side is poor at the border but improves closer to Palma.

To & From Songea

One or two vehicles daily depart from Majengo C area in Songea (Tsh12,000, three to four hours) to Mtomoni village and the Unity 2 bridge. Once across, take Mozambique transport to Lichinga (Tsh30,000, five hours). Pay in stages, rather than paying the entire Tsh40,000 Songea–Lichinga fare in Songea, as is sometimes requested.

Zambia

Border Crossings

- **Cassacatiza** (7am to 5pm) 290km northwest of Tete; main crossing.
- **Zumbo** (7am to 5pm) At the western end of Lake Cahora Bassa.

To & From Zambia

The Cassacatiza border is a seldom used but intriguing route between Mozambique and Zambia's South Luangwa National Park for those with their own vehicles. To cross the border via public transport: chapas go daily from Tete to Matema, from where there's sporadic transport to the border (allow about three hours from Tete to the border). On the other side, there are several vehicles daily to Katete (Zambia), and then on to Lusaka or Chipata.

The border post at Zumbo is accessed with difficulty from Mozambique via Fíngoę and is of interest primarily to anglers and birdwatchers heading to the western reaches of Lake Cahora Bassa. Once at Zumbo, the only possibility for onward transport to Luangwa (Zambia) or Kanyemba (Zimbabwe) is via private charter boat. The government pontoon is not running as of this writing.

Zimbabwe

Border Crossings

- **Espungabera** In the Chimanimani Mountains.
- **Machipanda** On the Beira Corridor linking Harare with the sea.
- **Mukumbura** (7am to 5pm) West of Tete.
- **Nyamapanda** On the Tete Corridor, linking Harare with Tete and Lilongwe (Malawi).

To & From Harare

From Tete there are frequent vehicles to Changara and on to the border at Nyamapanda, where you can get transport to Harare. Through buses between Blantyre and Harare are another option.

From Chimoio you can catch a direct chapa to the border at Machipanda (Mtc80, one hour), from where you'll need to take a taxi 12km to Mutare, and then get Zimbabwean transport to Harare.

The seldom-used route via the orderly little border town of Espungabera is slow and scenic, and an interesting dry-season alternative for those with a 4WD.

Mukumbura (4WD only) is of interest mainly to anglers heading to Cahora Bassa Dam. There is no public transport on the Mozambique side.

Getting Around

AIR

Airlines in Mozambique

Linhas Aéreas de Moçambique (p168) The national airline, with flights linking Maputo with Inhambane, Vilankulo, Beira, Chimoio, Quelimane, Tete, Nampula, Lichinga and Pemba. Always reconfirm your ticket, and check in early. Visa cards are accepted in most offices. Advance-purchase tickets are often significantly cheaper than last-minute fares, and there are many advertised specials. Sample one-way fares and flight frequencies: Maputo to Pemba (US$200, daily), and Maputo to Vilankulo (US$150, daily), Maputo to Lichinga (US$200, five weekly).

CR Aviation (www.craviation.co.mz) Scheduled and charter flights to the Bazaruto Archipelago, Quirimbas Archipelago, Inhaca and Gorongosa National Park.

BOAT

On Lake Niassa there is twice-weekly passenger service on the MV *Chambo* between Metangula, Cóbuè, Mbueca and several other villages along the Mozambican lakeshore.

BUS

- Direct services connect major towns at least daily, although vehicle maintenance and driving standards leave much to be desired.
- A large bus is called a *machibombo,* and sometimes also an *autocarro*. While there are several larger companies, most routes are served by small, private operators.
- Many towns don't have central bus stations. Instead, transport usually leaves from the bus-company garage, or from the start of the road towards the destination. Long-distance transport in general, and all transport in the north, leaves early – between 3am and 7am. Mozambican transport usually leaves quickly and close to the stated departure time.
- There is no luggage fee for large buses. For smaller buses and *chapas* (converted passenger trucks or minivans), if your bag is large enough that it needs to be stowed on the roof, you will be charged, with the amount varying depending on distance travelled and size of the bag, and always negotiable.
- Where there's a choice, always take buses rather than *chapas*.
- The more luggage on the roof, the slower the service.

Reservations

Etrago and Nagi Trans buses should be booked a day in advance. Otherwise, showing up on the morning of travel (about an hour prior to departure) is usually enough to ensure a place.

If you are choosy about your seat (best is in front, on the shady side), get to the departure point earlier.

Routes

Sample journey fares, times and frequencies:

ROUTE	FARE (MTC)	DURATION (HR)	FREQUENCY
Maputo–Vilanculos	950	10	daily
Nampula–Pemba	500	7	daily
Maputo–Beira	1700	17-18	daily
Lichinga–Maputo	4200	2-3 days	weekly

CAR & MOTORCYCLE

- A South African or international driving licence is required to drive in Mozambique. Those staying longer than six months will need a Mozambican driving licence.
- *Gasolina* (petrol) is scarce off main roads, especially in the north. *Gasóleo* (diesel) supplies are more reliable. On bush journeys, always carry an extra jerry can and top up whenever possible, as filling stations sometimes run out.
- Temporary import permits (US$2) and third-party insurance (US$10 to US$15 for 30 days) are available at most land borders, or in the nearest large town.
- In late 2016 Mozambique introduced *livre-trânsito* (free pass) cards. The cards – given to drivers following inspection at the border to minimise traffic-police stops – should be displayed in the front windscreen to show that the car has already been inspected.

Car Hire

- There are rental agencies in Maputo, Vilankulo, Beira, Nampula, Tete and Pemba, most of which take credit cards. Elsewhere, you can usually arrange something with upmarket hotels.
- Rates start at about US$100 per day for 4WD (US$80 for 2WD), excluding fuel.
- None of the major agencies offers unlimited kilometres.
- With the appropriate paperwork, rental cars from Mozambique can be taken into South Africa and Swaziland but not into other neighbouring countries. Most South African rental agencies don't permit their vehicles to enter Mozambique.

Insurance

- Private vehicles entering Mozambique must purchase third-party insurance at the border (from US$10 to US$15 for 30 days).
- It's also advisable to take out insurance coverage at home or (for rental vehicles) with the rental agency to cover damage to the vehicle, yourself and your possessions.
- Car-rental agencies in Mozambique have wildly differing policies (some offer no insurance at all, some that do may have high deductibles and most won't cover off-road driving); enquire before signing any agreements.

Road Rules

- Traffic in Mozambique drives on the left.
- Traffic already in a roundabout has the right of way.
- The driver and all passengers are required to wear a seat belt.
- It's prohibited to drive while using a mobile phone and required to drive with the vehicle's insurance certificate, and to carry a reflector vest and two hazard triangles.
- Speed limits (100km/h on main roads, 80km/h on approaches to towns and 60km/h

or less when passing through towns) are radar enforced.

- Fines for speeding and other traffic infringements vary, and should always be negotiated (in a polite, friendly way), keeping in mind that official speeding fines range from Mtc1000 up to Mtc5000.
- Driving on the beach is illegal.

LOCAL TRANSPORT

Chapa

- The main form of local transport is the *chapa*, the name given to any public transport that runs within a town or between towns and isn't a bus or truck. On longer routes, your only option may be a *camião* (truck). Many have open backs, and the sun and dust can be brutal; try for a seat in the cab.
- *Chapas* can be hailed anywhere, and prices are fixed. Intra-city fares average Mtc5 to Mtc7. The most comfortable and coveted seat (though you'll likely pay a bit more) is in the front, next to the window.
- *Chapa* drivers are notorious for their unsafe driving and there are many accidents. Bus is always a better option. Long-haul *chapas* usually depart early and relatively promptly, although drivers will cruise for passengers before leaving town.

Taxi

Apart from airport arrivals, taxis don't cruise for business, so you'll need to seek them out. While a few have functioning meters, you'll usually need to negotiate a price. Town trips start at Mtc150.

TRAIN

The only passenger train regularly used by tourists is the twice-weekly slow line between Nampula and Cuamba. Vendors are at all stations, but bring extra food and drink. Second class is reasonably comfortable, and most cabins have windows that open. Third class is hot and crowded. Book the afternoon before travel.

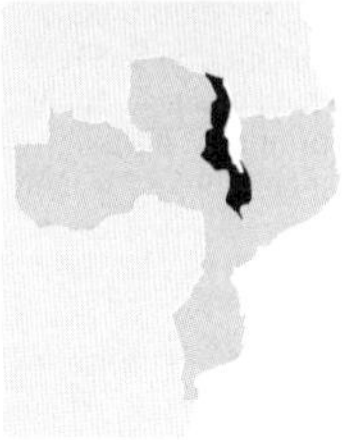

Malawi

POP 18,570,321

Includes ➡

Best Places to Sleep

- Kaya Mawa (p191)
- Mkulumadzi Lodge (p214)
- Mvuu Camp (p202)
- Chelinda Lodge (p185)

Best Places to Eat

- Casa Rossa (p203)
- Huntingdon House (p211)
- L'Hostaria (p207)
- Mushroom Farm (p184)

Why Go?

Apart from the legendary Malawian friendliness, what captures you first about this vivid country is its geographical diversity. Slicing through the landscape is Africa's third-largest lake: Lake Malawi, a shimmering mass of clear water, its depths swarming with colourful cichlid fish. Be it for diving, snorkelling, kayaking or just chilling, a visit to the lake is a must.

Suspended in the clouds in Malawi's deep south are the dramatic peaks of Mt Mulanje and the mysterious Zomba Plateau, both a hiker's dream, with mist-cowled forests and exotic wildlife. Further north is the otherworldly beauty of the Nyika Plateau, its rolling grasslands resembling the Scottish Highlands.

Malawi was once dismissed as a safari destination, but all that changed with a lion-reintroduction program at Majete Wildlife Reserve, which is now one of a few worthwhile wildlife-watching destinations nationwide.

When to Go

Lilongwe

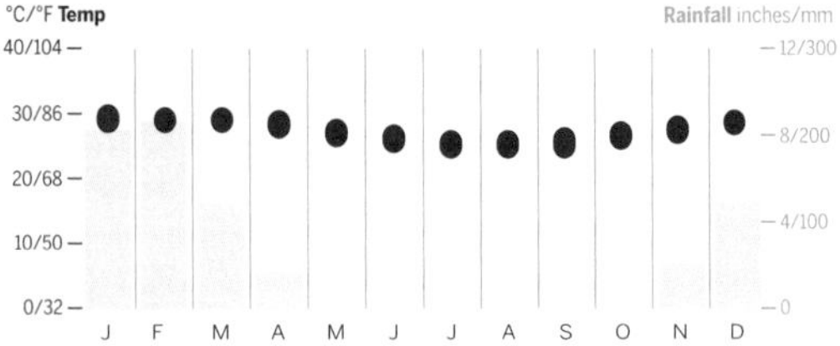

May–Jul Dry season, with cooler temperatures and lush vegetation.

Aug Interesting cultural festivals and good beach weather; the higher areas are chilly.

Sep & Oct End of the dry season: optimum wildlife-watching, but temperatures are high.

Malawi Highlights

1. **Lake Malawi** (p197) Kayaking across the bottle-green lake from ultra-chilled Cape Maclear to Mumbo Island.
2. **Majete Wildlife Reserve** (p213) Searching for reintroduced lions in Malawi's only Big Five park.
3. **Mt Mulanje** (p211) Scrambling up the twisted peaks and admiring the astounding views.
4. **Liwonde National Park** (p200) Spotting hippos and crocs on the Shire River and getting up close to elephants.
5. **Kaya Mawa** (p191) Escaping to this dreamy boutique hotel on Likoma Island.
6. **Nkhotakota Wildlife Reserve** (p194) Kayaking past crocs in the Bua River.
7. **Nyika National Park** (p185) Cycling the rugged grasslands, home to zebras and antelope.
8. **Nkhata Bay** (p188) Diving among cichlids and feeding fish eagles in northern Malawi's up-and-coming beach town.
9. **Livingstonia** (p184) Heading to the hills to find this atmospheric mission, home to fantastic ecolodges.

LILONGWE

Sprawling, chaotic and bustling with commerce, Lilongwe feels fit to burst. The nation's capital is initially a little underwhelming and it takes some time to get your bearings – you may wonder where the centre is – but once you've decided on your favourite restaurants, ferreted out the best malls and discovered those hidden leafy oases, the place grows on you.

◉ Sights

Lilongwe Wildlife Centre   WILDLIFE RESERVE
(Map p178; ☑0881 788999; www.lilongwewildlife. org; Kenyatta Rd; MK3500; ⊙8am-5pm, tours on the hour 9am-4pm) This 1.1-sq-km wilderness area is Malawi's only sanctuary for orphaned, injured and rescued wild animals, and plays an active role in conservation. Local residents include a one-eyed lion rescued from Romania, a python, two cobras, baboons, duikers, servals, and blue and vervet monkeys. The entry fee includes a one-hour tour of the enclosures.

Kamuzu Mausoleum   SHRINE
(Map p178; Capital Hill, Presidential Way; ⊙24hr) This marble and granite mausoleum is the final resting place of Malawi's 'president for life', Dr Hastings Kamuzu Banda. Between four pillars bearing the initials of his most prized principles – unity, loyalty, obedience and discipline – is a wrinkled portrait of the 'lion of Malawi'. Guides at the entrance will show you around in exchange for a small tip.

Parliament Building   NOTABLE BUILDING
(Map p178; Presidential Way; ⊙tours 7.30am-4.30pm Mon-Fri) To get up close to Malawi's movers and shakers, head to the home of the national parliament. It moved in 1994 from Zomba to the ostentatious palace of former president Banda on the outskirts of Lilongwe and now occupies this shiny new building near Capital Hill. Apply for a free guided tour by filling in a form at the gate two days beforehand (and only on weekdays).

🛏 Sleeping

Mabuya Camp   HOSTEL $
(Map p178; ☑01-754978; www.mabuyacamp.com; Livingstone Rd; camping/tent hire/dm US$7/9/12, r with/without bathroom US$45/30; P🛜🏊) Lilongwe's liveliest backpacker spot buzzes with a mix of travellers, overlanders and volunteers relaxing by the pool and in the large, shady gardens. There are dorms in the main house, as well as chalets, A-frame huts, en-suite rooms and camping pitches in the garden, with shared ablutions in thatched rondavels (round, traditional-style huts).

St Peter's Guesthouse   GUESTHOUSE $
(Map p181; ☑0995 299364; Glyn Jones Rd; incl breakfast dm MK4000, r MK8000-10,000; P) Anglican-owned St Peter's has four pleasant rooms next to a red-brick church. All rooms and the four-bed dorm are en suite. It's very peaceful, with a tranquil, leafy garden.

Lilongwe Golf Club   CAMPGROUND $
(Map p181; ☑01-753598; camping US$5; P🛜🛜🏊) This tranquil site is next to the green, and campers can use the bar-restaurant with its terrace, kids' playground and pool. There's a basic ablutions block and guards patrol the grounds. The golf club is off Glyn Jones Rd.

Kiboko Town Hotel   GUESTHOUSE $$
(Map p181; ☑01-751226; www.kiboko-safaris. com; Mandala Rd; s/d/tr incl breakfast from US$59/69/108; P🛜❄@🛜) This fresh upstairs guesthouse is right in the centre of Old Town, with a long veranda overlooking the Mandala St craft market. Staff are friendly and the 13 rooms are pleasant, with four-posters, ochre walls, fresh linen, mozzie nets and DSTV. There's also a terrace bar and a great **cafe** (Map p181; ☑01-751226; www. kibokohotel.com; Mandala Rd; mains MK4500; ⊙7am-5pm; P🛜🍴🍺) in the rear courtyard.

Korea Garden Lodge   HOTEL $$
(Map p181; ☑01-759774, 01-757854, 01-753467; www.kglodge.net; Tsiranana Rd; s/d from MK25,000/35,000, without bathroom MK18,000/22,000; P❄@🛜🏊) This good-value hotel has numerous rooms of varying standards; the more you pay, the larger and better equipped they get, and you can choose if you want an en-suite bathroom, TV, air-con and self-catering facilities. There's a tempting pool, flanked by a **restaurant** (☑01-753467; www.kglodge.net; 3056 Tsiranana Rd; mains MK5000; ⊙6.30am-9pm; P🛜) serving Asian food, and the grounds are replete with plants.

★Latitude 13°   BOUTIQUE HOTEL $$$
(☑0996 403159; www.latitudehotels.com; Mphonongo Rd, Area 43; r US$220; P🛜❄@🛜) Lilongwe's first world-class boutique hotel, this gated, nine-suite retreat raises the bar for Malawian accommodation. From the moment you step into its rarefied atmosphere of shadowy chic pulsing with glowing

pod lights you're transported right off the African continent.

★Kumbali Country Lodge LODGE $$$
(☎0999 963402; www.kumbalilodge.com; Capital Hill Dairy Farm, Plot 9 & 11, Area 44; s/d incl breakfast from US$200/240; P❄📶🏊) A short drive from the city centre, on a 650-hectare forest reserve, is a choice of swanky individual thatched chalets (Madonna has stayed here on her controversial visits to Malawi) with beautiful views of nearby Nkhoma Mountain.

Eating

Land & Lake Cafe CAFE $
(Map p181; ☎01-757120; Land & Lake Safaris, Area 3; mains MK3000; ⏰8am-4.30pm Mon-Fri, to 2pm Sat; P📶🧒) This garden cafe at Land & Lake Safaris' headquarters, off Laws Ave, serves croissants, bagels and English breakfasts, light lunches from quesadillas to spuds, and tempting desserts.

★Ad Lib INTERNATIONAL $$
(Map p181; ☎0994 350630; www.adlibglasgow.com; Mandala Rd; mains MK6000; ⏰9am-late) An adventurous extension of a hip Glaswegian diner chain, this popular local gathering spot has a covered street-front terrace and a jolly red-walled interior with a long bar. The menu gallops enthusiastically across a broad spectrum, including steaks, jerk chicken, fish and chips, wood-smoked meats, nachos, quesadillas, Angus-beef burger (recommended) and southern fried chicken popcorn.

★Koko Bean CAFE $$
(Map p178; ☎0994 263363; Lilongwe Wildlife Centre, Kenyatta Rd; mains MK5000; ⏰8am-5pm) Soundtracked by world music, this breezy urban sanctuary is surrounded by lawns, thatched shelters and a bar overlooking a sprawling jungle gym – perfect for a family visit. Come for breakfasts from French toast to hearty 'hangover' omelettes, with a pot of tea or coffee; sandwiches, wraps and burgers; and pizzas with zingy toppings.

★Ama Khofi CAFE $$
(Map p178; ☎0998 196475; Four Seasons Centre, Presidential Way; mains MK5000; ⏰7.30am-5pm Mon-Sat, 9am-5pm Sun; P📶🧒) Follow your nose to this delightful Parisian-style garden-centre cafe with wrought-iron chairs, a bubbling fountain and leafy surrounds. The menu has salads, main courses such as beef burgers and roast-beef sandwiches, and homemade sweet treats that include cakes and ice cream.

Drinking & Nightlife

Living Room CAFE, BAR
(Map p178; ☎0881 615460; www.facebook.com/thelivingroomlilongwe; mains MK4000, cocktails MK2000; ⏰8am-late) With woodcarvings on its shaded veranda, this tucked-away chill-out den (find it off Mzimba St) offers coffee, cocktails, board games and dishes from steaks to chambo and chips. Check Facebook for details of events, which include live music on Tuesdays and poetry on Wednesdays. The adjoining sports bar, Champions, opens at 11am; Amazon nightclub opens at 7pm on Friday and Saturday.

Chameleon Bar BAR
(Map p178; ☎0888 833114; Four Seasons Centre, Presidential Way; ⏰4-11pm Mon-Wed, to midnight Thu, to 1am Fri & Sat, 2-11pm Sun; 📶) This Scottish-owned watering hole faces **Buchanan's Grill** (Map p178; ☎0999 463686, 01-772859; www.buchanansgrill.com; Four Seasons Centre, Presidential Way; mains M6000, bar snacks MK4000; ⏰noon-2pm & 6-9pm Mon-Sat, noon-2.30pm Sun) in a leafy compound, with tables outside and a glass bar and purple walls within. It's popular with Malawians and expats both, and Sundays are big here, with live music from 2pm to 9.30pm. Karaoke is offered on the last Thursday of the month and soccer matches are screened.

Harry's Bar BAR
(Map p178; ⏰6pm-late) This hard-to-find wooden shack, located off Mzimba St, dishes up a bubbling atmosphere, live jazz in the garden and revolving entertainment. A Lilongwe institution and a must for any self-respecting hedonist.

Entertainment

Umunthu Theatre THEATRE
(Map p178; ☎01-757979; www.umunthu.com) In a converted warehouse off Paul Kagame Rd, Umunthu puts on regular live music, films, club nights and more, showcasing the best of Malawian talent. A variety show (MK500) takes place on Friday evening.

Shopping

★Four Seasons Centre MALL
(Map p178; Presidential Way; 📶) An oasis of fine dining and upmarket shopping, featuring clothing and design boutiques, a bar,

Lilongwe

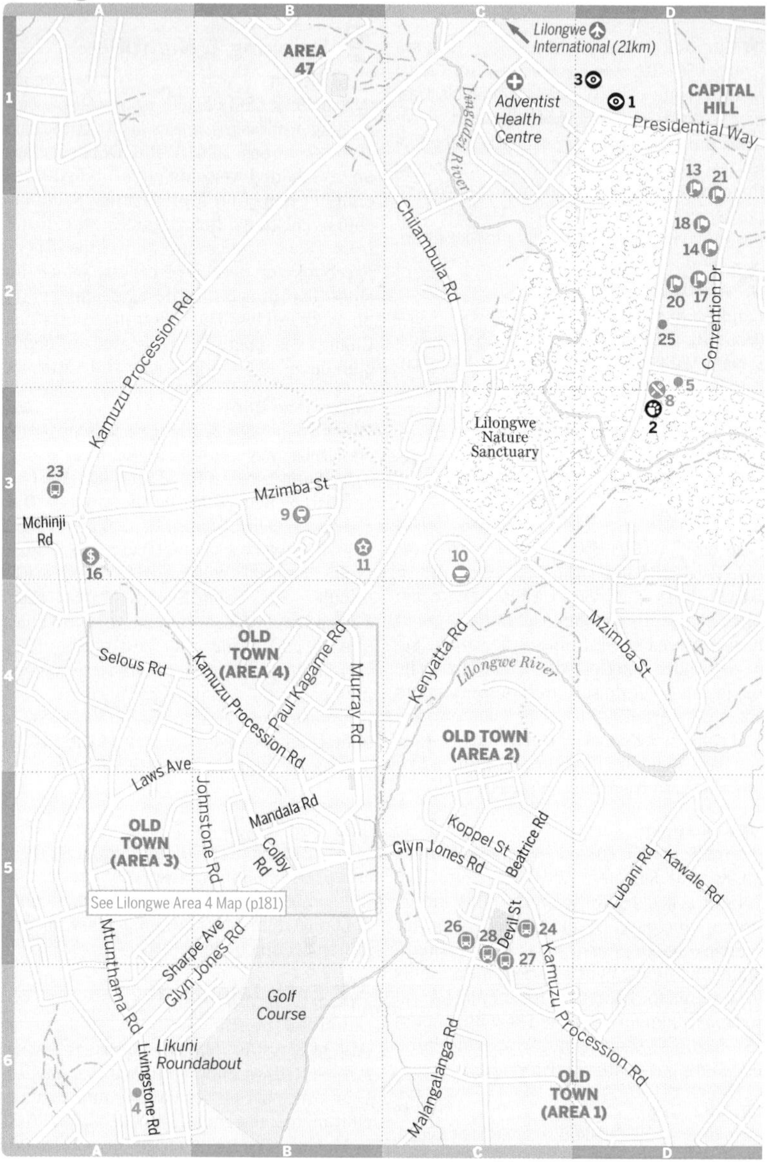

a restaurant and a cafe, Four Seasons is a restful one-stop shop. There's also a play park with a bouncy castle to keep nippers amused.

Lilongwe City Mall MALL

(Game Complex; Map p181; Kenyatta Rd) The best mall around for shops, fast-food joints, banks and other services, with a central location in Old Town. It also has branches of the mobile networks Airtel and TNM.

Lilongwe

Sights
1 Kamuzu Mausoleum D1
2 Lilongwe Wildlife Centre D3
3 Parliament Building D1

Activities, Courses & Tours
4 Adventure Office A6
5 Central African Wilderness Safaris D2

Sleeping
Mabuya Camp .... (see 4)
6 Sunbird Capital Hotel E1

Eating
Ama Khofi .... (see 12)
7 Buchanan's Grill F2
8 Koko Bean D2

Drinking & Nightlife
Chameleon Bar .... (see 7)
9 Harry's Bar B3
10 Living Room C3

Entertainment
11 Umunthu Theatre B3

Shopping
12 Four Seasons Centre F2

Information
13 British High Commission D1
14 German Embassy D2
15 Irish Embassy E2
16 Money Bureau A3
17 Mozambican High Commission D2
18 South African High Commission D2
19 Standard Bank E2
20 US Embassy D2
21 Zambian High Commission D1
22 Zimbabwean Embassy E2

Transport
23 AXA Coach Terminal A3
24 Buses to Dar es Salaam & Lusaka C5
25 Ethiopian Airlines D2
Kenya Airways .... (see 6)
26 Local Minibus Rank C5
27 Long Distance Minibuses C5
28 Main Bus Station C5
29 Malawian Airlines F2
30 South African Airways E1
31 Ultimate Travel E1

African Habitat ARTS & CRAFTS
(Map p181; 01-752363; grabifem@hotmail.com; Old Town Mall; 8.30am-5pm Mon-Fri, to 1pm Sat) Excellent for sculpture, woodcarvings, sarongs, cards and jewellery, as well as T-shirts and bags.

Craft Market MARKET
(Map p181; cnr Mandala & Kamuzu Procession Rds; 8am-4pm Mon-Sat) At these stalls outside the Old Town post office, vendors sell everything

from trinket woodcarvings, basketware and jewellery to traditional Malawian chairs.

Baobab Books BOOKS
(Map p181; ☎0999 280858; Uplands House, Kamuzu Procession Rd; ⏲8am-4.30pm Mon-Fri, to noon Sat) Excellent secondhand books hop with a wide range of novels, guidebooks, children's books and more. It also has a small cafe.

Information

IMMIGRATION

Immigration Office (Map p181; ☎01-750626; www.immigration.gov.mw; Murray Rd; ⏲7.30am-noon & 12.30-4pm Mon-Fri, to noon Sat)

MEDICAL

Adventist Health Centre (Map p178; ☎01-771543; ⏲casualty 24hr) Good for consultations, plus eye and dental problems. Off Presidential Way.

Daeyang Luke Hospital (☎01-711395; www.hospital.daeyangmission.org; Area 27; ⏲casualty 24hr, inpatients 8am-4.30pm Mon-Fri) Recommended private hospital. Off the M1 en route to the airport.

Michiru Pharmacy (Map p181; ☎01-754294; Nico Shopping Centre, Kamuzu Procession Rd; ⏲8am-5pm Mon-Fri, to 1pm Sat & Sun) Sells antibiotics and malaria pills as well as the usual offerings.

MONEY

Money Bureau (Map p178; ☎01-750875; www.fdh.co.mw; Crossroads Complex, Kamuzu Procession Rd; ⏲8am-4pm Mon-Fri, to noon Sat) Has good rates.

Standard Bank (Map p178; African Unity Ave, City Centre; ⏲8am-3pm Mon-Fri, 9-11am Sat) Change money and get a cash advances on Visa cards. There's a 24-hour ATM that accepts Visa, MasterCard, Cirrus and Maestro.

SAFE TRAVEL

During the day it's fine to walk around most of Old Town and City Centre, although City Centre is quieter at the weekend, so be on your guard then. Malangalanga Rd and the area around the main bus station and market can be dangerous, and walking to Old Town from there is not recommended. Muggers' haunts en route include the Kamuzu Procession Rd bridge between Area 2 and Area 3.

Watch out for your things while at the bus station, and if you arrive after dark take a taxi or minibus to your accommodation. Generally it isn't safe to walk around anywhere in the city after dark. Following a spate of carjackings, many local motorists jump red lights after dark.

Bus tickets should only be bought at the bus station.

Avoid Lilongwe Wildlife Centre after dark due to late-night hyena appearances.

TRAVEL AGENCIES

Ultimate Travel (Map p178; ☎01-776000; www.ultimatetravel.mw; President Walmont Hotel, Umodzi Park) offers city tours and nocturnal experiences of Lilongwe nightlife. For a day trip into the surrounding countryside, contact The **Adventure Office** (Map p178; ☎0996 347627; www.theadventureoffice.com; Mabuya Camp, Livingstone Rd) or **Land & Lake Safaris** (Map p181; ☎01-757120; www.landlake.net; Area 3). Travel agencies are also generally your best bet for tourist information.

Central African Wilderness Safaris (CAWS; Map p178; ☎01-771153; www.cawsmw.com; Woodlands Lilongwe, Youth Dr) The country's top safari operator specialises in trips to its high-end lodges in Liwonde and Nyika National Parks; also operates lodges in Lilongwe and the Chintheche Strip, and offers packages to Likoma Island and Zambia's South Luangwa National Park.

Ulendo Travel Group (☎01-794555; www.ulendo.net) Decades-old Ulendo is a one-stop travel shop for accommodation and car hire; **Ulendo Airlink** (☎01-794638; www.flyulendo.com) has flights head to hard-to-reach spots such as Likoma Island and the national parks; and a variety of expertly tailored tours and safaris in Malawi and Zambia are available. The reliable, specialist staff is a big selling point.

Getting There & Away

AIR

Ethiopian Airlines (Map p178; ☎01-772031; www.ethiopianairlines.com; Mantion Service Station Building, Kenyatta Rd; ⏲7.30am-4.30pm Mon-Fri)

Kenya Airways (Map p178; ☎01-774227; www.kenya-airways.com; Sunbird Capital Hotel, Chilembwe Rd)

Malawian Airlines (Map p178; ☎0992 991097, 01-774605; www.malawian-airlines.com; Golden Peacock Shopping Centre, Presidential Way)

South African Airways (Map p178; ☎01-772242; www.flysaa.com; Umodzi Park) Off Chilembwe Rd.

BUS

AXA (Map p178; ☎01-820100; www.axacoach.com; City Mall) buses run daily from outside its office to Blantyre (MK11,300, four hours), leaving at 7am, noon and 4.30pm. Buses leave around noon for Mzuzu (MK7000, four hours).

Destinations from the **main bus station** (Map p178; Malangalanga Rd, Area 2) include Mzuzu (MK4000, five hours), Blantyre (MK3500, four hours), Kasungu (MK2500, two hours), Nkhata

Lilongwe Area 4

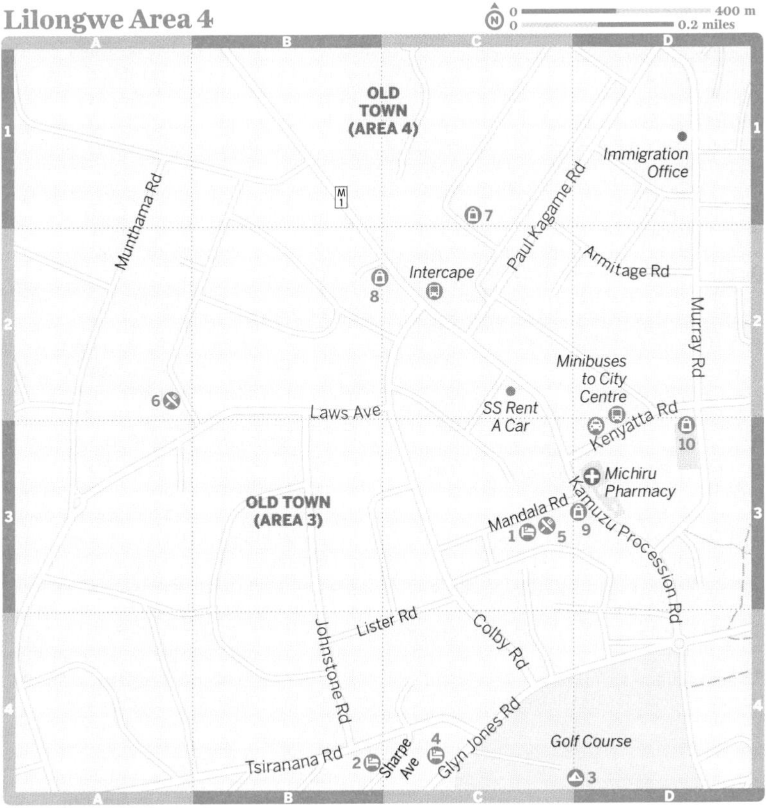

Lilongwe Area 4

Activities, Courses & Tours
Land & Lake Safaris .... (see 6)

Sleeping
1 Kiboko Town Hotel C3
2 Korea Garden Lodge B4
3 Lilongwe Golf Club D4
4 St Peter's Guesthouse C4

Eating
5 Ad Lib C3
Kiboko Town Hotel .... (see 1)
Korea Garden Restaurant .... (see 2)
6 Land & Lake Cafe A2

Shopping
7 African Habitat C1
8 Baobab Books B2
9 Craft Market D3
10 Lilongwe City Mall D3

Bay (MK4000, five hours) and Dedza (MK2000, one hour).

Long-distance minibuses (Map p178) depart from the main bus station area to nearby destinations such as Zomba (MK5000, four to five hours), Dedza (MK2000, 45 minutes to one hour), the Zambian border at Mchinji (MK2500, two hours), Mangochi (MK5000, 4½ hours), Limbe (for Blantyre; MK4000, three to four hours) and Nkhotakota (MK4000, three hours).

Intercape (Map p181; ☎0999 403398; www.intercape.co.za; Kamuzu Procession Rd; ⏲ticket office 5am-5pm Mon-Fri, to 2pm Sat, to 11am Sun) has modern buses to Jo'burg (MK36,000 to MK43,000, 36 hours), leaving daily from outside its office at 6am and departing Jo'burg daily at 8.30am. Intercape also operates a bus to Mzuzu (MK15,000 to MK23,000, five hours, daily except Friday and Sunday), which waits for the service from Jo'burg to arrive and leaves between 9pm and 11pm.

Kob's Coach Services (☎ in Zambia 260 977794073) leaves for Lusaka (Zambia) on Wednesday and Saturday at 5.30am, arriving at 5pm (MK20,000). **Taqwa Coach Company** (☎ in Zambia +260 977 114825) departs five evenings a week to Dar es Salaam (Tanzania; US$60, 30 hours) via Mzuzu, with onward connections to Nairobi (Kenya). In both cases, get there a good hour early for a decent seat. Both the Lusaka and the Dar es Salaam **services** (Map p178; Devil St) leave from Devil St, adjacent to the main bus station.

CAR

Avis (☎ 01-756105; www.avis.com) and Budget have offices at the **Sunbird Capital Hotel** (Map p178; ☎ 01-773388; www.sunbirdmalawi.com; Chilembwe Rd; s/d incl breakfast from US$142/172; P ⊖ ❄ @ ᯤ ≋). Local companies include the following:

Best Car Hire (☎ 01-751097; www.bestcarhiremalawi.com)

Chancy Mapples Car Hire (☎ 0888 323287, 0997 615442; www.car-hire-malawi.com)

Sputnik Car Hire (☎ 01-758253; www.sputnik-car-hire.mw)

SS Rent A Car (Map p181; ☎ 01-751478; www.ssrentacar.com; Kamuzu Procession Rd)

ℹ Getting Around

LOCAL TRANSPORT

The most useful local minibus route is between Old Town and City centre. The journey should cost around MK200; you can cross the whole city for MK300.

From Old Town, minibuses leave from next to Shoprite. They head north up Kenyatta Rd, and along Youth and Convention or Independence Dr. The minibus stand for the return journey from City Centre is at the northern end of Independence Dr.

You can also catch minibuses to Old Town and City Centre from the main bus station area.

TAXI

The best places to find taxis are at the big hotels and major shopping malls, including outside Old Town Shoprite. The fare between Old Town and City Centre is about MK6000, while a tuktuk should cost under MK4000. Negotiate a price with the driver first.

Mawaso Taxi Service (☎ 0999 161111, 0995 169772) Trips across town, airport pickups and drop-offs, and intercity journeys.

NORTHERN MALAWI

Remote northern Malawi is where ravishing highlands meet hippo-filled swamps, vast mountains loom large over empty beaches, and colonial relics litter pristine islands and hilltop villages. It's Malawi's most sparsely populated region and the first taste many travellers get of this tiny country after making the journey down from East Africa.

Karonga

Dusty little Karonga is the first town you'll come across on the journey down from Tanzania and, while it's unlikely to enrapture you, it suffices for a stop to withdraw some kwacha – and have a close encounter with a 100-million-year-old dinosaur. Karonga has the proud title of Malawi's 'fossil district', with well-preserved remains of dinosaurs and ancient humans. Its most famous discovery is the Malawisaurus (Malawi lizard) – a 9.1m-long, 4.3m-high fossilised dino skeleton found 45km south of town. See an impressive replica at the **Cultural & Museum Centre Karonga** (CMCK; ☎ 01-362579, 0888 515574; www.facebook.com/CMCK.Malawi; MK1000; ⏲ 8am-4.30pm Mon-Sat, from 2.30pm Sun).

Rooms at the **Sumuka Inn** (☎ 0999 444816; s/d standard MK13,000/18,000, deluxe MK15,000/20,000, executive MK17,500/22,500; P ❄) are badly in need of renovation – and a good clean – but it remains a friendly and reasonably comfortable stopover. You can have a hot shower here, a fridge of cold Carlsbergs awaits in reception, and the restaurant (mains MK3000) serves cooked breakfasts and basic meals such as chambo.

The **Safari Lodge** (☎ 01-362340; incl breakfast s/d standard MK5500/6500, executive MK9000/11,500) is a fallback option with spacious but basic rooms with tiled floors and a bar where drinkers watch the football.

ℹ Getting There & Away

AXA deluxe buses leave Karonga at noon daily for Blantyre (MK12,000, 18 hours), stopping in Mzuzu (MK4000, four hours) and heading down the lakeshore via Salima (MK11,150, 11 hours). Change in Mzuzu for Lilongwe. In the opposite direction, buses leave Blantyre around 5pm and reach Karonga around 11am the following day.

AXA has a **ticket office** (☎ 01-362787; www.axacoach.com) at Karonga bus station, in the market area 500m north of the museum.

Northern Malawi

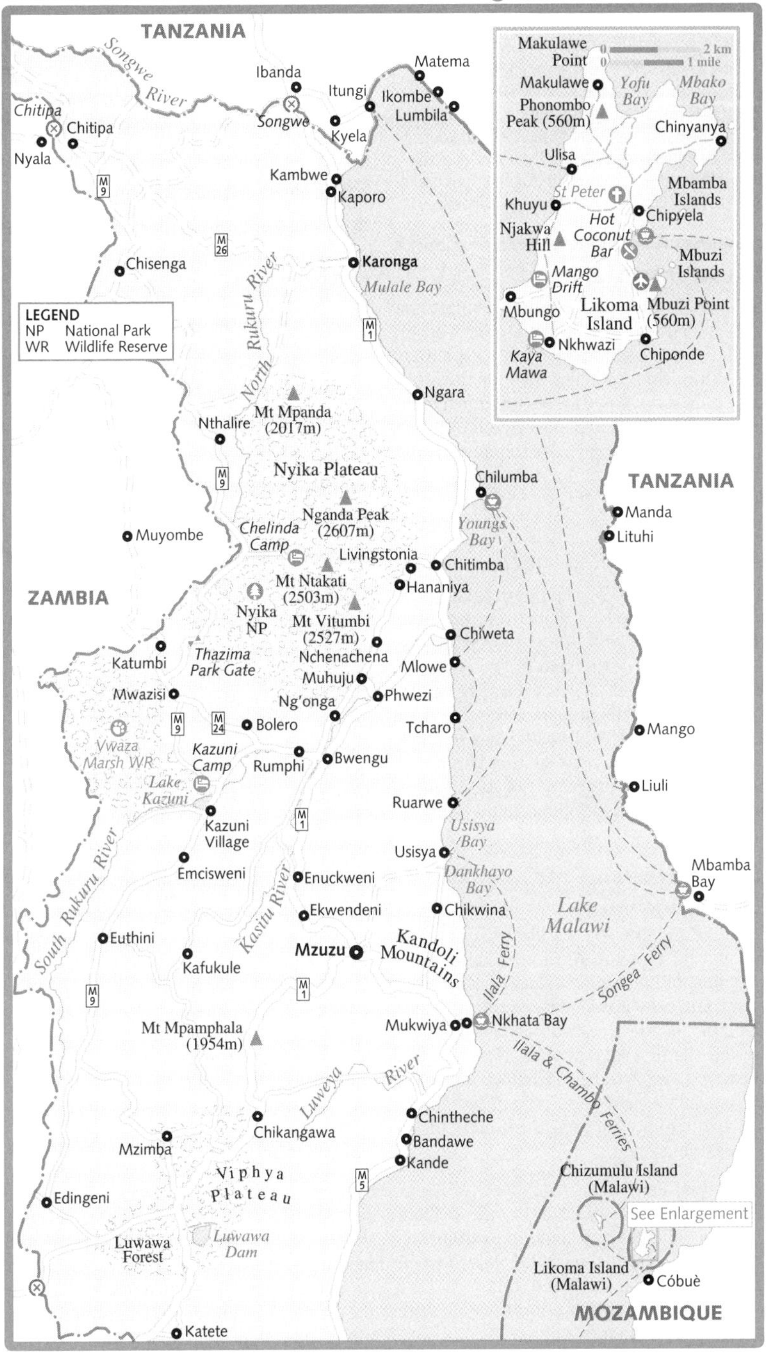

Minibuses run from the bus station to destinations including Mzuzu (MK4000, four hours) via Chitimba (MK2100, 1½ hours), and the Songwe border crossing to Tanzania (MK1200, one hour).

If you've got a 4WD you can cross into northern Zambia via Chitipa in northern Malawi. It's four hours from Karonga to Chitipa on a rough dirt road (there's no public transport, but you might be able to get a lift on a truck). After going through customs it is another 80km or four hours' drive to the Zambian border post at Nakonde.

Livingstonia

Built by Scottish missionaries, Livingstonia feels sanctified, special and otherworldly, with its tree-lined main street graced by crumbling colonial relics. But for the stunning mountain views, there's not much to do in town other than visit the museum, church and sundry historical curios. Experiencing this piece of mountaintop history, and staying at one of the nearby permaculture farms, will be a magical, peaceful chapter in your Malawian journey.

After two failed attempts at establishing a mission at Cape Maclear and at Bandawe (too many people kept dying from malaria), the Free Church of Scotland moved its mission 900m above the lake to the village of Khondowe. Called Livingstonia after Dr David Livingstone, the mission was built under the leadership of Dr Robert Laws in 1894. The town provides a fascinating glimpse of Malawi's colonial past: most of its old stone buildings are still standing, many used by the local university.

Sights

Stone House Museum MUSEUM
(☎01-368223; MK700; ⏰7.30am-4.30pm) The fascinating museum in Stone House (once the home of Livingstonia founder Dr Robert Laws, and now a national monument) tells the story of the European arrival in Malawi and the first missionaries. Here you can read Dr Laws' letters and books, including the old laws of Nyasaland, and peruse black-and-white photos of early missionary life in Livingstonia.

Manchewe Falls WATERFALL
This impressive waterfall thunders 125m into the valley below, about 4km from Livingstonia (towards the lake). Follow a small path behind the falls and there's a cave where, so the story goes, local people once hid from slave traders.

Livingstonia Church CHURCH
(☎01-311344; admission by donation) Dating from 1894, this mission church has a beautiful stained-glass window featuring David Livingstone with his sextant, his medicine chest and his two companions, with Lake Malawi in the background. You can climb the tower for a bird's-eye view of Livingstonia.

Sleeping & Eating

★**Lukwe EcoCamp** LODGE, CAMPGROUND $
(☎0999 434985; www.lukwe.com; camping US$6, s/d without bathroom US$15/25; P 📶) This serene, tasteful permaculture camp is about helping local farmers and being completely self-sufficient. Comfortable glass-fronted chalets and thatch-covered tents are set in leafy terraced gardens, with private balconies and shared solar- and donkey-boiler-heated showers, composting loos and self-catering kitchen. See the mountain drop into infinity and spy Manchewe Falls from the swing chair.

★**Mushroom Farm** LODGE, CAMPGROUND $
(☎0999 652485; www.themushroomfarmmalawi.com; camping US$5, dm US$8-10, s/d US$30/40, without bathroom from US$15/25; P 📶) Perched on the edge of the Livingstonia escarpment (aka an abyss!), this permaculture ecolodge and campsite is worth the arduous journey for the warm welcome and views that will have you manually closing your jaw. The safari tents, hardwood A-frames and dorms provide charmingly rustic accommodation; better still is the en-suite cob house with cliffside shower.

The bar-restaurant (mains US$5, pre-ordered dinner US$7) offers sweeping views and organic veggie fusion dishes such as tortilla wraps and Asian noodle salad. Activities on offer include yoga, woodcarving, guided day hikes (US$3 per person) to Livingstonia, Manchewe Falls and the Chombe Plateau, and coffee-plantation tours. The off-the-grid facilities include fire-heated shared showers, composting loo, solar-powered electricity and self-catering kitchen.

Hakuna Matata HOSTEL, CAMPGROUND $
(☎0991 092027, 0882 297779; www.facebook.com/chitimbahakunamatata; camping/dm MK3500/4900, s/d without bathroom MK7000/11,000; P 📶) At the foot of the mountain in lakeside Chitimba, this beach camp is an excellent launch pad for tackling the ascent to Livingstonia. The whitewashed rooms have mozzie nets and fans, and one

room has a private bathroom. Chat to the personable South African host, Willie, in the refreshingly shaded cafe (mains MK2000, pre-ordered dinner MK4000).

Getting There & Away

From the main north–south road between Karonga and Mzuzu, the road to Livingstonia (known as the Gorode) turns off at Chitimba, forcing its way up the escarpment. This twisting, ulcerated road is a test for the most steely drivers: a white-knuckle experience of 20 switchbacks and hairpins, with a boulder-strewn, mainly unpaved surface – at times single track – with the mountain abysmally close to you.

Don't attempt this in anything but a 4WD and *never* in rain. You can get a place in a shared pickup truck, which may involve a long wait for the vehicle to fill with passengers, for MK2000 (plus MK1000 per big backpack). The journey takes around 45 minutes, and pickups leave from the small station at the junction of the main M1 road and the Gorode.

Be warned that accidents are not uncommon in the shared pickups. A safer option is to hire a vehicle; organise this through your accommodation or call **Thomas** (☎0882 175409; up to 8 passengers MK20,000). Thomas lives in Livingstonia, so you may want to arrange the transfer in advance of your arrival in Chitimba. Alternatively, Willie at Hakuna Matata in Chitimba offers day trips in his bakkie (pickup) to Livingstonia for up to 10 people (US$10 per person, minimum charge US$60) – an easy and recommended option.

You can tackle the 15km trip up the mountain on foot, an ascent of just under 1000m that takes around three hours. Park your car, leave your bags and stock up on iced water at Hakuna Matata. There have been isolated incidents of muggings on the Gorode, so check on the latest situation and hire a guide if you're by yourself or setting off late. Enquire at Hakuna Matata, phone your accommodation or ask at the M1–Gorode junction for guide Stanley Zinyengo Gondwe, who can also arrange porters.

Coming from the south, another way to reach Livingstonia is to drive up the dirt road from Rumphi, for which you'll need a 4WD – that said, it's an easy, dusty and very pretty drive. You can also join this 78km route about halfway along by turning off the M1 at Phwezi. During the rainy season the dust turns to mud and even 4WDs may not make it.

Nyika National Park

It's a rough drive to these beguiling highlands, but Malawi's oldest reserve is worth every bump. Towering over 2000m above sea level, the 3200-sq-km **Nyika National Park** (person/car US$10/3; ⏰6am-6pm) is easily one of the country's most magical experiences. Turning burnt amber in the afternoon sun, the highland grass flickers with the stripes of zebras and is punctuated by glittering boulders that look like set dressing from a *Star Trek* movie.

Thanks to the top guides of **Central African Wilderness Safaris** (☎0881 085177, 01-771393; www.cawsmw.com), your chances of seeing animals on a morning wildlife drive (US$35 per person) or walk (US$20 per person) are extremely high.

The most exciting wildlife drives, however, are by night, with decent chances of your guide scoping out leopards. The current population of around 100 is one of the region's densest.

Wildlife viewing is good year-round, although in July and August the cold weather means the animals move off the plateau to lower areas. Birdwatching is particularly good between October and April, when migratory birds are on the move.

Sleeping & Eating

Chelinda Campground CAMPGROUND $
(☎0881 085177, 01-771393; www.cawsmw.com; camping US$15; P) Set in a secluded site with vistas of the plateau's rolling hills, this camp has permanent security, clean toilets, hot showers, endless firewood and shelters for cooking and eating. Self-caterers should stock up in Mzuzu or Rumphi. There's a small shop at Chelinda for National Parks staff, but provisions are often basic and supplies sporadic.

★**Chelinda Lodge** LODGE $$$
(☎01-771393, 0881 085177; www.cawsmw.com; s/d all-inclusive US$450/700; P ⊖ @ ᯤ) Sitting on a hillside in a clearing of pine trees, upmarket Chelinda is a traveller's dream. The main building crackles with fires at every turn, complemented by inviting couches, walls adorned with lush wildlife photography, pillars hung with woodcarvings, glittering chandeliers and high beams. Rates include park entrance fees and wildlife-watching activities.

★**Chelinda Camp** CHALET $$$
(☎0881 085177, 01-771393; www.cawsmw.com; s/d all-inclusive US$355/530; P ᯤ) Nestled into the lee of a valley beside a small lake, this Central African Wilderness Safaris lodge is insanely picturesque. Its bungalows have an unfussy '70s aspect to them and are ideal

Nyika National Park

for families, with small kitchen, cosy sitting room and stone fireplace. Rates include park entrance fees and wildlife-watching activities.

Getting There & Away

The main Thazima Gate (pronounced and sometimes spelled Tazima) is 55km northwest of Rumphi – about two hours' drive. Once inside the park, it's another 60km, two-hour drive to Chelinda. Especially from Rumphi to Thazima Gate, the corrugated road is appallingly bumpy; do call to check on its condition in the wet season. Petrol is available at Chelinda but in limited supply, so fill up before you enter the park.

It's possible to bring a mountain bike into Nyika; if you pick up a ride from Rumphi to Thazima, you can cycle the last 60km to Chelinda. An early start is recommended due to the distance.

Unfortunately, getting to Chelinda by public transport is tricky. From Rumphi, a truck or *matola* (pickup; MK3000) heading north to Chitipa could drop you at the turnoff to Chelinda, 16km west of the lodges and campground near the Zambian border. However, that will leave you somewhat stranded, and, when you make it to Chelinda, you will then have the return journey to tackle. On the bright side, taxi services in Mzuzu and Rumphi offer transfers; the main drawback, if the driver is hanging around and taking you back to Rumphi, is that you will have to pay for his or her accommodation.

If you are prepared to wait around, it may be possible to make an ad-hoc arrangement for staff from Chelinda to pick you up when they go shopping in Rumphi or Mzuzu.

Vwaza Marsh Wildlife Reserve

This compact, 1000-sq-km **reserve** (☎0991 912775, 0884 203964; moyoleonard52@gmail.com; person/vehicle US$10/3; ⏲6am-6pm) is home to plentiful wildlife, and ranges from large, flat areas of mopane (woodland) to open swamp and wetlands. The Luwewe River runs through the park, draining the marshland, and joins the South Rukuru River (the reserve's southern border), which flows into Lake Kazuni.

Lake Kazuni Safari Camp offers basic accommodation, and *matolas* run here from Rumphi, but visiting on a tour with the likes of Nkhata Bay Safaris (p189) is the easiest option.

The best time to visit is the dry season; just after the rainy season, the grass is high and you might go away without seeing anything.

If you're travelling by public transport, first get to Rumphi (reached from Mzuzu by minibus for MK2000). From Rumphi, *matolas* (pickups) travel to/from the Kazuni area and you should be able to get a lift to the main gate for around MK1500. Minibuses also ply this route to/from Kazuni village, and can drop you by the bridge, 1km east of the park gate and camp.

By car, head west from Rumphi. Turn left after 10km (Vwaza Marsh Wildlife Reserve is signposted) and continue for about 20km. Where the road swings left over the bridge, go straight on to reach the park gate and camp after 1km.

Lake Kazuni Safari Camp CABIN $
(0884 203964, 0991 912775; moyoleonard52@gmail.com; camping per site MK7500, r MK10,000; P) The camp's five simple en-suite, thatch-and-brick twin cabanas are perfectly positioned on the lakeshore; the animals are so plentiful that it feels as though you've stepped into a children's picture book. The camp is very basic and guests must bring their own food and drinks, including water; the accommodating staff will be happy to cook you dinner in the camp kitchen.

Mzuzu

Dusty, sprawling Mzuzu is Malawi's third-largest city, northern Malawi's principal town and the region's transport hub. Travellers heading along the M1 – across to Nkhata Bay, Nyika or Viphya, or up to Tanzania – are likely to spend a night or two here. With some good accommodation options, Mzuzu is an appealingly authentic and laid-back spot to experience everyday Malawian life.

Mzuzu has banks, shops, a post office, supermarkets, pharmacies, petrol stations and other facilities, which are especially useful if you've entered Malawi from the north.

Mzuzu Museum MUSEUM
(0884 201126, 0939 386624; M'Mbelwa Rd; MK500; 7.30am-noon & 1-4.30pm Mon-Sat; P) The city museum has displays on the people and the land of northern Malawi. Exhibits include traditional hunting implements, musical instruments, and photos of a paramount chief's coronation ceremony. If you're heading up to Livingstonia, there's an interesting exhibition telling the story of the missionaries who established the town.

Sleeping

★ **Macondo Camp** GUESTHOUSE $
(0991 792311; www.macondocamp.com; Chimaliro 4; camping MK3000, dm MK5000, s/d without bathroom MK14,000/17,000, apt MK35,000; P) Run by Italian couple and serial overlanders Luca and Cecilia, Macondo has cute rooms in the main house, tented chalets with wooden decks overlooking the lawn and banana trees, and an annexe with dorm beds.

Joy's Place HOSTEL $
(0991 922242, 0998 391358; www.facebook.com/joyinmzuzu; dm US$8, r/tr/q without bathroom US$25/30/35; P) Popular with the aid-work fraternity, these pleasantly decorated rooms with mozzie nets and bright bedspreads are hidden away in a suburban house. Choose between the eight-bed en-suite dorm and a private room sharing a bathroom with one other room. There's a relaxing lounge and a popular **restaurant** (0998 391358, 0991 922242; mains MK3500; 7am-8pm; P).

Umunthu Camp LODGE $
(0992 417916, 0881 980019; umunthucamp@gmail.com; dm/r MK5000/12,000; restaurant 7am-9pm Tue-Sun; P) The brainchild of South African couple Andries and Farzana, Umunthu has coolly decorated, sparsely furnished rooms and a four-bed dorm with adjoining bathroom. The bar-restaurant (mains MK5000) draws on the resident kitchen garden, serving dishes including pizza, pasta, burgers and steaks. It's behind Shoprite supermarket, signposted from the main drag.

Sunbird Mzuzu HOTEL $$$
(01-332622; www.sunbirdmalawi.com; Kabunduli Viphya Dr; s/d/ste incl breakfast from US$120/150/240; P) Easily the city's plushest digs, this large hotel in imposing

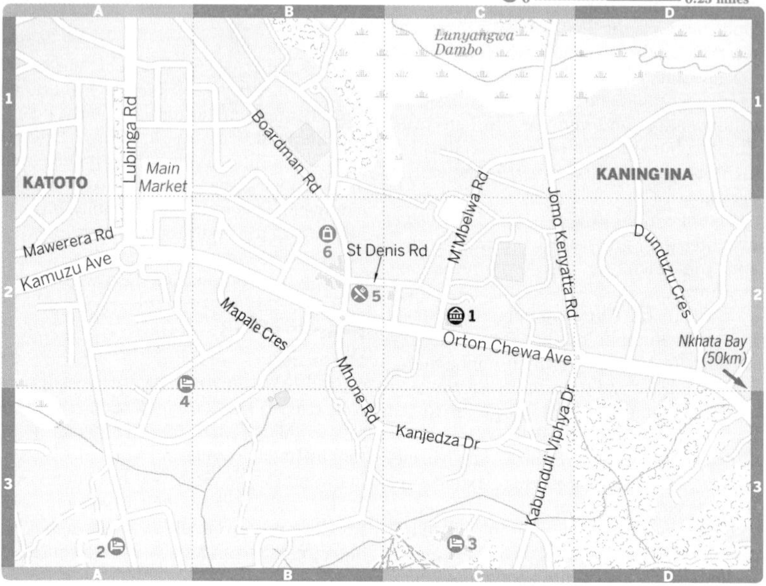

Mzuzu

Sights
1 Mzuzu Museum ... C2

Sleeping
2 Joy's Place ... A3
3 Sunbird Mzuzu ... C3
4 Umunthu Camp ... A2

Eating
Joy's Place ... (see 2)
5 Soul Kitchen ... B2

Shopping
6 Hardware Market ... B2

grounds has huge rooms with deep-pile carpet, flat-screen DSTV, fridge and views of Mzuzu's golf course. As you'd expect from Sunbird, the service is friendly and efficient and the place is of an international standard.

Eating

Soul Kitchen MALAWIAN $
(☎0884 957150; St Denis Rd; mains MK2000; ⏰7am-10pm Mon-Sat) Watch Mzuzu go by on Soul Kitchen's shaded stoep with a barbecue smoking away at one end and a view of the city's only traffic light. Barbecued chicken, chambo, omelette and T-bone steak are on the menu.

★ **Macondo Camp** ITALIAN $$
(☎0991 792311; mains MK4500; ⏰7am-9pm; P 📶) This Italian restaurant offers treats such as homemade pasta made daily, Parmesan flown from Italy and monthly live music on the stoep. Dishes include pizza, steaks, spring rolls and the ever-popular ravioli with blue cheese, which can be accompanied by a good selection of Italian and South African wines. It's at the namesake guesthouse northeast of central Mzuzu.

Getting There & Away

AXA buses leave at 5pm for Blantyre (MK8000, 13 hours) via the lakeshore, and at 7am for Karonga (MK4000, four hours). AXA departs at 7pm for Lilongwe (MK7000, four hours).

Minibuses and shared taxis go to Nkhata Bay (MK1500, one to two hours), Karonga (MK4000, four hours), Chitimba (MK2000, 2½ hours), Rumphi (MK2000, one hour) and the Tanzanian border (MK5200, five hours).

If you need to repair your vehicle, there's a well-stocked **Hardware Market** (Boardman Rd), where the many shopkeepers can sell you all manner of parts and recommend mechanics.

Nkhata Bay

Nkhata Bay has an almost Caribbean feel, with its fishing boats buzzing across the green bay, market stalls hawking barbecued fish, and reggae filling the languorous afternoons. There are also loads of activities to enjoy before you hammock flop, be it snorkelling, diving, fish-eagle feeding, kayaking or forest walks.

Sights & Activities

Chikale Beach BEACH

On the southern side of Nkhata Bay, Chikale Beach is a popular spot for swimming and lazing on the sand, especially at weekends. After church on Sunday, the locals set up a speaker stack and enjoy a few beers.

Monkey Business KAYAKING

(☎0999 437247; monkeybusinesskayaking.blogspot.co.za; Butterfly Space) Monkey Business, at Butterfly Space hostel, can organise paddling excursions personally tailored to your needs – anything from half a day to a few days down the coast.

Aqua Africa DIVING

(☎0999 921418; www.aquaafrica.co.uk) This dependable British-run outfit offers dives for certified divers (from US$50) and numerous courses, including the three- to four-day PADI Open Water course (US$380 including all materials). Colourful cichlid fish, the kind you've probably seen in a dentist's aquarium, swim throughout the lake, but more spectacular are the schools of dolphinfish that are drawn to your torch (flashlight) on night dives.

Nkhata Bay Safaris TOURS

(☎0999 265064; www.nkhatabaysafaris.com; 4-day tour for 2 people camping/chalets US$655/755) Run by a Malawian team headed by Davie, this tour operator offers four- to 10-day trips to Vwaza Marsh Wildlife Reserve, Nyika National Park, Livingstonia and further afield. It can help with local activities, transport and accommodation bookings, and has recently introduced day and overnight wildlife-watching tours to Vwaza and overnight safaris to Nkhotakota Wildlife Reserve (US$275 per person).

Sleeping

★**Mayoka Village** LODGE $

(☎0999 268595, 01-994025; www.mayokavillagebeachlodge.com; camping/d US$5/12, chalet s/d US$30/45, f US$50-70, s/d/tr/q without bathroom US$20/35/45/60; P wi-fi) Cleverly shaped around the rocky topography of a cliff, boutique-style Mayoka cascades down in a series of beautiful bamboo-and-stone chalets. There are myriad romantic nooks for taking in the lake below or grabbing some rays on sunloungers. The waterfront bar-restaurant (mains MK2500) is a beach hideaway serving cocktails and dishes from wraps and burgers to Malawian red-bean stew.

Butterfly Space HOSTEL $

(☎0999 265065, 0999 156335; www.butterfly-space.com; camping/dm MK1500/3000, chalets per person with/without bathroom MK8000/7000; P @ wi-fi) Run by Alice and Josie, inspiring, colourful and socially committed Butterfly is a rare backpackers' oasis. There's a *palapa*-style lounge or spacious beachfront bar to chill in, a private beach, an internet cafe, a media centre, a self-catering block and a restaurant serving authentic Tongan cuisine, as well as sandwiches, chapattis, pasta and burgers (mains MK2000, pre-ordered dinner MK3000).

Aqua Africa GUESTHOUSE $$

(☎0999 921418; www.aquaafrica.co.uk; standard s/tw US$30/40, deluxe s/d incl breakfast US$60/80; ⏲restaurant 7am-6pm; P ❄ wi-fi) With whitewashed rooms featuring polished stone floors, step-in mozzie nets and blue curtains opening onto balconies overlooking the bay, this dive school's four rooms often host its students. The Dive Deck Cafe, complete with wicker loungers and viewing deck, has an excellent menu ranging from full breakfasts to nachos, Cajun chicken, fish burgers and peanut-coated chicken strips (mains MK2500).

Njaya Lodge LODGE $$

(☎01-352342, 0999 948673, 0884 743647; www.njayalodge.com; d, tr & q US$60, cottages US$70, r without bathroom per person US$15; P wi-fi) Set in terraced gardens bursting with frangipanis and palms, with manicured lawns tumbling down to the spearmint water, Njaya has a range of accommodation from garden chalets on the hillside to striking stone cottages right by the lake. It's a little run-down but in a wonderful secluded location.

Eating & Drinking

Crest View MALAWIAN $

(☎0881 174804; mains MK2000; ⏲6am-9pm; ✎) Thrifty travellers appreciate this local hangout with football on the TV and a good view

Nkhata Bay

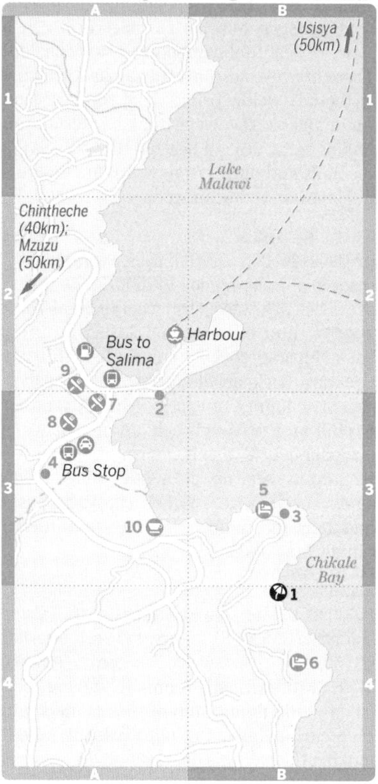

Nkhata Bay

Sights

1 Chikale Beach B4

Activities, Courses & Tours

2 Aqua Africa A3
3 Monkey Business B3
4 Nkhata Bay Safaris A3

Sleeping

Aqua Africa .... (see 2)
Butterfly Space .... (see 3)
5 Mayoka Village B3
6 Njaya Lodge B4

Eating

7 Crest View A3
8 Kaya Papaya A3
9 Peoples Supermarket A2

Drinking & Nightlife

10 One Love A3

of the action happening on the main street. *Nsima* (a filling porridge-like dish made from white maize flour and water) with beans, omelettes and other local favourites are on the menu.

Peoples Supermarket SUPERMARKET $
(6.30am-7pm Mon-Fri, to 6pm Sat, 8am-5pm Sun) For self-catering, the Peoples Supermarket on the main drag sells toiletries, biscuits and milk.

One Love CAFE $
(0996 955164; www.facebook.com/onelove-handmadeart) At One Love, with an unbeatable view of the bay, Kelvin the Rasta serves cold beers and simple dishes such as chapattis, *nsima* and beans (mains MK1300). He also sells his woodcarvings and drums. Hours are variable, so call ahead before making a special trip.

★ **Kaya Papaya** THAI $$
(0888 576489, 0993 688884; mains MK4000; 11am-10pm, last food orders 8.45pm;) Close to the harbour, with a big upstairs balcony overlooking the main street, Kaya Papaya has an appealing Afro-Asian-fusion chic that's matched by a menu of zesty salads, pizza and Thai fare such as green curry, chicken satay and stir-fries. If you're still hungry, try a banana pancake.

Information

Travellers have been mugged when walking outside the town centre (in particular to and from Chikale Beach and the surrounding lodges at night), so take extra care when walking this route as it's unlit and can be quite deserted. Muggings have subsided thanks to police efforts, but it's best to walk with another guest or a staff member from your lodge after dark.

Most travellers will encounter a fair amount of hassle from Rastas and beach boys offering a bewildering range of services and stimulants. If you're not interested, be polite but firm and they should leave you alone.

Getting There & Away

Most transport leaves from the bus stop in the market area. AXA runs to Karonga via Mzuzu, leaving around 5.30am, and down the lake to Blantyre via Salima, departing around 6.30pm. Minibuses run to Nkhotakota (MK1500, five hours), Chintheche (MK950, one hour) and Mzuzu (MK1000, 1½ hours). There are also regularly departing and less cramped shared taxis (MK1500 to Mzuzu) and a daily bus to Salima (MK8000, nine hours, 5am), which respectively leave from the main bus stop and from outside the Admarc maize store.

To reach Lilongwe the quickest option is to head down the lake to Salima and change; alternatively, travel inland to Mzuzu and pick up a service going south.

Another option is to privately hire a taxi; you can likely share with someone from your accommodation heading in the same direction. Mzuzu costs MK12,000 (MK20,000 return) and Lilongwe MK100,000. **Noba Taxi** (☎ 0995 260191) is a trustworthy and well-priced operation.

The *Ilala* (p223) ferry leaves from the **harbour** (☎ 0882 870392) and heads north up the lakeshore to Chilumba on Sunday morning. Returning south, it departs Nkhata Bay for Chizumulu and Likoma Islands on Monday evening. Tanzania's Songea ferry crosses from Mbamba Bay (Tanzania) and the MV *Chambo* (p223) ferry sails from Metangula (Mozambique) via Likoma and Chizumulu on Wednesday, returning from Nkhata Bay on Thursday morning. This should mean you can catch the *Chambo* to the islands on Thursday and return to Nkhata Bay on the *Ilala* on Saturday...but there are no guarantees.

Drivers can fill up at the petrol station on the main road.

Likoma Island

Blissful Likoma Island – situated on the Mozambican side of Lake Malawi but part of Malawi – measures 17 sq km and is home to around 9000 people.

Likoma's flat and sandy south is littered with baobabs and offers an uninterrupted panoramic view of Mozambique's wild coast. The island's main drawcards are its abundance of pristine beaches and the attendant snorkelling, diving and water sports, but there's a healthy dose of other activities, both cultural and physical, to fill several days here.

Sights & Activities

Swimming is a must on Likoma and is best on the long stretches of beach in the south. The tropical-fish population has been unaffected by the mainland's overfishing, and the snorkelling is excellent. Snorkels are on hand at the island's accommodation options, which can arrange scuba diving and PADI courses too.

A range of water sports is also available through accommodation, from learning to kitesurf to waterskiing and wakeboarding.

The island's compact but diverse area is perfect for walking and mountain biking; you can bring bikes across on the ferry or hire them from accommodation.

Cathedral of St Peter CHURCH

(Chipyela; ⏲ dawn-dusk) Likoma's huge Anglican cathedral (1911), said to be the same size as Winchester Cathedral, should not be missed. Its stained-glass windows, crumbling masonry and sheer scale are testament to the zeal of its missionary creators' religious conviction.

Climb the tower for spectacular views. If you're lucky you might meet the charming verger, who'll happily give you a tour, and you're welcome to join in the vibrant service on Sunday morning. The cathedral is less than 500m inland (and uphill) from the ferry terminal.

Sleeping & Eating

★ **Mango Drift** HOSTEL **$$**

(☎ 0999 746122; www.mangodrift.com; camping US$6, tent rental US$1, dm US$8, s/d US$60/70, without bathroom US$25/30; @ wi-fi) Far from backpacker hardship, this affordable island idyll is one of Malawi's most luxurious hostels. Its stone chalets are the closest you'll come to boutique this side of US$100, with hibiscus petals scattered on snow-white linen, wicker furniture, sundown verandas and loungers on the sand. The shared toilets and shower block are no less immaculate.

★ **Kaya Mawa** BOUTIQUE HOTEL **$$$**

(☎ 0999 318360; www.kayamawa.com; full board per person from US$415; air-con @ wi-fi) Remember Scaramanga's pad in *The Man with the Golden Gun*? Kaya Mawa, set on an amber-coloured beach lapped by turquoise water, is the ultimate location to live out your inner Bond fantasy. Its cliffside chalets, cleverly moulded around the landscape, are so beautiful you'll never want to leave.

Getting There & Away

Ulendo Airlink flies daily to Likoma from Lilongwe (adult/child one way US$295/211), with further scheduled departures from several other locations. The second option is to charter a flight; from Lilongwe, the one-way fare is US$365 for adults and US$260 for children, with a minimum of two passengers. Note that this does not give you exclusive use of the aircraft. The third, most affordable option is to check the 'bid to fly' section of Ulendo Airlink's website and make an offer for a seat on one of the listed flights.

The *Ilala* ferry stops at Likoma Island twice a week, usually for three to four hours, so even if you're heading elsewhere, you might be able to nip ashore to have a quick look at the cathedral. Check with the captain before you leave the boat. The ferry sails Nkhotakota–Likoma Island–Chizumulu Island–Nkhata Bay on Saturday, returning south on Monday/Tuesday. Additionally, the *Chambo* ferry sails Metangula (Mozambique)–Likoma Island–Chizumulu Island–Nkhata Bay on Wednesday, returning on Thursday. There's also a Metangula–Likoma MV *Chambo* service on Saturday, which returns on Sunday.

Dhows sail in the morning from Mdamba to Cóbuè (Mozambique). The fare is around MK2000; for a little extra they can pick you up or drop you off at Mango Drift. It is sometimes possible to catch a local boat to Chizumulu Island for around MK1000 per person, or to privately hire a boat with an engine (MK25,000 to MK30,000); ask your accommodation.

The lodges pick guests up from flight and ferry arrivals.

Chizumulu Island

Stretches of azure water and white rocky outcrops give Chizumulu Island – floating around 10km west of the larger Likoma Island – a Mediterranean flavour, while the backdrop of dry scrub is positively antipodean. Few travellers make it to Chizumulu thanks to its remote location and ferry schedules. However, you may stop off on a cruise or on the ferry en route between Likoma and Nkhata Bay.

The *Ilala* ferry stops right outside Wakwenda Retreat. It normally sails Nkhotakota–Likoma Island–Chizumulu Island–Nkhata Bay on Saturday, returning south on Monday/Tuesday. Additionally, the MV *Chambo* ferry sails Metangula (Mozambique)–Likoma Island–Chizumulu Island–Nkhata Bay on Wednesday, returning on Thursday.

This makes it possible to arrive at Chizumulu from Nkhata Bay early on Tuesday morning on the *Ilala,* and return to Nkhata Bay on the Wednesday on the MV *Chambo.* Alternatively, you can arrive at Chizumulu on Thursday on the MV *Chambo,* returning to Nkhata Bay on Saturday on the *Ilala.*

There are now no daily dhow ferries between the two islands, though it's possible to find a local boat over to Likoma for MK1000 per person – if one is heading across (no guarantees). The trip can take anywhere from one to three hours depending on the weather; it's an extremely choppy ride when the wind is blowing, and potentially dangerous if a storm comes up. If you're unsure, ask at Wakwenda Retreat for advice. It's also possible to privately hire a boat with an engine for MK25,000 to MK30,000.

Wakwenda Retreat (☎SMS only 0999 348415; www.facebook.com/wakwenda; camping/dm US$5/7, s/d without bathroom US$15/20), sometimes known as Nick's Place, smack bang on a postcard-perfect beach, is utter chill-out material. The bar occupies an outcrop of rocks by the water's edge with multilevel decks, featuring sunloungers and a plunge pool. The campsite is clustered around a massive, hollow baobab tree, which you can camp inside, and there are huts with verandas too.

CENTRAL MALAWI

This small corner of Malawi is chiefly famed for its dazzling white beaches, like the backpacker magnet, Cape Maclear, and for its desert islands like Mumbo and Domwe – both reached by sea kayak or boat. Nkhotakota Wildlife Reserve, its wildlife stocks increased by a major elephant translocation, has fine lodges and good access from the coast. North of here is the Viphya Plateau, a haunting wilderness of mountains, grasslands and mist-shrouded pines. For cultural appeal, meanwhile, you can't beat the Kungoni complex and mission buildings in Mua.

Viphya Plateau

The Viphya Plateau forms the spine of central and northern Malawi, snaking a cool path through the flat scrubland, dusty towns and sunny beaches that reign on either side. Tightly knit forests give way to gentle valleys and rivers, and huge granite domes rise softly from the earth like sleeping beasts. Indigenous woodland bristles with birds and wildflowers, monkeys dart through the trees and antelope can often be seen.

Buses and *matolas* (pickups) can drop off and pick up at the Luwawa Forest Lodge turnoff on the M1; the bus costs MK5000 from Lilongwe. Returning south, *matolas* regularly pass by on the M1 between 8am and 9am.

There's no public transport to Luwawa Lodge, so you'll have to walk from the Luwawa turnoff or call the lodge for a pickup (US$10 per group).

Central Malawi

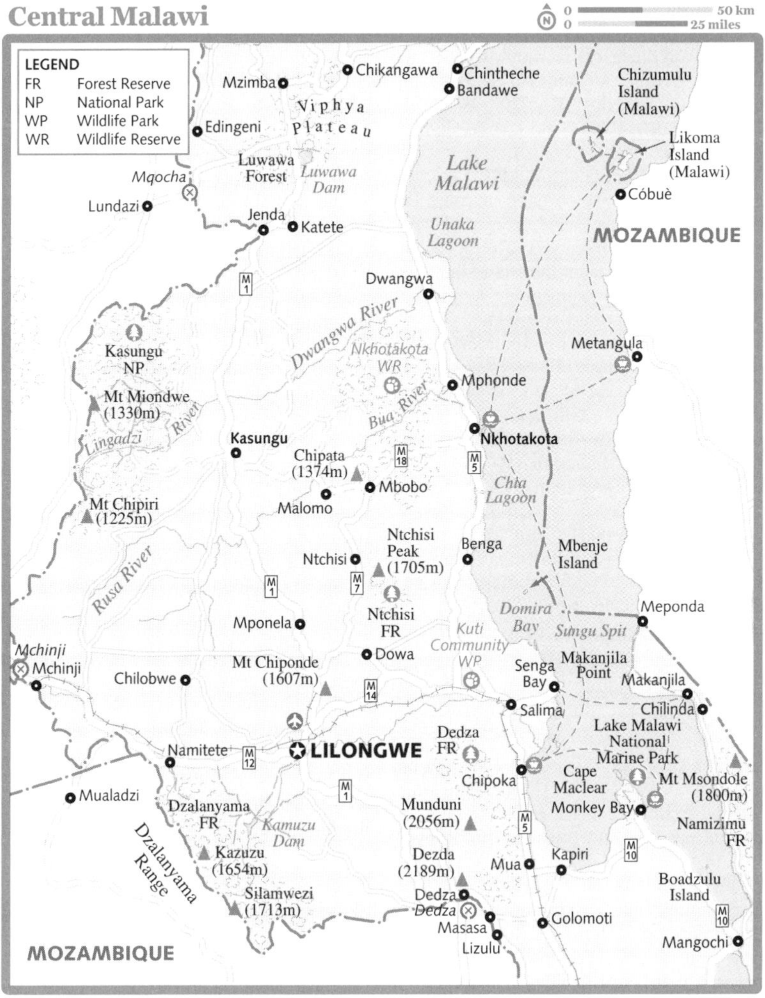

★ **Luwawa Forest Lodge** LODGE, CAMPGROUND $$

(☎01-342333, 0999 512645; www.luwawaforestlodge.net; camping US$8, dm US$14, r without bathroom per person US$40, chalets incl breakfast/half-board/full board per person US$80/105/120, cottages US$120-160; P 📶) Set at 1585m, homey Luwawa sits in a clearing of pine trees, its manicured gardens spilling with colourful flowers and morning mist. There are seven chalets and cottages, perfect for families (as they sleep up to five), with bunks, bathrooms, self-catering facilities and swallow-you-up four-posters, as well as more affordable rooms, dorms and a shaded camping area.

Nkhotakota

One of the oldest market towns in Africa, unassuming Nkhotakota had a significant and sinister part to play in Malawi's history. In the 1800s the town was home to a huge slave market, set up by Swahili-Arab trader Jumbe Salim-bin Abdullah. From here thousands of unfortunate captives were shipped annually across the lake to Tanzania, before being forced to march to the coast.

Today the town is strung out over 4km between the busy highway and the lake. If you do arrive on the ferry or stumble from a bus, there are a couple of historical sights – especially the **Livingstone Tree** and **All Saints Church** (⌚dawn-dusk) – and lakeside lodges, but if you can it's better to continue straight to the nearby Nkhotakota Wildlife Reserve.

The *Ilala* ferry stops here en route between Monkey Bay and Likoma Island, heading north to Likoma on Saturday morning and returning from the island on Tuesday morning, before continuing south from Nkhotakota on Tuesday evening.

AXA buses pass through around midnight daily, heading to Blantrye via Salima and to Karonga via Mzuzu. Minibuses go to Salima (MK1500, two hours) and Nkhata Bay (MK3500, five hours). Waiting for a direct service to Lilongwe (MK2200, four hours) may be slower than going to Salima and changing there.

Buses and minibuses stop close to the **Puma garage**: services to Nkhata Bay stop just north of this petrol station; those to Salima and Lilongwe stop to the south; and those to Kasungu stop to the west, at the beginning of the Kasungu road.

Nkhotakota Pottery Lodge LODGE $$
(☎0999 380105, 0997 189064; www.nkhotakota-pottery-lodge.com; camping/dm US$10/15, s/d from US$36/54; P) This German-run lodge offers 10 simple garden rooms, each with mozzie net, fan and private veranda overlooking the lake, and a six-bed dorm next to 200m of sandy beach. Superior rooms have kitchenettes. There's a bar-restaurant where live music and dance performances are sometimes staged, with breakfast (US$8 per person), half board (US$20) and full board (US$26) available.

Sitima Inn HOTEL $$
(☎0999 260005; www.sitimainn.com; camping/dm MK4500/7500, s/d incl breakfast from MK30,000/48,750, without bathroom from MK15,000/26,250; P) Within staggering distance of the *Ilala* ferry, this low-slung cream building with art-deco aspirations is quirky to say the least, incorporating old boat materials, car doors and nautical motifs. Despite the faint hint of decline, rooms are mostly neat, pleasantly decorated and houseproud. There are also two basic four-bed dorms and a slightly tacky suite.

Nkhotakota Wildlife Reserve

West of the main lakeshore road lies **Nkhotakota Wildlife Reserve** (☎0999 521741; www.african-parks.org; person/car US$10/3; ⌚6am-6pm), comprising 1800 sq km of rough, inhospitable terrain inhabited by animals from elephants to buffaloes.

The best way to experience the bush is by staying at one of the reserve's two excellent lodges and walking with a guide, or by kayaking down the Bua River from Tongole, your heart in your mouth as crocs upstream slip soundlessly into the murk to come and take a closer look.

The turnoff to the reserve's main gate is 10km north of Nkhotakota town. Public transport along the coast road north of Nkhotakota can you drop you at this turnoff, from where the gate is 10km away along a dirt track. You can walk to the gate, but you can't walk in the park unaccompanied. If you are staying at Bua River Lodge, SMS or email 24 hours ahead (don't call, because mobile reception at the lodge is bad) to be picked up from the turnoff (US$5 per person) or Nkhotakota (US$10).

Ulendo Airlink (p223) offers charter flights to the reserve from Lilongwe and Likoma Island (adult/child one way US$271/194 each; minimum two passengers). The airstrip is near Tongole Wilderness Lodge. Note that you are not guaranteed exclusive use of the aircraft. A more affordable option is to check the 'bid to fly' section of Ulendo Airlink's website and make an offer for a seat on one of the listed flights.

★ **Tongole Wilderness Lodge** LODGE $$$
(☎0999 055778, 01-209194; www.tongole.com; per person with full board US$435; P) Built with local materials, this eco-conscious lodge sits at elevation above the Bua River, a well-worn elephant crossing. Its thatched, near-church-high lodge is crowned by a mezzanine walkway leading to an aerial viewpoint – the perfect place to balance a G&T and binoculars. Huge chalets include plunge baths, marble basins, rain showers, wooden decks and wrought-iron doors with widescreen views.

Bua River Lodge LODGE, CAMPGROUND $$$
(☎0995 476887, 0885 181834; www.buariverlodge.com; camping US$10, with full board island/riverside tents US$150/110, hillside r US$85; P) Run by likeable Englishman (and Eric Sykes lookalike) John, Bua River – perched

above a beautiful boulder-strewn section of the river – is an adult Neverland. By night, trails lit by solar lanterns deter nosy wildlife and snake their way to safari tents kitted out with alfresco rain showers, African-chic decor, thick duvets and locally carved chairs.

Senga Bay

Sitting at the tip of a broad peninsula jutting into the lake, Senga Bay thrums with music by night; by day, fishing nets dry on the beach, boats are propped up photogenically on the shore and backstreets are vivid with playing kids. The trickle of travellers who pass through may find the fishing and conference town a little workaday, but it's a pleasant spot to break a journey along the lake, with some great accommodation and a more authentic feel than nearby Cape Maclear.

Sights

Lodges and guides can organise activities including windsurfing, snorkelling, boat trips, spotting otters by kayak and learning to dive.

Nonguests can use the beach and facilities at Steps Campsite, but be warned that it gets extremely busy at weekends.

Stuart M Grant Tropical Fish Farm AQUARIUM
(Red Zebra Tours; ☎0999 568425; www.lakemalawi.com; Kambiri Point, South Senga Bay) About 10km south of Senga Bay is Stuart Grant's tropical fish farm, which breeds and exports cichlids. If you're interested you can do a half-hour tour of the farm and its several hundred tanks.

Sleeping & Eating

★ **Cool Runnings** HOSTEL, CAMPGROUND $
(☎0999 915173, 01-263398; www.facebook.com/Cool-Runnings-Malawi-183925861628566; camping/safari tents/dm US$5/8/10, fixed trailers per person US$12, r US$35; P 📶) The smiley yellow faces leading to this excellent-value beachside guesthouse say it all. Like a home away from home and run by warm host Sam, Cool Runnings offers accommodation in a cute old house, a fixed trailer, a grassy campsite, a three-bed safari tent, and what could be Malawi's two nicest dorms, each containing two beds.

Steps Campsite CAMPGROUND $
(☎01-263444, 01-263222; captitalres@sunbirdmalawi.com; camping MK3000, day use MK1500; P) Perfectly situated by the giant boulders that bookend the golden stretch of beach, this campsite is owned by Sunbird Hotels and benefits from its premier-level service. It's better during the week, as it fills with locals and visitors from Lilongwe over the weekend.

Mufrasa Backpacker Lodge LODGE $$
(☎0888 919098, 0999 667753; camping MK4000, dm MK5000, r with/without bathroom from MK17,000/12,000; P) This faded banana-and-pastel-green beachfront place has a sandy patio with scattered loungers, a little bar and a Caribbean vibe. Clean rooms have vividly coloured linen, and African art on the walls, and are tantalisingly close to the lull of the surf.

Red Zebra Cafe MALAWIAN $
(☎0999 212328; mains MK3000; ⏰6am-9.30pm; P 🖉) Situated in a garden off the main road, this local eatery serves simple dishes such as chicken, beef and veggie curries, chambo and omelettes. Eat within its colourful interior or alfresco.

Information

Take great care when swimming near the large rocks at the end of the beach at Steps Campsite; there's a surprisingly strong undertow. Flags advise on whether it's safe to swim.

Some beaches here, especially at the bay's southern end, are flat, sheltered and reedy: perfect conditions for bilharzia snails, so check with your accommodation if it's safe to swim.

During the wet season, seek local advice before swimming in the lake at dusk and after dark, as crocs are occasionally at large.

Getting There & Away

From Salima, minibuses and *matolas* (pickups) run to Senga Bay (MK500), dropping you in the main street. If you want a lift all the way to Steps Campsite, negotiate an extra fee with the driver. A private taxi costs MK3500 to MK5000 from Salima, depending on where you want to be dropped.

From Lilongwe, buses (MK1700, two hours) and minibuses (MK1500), the latter departing more frequently but more packed, run to Salima. AXA buses stop at Salima bus station, which has an AXA office, en route up/down the lake between Mzuzu and Blantyre.

If you're travelling to/from Cape Maclear, consider chartering a boat; it's not too expensive if you get a group together (US$220 through Cool Runnings guesthouse). There's also the *Ilala* ferry, which sails to Monkey Bay on Wednesday morning, and heads north from Monkey Bay to

WORTH A TRIP

MUA

Sitting on a hill aglow with flame trees, Mua is a rare treat; its red-brick terracotta-tiled mission seems transplanted from Tuscany, its **church** strangely beautiful. The Roman Catholic mission was established in 1902, and a visit to its sepia-tinted structures is complemented by the excellent **Kungoni Centre of Culture & Art** (☎01-262706, 0999 035870; www.kungoni.org; ⏲7.30am-4pm Mon-Sat). With the **Chamare Museum** offering gripping insights into the culture of Malawi's various ethnic groups, plus the nearby **Kungoni Art Gallery**, Mua could be an unexpected highlight of your trip. For accommodation, try **Namalikhate Lodge** (☎01-262706; www.kungoni.org; camping MK5000, s/d MK17,000/22,000; ⏲restaurant 7.30am-6.30pm; P).

Mua is about 50km south of Salima on the road to Balaka. The Mua Mission is about 2km from the main road and is signposted (the Mua Mission Hospital sign is clearest). The road uphill is quite rough, so call ahead to check on its current condition if you're driving a 2WD.

From the turnoff on the main road, you can catch passing minibuses heading to Salima (MK1200, one hour) and Monkey Bay (MK3000, two hours).

Senga Bay and beyond on Friday. Additionally the weekly MV Chambo (p223) ferry sails to/from Metangula (Mozambique) via Makanjila.

Self-drivers can fuel up at the petrol station.

Monkey Bay

Hidden behind the Cape Maclear headland, sultry Monkey Bay is enchantingly slow: languid locals, a petrol station and a few shops are all that you'll find here. It's backpacker country, with two beachfront traveller joints, and the harbour is the launch pad for the *Ilala* ferry's long journey up the lake. Fish, snorkel or hammock flop – whatever you do, you may need to recalibrate your calendar.

From Lilongwe, buses run to Monkey Bay, usually via Salima and the southern lakeshore (MK3000, four hours). It's probably quicker to catch a minibus to Salima (MK1700, two hours), where you should find a minibus or *matola* (pickup) going direct to Monkey Bay.

From Blantyre, it's easiest to reach Monkey Bay by minibus with a change in Mangochi (total MK6000, five to six hours).

The *Ilala* ferry leaves **Monkey Bay Harbour** (☎0881 100018, 0996 784594) on Friday morning and heads up the lake to Senga Bay and points north, arriving back on Wednesday afternoon.

Ulendo Airlink (p223) flies a few days a week to Monkey Bay and the Makokola airstrip, between Monkey Bay and Mangochi, from Lilongwe (adult/child US$220/159), Likoma Island, Liwonde National Park and Majete Wildlife Reserve. Charter flights are also available, as are discounted seats on upcoming departures; check the 'bid to fly' section of Ulendo Airlink's website.

Mufasa Ecolodge HOSTEL, CAMPGROUND $
(☎0993 080057; www.facebook.com/MufasaRusticLodgeBackpackers; camping/tent hire/dm MK3000/3500/5000, s/d without bathroom MK8000/12,000; P 📶) This traveller's magnet is the main reason to hang around in Monkey Bay, with a sheltered beach bookended by smooth boulders and campsites on the sand or mountainside. Rooms are basic bamboo affairs, but the beach bar is appealing, with lounging cushions, wicker swing chairs and a relaxed vibe. Come dusk expect communal fires, drum circles and backpacker bonhomie.

Norman Carr Cottage BOUTIQUE HOTEL $$$
(☎0888 355357, 0999 207506; www.normancarrcottage.com; s/d all-inclusive from US$145/240; P ❄ 📶 🏊) Balancing simplicity, character and luxury, this beach retreat's six suites and two-bedroom family cottage have massive handmade king-size beds, small living areas and open-air garden showers. The beach and gardens are full of hanging chairs and sun beds and there's a beachside pool and whirlpool – perfect for a Malawian gin and tonic.

Cape Maclear

A long stretch of powder-fine sand bookended by mountains and lapped by dazzling water, Cape Maclear deserves all the hype thrown at it. By day the bay glitters a royal blue, studded with nearby islands and puttering, crayon-coloured fishing boats.

Especially in the early morning, the tideline is a hub of local life, with women washing clothes and their children, while fisherfolk spread out vermilion nets to dry and tourists emerge onto the verandas of nearby beach cabanas. Come afternoon the sleepy lanes ring with music from backstreet gospel choirs, while the evenings fill with reggae from the tinny sound system of that bar under the baobab. Much of the surrounding area is part of **Lake Malawi National Park** (person/car US$10/3), a Unesco World Heritage Site.

Activities

Water Sports

Cape Maclear Scuba DIVING
(☎0999 952488; www.capemaclearscuba.com; Thumbi View Lodge; casual dive US$50, PADI Open Water course US$400) With a reputation for affordability, this outfit offers casual dives and PADI courses from the toe-dipping Discover Scuba (US$70) to the Advanced Open Water and Dive Master.

Danforth Yachting SAILING, DIVING
(☎0999 960770, 0999 960077; www.danforthyachting.com) Fancy sailing to Likoma and Chizumulu Islands? Book two weeks ahead to charter the *Mufasa* for anything from two days to a fortnight, with rates starting at US$225 per person per night (US$900 minimum), including full board and activities such as snorkelling and fishing. No children under 16.

Kayak Africa KAYAKING
(☎0999 942661, in South Africa 21-783 1955; www.kayakafrica.co.za) For a longer paddle expedition, Kayak Africa is great, as you can arrange to kayak to one of its beautiful camps on Domwe and Mumbo Islands, or even between them. The islands are respectively 5km and 10km offshore, and separated by 7km of lake.

Hiking

There's a range of hikes and walks in the hills. Entry into the national park is US$10, which you can pay at the **Lake Malawi National Park Headquarters** (Otter Point Rd; ⏰7.30am-noon & 1-5pm Mon-Sat, 10am-noon & 1-4pm Sun) or the nearby gate, and the rate for a Cape Maclear Tour Guides Association guide is US$15 per person. It's better to hire a guide.

The main path starts by the **Missionary Graves** and leads up through woodland to a col below **Nkhunguni Peak**, the highest on the Nankumba peninsula, with great views over Cape Maclear, the lake and surrounding islands. It's six hours return to the summit; plenty of water and a good sun hat are essential.

Another interesting place to visit on foot is **Mwala Wa Mphini** (Rock of the Tribal Face Scars), which is just off the main dirt road into Cape Maclear, about 5km from the Lake Malawi National Park Headquarters. This huge boulder is covered in lines and patterns that seem to have been gouged by long-forgotten artists but are simply a natural geological formation.

Volunteering

Panda Garden VOLUNTEERING
(☎0993 229822; www.heeedmalawi.net; ⏰7am-5pm) This environmental NGO offers volunteering opportunities such as gardening and bilharzia research on the lake, including identifying host-carrying snail areas (scuba divers welcome).

Billy Riordan Memorial Clinic MEDICAL
(Otter Point Rd; consultations child/adult US$50/100, out of hours US$60/125; ⏰minor complaints 8am-noon & 2-4pm Mon-Fri, emergency 10am-noon & 3-4pm Sat & Sun) Set up by an Irish charity (www.billysmalawiproject.org), and run by medical volunteers and more than 30 local staff.

Sleeping

★**Funky Cichlid** HOSTEL $
(☎0999 969076; www.thefunkycichlid.com; camping/dm US$5/10, s/d without bathroom from US$20/30; P 📶) With its cheeky logo of a cichlid clad in sunglasses, this backpacker beach resort is Cape Mac's top spot to chill by day and party by night. Cool whitewashed rooms and six- to eight-bed dorms

CAPE MACLEAR TOUR GUIDES ASSOCIATION

All guides registered with the Cape Maclear Tour Guides Association work to a set price list and circulate at different resorts along the beach on a regular basis, so it's more than likely you'll be *softly* approached by one within an hour or two of arrival. Note that the association excludes entrance fees to **Lake Malawi National Park** from its prices. Most tours and activities have a minimum of three people (you can pay the difference if there are only one or two of you).

Cape Maclear

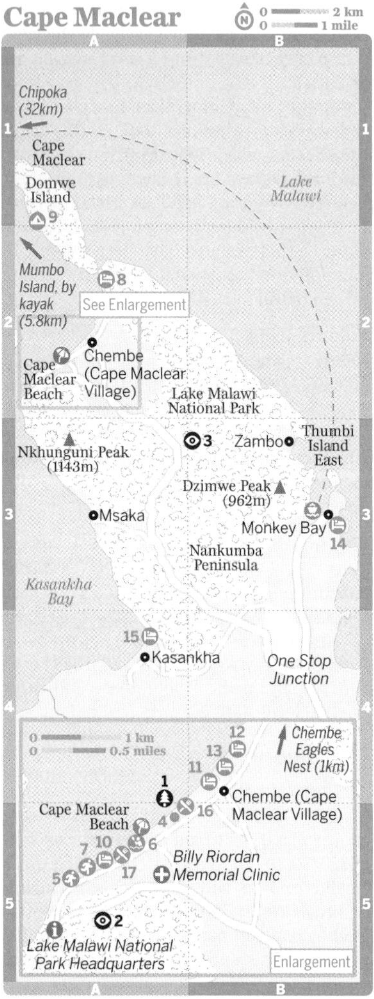

Cape Maclear

Sights

1 Lake Malawi National Park A4
2 Missionary Graves A5
3 Mwala Wa Mphini B3

Activities, Courses & Tours

4 Cape Maclear Scuba A5
5 Danforth Yachting A5
6 Kayak Africa A5
7 Panda Garden A5

Sleeping

Cape Maclear EcoLodge .... (see 7)
8 Chembe Eagles Nest A2
9 Domwe Island Adventure Camp A1
10 Funky Cichlid A5
11 Gecko Lounge B4
12 Malambe Camp B4
13 Mgoza Lodge B4
14 Mufasa Ecolodge B3
15 Pumulani A4
Thumbi View Lodge .... (see 4)
Tuckaways Lodge .... (see 11)

Eating

Gecko Lounge .... (see 11)
Mgoza Restaurant .... (see 13)
16 Mphipe Lodge A5
17 Thomas's Grocery, Restaurant & Bar A5
Thumbi View Lodge .... (see 4)

are decorated with funky murals, with well-maintained shared ablutions and packages available including breakfast, full or half board, drinks and water sports.

★ Tuckaways Lodge HOSTEL $

(☎0993 405681; www.geckolounge.net; s/d/f without bathroom US$25/40/100; P) Affiliated with the neighbouring Gecko Lounge, this neat and well-maintained compound offers a family room and five twin or double bamboo cabins with walk-in mozzie nets and decks overlooking the beach. Waking up to a waiting flask of tea to enjoy as you take in the morning views is a cracking start to the day.

Cape Maclear EcoLodge LODGE $

(☎0999 140905; www.heeedmalawi.net; d/f from US$45/75, s/d without bathroom from US$20/35; P ❄ 📶) Part of a non-profit NGO, these simple rooms open onto little terraces with cane chairs bedecked with colourful cushions, overlooking a leafy garden at the quiet end of the beach. There is a range of rooms, a restaurant and numerous water-based activities on offer, including diving with the on-site operator.

Malambe Camp HOSTEL $

(☎0999 258959; www.malambecamp.co.uk; camping/tent hire/dm MK1500/2500/3000, hut without bathroom s/d MK5000/6500; 📶) This backpacker hit has shaded pitches right on the beach, a spotless ablution block, and a cool cafe-bar with a covered dining area ringed by pot plants and dotted with wicker chairs. Choose from simple huts constructed from reed mats, and an eight-bed reed dorm.

Gecko Lounge LODGE $$
(☎0999 787322; www.geckolounge.net; dm/r/chalet q US$15/75/90; P 📶) A firm family favourite and with good reason, Gecko's self-catering chalets are right on the manicured beach. Each has a double and a bunk bed, fridge, fan, tile floor, mozzie nets and private veranda, as well as plenty of hammocks and swing chairs outside. Equally pleasant are the subdivided eight-bed dorm and the double and family rooms, replete with African decor.

The thatch- and wicker-accented **restaurant** (☎0999 787322; www.geckolounge.net; mains MK6000; ⏱8am-8pm; 📶) is popular for its tasty pizzas and burgers, as well as being the perfect sundowner spot. You can also rent kayaks and snorkel gear, making Gecko a winning beachfront option.

Chembe Eagles Nest LODGE, CAMPGROUND $$
(☎0999 966507; www.chembenest.com; camping US$10, chalets incl breakfast US$85; P @ 📶) At the far northern end of Cape Maclear Beach, this lodge sits in an idyllic spot on a beautiful and very clean, broad stretch of private beach, strewn with palm trees and shaded tables, and nestled against the side of the hills. Chalets have cool, tiled floors, thatched roofs and granite bathrooms with hot showers; campsites have power points.

★ **Pumulani** LODGE $$$
(☎01-794491; www.robinpopesafaris.net; per person all-inclusive US$355-470; ⏱Apr-Jan; P ❄ @ 📶) Pumulani is a stylish lakeside lodge with nature-inspired rooms – think grass roofs and huge windows to let in the light, views of the surrounding forest and lake, and massive wooden terraces from which to gaze at the clear waters and sweep of golden sand below. The food, served in the open bar-restaurant, is equally amazing.

★ **Mumbo Island Camp** CAMPGROUND $$$
(☎0999 942661, in South Africa 21-783-1955; www.kayakafrica.co.za; per person all-inclusive US$260) Situated exclusively on Mumbo Island, this eco-boutique camp has chalets and a walk-in tent on wooden platforms (with en-suite bucket showers and eco-loos), tucked beneath trees and above rocks, with spacious decks and astounding views. Accommodation rates include boat transfers, full board, kayaking, snorkelling and guided hikes.

★ **Domwe Island Adventure Camp** CAMPGROUND $$$
(☎0999 942661, in South Africa 21-783-1955; www.kayakafrica.co.za; camping US$30, safari tents per person US$60) Domwe is the smaller and more rustic of Kayak Africa's two neighbouring island lodges, run on solar power and romantically lit by paraffin lamps. It's self-catering, with furnished safari tents, kitchen, shared eco-showers and composting toilets. It has a bar and a beautiful staggered dining area, open to the elements and set among boulders. Food can be provided on request.

Eating

Thumbi View Lodge CAFE $
(☎0998 599005, 0997 463054; www.thumbiviewlodge.com; mains MK3000; ⏱7am-8pm) On the lane opposite Thumbi View's gate, this cafe serves light meals and snacks such as vegetable curry, spaghetti Bolognese, lasagne, fish, burgers and toasted sandwiches. Book by 1pm to join the set dinner, which typically consists of Indian or South African dishes such as slow-cooked oxtail from the owners' homeland, in the main lodge.

Mphipe Lodge ITALIAN $
(☎0884 997481; www.andiamotrust.org; mains MK2500; ⏱7am-9pm; P) For a different take on lake fish, Mphipe serves it in pasta dishes. Malawian staples such as *kampango* (catfish) and *nsima* (a porridge-like dish made from maize flour) are also on the menu. The lodge funds a children's hospital in Balaka.

Mgoza Restaurant INTERNATIONAL $
(☎0995 632105; www.mgozalodge.com; mains MK2000; ⏱kitchen 7am-9.15pm, bar to 10pm; 📶) With shaded *palapa* (palm-leaf) shelters in a garden facing the lake, this is a cool spot to chat in the friendly bar or take dinner outside.

Located at Mgoza Lodge, the restaurant serves up great full English breakfasts, healthy fruit smoothies and, come evening, fresh fish and great burgers loaded with fried onions. The garden is an atmospheric dinner-time setting.

Thomas's Grocery, Restaurant & Bar MALAWIAN $
(☎0999 270602, 0999 468383; dishes MK1800; ⏱8am-7pm Mon-Sat, bar to 11.30pm daily) This local gathering place comprises a shop and a bar with shaded seating and a reggae soundtrack. Simple dishes such as omelette, spaghetti, and beans with chapati or *nsima*

are offered, and the shop sells biscuits, toiletries and basic provisions.

Getting There & Away

By public transport, first get to Monkey Bay, from where a *matola* (pickup) to Cape Maclear costs MK1000 and a motorbike costs MK1500. The journey takes about an hour and they drop at the lodges.

Approaching by car on the M10 tar road, the road to Cape Maclear (signposted) turns west off the main drag about 5km before Monkey Bay. The first third of the 18km road to Cape Maclear is badly corrugated, but thereafter it's a smooth, tarred ride.

If you're heading to/from Senga Bay, ask around about chartering a boat. The Cape Maclear Tour Guides Association charges US$300, which, if split between several people, is a good alternative to the long, hard bus ride. Monkey Bay is US$200.

To catch a *matola* or motorbike in Cape Maclear, ask your lodge to call a driver, as there is no official bus station. As usual, *matolas* leave on a fill-up-and-go basis.

SOUTHERN MALAWI

Southern Malawi is home to the country's commercial capital, Blantyre, and incredibly diverse landscapes. These include mist-shrouded Mt Mulanje, Malawi's highest peak, and the Zomba Plateau, a stunning highland area. Safari-lovers can experience luxury and adventure combined in two of the country's best wildlife reserves: Liwonde and Majete, the country's only Big Five Park.

Liwonde

Straddling the Shire River, Liwonde is the main gateway to Liwonde National Park. The river divides the town in two, with the market and most services found on the eastern side, along with the turnoff to the park. If you're unable to stay in the park, it's possible to use Liwonde as a base for a short safari by road or river.

Regular minibuses run along the main road through town to/from Zomba (MK1000, 45 minutes), Limbe (for Blantyre; MK2500, three hours), Mangochi (MK2500, two hours) and the Mozambique border at Nayuchi (MK3000, 2½ to three hours).

There are two petrol stations east of the river en route to the Liwonde National Park turnoff.

Shire Camp LODGE $

(☎0999 210532, 0884 629214; camping/dm/r US$5/10/20; P) Shire Camp's faded bamboo-and-brick cabanas in varying states of repair have tiled floors, fans, hot-water bathrooms and netted breeze vents. The three-bed ensuite dorm is the best option. Right on the river, the colourful thatched bar-restaurant (mains MK3000) serves basic meals such as chambo, omelettes, burgers and pasta.

The campsite is less appealing, with hard, rocky ground and a basic ablutions block. Shire Camp can take you on a 2½-hour river safari (US$35 per person, two people minimum), which heads into Liwonde National Park. The camp is on the river's west bank. Take the dirt road next to the National Bank; follow the sign to Hippo View Lodge.

Hippo View Lodge HOTEL $$

(☎01-542116/8; www.hippoviewlodge.com; incl breakfast s/d superior MK35,000/55,500, deluxe MK48,000/65,500; P ❄ 📶 🏊) This 111-room behemoth does its best to banish a lingering feeling of faded grandeur, with rooms in blocks overlooking riverside gardens shaded by palms and a huge baobab. Superior rooms have tiled floor, fridge, phone and plasma-screen TV; it's worth upgrading to the more attractive and modern deluxe rooms, with larger bathrooms and tea and coffee.

Liwonde National Park

Set in 584 sq km of dry savannah and forest alongside the serene Shire River, the relatively small **Liwonde National Park** (www.african-parks.org; person/car US$20/4; ⏲6am-6pm) is one of Africa's best spots for river-based wildlife watching, with around 550 elephants, 2000 hippos and innumerable crocs. Animals including black rhinos, buffaloes and sable antelopes are found on dry land, where the terrain rolls from palm-studded flood plains and riverine forests to mopane and acacia woodlands interspersed with candelabra succulents.

The park's excellent lodges offer a fantastic range of wildlife-spotting drives, walks and boat trips.

Njobvu Cultural Village CULTURAL

(☎0888 623530; www.njobvuvillage.org; r incl breakfast per person US$16, all-inclusive US$50) 🍃 Near Liwonde National Park's Makanga Gate, Njobvu offers visitors a rare opportunity to stay in a traditional Malawian village,

Southern Malawi

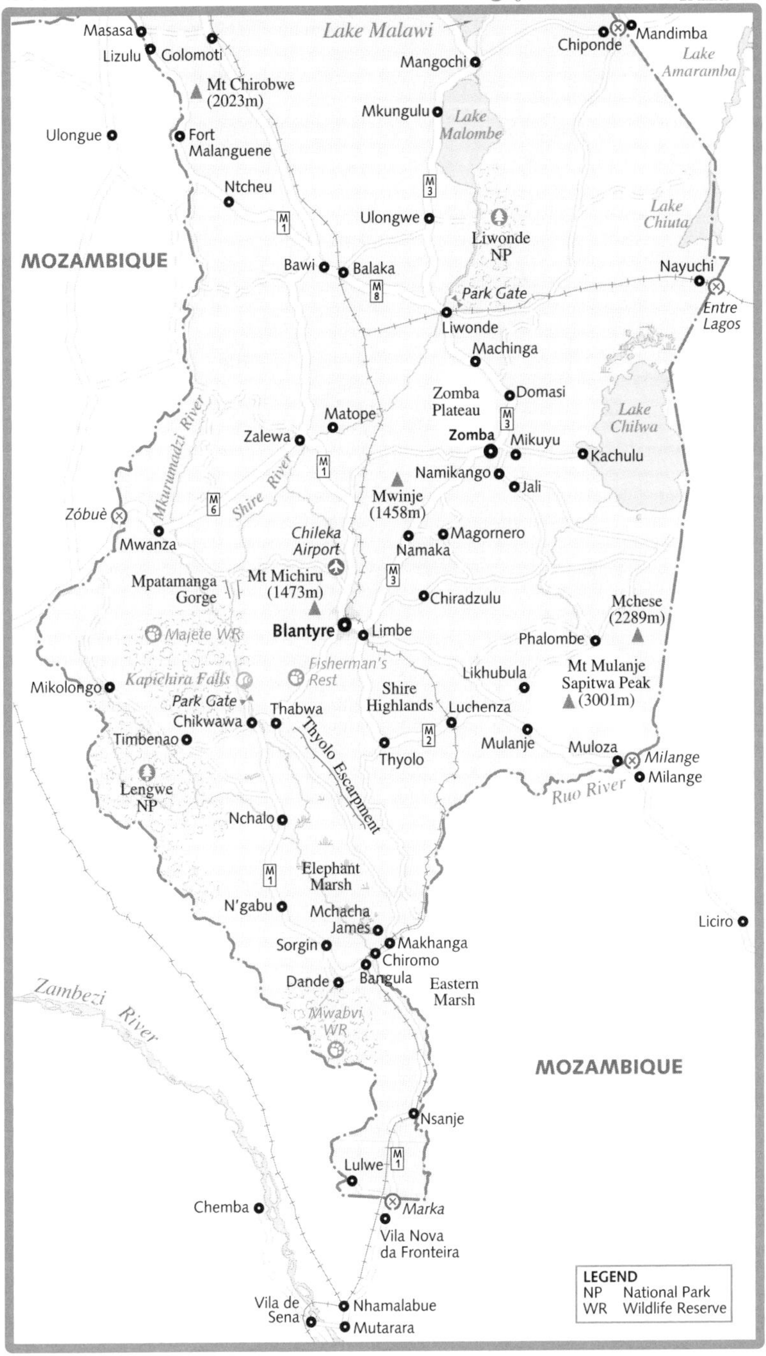

MALAWI SOUTHERN MALAWI

LIWONDE RHINO SANCTUARY

The **rhino sanctuary** (☎01-821219, 01-771393; www.cawsmw.com; US$80) is a fenced-off area within Liwonde National Park, developed for breeding rare black rhinos, and expanded to protect other mammal species from poaching. With a scout from Mvuu Camp or Mvuu Lodge in the park, you can go on a three-hour hike, searching for the rhinos in the 48-sq-km reserve.

In late 2016 10 black rhinos were living in the enclosure, along with populations of Lichtenstein's hartebeest, Cape buffalo, Burchell's zebra, eland and roan antelope.

sleeping in mud-brick huts (with or without a mattress – your choice!). During the day you are invited to take part in the villagers' daily lives, visiting traditional doctors and the village school, and eating local food such as the porridge-like *nsima*.

Sleeping

★**Bushman's Baobabs** LODGE, CAMPGROUND $$
(☎0995 453324, 0884 659901; www.bushmansbaobabs.com; camping US$7.50, dm US$15, s US$65-85, d US$90-120, tr/f US$180/240, s/d without bathroom US$25/50; P) The former Chinguni Hills Lodge is a fun place to experience a night in the bush and a safari. In an accessible location in the south of the park, Bushman's offers 14-bed dorms, thatched A-frame tents, luxurious en-suite tents, en-suite chalets, and campsites with barbecue spots and a self-catering kitchen. Wildlife drives, walks, and boat and canoe trips are offered.

Liwonde Safari Camp LODGE, CAMPGROUND $$
(☎0881 813240; www.liwondesafaricamp.com; camping/dm US$10/15, safari tent s/d US$40/60; P) This rustic camp is immersed in the park, with stilted safari tents, dorm and campsite sharing ablutions and a self-catering kitchen. There's a plunge pool, a thatched bar, meals (buffet dinner US$15), and – if you don't spot animals from the viewing decks – wildlife walks (US$5 per person), drives and boat trips (US$25 per person).

★**Mvuu Camp** LODGE $$$
(☎01-821219, 01-771393; www.cawsmw.com; camping US$15, chalets all-inclusive s/d US$360/520; P@☎) Run by the excellent Central African Wilderness Safaris, Malawi's premier safari operator, Mvuu sits on the river in the realm of myriad hippos and crocs. The camp comprises a main restaurant building and, nearby, scattered chalets with cosy interiors, step-in mozzie nets, comfy beds, immaculate linen and stone-walled bathrooms.

Getting There & Away

The main park gate is 6km east of Liwonde town. From the gate to Mvuu Camp is 28km along the park track (closed in the wet season); a 4WD vehicle is recommended for this route. The park lodges offer transfers from Liwonde.

Another way in for vehicles is via the dirt road (open all year) from Ulongwe, a village between Liwonde town and Mangochi. This leads for 14km through local villages to the park's western boundary. A few kilometres inside the park is a car park and boat jetty, where a watchman hoists a flag to arrange a boat from Mvuu Camp or Mvuu Lodge to collect you. This service is free if you're staying at the camps.

Alternatively, if you book in advance to stay at Mvuu Camp or Mvuu Lodge, you can organise a boat transfer–safari from Hippo View Lodge in Liwonde town for US$80.

For those without wheels, the best option is to get any bus or minibus between Liwonde town and Mangochi and get off at Ulongwe (make sure you say this clearly, or the driver may think you want to go to Lilongwe). In Ulongwe, locals wait by the bus stop and will sometimes take you by bicycle to the park (this takes about an hour and costs around MK4500).

Ulendo Airlink (p223) flies a few days a week to the Liwonde National Park airstrip (near Mvuu Camp and Mvuu Lodge), from Lilongwe (adult/child US$295/211), Likoma Island and Monkey Bay. Charter flights are also available, as are discounted seats on upcoming departures; check the 'bid to fly' section of Ulendo Airlink's website.

Zomba

With its chilly elevation and atmospheric old colonial and missionary buildings nestled in the wooded foothills, Zomba is hauntingly special – like a chapter of the British Empire hanging by a tenuous thread. It has the typical chaos of a dusty market town, but the higher you climb towards the Zomba Plateau, the more stunning and pristine the scenery becomes. The capital from 1891 to 1974 of British Central Africa, Nyasaland and, finally, Malawi, it's home to wide, tree-lined streets and an easy charm. This is perhaps Malawi's most appealing city, and a great base for exploring the plateau to the north.

African Heritage ADVENTURE, CULTURAL (Luso Lathu Art & Coffee Shop; ☎0999 235823; www.africanheritage.mw; Zomba Gymkhana Club) This craft shop doubles as a tourism hub, offering guided tours, shuttles to the Zomba Plateau (US$10), mountain-bike rental (MK1000 per hour) and a detailed plateau map (MK1000). Half-day tours cover the plateau and historical Zomba, while longer itineraries go further afield to Mt Mulanje, Mua, Lake Chilwa and beyond.

Sleeping & Eating

Pakachere Backpackers & Creative Centre HOSTEL $ (☎0994 685934, 0882 858089; www.pakachere.com; camping/tent hire/dm US$5/7/10, r/tr US$40/45, r without bathroom US$35; P 📶) This locally run hostel is nicely decorated, and has craftwork for sale and a bar-restaurant opening onto a garden with thatched seating areas. The spacious rooms are worn but clean, with tiled floors and mozzie nets, and there's six-bed dorm and an en-suite 10-bedder with secure storage space.

★**Casa Rossa** GUESTHOUSE, CAMPGROUND $$ (☎0991 184211, 0881 366126; www.casarossamw.com; Mountain Rd 5; incl breakfast camping US$5, r US$50-60, without bathroom US$40; P 📶) Named after its oxblood veranda overlooking town, this Italian-owned guesthouse offers hillside tranquillity and the best **restaurant** (mains MK3100-8100; ⏱9am-9pm Tue-Sun, residents only Mon; P 📶 🍷) around. Rooms in the old colonial house are simple but comfortable and the campsites in the leafy garden have electricity, fireplace and two barbecues.

★**Annie's Lodge** LODGE $$ (☎01-527002, 01-951636; www.annieslodge.com; Livingstone Rd; incl breakfast s US$40-70, d US$50-80; P ❄ 📶) Set in the foothills of the Zomba Plateau, Annie's has a bar-restaurant with an appealing terrace for a sundowner, and black-and-white-brick chalets with green tin roofs, engulfed in palm trees and flowers. The 40-plus rooms are carpeted, clean and welcoming, with DSTV, bathroom and fan or air-con.

Getting There & Away

Zomba is on a main route between Lilongwe and Blantyre. The bus station is in the town centre, off Namiwawa Rd. Minibuses depart every hour or so to Limbe (for Blantyre; MK1500, one hour) and Lilongwe (MK6000, five hours), and head to Liwonde (MK1000, 45 minutes). There are more services in the morning.

Alternatively, you can privately hire a taxi; the fare to Blantyre is MK30,000. Organise it through your accommodation; they may know of another guest or local going in the same direction who can share the ride.

For Mt Mulanje, there is a daily National Bus Company service at 11am to Phalombe (MK1500, 1½ hours), where you can pick up a minibus to Mulanje.

Zomba Plateau

Rising nearly 1800m behind Zomba town, and carpeted in thick stands of pine, the Zomba Plateau is beguilingly pretty. As you ascend the snaking road past wildflowers, stoic locals heaving huge burdens of timber, and roadside strawberry vendors, the place almost feels like alpine France; then a vervet monkey jumps out, a pocket of blue mist envelops your car, and you remember you're in Africa. This gorgeous highland paradise, replete with streams, lakes and tumbling waterfalls, is home to monkeys, bushbucks, and birds including mountain wagtails and Bertram's weavers.

The plateau can be covered on foot, mountain bike or car (4WD only on the back roads), with myriad winding trails that ring and cross the mountain. It's divided in two by the Domasi Valley. The southern half has a tarred road to the top, a hotel, several picnic places, waterfalls and viewpoints, and a network of driveable tracks and hiking paths.

Plateau Stables HORSE RIDING (☎0993 764600; www.plateaustables.com; per person per hour US$40) Opposite Mulunguzi Dam, this long-running stable offers one- to five-hour plateau excursions on well-kept horses. In the wet season (mid-November to mid-March), phone ahead to check that weather conditions are suitable.

Sleeping

Ku Chawe Trout Farm CAMPGROUND, BUNGALOWS $ (P) This campsite is ideally located in the lee of a valley amid a giant gum- and cedar-tree clearing. In late 2016 it was showing signs of not being well maintained and was undergoing a change of management.

Zomba Plateau (Southern Section)

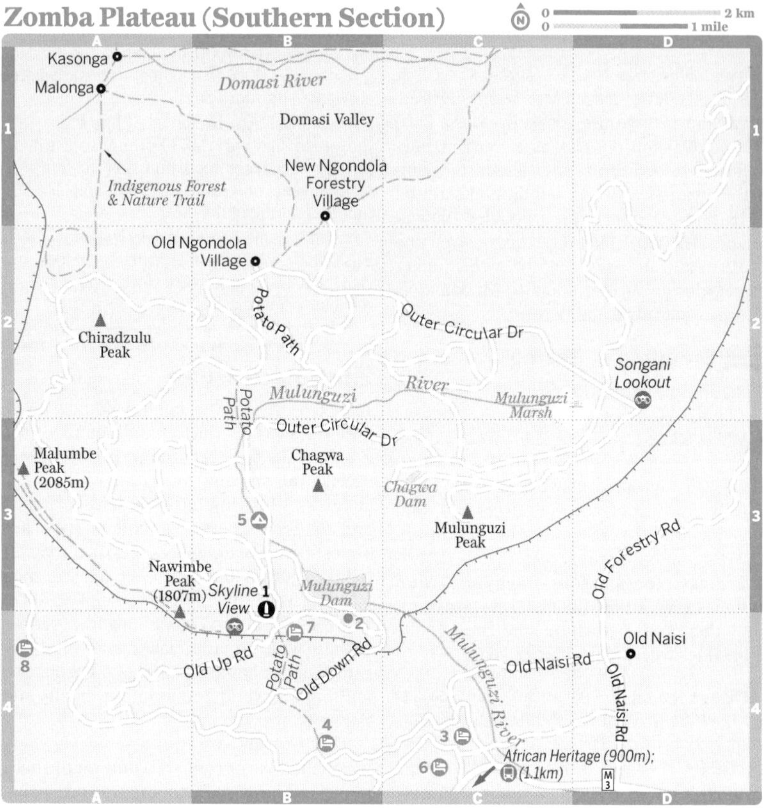

Zomba Plateau (Southern Section)

Sights

1 Model Hut B3

Activities, Courses & Tours

2 Plateau Stables B4

Sleeping

3 Annie's Lodge C4
4 Casa Rossa B4
5 Ku Chawe Trout Farm B3
6 Pakachere Backpackers & Creative Centre C4
7 Sunbird Ku Chawe B4
8 Zomba Forest Lodge A4

Eating

Casa Rossa .... (see 4)

If you're keen to camp on the plateau, Enquire in Zomba or at the nearby **Sunbird Ku Chawe** (☎01-773388, 01-514211; www.sunbirdmalawi.com; incl breakfast s US$127-203, d US$157-233;) hotel whether the campsite is functional again.

★ **Zomba Forest Lodge** GUESTHOUSE $$$
(☎0997 593325, 0992 802702; www.zombaforestlodge.com; per person with full board US$110; P) Book at least a day ahead to stay at this four-room guesthouse owned by British-Malawian couple Tom and Petal. Woodcarvings and Tom's artwork decorate the Afro-chic rooms, and candles, paraffin and solar power light the off-the-grid property. Hike up to the plateau or wander the 8-hectare grounds, with its 3.5km of walking trails and indigenous rainforest along the stream.

Blantyre & Limbe

Founded by Scottish missionaries in 1876, and named after the town in South Lanarkshire, Scotland, where explorer David Livingstone was born, Blantyre is Malawi's second-largest city. It's more appealing and cohesive than Lilongwe thanks to its compact size and hilly topography, and though there's not much to do here, it makes a good springboard for exploring Majete Wildlife Reserve and Mt Mulanje.

Attached to the Blantyre's eastern side, **Limbe** is home to a grand old mission church, a minibus station and a golf club. Unlike Blantyre, however, which has seen a finessing of its restaurants and hotels, Limbe has fallen into disrepair over the last couple of decades. You may have to change minibuses here, but it's best to head straight on.

Malawi's commercial and industrial hub, Blantyre has the country's best and most diverse choice of restaurants, a small selection of lively watering holes and a smattering of sights. Add to that tour operators, banks, internet cafes and other practicalities, and Blantyre makes a pleasant stopover.

Sights & Activities

Mandala House HISTORIC BUILDING

(Map p208; ☎01-871932; Kaoshiung Rd; ⌚8.30am-4.30pm Mon-Fri, to 12.30pm Sat) This is the oldest building in Malawi, built in 1882 as a home for the managers of the African Lakes Corporation. It's a quietly grand colonial house, encased in wrap-around verandas and set in lovely gardens. Inside are the inviting Mandala Cafe (p207), an eclectic art gallery (p207) and the **Society of Malawi Library & Archive** (Map p208; ☎01-872617; www.societyofmalawi.org; 1st fl, Mandala House, Kaoshiung Rd; ⌚9am-4pm Mon-Fri) FREE.

Museum of Malawi MUSEUM

(Chichiri Museum; Map p206; ☎01-873258; Kasungu Cres; adult/child under 13yr MK500/100; ⌚7.30am-4.30pm) Malawi's interesting national museum has a few gems, including a royal ceremonial stool dating from the 16th century and a display on Gule Wamkulu dances. The museum is between central Blantyre and Limbe, accessed from Moi Rd opposite Chichiri Shopping Mall. Take a minibus headed for Limbe and ask to be let off at the museum.

St Michael and All Angels Church CHURCH

(CCAP Church; Map p208; www.stmichaelchurchmw.com; ⌚services 6am, 7am, 8.30am, 10.30am & 5pm Sun) This magnificent red-brick Church of Central Africa Presbyterian building was preceded by a simpler structure, built by Scottish missionary Reverend DC Scott in 1882. In 1888 the missionaries started work on a new, more impressive church with elaborate brickwork moulded into arches, buttresses, columns and towers, topped with a grand basilica dome. The church is off Old Chileka Rd.

Blantyre Sports Club GYM

(Map p208; ☎01-835095, 01-821172; btsportsclub@africa-online.net; day membership adult/child under 18yr MK5500/1000; ⌚6am-10pm, pool & golf course to 5pm) Established in 1896, and

DON'T MISS

HIKING ON THE ZOMBA PLATEAU

The southern half of the plateau is ideal for hiking. The network of tracks can be confusing, though, so for more help with orientation there's a 3D map of the plateau in the **Model Hut** (⌚8.30am-4.30pm).

The **Potato Path** is the most popular hike at Zomba. It's a direct route from town all the way up to the plateau. To find the path, head up the main road to the plateau and turn right at the firebreak line just past Casa Rossa guesthouse. From here a few paths climb steeply through woodland and converge on the plateau near the Sunbird Ku Chawe hotel (45 minutes).

From near the Sunbird Ku Chawe, the Potato Path goes straight across the southern half of the plateau, sometimes using the park tracks, sometimes using narrow shortcuts, and leads eventually to Old Ngondola village, from where it descends steeply into the Domasi Valley.

Allow two to three hours for the ascent, and about 1½ hours coming down.

Greater Blantyre & Limbe

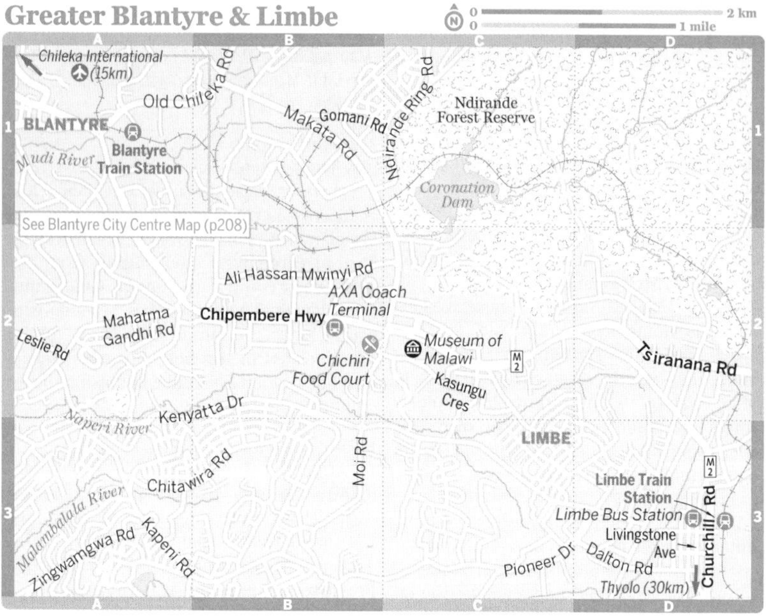

with a faint whiff of colonialism, this is a great place to work up a sweat or keep the kids amused. There's a restaurant and bar, and you can pay supplements to use the pool (adult/child MK2000/1000), gym, and tennis, squash and nine-hole golf courses. It's off Victoria Ave.

Sleeping

★Doogles HOSTEL $
(Map p208; ☎0999 186512; www.dooglesmalawi.com; Mulomba Pl; dm US$15, r US$30-45; P@🛜≋) Doogles is popular with discerning travellers of all stripes, its inviting pool and bar ringed by walls with a cool sunset-safari design. From there, the complex leads to a big TV lounge, lush gardens, super-fresh en-suite rooms with shower, clean six-bed dorms, and thatched en-suite chalets with mozzie nets and fans.

Blantyre Lodge HOTEL $
(Map p208; ☎01-834460; Old Chileka Rd; s/d incl breakfast MK10,500/14,000; P❄🛜) So-so en-suite rooms with grotty bedspreads, TV, bare white walls and a few sticks of furniture. But it's close to the main bus station. Opt for a room out the back, away from the main drag.

Henderson Street Guest House GUESTHOUSE $
(Map p208; ☎01-823474; 19 Henderson St; incl breakfast s/d standard MK12,000/14,000, executive MK15,000/17,000; P🛜) Five minutes' walk from the town centre, this old-fashioned place sits in a leafy garden and has a welcoming veranda. The seven rooms are tired but clean and cosy, with a mishmash of old and new furniture, small TV, and tiled bathroom with shower.

Hotel Victoria HOTEL $$
(Map p208; ☎01-823500; www.hotelvictoriamw.com; Lower Sclater Rd; s/d incl breakfast from MK45,000/50,000; P❄@🛜≋) Upmarket Victoria attracts corporate types and aid workers with its pool, marble lobby and air-conditioned restaurant. Eighty rooms enjoy plump pillows, thick carpet, DSTV, writing desk, fridge and less impressive bathroom. Deluxe and larger executive rooms are a big step up, with flat-screen TV, office chair, and bathroom with oval tub and shower. Ask for one away from Victoria Ave.

Kabula Lodge LODGE $$
(☎01-821216; www.kabulalodge.co.mw; Kabula Hill; incl breakfast s/d from US$40/50, without bathroom US$20/30; P❄🛜) Hidden down a dirt

road off Michiru Rd, on the crest of a hill northwest of the city centre, friendly Kabula enjoys peace aplenty and scenic mountain views from its breakfast terrace. Executive rooms are equally pleasing, with wrought-iron beds, minimal decor, DSTV, fridge and air-con, but some rooms and shared bathrooms are basic, so ask to see a few.

Malawi Sun Hotel HOTEL $$$
(Map p208; 01-824808; www.malawisunhotel.com; Robins Rd; incl breakfast s/d standard US$100/125, executive US$145/170;) This comfortable hotel has a small African-style lounge with mountain views, a tempting swimming pool and a food court. The 73 rooms are decent, with DSTV, comfy beds, fridge, tea and coffee. It's worth upgrading to executive from standard (also called 'ethnic' for their Malawian decorative touches); shoot for a balcony overlooking the hills.

Eating

Food Court FAST FOOD $
(Map p208; 0997 915519; www.malawisunhotel.com; Malawi Sun Hotel, Robins Rd; Blue Savannah mains MK2000; 8am-9pm) With striking views of the mountains, this breezy alfresco courtyard is surrounded by a bakery (Bread Basket), a fast-food joint (Blue Savannah) and an ice-cream parlour (Scoops & Shakes), the latter selling iced coffees, milkshakes and ice-cream cones.

Chichiri Food Court FAST FOOD $
(Map p206; Chichiri Shopping Mall, Chipembere Hwy) This alfresco food court is popular with families for its play area and bouncy castle. The fast-food outlets here include a pizzeria (Jungle Pepper), ice-cream parlours and fried-chicken joints.

★ **L'Hostaria** ITALIAN $$
(Map p208; 0888 282828; www.facebook.com/hostariaMW; Sharpe Rd; mains MK5500; noon-2pm & 6.30-9pm Tue-Sun;) In an atmospheric old house with black-and-white floors and a large veranda overlooking a lawn, L'Hostaria offers Italian recipes and fresh produce that attract local expats in the know. Come for a relaxing evening and wood-fired pizzas, homemade pastas and steaks.

★ **Mandala Cafe** CAFE $$
(Map p208; 01-871932; Mandala House, Kaoshiung Rd; mains MK5000-6000; 8.30am-4.30pm Mon-Fri, to 12.30pm Sat;) Sit on a breezy stone terrace in the grounds of Mandala House (p205), or inside at this chilled cafe adorned with artworks and guidebooks. Regulars love the Italian cuisine, fillet steak, Thai chicken, freshly brewed coffee, iced tea and gelato. A real oasis.

★ **21 Grill on Hanover** STEAK $$
(Map p208; 01-820955; Protea Hotel Ryalls, 2 Hanover Ave; mains MK7000; 11am-3pm & 4-10pm Mon-Fri, from 4pm Sat & Sun;) Established in 1921, this historical restaurant is one of Malawi's more sophisticated eateries, occupying a library-like room with salmon-coloured seats and ornate carpets. The menu focuses on meat dishes, from South African Karoo lamb curry to flaming Jack Daniel's steak, but it also has a good selection of fish, pasta, salad and decadent desserts.

★ **Casa Mia** INTERNATIONAL $$$
(01-827871; www.blantyreaccommodation.com; Kabula Hill Rd; mains MK5000-11,000; 6.30am-9.30pm;) Don your smarts for dinner at this classy guesthouse restaurant. The wine-stacked interior, with its antique Cinzano prints, white tablecloths and expat clientele, is a pleasant environment for dishes ranging from steaks and carbonara to red wine–marinaded Karoo lamb and chambo Thermidor. Lunch on the breezy terrace is more casual.

Drinking & Nightlife

Kwa Haraba CAFE
(Map p208; 0994 764701, 0993 801564; www.facebook.com/KwaHaraba-138690532886703/; Phekani House; 7.30am-5pm Sun-Tue & Thu, to 8pm Wed, to 10pm Fri & Sat) This craft shop and cafe serves fresh juices bursting with goodness and light meals such as feta pizza, ham and cheese pita sandwiches, salads and toasted sandwiches. The wonderful masks, paintings, secondhand paperbacks and fabric make a creative environment. Cocktails and music from 6pm Friday and Saturday, and poetry between 6pm and 7pm Wednesday. Phekani House is off Glyn Jones Ave.

Shopping

Mandala House ARTS & CRAFTS
(Map p208; 01-871932; Kaoshiung Rd; 8.30am-4.30pm Mon-Fri, to 12.30pm Sat) Situated in Mandala House (p205), the oldest colonial dame in the city, this eclectic gallery features vividly coloured, contemporary

Blantyre City Centre

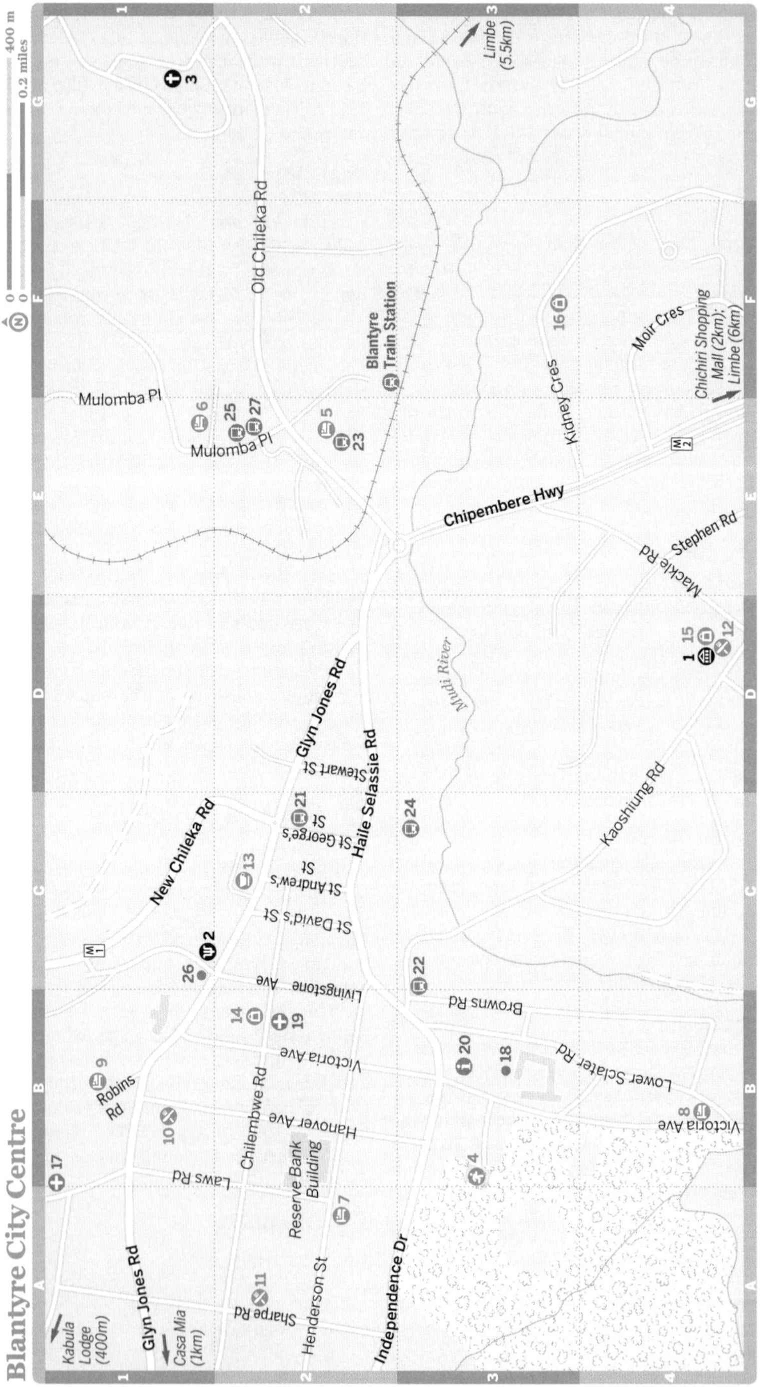

Blantyre City Centre

Sights
1 Mandala House D4
2 Shree Hindu Temple C1
Society of Malawi Library & Archive .... (see 15)
3 St Michael and All Angels Church G1

Activities, Courses & Tours
4 Blantyre Sports Club B3

Sleeping
5 Blantyre Lodge E2
6 Doogles E1
7 Henderson Street Guest House A2
8 Hotel Victoria B4
9 Malawi Sun Hotel B1

Eating
10 21 Grill on Hanover B1
Food Court .... (see 9)
11 L'Hostaria A2
12 Mandala Cafe D4

Drinking & Nightlife
13 Kwa Haraba C2

Shopping
Central Africana Bookshop .... (see 16)
14 Craft Stalls B2
15 Mandala House D4
16 Uta Waleza Centre F3

Information
17 Blantyre Adventist Hospital B1
18 Immigration Office B3
Jambo Africa .... (see 16)
19 One Stop Pharmacy B2
20 Tourist Office B3

Transport
21 AXA House Coach Terminal C2
22 City Bus Station C3
23 Intercape E2
24 Mibawa Bus Depot C3
25 National Bus Company E2
26 SS Rent A Car C1
27 Wenela Bus Station E2

work by local artists, as well as sculpture, old maps and prints, and huge, carved wooden thrones.

Central Africana Bookshop BOOKS
(Map p208; ☎01-876110; www.centralafricana.com; Uta Waleza Centre, Kidney Cres; ⏰8am-5pm Mon-Fri, 9am-1pm Sat) This long-running bookshop on two levels has an excellent selection of Africana, ranging from dusty old tomes to coffee-table books, and from novels and guidebooks to a section dedicated to Livingstone.

Uta Waleza Centre MALL
(Map p208; Kidney Cres) With a few design shops and an excellent bookshop, Uta Waleza is a good place to buy presents and souvenirs.

Craft Stalls ARTS & CRAFTS
(Map p208; Chilembwe Rd; ⏰8am-4pm Mon-Sat) There are good craft stalls under an awning next to the salmon-coloured Malawi Savings Bank building. The work on sale is excellent and browsing is refreshingly hassle free.

Information

IMMIGRATION

Immigration Office (Map p208; ☎01-823777; www.immigration.gov.mw; Government Complex, Victoria Ave; ⏰7.30am-noon & 12.30-4pm Mon-Fri, to noon Sat) For visa extensions or temporary-residency applications.

MEDICAL SERVICES

Blantyre Adventist Hospital (Map p208; ☎hospital 01-820006, medical appointments 01-820399; Kabula Hill Rd; ⏰casualty 24hr) This private hospital and medical and dental clinic charges MK5400 for a doctor's consultation and MK2000 for a malaria test. Cash only.

One Stop Pharmacy (Map p208; ☎0888 860230, 01-824148; Chilembwe Rd; ⏰8am-5.30pm Mon-Fri, 9am-2pm Sat) This well-stocked pharmacy sells bilharzia tablets (if you've been swimming in the lake), as well as malaria prophylaxis.

TOURIST INFORMATION

Jambo Africa (Map p208; ☎0882 904166, 0111 572709; www.jambo-africa.com; Uta Waleza Centre, Kidney Cres; ⏰8am-5pm Mon-Fri, 9am-noon Sat) A great one-stop shop for travel tickets, car hire, excursions and accommodation, Jambo owns a park lodge and two self-catering cottages on the lake. It has a second office next to the Shree Hindu Temple (Map p208; ☎01-820761; Glyn Jones Rd).

Tourist Office (Map p208; ☎01-827066; Government Complex, Victoria Ave; ⏰7.30am-4.30pm Mon-Fri) In a cottage-like tax building dating to 1939, this small office covers the whole country. It stocks a few leaflets and maps, sells wall maps of Malawi (MK5000), and can offer enthusiastic, though not always particularly helpful, advice.

Getting There & Away

AIR

Blantyre's **Chileka International Airport** (☎ 01-827900) is about 15km north of the city centre. A taxi to the city costs around MK15,000, but agree on a price with the driver first. The price can be negotiated down a bit if you're going from the city to the airport. If your budget doesn't include taxis, frequent local buses between the City Bus Station and Chileka Township pass the airport gate (the fare's around MK2000).

BUS & MINIBUS

Blantyre's main bus station for long-distance buses is **Wenela Bus Station** (Map p208; Mulomba Pl), east of the centre. Companies including **National Bus Company** (Map p208; ☎ 0888 561365; Wenela Bus Station, Mulomba Pl) have daily services to Lilongwe (MK3500, four hours), Mzuzu (MK7500, nine to 10 hours), Zomba (MK1500, 1½ to two hours), Mulanje (MK1500, 1½ hours) and Karonga (MK10,500, 14 hours).

AXA buses depart from the **terminal** (Map p206; Chipembere Hwy) next to the Chichiri Shopping Mall, then pick up at the central **office** (Map p208; ☎ 01-820411, 01-820100; www.axacoach.com; St George's St; ⏲ ticket office 6am-5pm) en route to Lilongwe (MK11,300). These Super Executive coaches leave in both directions at 7am and 4.30pm. Cheaper Special and Executive buses to/from Mzuzu (Special MK11,550, Executive MK12,600) via Lilongwe (MK6350, MK8100) leave in both directions at 7am and 6pm. Buses taking the lakeshore route to Mzuzu don't work to a fixed schedule but leave when they're full, normally around 5pm. For all services, it's best to book ahead.

Most intercity minibuses leave from **Limbe Bus Station** (Map p206), off Livingstone Ave; it's normally fastest to take a minibus there (MK200, 15 minutes), either from the **Mibawa depot** (Map p208) or the roadside, then pick up a long-distance service. A taxi there costs around MK4000. Routes from Limbe include Zomba (MK1500, one hour), Mulanje (MK1500, 1¼ hours) and Mangochi (for Monkey Bay; MK4000, five hours).

Minibuses to Chikwawa (for Majete Wildlife Reserve; MK1500, 1½ hours) depart from Blantyre's **City Bus Station** (Map p208).

The car park next to Blantyre Lodge is the pickup and drop-off point for long-distance bus companies headed for Jo'burg. **Intercape** (Map p208; ☎ 0999 403398; www.intercape.co.za; Blantyre Lodge, Old Chileka Rd) goes to Jo'burg at 8am daily (MK45,000, two days).

CAR

Avis (☎ 01-622719), Budget and **SS Rent A Car** (Map p208; ☎ 01-822836; www.ssrentacar.com; Glyn Jones Rd) have offices in the city.

Mulanje

Mulanje is famous for both its infinity of emerald-green tea plantations, and the achingly pretty Mt Mulanje – a massif of some 20 peaks reaching over 2500m. The town makes a reasonable base for forays into the massif, with a good lodge and a few eateries along the main road.

A daily National Bus Company bus runs to/from Blantyre (MK1500, 1½ hours), as do regular minibuses to/from Limbe (MK1500, 1½ hours); on the minibus, you may have to change in Thyolo. If you're heading for the border with Mozambique, minibuses and matolas (pickups) run to Muloza (MK800, 30 minutes).

Mulanje Infocentre TOURIST INFORMATION
(☎ 0888 122645, 01-466466; infomulanje@sdnp.org.mw; Phalombe Rd, Chitakale Trading Centre; ⏲ 8am-5pm Mon-Fri, by appointment Sat & Sun) The best source of information about hiking on Mt Mulanje and beyond, with helpful staff and documentation. They can book the Mulanje forestry huts and organise guides and porters, as well as tours to local waterfalls, tea estates and villages, the latter potentially including a Gule Wamkulu ceremony (with notice).

Sleeping & Eating

Kokotowa Executive Lodge LODGE $
(☎ 01-466743; Chitakale Trading Centre; incl breakfast s/d/tr standard MK10,000/11,500/13,000, executive MK12,000/13,000/15,000; P @) Popular for conferences, Kokotowa's 12 rooms (with more coming) are basic but clean, spacious and comfortable, with large beds, plentiful furniture and fans. The whole shebang is arranged around a courtyard with bar, restaurant and secure parking. Find it off the M2, on the Blantyre side of the Chitakale junction; follow the sign for the altogether less impressive Chididi Motel.

Mulanje Motel MOTEL $
(☎ 01-466245; M2; r MK5000; P) Mulanje Motel's 18 basic but clean rooms have flowery bedding, fan and functional if frugal bathroom; those in the rear annexe are rather dingy. Around the front courtyard are a restaurant and a bar with pool table.

★ Kara O'Mula LODGE $$

(☎01-466515; www.karaomula.com; incl breakfast s/d US$50/65, chalets US$65/75; P 📶 🏊) Hidden up a dirt track right beneath Mt Mulanje, this delightful eyrie cloaked in lush vegetation has a swimming pool (fed by fresh water from a small waterfall), a cosy thatched bar, back-up power and a long veranda to savour the wonderful views of mountains and tea estates. It's homey, welcoming and the perfect base from which to hike.

★ Huntingdon House HISTORIC HOTEL $$$

(☎0882 599717, 0993 121854; www.huntingdon-malawi.com; Satemwa Tea and Coffee Estate, Thyolo; per person all-inclusive US$325, self-catering bungalows US$225; P 🚭 📶) Between Mulanje and Blantyre, this atmospheric colonial homestead, still run by the founding family, offers accommodation among the emerald-green fields of a Shire Highlands tea estate. Book ahead to stay in one of the five rooms, with their coat stands, claw-footed bathtubs and pervasive mood of calm, and enjoy the excellent **restaurant** (1-/2-course lunch MK5500/7000, afternoon tea MK7500, dinner MK12,000; ⏲noon-8pm; P 📶 🍷) and **tea tastings** (☎01-473500; tastings per person US$10; ⏲tastings 10.30am-3.30pm Mon-Fri, by appointment Sat & Sun), guided walks and mountain biking.

Mulanje Pepper PIZZA $$

(☎0999 826229, 0888 826229; www.junglepeppperpizza.com/mulanje; Phalombe Rd, Chitakale Trading Centre; pizzas MK4500-5600; ⏲11am-9pm Wed-Mon) Underneath Mulanje Infocentre, the former Pizzeria Basilico (and country cousin of Blantyre's Jungle Pepper) serves an excellent selection of wood-fired pizzas (you can see them rolling the dough before your very eyes), as well as a range of pastas and grills. It has a breezy terrace overlooking the street.

Mt Mulanje

A huge hulk of twisted granite rising majestically from the surrounding plains, Mt Mulanje towers over 3000m high. All over the mountain are dense green valleys and rivers that drop from sheer cliffs to form dazzling waterfalls. The locals call it the 'Island in the Sky', and on misty days (and there are many) it's easy to see why: the massif is shrouded in a cotton-wool haze, its highest peaks bursting through the cloud to touch the heavens.

Some people come to the base of the mountain just for a day visit, but the stunning scenery, easy access, clear paths and well-maintained huts make Mulanje a fine hiking area worthy of a few days. While here, look out for the endemic Mulanje cedar, which can grow up to 40m high. The abundant wildlife also includes klipspringers, duikers, vervet and blue monkeys, rock hyraxes (dassies), black eagles, buzzards, hawks and kestrels.

On the second Saturday in July, the 20-year-old **Mt Mulanje Porters Race** follows a gruelling, rocky route over the country's highest peak. It was originally only for porters and guides, but these days anyone can take the 22km challenge. Contact Mulanje Infocentre (p210) for details.

🛏 Sleeping

Below the Mountain

Likhubula Forest Lodge LODGE $

(☎0888 773792, 0111 904005; Likhubula; camping MK3500, s/d from MK12,100/14,100; P) This faded but lovely old colonial house has lots of character: a homey kitchen, five clean rooms (two with their own bathroom), a veranda, a communal lounge with rocking chairs, and a nightly fire crackling. The easy charm of the staff and the recommended food make it a memorable place to overnight, with breakfast, half board and full board available.

Thuchila Tourist Lodge LODGE $

(☎0881 327988; www.facebook.com/thuchilatourist.lodge; camping MK5000, incl breakfast

HIKING ON MT MULANJE

There are about six main routes up and down Mulanje. The three main ascent routes go from Likhubula: the **Chambe Plateau Path** (also called the Skyline Path), the **Chapaluka Path** and the relatively easy **Lichenya Path** (aka the Milk Run). Other routes, more often used for the descent, are Thuchila Hut to Lukulezi Mission, Sombani Hut to Fort Lister Gap, and Minunu Hut to the Lujeri Tea Estate.

Once you're on the massif, a network of paths links the huts and peaks, and many permutations are possible. It takes anything from two to six hours to hike between one hut and the next.

Mt Mulanje

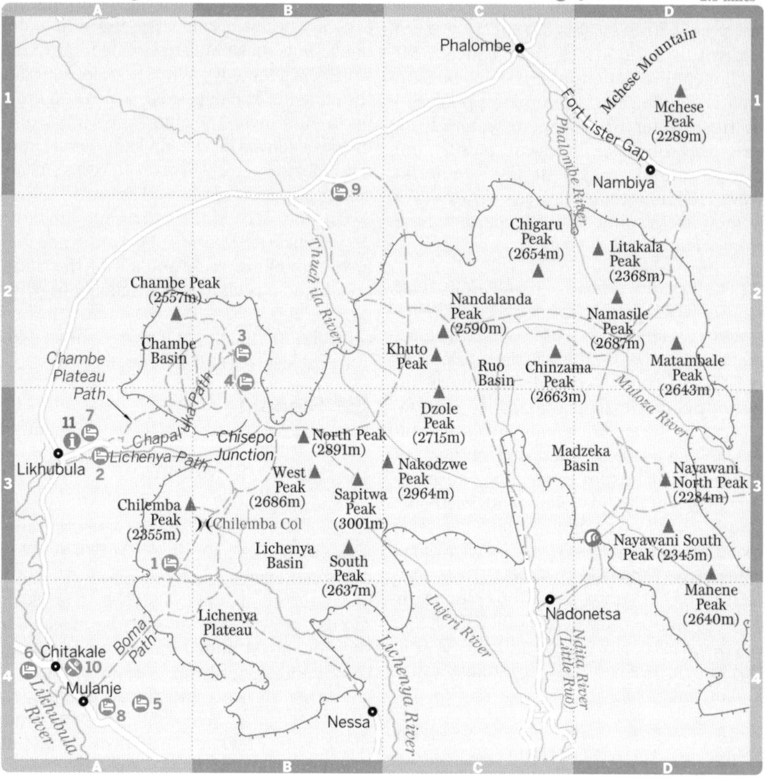

Mt Mulanje

Sleeping

1 CCAP Cottage A3
2 CCAP Guesthouse A3
3 Chambe Hut B2
4 France's Cottage B2
5 Kara O'Mula A4
6 Kokotowa Executive Lodge A4
7 Likhubula Forest Lodge A3
8 Mulanje Motel A4
9 Thuchila Tourist Lodge B1

Eating

10 Mulanje Pepper A4

Information

11 Likhubula Forestry Office A3
Mulanje Infocentre .... (see 10)

s/d MK15,000/17,000, without bathroom from MK6000/7500; P 📶) This rustic lodge has an edge-of-the-world feel (maybe it's the caged baboons outside), with lush gardens nestled in the shadow of the massif. There are basic rooms with shared bathroom, while comfortable blue-walled en-suite chalets further up the slope have fridge, fan and a swimming hole below. The bar-restaurant (mains MK2000) serves curries, chambo, *nsima* and the like.

CCAP Guesthouse GUESTHOUSE $
(☎0888 863632, 0881 188887; www.ccapblantyre-synod.org/ccap-likhubula-mulanje.html; Likhubula; camping US$5, dm US$11, s/d/q from US$47/55/93, r without bathroom per person US$16) The CCAP (Church of Central Africa Presbyterian) Mission, after the Likhubula gate, has cosy rooms, four- and 12-bed dorms, and one- and two-bedroom self-catering chalets (number one is homey). The friendly guesthouse among jacaranda trees is a pleasant place to rest after a long hike. Breakfast (US$4), and lunch and dinner (US$6), are available to both guests and nonguests.

On the Mountain

There are eight forestry huts on Mulanje: Chambe, Chisepo, Lichenya, Thuchila, Chinzama, Minunu, Madzeka and Sombani. Each is equipped with benches, tables and open fires with plenty of wood. Some have sleeping platforms (no mattresses); in others you just sleep on the floor. You provide your own food, cooking gear, candles, sleeping bag and stove (although you can cook on the fire). A caretaker chops wood, lights fires and brings water, for which a small tip should be paid. Payments must be made at Likhubula Forestry Office – show your receipt to the hut caretaker.

CCAP Cottage CHALET $

(☎0888 863632, 0881 188887; per person US$8) On the Lichenya Plateau, this basic cottage is a step up from the forestry huts found elsewhere in the mountains, with utensils in the kitchen, plus mattresses and blankets. You can make reservations at the CCAP Guesthouse, from where the cottage is a six-hour walk.

France's Cottage CHALET $

(☎0888 122645; www.mcm.org.mw/mulanje_huts.php; per person camping/cottages MK500/1000) This historical two-bedroom cottage sleeps six and comes with a living room complete with cooking fireplace. There are two single beds and two bunks. It's in the Chambe Basin near the **Chambe Hut** (per person camping/huts MK500/1000). Book through the Mulanje Infocentre or Likhubula Forestry Office – show your receipt to the hut caretaker.

ℹ Information

Hiking on Mt Mulanje is controlled by the **Likhubula Forestry Office** (☎0111 904005, 0888 773792; ⏲7.30am-4.30pm), at the small village of Likhubula, about 15km north of Mulanje town centre. Entry fees payable at the gate are MK1000 per person, MK500 per vehicle, and MK1000 per day for parking. Register here with Macdonald and the friendly staff, and make reservations for the mountain huts (or call in advance). The office can also advise day-trippers about short hikes on the lower slopes.

Also excellent for information and bookings is the Mulanje Infocentre. Emmie and the knowledgeable staff provide all pertinent information about hiking on the mountain and have a good reference library of books and maps.

Mulanje is a big mountain with notoriously unpredictable weather. After periods of heavy rain streams can become swollen and impassable – do not try to cross them! You should wait until the flood subsides or adjust your route to cross in safety further upstream. Also be aware that much of the mountain's granite surface can become very slippery and dangerous when wet. Even during the dry season, it's not uncommon to get rain, cold winds and thick mists, which make it easy to get lost.Between May and August, periods of low cloud and drizzle (called chiperone) can last several days, and temperatures drop below freezing. Always carry a map, a compass and warm and waterproof clothing in case the weather changes.

Mountain Club of Malawi (☎0888 842701, 01-821269; www.mcm.org.mw) Comprehensive source of info on hiking, mountain biking and rock climbing in the massif.

ℹ Getting There & Away

The dirt road to Likhubula turns off the main sealed Blantyre–Mulanje road at Chitakale Trading Centre, about 2km northwest of the centre of Mulanje town – follow the signpost to Phalombe.

If you're coming from Blantyre on the bus, ask to be dropped at Chitakale. From there, you can pick up a *matola* (pickup), minibus (MK1000) or bicycle taxi (MK700) to Likhubula. Alternatively you can walk (11km, two to three hours); it's a pleasant hike with good views of the southwestern face of Mulanje on your right.

Majete Wildlife Reserve

Malawi's only Big Five park, this rugged wilderness of hilly miombo (woodland) and savannah hugs the west bank of the Shire River. Since African Parks took over its management in 2003, things have really been looking up for the once heavily poached reserve. A perimeter fence has been erected, and accommodation and roads have been massively upgraded. With Majete's lion-reintroduction program, the **park** (☎0999 521741; www.african-parks.org; person/vehicle US$20/4; ⏲6am-6pm) is now a conservation case study and an exciting destination.

Majete lies west of the Shire River, some 70km southwest of Blantyre. Take the M1 to Chikwawa, from where signs will direct you 20km to the reserve along 2WD-accessible roads. By public transport, the nearest you can get is Chikwawa.

Regular minibuses run from Blantyre to Chikwawa (MK1500, 1½ hours). From there, the easiest option is to arrange a transfer with your lodge, but you can privately hire a *matola* (pickup; MK6000 to MK8000).

Ulendo Airlink (p223) flies a few days a week between the reserve airstrip, 1.5km west of the gate, and destinations including Lilongwe (adult/child US$341/243) and Likoma Island. Charter flights are also available, as are discounted seats on upcoming departures; check the 'bid to fly' section of Ulendo Airlink's website.

Community Campsite CAMPGROUND $
(0999 521741; www.african-parks.org; camping/tent hire US$10/25, gazebo s/d US$12/15; P) Enabling visitors on a budget to stay in the reserve and fully immerse themselves in the wildlife-viewing activities, this campground has shady places to pitch up, park or sleep on a stilted gazebo under the stars. There's drinkable borehole water, a thatched bar, clean ablution blocks and hot showers, as well as barbecues, cooking utensils and free firewood.

★**Mkulumadzi Lodge** LODGE $$$
(01-794491; www.mkulumadzi.com; per person all-inclusive US$445; P) Romantically reached by a suspension bridge over a croc-infested river, this extraordinary lodge is a fusion of African tradition and boutique chic. The eight chalets are artfully blended with the bush, with grass roofs, step-in rain showers and windows offering widescreen views of the Shire River as you flop in a sunken, candlelit bath.

★**Thawale Camp** LODGE $$$
(0999 521741; www.african-parks.org; chalets per person with half board/full board/full board plus activities from US$138/150/180; P) Situated around a watering hole frequented by antelopes and warthogs, this upmarket bush camp is about 3km inside the reserve from the main entrance. The standard, luxury and family tented chalets on raised wooden platforms feel safari-ready with their khaki sheets, outside barbecues and private verandas overlooking the floodlit watering hole.

UNDERSTAND MALAWI

Malawi Today

The smiles travellers encounter in 'the warm heart of Africa' belie a country grappling with the disasters of drought, flooding and food shortages. These environmental challenges are set against a background of political corruption, unsustainable population growth and deforestation, and one of the world's highest HIV/AIDS infection rates at about 10%. Going into 2017, leadership difficulties continue to dominate headlines. However, there is good news in the conservation sector, with animal translocations proceeding apace. Among the highlights: 250 elephants are set to be translocated from Majete to Nkhotakota in 2017 and Liwonde's rhino sanctuary continues to conserve endangered black rhinos.

History

The Difaqane ('The Crushing)'

Also known as the *Mfecane,* meaning the 'crushing' or 'scattering', the period between 1815 and about 1840 saw indigenous tribes in Southern Africa involved in internecine, bloody struggles. Much of this can be attributed to one man, Shaka, king of the Zulu tribe. In the early 19th century there were three centralised kingdoms: the Ngwane, Mdwandwe and Mthethwe. In 1869 Shaka, ruler of the Mthethwe, revolutionised military warfare by replacing the throwing spear with a stabbing spear and surrounding his enemy in a tight horseshoe then closing in on them. Very soon widespread massacres spread across Southern Africa, depopulating countries and killing some two million people.

Among those that fled were the Mdwandwe clan, who headed for Mozambique, coercing the local Tonga people to form a cooperative army with them – the Jere-Ngoni. By 1825, blazing their own trail of carnage, the Jere-Ngoni entered Malawi, terrorising the Yao people near the lake and the Tumbuka people to the north, raiding villages, butchering old men and forcibly enlisting young men. The army settled on Lake Malawi and were to remain there until their Mdwandwe chief's death in 1845. This bloody period is remembered as 'The Killing'.

The Dark Days of Slavery

Slavery, and a slave trade, had existed in Africa for many centuries, but in the early 19th century demand from outside Africa increased considerably. Swahili-Arabs, who dominated the trade on the east coast of Africa, pushed into the interior, using powerful local tribes such as the Yao to raid and capture their unfortunate neighbours. Several trading centres were established in Malawi, including Karonga and Nkhotakota – towns that still have a Swahili-Arab influence today.

Livingstone & the First Missionaries

The first Europeans to arrive in Malawi were Portuguese explorers who reached the interior from Mozambique in the early 1600s. Its most famous explorer, though, was David Livingstone from Scotland, whose exploration heralded the arrival of Europeans in a way that was to change Malawi forever.

In 1858, when Livingstone found his route up the Zambezi blocked, he followed a major tributary called the Shire into southern Malawi, reaching Lake Malawi in September 1859 – and providing fodder for thousands of tourist brochures to come by reportedly dubbing it the 'lake of stars'.

Livingstone died in Zambia in 1873. In 1875 a group from the Free Church of Scotland built a new mission at Cape Maclear, which they named Livingstonia, and in 1876 the Established Church of Scotland built a mission in the Shire Highlands, which they called Blantyre. Cape Maclear proved to be malarial, so the mission moved to Bandawe, then finally in 1894 to the high ground of the eastern escarpment. This site was successful; the Livingstonia mission flourished and is still there today.

The Colonial Period

By the 1880s competition among European powers in the area was fierce. In 1889 Britain allowed Cecil Rhodes' British South Africa Company to administer the Shire Highlands, and in 1891 the British Central Africa (BCA) Protectorate was extended to include land along the western side of the lake. In 1907 the BCA Protectorate became the colony of Nyasaland.

Colonial rule brought an end to slave traders and intertribal conflicts, but also introduced a whole new set of problems. As the European settlers' demand for land grew, the hapless local inhabitants found themselves labelled 'squatters' or tenants of a new landlord, and were forced to seek work on the white-settler plantations or to become migrant workers in Northern and Southern Rhodesia (present-day Zambia and Zimbabwe) and South Africa. By the turn of the 19th century some 6000 Africans were leaving the country every year; this had escalated to 150,000 by the 1950s.

Transition & Independence

After WWI the British began allowing the African population a part in administering the country, although it wasn't until the 1950s that Africans were actually allowed to enter the government.

In 1953, in an attempt to boost its sluggish development, Nyasaland was linked with Northern and Southern Rhodesia in the Federation of Rhodesia and Nyasaland. But the federation was opposed by the pro-independence Nyasaland African Congress (NAC) party, led by Dr Hastings Kamuzu Banda. The colonial authorities declared a state of emergency and Banda was jailed.

By mid-1960 Britain was losing interest in its colonies. Banda was released, and he returned to head the now renamed Malawi Congress Party (MCP), which won elections held in 1962. The federation was dissolved, and Nyasaland became the independent country of Malawi in 1964. Two years later, Malawi became a republic and Banda was made president.

Banda: Hero to Villain

Banda swiftly forced members of the opposition into exile, banning political parties, declaring himself 'president for life' and outlawing the foreign press. Miniskirts, women in trousers, long hair for men and other such signs of Western cultural influence were also banned.

Alongside this move towards dictatorship, Banda remained politically conservative, giving political support to apartheid-era South Africa, which, in turn, rewarded Malawi with aid and trade.

With the end of the Cold War in the 1990s, South Africa and the West no longer needed to support Banda, and within the country opposition was swelling. In 1992 the Catholic bishops of Malawi condemned the regime and called for change, and demonstrations, both peaceful and violent, added their weight to the bishops' move. As a final blow, donor countries restricted aid until Banda agreed to relinquish total control.

In June 1993 a referendum was held for the people to choose between a multiparty political system and Banda's autocratic rule. Over 80% of eligible voters took part; those

LOCAL KNOWLEDGE

GULE WAMKULU

Performed at funerals, major celebrations and male initiation ceremonies, Gule Wamkulu or 'Great Dance' is the most popular dance among the Chewa. It can't be performed by just anyone; only members of a secret society, sometimes called the Nyau brotherhood, are allowed to participate. Dancers perform clad in magnificent costumes and brightly painted masks made from cloth, animal skins, wood and straw. Each dancer represents a particular character (there are more than 150 Gule Wamkulu characters): a wild animal, perhaps, or an ancestral spirit, sometimes even a modern object such as a car or a plane. Each character has its own meaning – for example, lions represent strength and power and often appear at the funeral of a chief.

Supported by an entourage of drummers and singers, the dancers achieve a state through which they can summon up the spirits of animals or dead relatives. As the drumbeats quicken, they perform dances and movement with incredible energy and precision. Some of this is pure entertainment, some of it is a means of passing on messages from ancestral spirits, and some of it aims to scare the audience – as a moral lesson or a warning. Through acting out mischievous deeds, the Gule Wamkulu characters are showing the audience, as representatives of the spirit world, how not to behave.

There are both individual and group performances and they take place during the day and at night – when the audience watches from afar. The dance is widespread in central and southern Malawi and is also performed in Zambia's Eastern Province and the Tete province of Mozambique.

voting for a new system won easily, and Banda accepted the result.

The 1990s: Fresh Hope

At Malawi's first full multiparty election in May 1994, the victor was the United Democratic Front (UDF), led by Bakili Muluzi. He quickly closed political prisons, encouraged freedom of speech and print, and initiated free primary-school education; he also undertook several economic reforms with the help of the World Bank and the IMF.

In November 1997 Dr Banda died. His age was unknown, but he was thought to be 99.

In 2002, after failing to pass a bill that would have given him life presidency, Muluzi chose Bingu wa Mutharika as his successor, and in 2004 Mutharika duly won the election. The new leader resigned from the UDF and set up his own party, the Democratic Progressive Party (DPP). A massive famine in 2005 saw Malawi bear the brunt of crop failure and drought in the region. In 2006, under the Highly Indebted Poor Country Initiative, Malawi qualified for debt relief.

Mutharika: Malawi's New Dictator

In 2010 Mutharika expelled his deputy, Joyce Banda, from the party, but he had no choice but to retain her as vice-president as she was elected in 2009 as his running mate. Then in 2011 a diplomatic spat erupted between Mutharika and the UK after a leaked British document accused him of being autocratic. Mutharika hit back, expelling the British High Commissioner; immediately, Malawi's biggest donor froze millions of dollars of aid.

By the end of 2011, Malawi was crippled by soaring fuel prices of up to 150% and terrible shortages that ground the country's already ailing industry to a halt. Foreign exchange was also banned as Mutharika took the inflammatory measure of inflating Malawi's currency on the international markets.

On 5 April 2012 Mutharika suffered a heart attack. In the following days, the army placed a cordon around Joyce Banda's house to assist her constitutional succession to power (lest Mutharika's supporters enact a coup). She was sworn in as Malawi's first female president on 7 April.

Joyce Banda: Unfulfilled Promise

In 2012 Banda took some very brave steps to get her house in order: first, she devalued the kwacha by 40%; next, she sold the US$15 million presidential jet, saving the poor country US$300,000 a year in maintenance and insurance. Meanwhile, she proved herself a shrewd international diplo-mat; foreign funding to Malawi swiftly resumed, with the IMF agreeing to a donation of US$157 million.

Banda's presidency lasted until 2014, when her predecessor's brother, Peter Mutharika, was voted in. Her two-year term was rocked by the 'cashgate' scandal, which saw international aid temporarily frozen when up to US$100 million disappeared from government coffers. She is reportedly planning to run in the 2019 election.

Culture

Malawi's main ethnic groups are Chewa, dominant in the centre and south; Yao in the south; and Tumbuka in the north. Other groups include the Ngoni (also spelt Angoni), inhabiting parts of the central and northern provinces; the Chipoka (or Phoka) in the central area; the Lambya; the Ngonde (also called the Nyakyusa) in the northern region; and the Tonga, mostly along the lakeshore.

There are small populations of Asian and European people living mainly in the cities and involved in commerce, farming (mainly tea plantations) and tourism. The Indian community is well established, with many businesses owned and run by Indians, while the Chinese population is growing.

Around 83% of Malawians are Christians. Some are Catholic, while many follow indigenous Christian faiths that have been established locally.

Malawi has a significant Muslim population of around 13%, mostly living in the south. Alongside the established churches, many Malawians also follow traditional animist religions.

DON'T MISS

LAKE OF STARS MUSIC FESTIVAL

One of the region's largest spectacles, this three-day **music festival** features live acts from around Africa and Europe. It takes place in a different lakeshore venue each year, with proceeds benefiting charity. Booking accommodation well in advance is essential, but there are normally camping spots available until the last minute.

The Arts

Literature

Poetry is very popular. The late Steve Chimombo was a leading poet whose collections include *Napolo and Other Poems*. His most highly acclaimed work is a complex poetic drama, *The Rainmaker*. Another returned exile, Jack Mapanje, published his first poetry collection, *Of Chameleons and Gods*, in 1981.

Malawi's most acclaimed novelist is the late Legson Kayira, whose semi-autobiographical *The Looming Shadow* and *I Will Try* earned him acclaim in the 1970s. A later work to look out for is *The Detainee*. Another novelist is Sam Mpasu; also a politician, he served a two-year jail sentence following a corruption scandal in the 2000s. His *Nobody's Friend* was a comment on the secrecy of Malawian politics – it earned him an earlier two-year prison stint in 1975. After his release he wrote *Political Prisoner 3/75* and later became minister for education in the new UDF government.

MUST READ: THE BOY WHO HARNESSED THE WIND

When the 2001 drought brought famine, and terrible floods decimated his parents' crops, 14-year-old William Kamkwamba was forced from school. While he was educating himself at his old primary school, one book in particular spoke to him; it was about electricity generation through windmills.

A lightbulb moment flashed. Exhausted from his work in the fields every day, William picked around for scrap and painstakingly began his creation: a four-bladed windmill. Soon neighbours were coming to see him to charge their phones on his windmill.

When news of William's invention spread, people from across the globe offered to help him. He was shortly re-enrolled in college and travelling to America to visit wind farms, and he has since been mentoring children on how to create their own independent electricity sources. *The Boy Who Harnessed The Wind* (by William Kamkwamba and Bryan Mealer) is his amazing story, published in 2009.

Natural Environment

Pint-sized, landlocked Malawi is wedged between Zambia, Tanzania and Mozambique, measuring roughly 900km long and between 80km and 150km wide, with a total area of 118,484 sq km.

Lying in a trough formed by the Rift Valley, Lake Malawi makes up over 75% of Malawi's eastern boundary. West and south of the lake, escarpments rise to high plateaus covering much of the country.

Wildlife

In 2012 Malawi began reintroducing lions at Majete Wildlife Reserve, finally giving the country its 'Big Five' stamp. Many people head for Liwonde National Park, noted for its herds of elephants and myriad hippos. Along with Majete, it's the only park in the country where you might see rhinos.

Elephants are also regularly seen in Nkhotakota Wildlife Reserve, Majete and Nyika National Park. Nyika has the country's largest population of leopards and Nkhotakota has been bolstered by a historic elephant translocation from Liwonde and Majete. Vwaza Marsh Wildlife Reserve is known for its hippos, as well as elephants, buffaloes and antelope, but is currently in poor shape due to unsatisfactory management.

Lake Malawi has more fish species than any other inland body of water in the world, with a total of over 1000, of which more than 350 are endemic. The largest family of fish in the lake is the Cichlidae (cichlids).

For birdwatchers, Malawi is rewarding: over 600 species have been recorded in the country, and birds rarely spotted elsewhere in Southern Africa are easily seen here, including the Böhm's bee-eater, wattled crane and African skimmer.

National Parks

Malawi has five national parks. These are (from north to south) Nyika, Kasungu, Lake Malawi (around Cape Maclear), Liwonde and Lengwe. There are also four wildlife reserves – Vwaza Marsh, Nkhotakota, Mwabvi and Majete – meaning that 16.8% of Malawi's land is protected.

Most parks and reserves cost US$10 per person per day (each 24-hour period), plus US$3 per car per day. Citizens and residents pay less. All fees are payable in kwacha or US dollars.

SURVIVAL GUIDE

Directory A–Z

ACCOMMODATION

There are generally good selections of backpacker hostels and top-end accommodation but fewer midrange guesthouses and hotels. One tip: consider sharing a bathroom; many budget and midrange options have lovely rooms with a bathroom for every two rooms. Camping offers affordable access to high-end lodges, as many have campsites.

ACTIVITIES

Birdwatching

Malawi is a great destination for birding, with over 600 species recorded here. The best place to start is the national parks. Liwonde is an excellent spot, with particularly good birdlife along the river, and the forests in Nyika are also good. For water birds, Elephant Marsh in Malawi's far south is your surest bet. Land & Lake Safaris (p180) in Lilongwe can organise birdwatching tours around the country.

Cycling

Several lakeshore lodges hire out mountain bikes from about US$10 a day. Great mountain-biking areas include Nyika National Park, with its hilly landscape and good network of dirt tracks, and the Viphya Plateau. These areas' lodges offer rental bikes.

Diving, Snorkelling & Other Water Sports

Lake Malawi's population of colourful fish attracts travellers to come scuba diving. The lake is reckoned by experts to be among the best freshwater diving areas in the world, and one of the cheapest places to learn how to dive. The water is warm, and (depending on the season) visibility and weather conditions are usually good. Places where you can hire scuba gear and take a PADI Open Water course include Nkhata Bay, Cape Maclear, Likoma Island and Senga Bay. If you don't want to dive you can still enjoy the fish: snorkelling gear can be hired from dive centres, and lakeside hotels rent out snorkels.

SLEEPING PRICE RANGES

The following price ranges refer to an en-suite double room excluding breakfast, in high season.

$ less than MK35,000 (US$50)

$$ MK35,000–MK70,000 (US$50–US$100)

$$$ more than MK70,000 (US$100)

Upmarket lodges along the lake have facilities for waterskiing or windsurfing. You can also go sailing, or join luxurious 'sail safaris' where everything is done for you – Danforth Yachting (p197) and Pumulani (p199) in Cape Maclear on the southern lakeshore can both organise this. Kayaking is available at Cape Maclear and Nkhata Bay and at many of the lodges dotting the lakeshore.

Hiking & Rock Climbing

The main areas for hiking are Mt Mulanje and the Nyika Plateau. Other areas include the Zomba Plateau, and various small peaks around Blantyre. Mulanje is Malawi's main rock-climbing area, with some spectacular routes and Africa's longest vertical rock wall, although local climbers also visit smaller crags and outcrops. Rock climbing can also be arranged in Livingstonia and the Viphya Plateau.

The Mountain Club of Malawi (p213) provides a wealth of information about hiking and climbing on Mt Mulanje.

BUSINESS HOURS

Banks Usually 8am to 3.30pm weekdays.

Bars Noon to 11pm.

Post offices Generally 7.30am to 5pm weekdays, sometimes with a break for lunch. In Blantyre and Lilongwe, they're open Saturday morning too.

Restaurants If they don't serve breakfast, 11am to 10pm.

Shops and offices 8am to noon and 1pm to 5pm weekdays. Many shops also open Saturday morning.

CHILDREN

Child care Easy to arrange informally through your hotel.

Restaurant high chairs Available at many big-city restaurants.

Nappies & Formula Widely available in major cities, but not elsewhere.

Warning Never let your children swim in Lake Malawi from just before dusk into the night. There are many tragic stories about kids who outstayed their welcome and got taken by crocs and hippos, who come out at this time.

EMBASSIES & CONSULATES

Australia Contact the Australian Embassy in Harare, Zimbabwe.

Canada Contact the Canadian High Commission in Maputo, Mozambique.

France Contact the French Embassy in Harare, Zimbabwe.

New Zealand Contact the New Zealand High Commission in Pretoria, South Africa.

The following are in Lilongwe:

British High Commission (Map p178; ☎01-772400; www.gov.uk; City Centre)

German Embassy (Map p178; ☎01-772555; www.lilongwe.diplo.de; Convention Dr, City Centre)

Irish Embassy (Map p178; ☎0888 207543; www.dfa.ie/irish-embassy/malawi; 3rd fl, Arwa House, African Unity Ave, City Centre)

Mozambican High Commission (Map p178; ☎01-774100; www.minec.gov.mz; Convention Dr, City Centre)

Netherlands Honorary Consulate (☎0999 960481; https://zimbabwe.nlembassy.org; Heavenly Close, Area 10)

South African High Commission (Map p178; ☎01-773722; www.dirco.gov.za; Plot 19)

US Embassy (Map p178; ☎01-773166; lilongwe.usembassy.gov; 16 Kenyatta Rd, City Centre)

Zambian High Commission (Map p178; ☎01-772590; www.facebook.com/zambiahighcommissionlilongwe; City Centre)

Zimbabwean Embassy (Map p178; ☎01-774988, 01-774413; www.zimfa.gov.zw; Area 13)

INTERNET ACCESS

Across the country, most accommodation and restaurants catering to foreigners offer wi-fi, generally operated by Skyband (www.skyband.mw). The advantage of this system is that you can buy a voucher (typically MK2000 for 500MB) and use it at multiple locations. The disadvantage is that Skyband hot spots can be hit and miss, so many residents prefer to access the internet on their phone using an Airtel (http://africa.airtel.com) SIM card. TNM (www.tnm.co.mw) SIM cards are not as good for surfing the web. Mobile-phone data typically costs MK5000 for 1GB, valid for 30 days.

Wi-fi is rarely free in budget accommodation but may be in midrange and top-end places. You'll find internet cafes in Lilongwe, Blantyre and most towns.

MONEY

Take some US dollars and a back-up card. ATMs are widespread and credit cards accepted. Power cuts scupper both; keep a reserve supply of cash.

EATING PRICE RANGES

The following price ranges refer to a standard main course.

$ less than MK3500 (US$5)

$$ MK3500–MK7000 (US$5–US$10)

$$$ more than MK7000 (US$10)

ATMs

Standard and National Banks are the best bet for foreigners wishing to withdraw cash, and their ATMs accept Visa, MasterCard, Cirrus and Maestro cards. ATMs are found in most cities and towns including Lilongwe, Blantyre, Mzuzu, Karonga, Liwonde, Salima, Mangochi, Zomba and Nkhata Bay. Visa is most widely accepted.

ATMs dispense a maximum of MK40,000 per withdrawal, but you can insert your card three times in a row, thus ending up with MK120,000 (US$168). Your bank at home will charge you for each transaction. Alternatively you can go into the bank and withdraw your card limit in kwacha, although you will have to queue and the tellers are sometimes reluctant.

It's worth taking at least one back-up card, as the banks often experience network problems: for example, sometimes foreign credit cards work in the ATMs but debit cards don't.

Cash

Malawi's unit of currency is the Malawian kwacha (MK). This is divided into 100 tambala (t).

Banknotes include MK1000, MK500, MK200, MK100, MK50, MK20, MK10 and MK5. Coins are MK10, MK5, MK1, 50t, 20t, 10t, 5t, 2t and 1t, although the small tambala coins are virtually worthless.

At big hotels and other places that actually quote in US dollars you can pay in hard currency or kwacha at the prevailing exchange rate. As the US dollar is stronger than the kwacha, you will save money by paying with dollars where possible.

ATMs and card machines generally don't work during the frequent power cuts, so carrying a wad of kwacha, and preferably US dollars too, is wise.

Credit & Debit Cards

You can use Visa cards at some but not all of the large hotels, high-end lodges and top-end restaurants (be warned that this will add a 5% to 10% surcharge to your bill). MasterCard is less commonly accepted.

Inform your bank that you will be travelling in Malawi.

Exchange Rates

Australia	A$1	MK541
Canada	C$1	MK532
Euro Zone	€1	MK783
Japan	¥100	MK680
New Zealand	NZ$1	MK511
South Africa	ZAR10	MK515
UK	UK£1	MK869
USA	US$1	MK713

For current exchange rates, see www.xe.com.

PUBLIC HOLIDAYS

When one of these dates falls on a weekend, normally the following Monday is a public holiday. Islamic holidays are also observed throughout Malawi by the Muslim population.

New Year's Day 1 January

John Chilembwe Day 15 January

Martyrs' Day 3 March

Easter March/April – Good Friday, Holy Saturday and Easter Monday

Labour Day 1 May

Kamuzu Day 14 May

Independence Day 6 July

Mother's Day October, second Monday

Christmas Day 25 December

Boxing Day 26 December

SAFE TRAVEL

Malawi is one of the safest African countries for travellers, but you should still be reasonably cautious and employ common sense.

- The cities are most dangerous. Catch taxis and don't wander around at night.
- Much of the danger comes from the chaotic roads and unfit vehicles; drive carefully, and bail out if a minibus feels excessively unsafe.
- Take care to avoid environmental hazards such as bilharzia and traveller's diarrhoea.

Wildlife

Potential dangers at Lake Malawi include encountering a hippo or crocodile after dusk, when they come up onto beaches. The Shire River is replete with crocodiles, and locals disappear in dugouts on a regular basis, so be careful of dipping your hand in the water while on a river safari. Popular tourist beaches are safe, although, just to be sure, you should seek local advice before diving in. Avoid sheltered, reedy beaches where bilharzia host snails are found. The most dangerous animals in Malawi are the mosquitoes that transmit malaria.

TELEPHONE & MOBILE PHONES

Mobile phones are in use everywhere, and coverage is extensive. The major networks are Airtel and TNM, with 099 and 088 prefixes respectively. TNM has better coverage in rural areas and is popular with locals. Airtel is popular among expats and travellers; it also has good coverage, and works better in the cities, especially for using the internet and social-media apps.

SIM cards are readily available from street vendors for around MK1000. If you need to cut the card to fit your phone, there will invariably be someone nearby ready to whip out his cutter for MK500 or so. You can buy top-up scratchcards from vendors and shops. Cards generally come in maximum denominations of MK1000. Mobile-phone data typically costs MK5000 for 1GB, valid for 30 days.

Emergency & Important Numbers

Country code	☎265
International access code	☎00
Ambulance	☎998
Police	☎997
Fire	☎999

TIME

Malawi follows Central Africa Time, which is two hours ahead of Greenwich Mean Time (GMT/UTC). There is no daylight saving time.

TOURIST INFORMATION

There are tourist-information offices in Blantyre and Lilongwe, but you're much better off asking for advice from your accommodation or a travel agency. Outside Malawi, tourism promotion is handled by UK-based **Malawi Tourism** (☎ in the UK 0115-972 7250; www.malawitourism.com), which responds to enquiries from all over the world.

VISAS

Most nationalities require a visa, which is issued (in most cases) upon arrival at the airport or major land border.

A one-month single-entry visa costs US$75, six- and 12-month multiple-entry visas cost US$150 and US$250 respectively; a seven-day transit visa costs US$50. Card payments should be possible at the airports, but it would be wise to have the fee handy in cash US dollars. You can apply in advance through your local Malawian embassy, but it is more expensive (US$100 for a single-entry visa).

Check the Malawian Department of Immigration website, www.immigration.gov.mw/visa.html, for more info. At the time of writing, the site advised travellers to apply in advance or, if that was not possible, to obtain a letter of authorisation. However, this directive was not being enforced and was likely to be dropped. There was also discussion of establishing an electronic visa system, so it would be worth checking with your accommodation for updates.

Once in Malawi, travellers with a one-month single-entry visa can apply to extend it to three months total at the immigration offices in Lilongwe, Blantyre and Zomba. This costs MK5000 per month cash. Temporary-residence permits, lasting up to six months and available in Lilongwe and Blantyre, cost US$100.

VOLUNTEERING

There are numerous volunteer opportunities in Malawi. A good initial contact is **Volunteer Abroad** (www.volunteerabroad.com), which has listings of current options. Otherwise, local grass-roots opportunities include the following:

Billy Riordan Memorial Trust (www.billys-malawiproject.org) Has an established clinic in Cape Maclear and provides medical care in the area. The trust needs medical volunteers (doctors, dentists, nurses, lab technicians etc).

Butterfly Space (p189) Involved in a number of projects in Nkhata Bay, as is neighbouring Mayoka Village.

Cool Runnings (p195) Involved in a variety of projects in the Senga Bay area.

Panda Garden (p197) Based in Cape Maclear, Panda Garden is always on the lookout for divers and others to help with bilharzia research in the lake.

Ripple Africa (www.rippleafrica.org) Recruits volunteer teachers, doctors, nurses and environmental workers for projects in the Chintheche district.

Wildlife Action Group (www.wag-malawi.org) Uses volunteers to assist in the management and maintenance of forest reserves near Salima.

Getting There & Away

AIR

There are no direct flights to Malawi from Europe or the United States. The easiest way to reach the country by air is via Kenya, Ethiopia or South Africa.

Lilongwe International Airport (Kamuzu International Airport; LLW; ☎0992 991097) A taxi or airport shuttle to/from town costs US$35. It's a standard charge, advertised on a board in the arrivals terminal, and taxi drivers meet incoming flights. You can also arrange a transfer in advance through your accommodation.

Chileka International Airport (Blantyre) A taxi from the airport to the city costs around MK10,000, but agree on a price with the driver first. The price can be negotiated down if you're going from the city to the airport. Frequent local buses between the City Bus Station and Chileka Township also pass the airport gate (around MK2000).

Airports & Airlines

Lilongwe International Airport 25km north of Lilongwe City Centre, handles the majority of international flights, while **Chileka International Airport**, 15km north of central Blantyre, also receives numerous flights.

The country's national carrier relaunched as Malawian Airlines in 2012, when its previous incarnation, Air Malawi, went into liquidation and the government partnered with Ethiopian Airlines.

Ethiopian Airlines (☎01-772031; www.ethiopianairlines.com) Flies daily from Addis Ababa (Ethiopia) to both Lilongwe and Blantyre.

Kenya Airways (☎01-824524, 01-774227; www.kenya-airways.com) Links both Lilongwe and Blantyre with Nairobi (Kenya) four days a week.

Malawian Airlines Has a decent regional network, with flights heading to Dar es Salaam (Tasmania), Johannesburg (South Africa), Lusaka (Zambia) and Harare (Zimbabwe) from Blantyre and Lilongwe.

Proflight Zambia (☎01-700444; www.proflight-zambia.com) Flies Lilongwe to Lusaka (Zambia) six days a week.

South African Airways (☎01-772242, 01-620617; www.flysaa.com) Flies three days weekly between Blantyre and Johannesburg (South Africa), and six days weekly between Lilongwe and Johannesburg (with connections to Durban, Cape Town etc).

LAND

Overland, travellers can enter the country from Zambia, Mozambique or Tanzania. Indeed, Malawi is a popular staging post for overland trucks heading between Nairobi and Cape Town. Most border posts close from 6pm to 7am.

Bus

It's possible to cross into Malawi by bus from Tanzania, Zambia, Zimbabwe and South Africa, and there are direct services from Johannesburg (South Africa), Dar es Salaam (Tanzania), Lusaka (Zambia) and Harare (Zimbabwe) to Blantyre and Lilongwe. When crossing the border you will have to get off the bus to pass through customs and pay for your visa.

Mozambique

South

Take a minibus to the Mozambican border crossing at Zóbuè and then a minibus to Tete, from where buses go to Beira and Maputo. You could also get a Blantyre–Harare bus to drop you at Tete.

Central

There are daily buses from Blantyre to the Mozambican border at Marka; failing that, take a bus to Nsanje and continue by minibus or *matola* (pickup). It's a few kilometres between the border crossings – you can walk or take a bicycle taxi – and you can change money on the Mozambique side. From here pickups go to Mutarara and over the bridge to Vila de Sena.

North

There are three border crossings from Malawi into northern Mozambique: Muloza, from where you can reach Mocuba in Mozambique, and Nayuchi and Chiponde, both of which lead to Cuamba in Mozambique.

Regular buses run from Blantyre, via Mulanje, to Muloza. From here, it's 1km to the Mozambican border crossing, then another few kilometres into Milange. From Milange there's usually a *chapa* (pickup or converted minibus) or truck about every other day in the dry season to Mocuba, where you can find transport on to Quelimane or Nampula.

Further north, minibuses and *matolas* run a few times per day between Mangochi and the border crossing at Chiponde. It's then 7km to the Mozambican border crossing in Mandimba and the best way to get there is by bicycle taxi. Mandimba has a couple of *pensãos* (pensions), and there's at least one vehicle daily, usually a truck, between here and Cuamba.

The third option is to go by minibus from Liwonde to the border at Nayuchi. From Nayuchi, where there are moneychangers, you can walk to Entre Lagos, and then get a *chapa* to Cuamba.

South Africa

A number of bus companies run services from Lilongwe and Blantyre to Johannesburg. The best option is **Intercape** (p181), which operates daily services between Jo'burg and both Blantyre and Lilongwe, with a service continuing north five days a week from the latter to Mzuzu.

Buses from Lilongwe leave from outside the petrol station on Paul Kagame Rd in Old Town. In Blantyre, most Johannesburg-bound buses depart from the car park outside Blantyre Lodge.

Tanzania

If you're going in stages, Mbeya in southern Tanzania is handy for crossing to/from northern Malawi. Buses and minibuses ply the M1 between Mzuzu and Karonga, from where you can get a minibus or taxi to the Songwe border crossing. It's 200m across the bridge to the Tanzanian border crossing.

Once on the Tanzanian side of the border, minibuses travel 115km north to Mbeya, where you will need to overnight before continuing on the next morning to Dar es Salaam. You can change money with the bicycle-taxi boys, but beware of scams.

Zambia

Four direct **Kob's Coach Services** (p182) buses per week link Lilongwe and Lusaka (MK20,000, 12 hours), departing from Devil St on Wednesday and Saturday mornings. Regular minibuses run between Lilongwe and Mchinji. From here, it's 12km to the border. Local shared taxis shuttle between Mchinji and the border crossing.

From the Zambian side of the border, shared taxis run to Chipata, about 25km northwest of the crossing, from where you can reach Lusaka or South Luangwa National Park.

SAMPLE FERRY ROUTES & FARES

Following are sample fares from Nkhata Bay.

DESTINATION	OWNER'S CABIN	STANDARD CABIN	UPPER DECK	2ND	ECONOMY
Nkhotakota	MK25,770	MK19,850	MK12,490	MK7160	MK5120
Monkey Bay	MK44,800	MK34,440	MK20,450	MK11,860	MK8120

LAKE

Dhows sail in the morning from Mdamba on Likoma Island (Malawi) to Cóbuè (Mozambique). If you're planning to visit Mozambique you must get a visa in advance and be sure to get your passport stamped at Malawian immigration in Mdimba.

In the market by the cathedral in Cóbuè there's an immigration office for your entry/exit formalities. Right beside the office are the boatmen.

Mozambique

Operated by the **Malawi Shipping Company** (p169), the *Chambo* connects Metangula (Mozambique) with Likoma Island, Chizumulu and Nkhata Bay. It leaves Metangula at 5am on Wednesday, and reaches Likoma around 11.30am, Chizumulu around 12.30pm and Nkhata Bay around 2pm.

On the return journey, it leaves at 5am on Thursday, stops in Chizumulu around 7.30am and Likoma around 9am, and departs Likoma around 2pm to reach Metangula around 8pm.

There's also a Saturday service just to/from Likoma, leaving Metangula at 5am and arriving on the island around 11.30am. It returns on Sunday at 1.30pm, arriving in Metangula around 8pm.

The *Chambo* also heads south from Metangula to Chipoka via Makanjila and Senga Bay, leaving at 5am on Monday, passing Senga Bay around 6.30pm and arriving in Chipoka around 9pm. It returns north at 5am on Tuesday, passing Senga Bay around 7am and reaching Metangula around 8pm.

Malawian and Mozambican immigration officers both board the *Chambo* to issue exit/entry stamps and visas. You can check for timetable changes at www.malawitourism.com.

Tanzania

The Tanzanian *Songea* (www.mscl.go.tz) sails south, at 1pm on Thursday, from Itungi via Liuli and Mdamba Bay (all in Tanzania) to Nkhata Bay. A 1st-class ticket from Mdamba Bay to Nkhata Bay costs around US$5.

Getting Around

AIR

Malawian Airlines (☎01-827900, 01-774605; www.malawian-airlines.com) The national carrier operates daily flights between Lilongwe and Blantyre (US$50, one hour), a good alternative to the bus. Its booking system isn't always reliable, so it's worth confirming your flight by phone or at an office.

Ulendo Airlink (☎01-794638; www.flyulendo.com) The aviation wing of Ulendo Travel Group operates scheduled and charter flights on safe twin-prop planes to locations including Likoma Island and all the major wildlife parks. Check the 'bid to fly' section of Ulendo Airlink's website for discounted seats on upcoming flights.

BOAT

The *Ilala* ferry chugs passengers and cargo up and down Lake Malawi once a week in each direction. Travelling between Monkey Bay in the south and Chilumba in the north, it makes nine stops at lakeside villages and towns in between, as well as at Likoma and Chizumulu Islands. Many travellers rate this journey (or a leg of it) as a highlight of the country, although there are occasionally nasty storms. If you're unlucky, be prepared for some pitching and rolling. The boat dates from 1949 and is certainly no cruise liner, so it's better to regard it as a practical method of getting from A to B than an experience in itself.

When the *Ilala* stops at lakeside towns or villages, the water is too shallow for it to come close; the lifeboat is used to ferry passengers ashore. In both directions, the ferry docks at Nkhata Bay for seven hours and traders come aboard, selling food, drinks and newspapers. The whole trip, from one end of the line to the other, takes about three days. You can normally download the latest schedules from Malawi Tourism.

Classes & Reservations

The classes are the exclusive Owner's Cabin, Standard Cabin, Upper Deck, Second and Economy. The standard cabins were once luxurious, and are still in reasonable condition. This class and the upper deck are popular with travellers, due largely to the sociable bar. There are also seats, a shaded area and mattresses for hire on the upper deck. Second and Economy classes are dark, crowded and permeated by engine fumes, and are not recommended.

Cabin and Upper Deck class passengers can dine in the ferry's restaurant, which serves beef curry, peri-peri chicken and the like. Dishes such as beans, rice and vegetables are served from a galley on the economy deck.

Reservations are usually required for Cabin class, and are recommended to ensure a comfortable journey.

BUS

Malawi's best bus company is **AXA Coach Service** (☎ 01-820100; www.axacoach.com), with three classes of vehicle: Super Executive, Executive and Special. The former is a luxury nonstop service with air-con, toilet, comfortable reclining seats, USB ports, reading lights, good drivers, snacks, fresh coffee and even an on-board magazine. Services operate between Blantyre and Lilongwe twice a day, leaving every morning and afternoon from special departure points in each city (not the main bus stations).

The Executive and Special services are the next in line. These buses have air-con and reclining seats as well as TVs, but they don't have toilets. They ply the route between Blantyre and Karonga via Lilongwe and Mzuzu daily, serving the main towns, with limited stops elsewhere.

Other smaller bus companies, including the National Bus Company, have daily services up and down the lake and between the country's main centres. These are marginally more comfortable than minibuses, but no more efficient, and they generally cost the same.

Minibuses are the most popular option because they leave regularly throughout the day. They operate on a fill-up-and-go basis; you can speed up the process, and buy yourself some comfort, by purchasing two seats. Direct long-distance minibuses are becoming less common; you will likely have to change once or twice on a long-distance journey up the lakeshore or M1. You can still buy a long-distance ticket – the driver should transfer your fare to the connecting service – but it is wiser to only pay as far as the place where you will change minibuses.

In rural areas, the frequency of buses and minibuses drops dramatically – sometimes to nothing. In cases like this, the 'bus' is often a truck or pickup, with people just piled in the back. In Malawi this is called a *matola*.

CAR & MOTORCYCLE

The majority of main routes are sealed, though off the main routes roads are rutted and potholed, making driving slow and dangerous. Secondary roads are usually graded dirt. Some are well maintained and easy to drive on in a normal car; others are bad, especially after rain, and slow even with a 4WD. Rural routes are not so good, and after heavy rain are often impassable. Several lodges along the lakeshore have poor access roads that need a 4WD. The same goes for the country's national parks and wildlife reserves.

TAXI

You can often share a taxi instead of waiting for the minibus to depart – a safer, more comfortable and faster option.

Privately hiring a taxi will likely work out cheaper than renting a car with a driver, plus removing driving stress and giving you an unofficial guide and interpreter. **High Class Taxi Services** (☎ 0888 100223, 0999 356920; justinchimenya@yahoo.com) in Blantyre and **Mawaso Taxi Service** (☎ 0999 161111, 0995 769772; plizimba@gmail.com) in Lilongwe both offer multiday services.

TRAIN

Central Eastern African Railways (CEAR; ☎ 01-840841; www.cear.mw) operates the following services. The trains are slow and unreliable, so buses and minibuses are a better option. The following journeys cost MK2100 in business class.

Limbe–Balaka via Blantyre (11½ hours) Departs 7am Wednesday, returns 6am Friday.

Balaka–Nayuchi via Liwonde (six hours) Departs 6am Thursday, returns 1.30pm.

Limbe–Makhanga (9¾ hours) Departs 9am Saturday, returns 7am Sunday.

Survival Guide

Health

While the region has an impressive selection of tropical diseases, it's more likely you'll get a bout of diarrhoea or a cold than a more exotic malady. Stay up to date with your vaccinations and take basic preventive measures, and you'll be unlikely to succumb to any of the serious health hazards.

Before You Go

Insurance

Find out in advance whether your insurance plan will make payments directly to providers or will reimburse you later for overseas health expenditures. Most doctors and clinics in the region expect up-front payment in cash.

It's vital to ensure that your travel insurance will cover any emergency transport required to get you at least to Johannesburg (South Africa), or all the way home, by air and with a medical attendant if necessary.

If your policy requires you to pay first and claim later for medical treatment, be sure to keep all documentation. Some policies ask you to call back (reverse charges) to a centre in your home country where an immediate assessment of your problem is made. Since reverse-charge calls aren't possible in many parts of the region, contact the insurance company before setting off to confirm how best to contact it in an emergency.

Recommended Vaccinations

The World Health Organization (www.who.int/en/) recommends that all travellers be covered for diphtheria, tetanus, pertussis, measles, mumps, rubella and polio, as well as for hepatitis B, regardless of their destination.

According to the US Centers for Disease Control & Prevention (www.cdc.gov), the following additional vaccinations are recommended for the region: hepatitis A, rabies and typhoid, and boosters for tetanus, diphtheria and measles. A yellow-fever vaccination certificate is not officially required to enter any of the three countries unless you are entering from an infected area (which are found in several neighbouring countries), but carrying one is advised; the certificate is often requested.

Medical Checklist

Carry a medical and first-aid kit to help yourself in the case of minor illness or injury. Possible items to include:

- Antibiotics (prescription only), eg ciprofloxacin (Ciproxin) or norfloxacin (Utinor)
- Antidiarrhoeal drugs (eg loperamide)
- Acetaminophen (paracetamol) or aspirin
- Antibacterial ointment (eg Bactroban) for cuts and abrasions (prescription only)
- Anti-inflammatory drugs (eg ibuprofen)
- Antihistamines (for hay fever and allergic reactions)
- Antimalaria pills
- Steroid cream, such as hydrocortisone (for allergic rashes)
- Bandages, gauze, gauze rolls
- Adhesive or paper tape
- Scissors, safety pins, tweezers
- Thermometer
- Pocket knife
- Insect repellent containing DEET for the skin
- Insect spray containing Permethrin for clothing, tents and bed nets
- Sunblock
- Oral rehydration salts
- Iodine tablets (for water purification)
- Sterile needles, syringes and fluids if travelling to remote areas
- Self-diagnostic kit that can identify malaria in the blood from a finger prick, and emergency treatment

Other Preparations

- Get a check-up from your dentist and also your doctor if you have any regular medication or chronic illness, such as high blood pressure or asthma.
- Organise spare contact lenses and glasses (and take

your optical prescription with you).

- Get a first-aid and medical kit together and arrange necessary vaccinations.
- Consider registering with the International Association for Medical Advice to Travellers (www.iamat.org), which provides directories of certified doctors.
- If you'll be spending much time in remote areas (ie anywhere away from capitals and major cities or tourist centres), consider doing a first-aid course (contact the Red Cross or St John Ambulance) or attending a remote-medicine first-aid course, such as that offered by the Royal Geographical Society (www.wildernessmedicaltraining.co.uk).
- Carry medications in their original (labelled) containers. A signed and dated letter from your physician describing all medical conditions and medications, including generic names, is also a good idea.
- If carrying syringes or needles, be sure to have a physician's letter documenting their medical necessity.

Websites

General information:

Fit for Travel (www.fitfortravel.scot.nhs.uk)

International Travel and Health (www.who.int/ith) A free, online publication of the World Health Organization.

Lonely Planet (www.lonelyplanet.com)

MD Travel Health (www.mdtravelhealth.com)

Government travel-health websites:

Australia www.smartraveller.gov.au

Canada www.phac-aspc.gc.ca

UK http://www.nhs.uk/Livewell/TravelHealth/Pages/Travelhealthhome.aspx

USA www.cdc.gov/travel

Further Reading

- *Wilderness and Travel Medicine* by Eric A Weiss (2012)
- *How to Shit Around the World: The Art of Staying Clean & Healthy While Travelling* by Jane Wilson-Howarth (2006)
- *Healthy Travel: Africa* by Isabelle Young and Tony Gherardin (2008)
- *How to Stay Healthy Abroad* by Richard Dawood (2002)
- *Travel with Children* by Sophie Caupeil et al (2015)

In Africa

Availability & Cost of Health Care

Capital cities are generally the only places with good emergency medical services. For Western standards, expect to pay Western prices.

If you become seriously ill, seek treatment in the capital city or in South Africa, or return home. If you fall ill in an unfamiliar area, ask staff at a top-end hotel or resident expatriates where the best nearby medical facilities are. In an emergency contact your embassy.

Well-stocked pharmacies are found in capital cities and some major towns. These will invariably carry medications to treat malaria and other basics, though it's best to bring whatever you think you may need from home.

Always check the expiry date before buying medications, especially in smaller towns.

There is a high risk of contracting HIV from infected blood transfusions. The BloodCare Foundation (www.bloodcare.org.uk) is a useful source of safe, screened blood, which can be transported to any part of the world within 24 hours.

Infectious Diseases

Following are some of the diseases that are found in the region, although with a few basic preventive measures, it's unlikely that you'll succumb to any of these.

CHOLERA

Cholera is usually only a problem during natural or artificial disasters (eg war, floods or earthquakes), although small outbreaks can possibly occur at other times. Travellers are rarely affected. Cholera is caused by bacteria and spread via contaminated drinking water. The main symptom is profuse watery diarrhoea, which causes debilitation if fluids are not replaced quickly. An oral cholera vaccine is available in the USA, but it is not particularly effective. Most cases of cholera can be avoided by careful selection of good drinking water and by avoiding potentially contaminated food. Treatment is by fluid replacement (orally or via a drip), but sometimes antibiotics are needed. Self-treatment is not advised.

TRADITIONAL MEDICINE

Reliable statistics are difficult to find concerning the number of Southern Africans who rely on traditional medicine. However, especially when travelling in rural areas, you may well hear about or meet traditional healers. While most traditional medicine is inconsistent and unregulated, there is a vast and impressive store of local knowledge regarding medicinal uses of plants, and it is always worth asking if you could meet the local healer or be given an introduction to local plants and traditional medicinal practices.

DENGUE FEVER (BREAKBONE FEVER)

Dengue fever is spread through the bite of the mosquito. It causes a feverish illness with headache and muscle pains similar to those experienced with a bad, prolonged attack of influenza. There might be a rash. Self-treatment: paracetamol and rest.

DIPHTHERIA

Diphtheria is spread through close respiratory contact. It usually causes an elevated temperature and a severe sore throat. Sometimes a membrane forms across the throat, resulting in the need for a tracheostomy to prevent suffocation. Vaccination is recommended for those likely to be in close contact with the local population in infected areas. This more important for long stays than for short-term trips.

FILARIASIS

Tiny worms migrating in the lymphatic system cause filariasis. The bite from an infected mosquito spreads the infection. Symptoms include localised itching and swelling of the legs and/or genitalia. Treatment is available.

HEPATITIS A

Hepatitis A is spread through contaminated food (particularly shellfish) and water. It causes jaundice and, although it is rarely fatal, it can cause prolonged lethargy and delayed recovery. If you've had hepatitis A, you shouldn't drink alcohol for up to six months afterwards, but once you've recovered, there won't be any long-term problems. The first symptoms include dark urine and a yellow colour to the whites of the eyes. Sometimes a fever and abdominal pain might be present. Hepatitis A vaccine (Avaxim, VAQTA, Havrix) is given as an injection: a single dose will give protection for up to a year, and a booster after a year gives protection for 10 years. Hepatitis A and typhoid vaccines can also be given as a single-dose vaccine (hepatyrix or viatim).

HEPATITIS B

Hepatitis B is spread through infected blood, contaminated needles and sexual intercourse. It can also be spread from an infected mother to the baby during childbirth. It affects the liver, causing jaundice and occasionally liver failure. Most people recover completely, but some people might be chronic carriers of the virus, which could lead eventually to cirrhosis or liver cancer. Those visiting high-risk areas for long periods or those with increased social or occupational risk should be immunised. Many countries now routinely give hepatitis B as part of childhood vaccinations. It is given singly or can be given at the same time as hepatitis A (hepatyrix).

A course will give protection for at least five years. It can be given over four weeks or six months.

HIV & AIDS

Human immuno-deficiency virus (HIV), the virus that causes acquired immune deficiency syndrome (AIDS), is a significant problem in the region. The virus is spread through infected blood and blood products, by sexual intercourse with an infected partner and from an infected mother to her baby during childbirth and breastfeeding. It can be spread through 'blood to blood' contacts, such as with contaminated instruments during medical, dental, acupuncture and other body-piercing procedures, and through sharing intravenous needles. At present there is no cure; medication that might keep the disease under control is available, but these drugs are often unavailable for most locals and not readily available for travellers, either. If you think you might have been infected with HIV, a blood test is necessary; a three-month gap after exposure and before testing is required to allow antibodies to appear in the blood.

MALARIA

Malaria is prevalent in all three countries, and is especially a risk in Mozambique. Infection rates are higher during the rainy season, but the risk exists year-round and it is extremely important to take preventive measures, even if you will just be travelling for a short time.

Malaria is caused by a parasite in the bloodstream spread via the bite of the female Anopheles mosquito. There are several types of malaria, falciparum malaria being the most dangerous and the predominant form in parts of the region. Infection rates vary with season and climate, so check out the situation before departure. Unlike most other diseases regularly encountered by travellers, there is not yet a vaccine for malaria. However, several drugs are used to prevent malaria and new ones are in the pipeline. Up-to-date advice from a travel-health clinic is essential, as some medication is more suitable for some travellers than others. The pattern of drug-resistant malaria is changing rapidly, so what was advised several years ago might no longer be the case.

Malaria can present in several ways. The early stages include headaches, fevers, generalised aches and pains, and malaise, which could be mistaken for flu. Other symptoms can include abdominal pain, diarrhoea and a cough. Anyone who develops a fever in a malarial area should assume malarial infection until a blood test proves negative, even if you have been taking antimalarial medication. If not treated, the next stage could develop within 24 hours, particularly if falciparum malaria is the parasite: jaundice, then reduced consciousness and coma (also known as cerebral malaria), followed by death. Treatment in hospital is essential; the death rate might still be as high as 10% even in the best intensive-care facilities.

Prevention & Treatment

Many travellers are under the impression that malaria is a mild illness, that treatment is always easy and successful, and that taking antimalarial drugs causes more illness through side effects than actually getting malaria. This is unfortunately not true. Side effects of the medication depend on the drug being taken. Doxycycline can cause heartburn and indigestion; mefloquine (Larium) can cause anxiety attacks, insomnia and nightmares, and (rarely) severe psychiatric disorders; chloroquine can cause nausea and hair loss; proguanil can cause mouth ulcers; and Malarone is expensive. The side effects are not universal and can be minimised by taking medication correctly (eg with food). Also, some people should not take a particular antimalarial drug (eg people with epilepsy should avoid mefloquine, and doxycycline should not be taken by pregnant women or children younger than 12).

If you decide that you really do not wish to take antimalarial drugs, you must understand the risks and be obsessive about avoiding mosquito bites. Use nets and insect repellent, and report any fever or flu-like symptoms to a doctor as soon as possible. Some people advocate homeopathic preparations against malaria, such as Demal200, but as yet there is no conclusive evidence that this is effective and many homeopaths do not recommend their use.

People of all ages can contract malaria and falciparum causes the most severe illness. Repeated infections might result eventually in less serious illness. Malaria in pregnancy frequently results in miscarriage or premature labour. Adults who have survived childhood malaria have developed immunity and usually only develop mild cases of malaria; most Western travellers have no immunity at all. Immunity wanes after 18 months of non-exposure, so even if you have had malaria in the past and used to live in a malaria-prone area, you might no longer be immune.

If you will be away from major towns, it's worth considering taking standby treatment, although this should be seen as emergency treatment only and not as routine self-medication. It should be used only if you will be far from medical facilities and have been advised about the symptoms of malaria and how to use the medication. If you do resort to emergency self-treatment, medical advice should be sought as soon as possible to confirm whether the treatment has been successful. In particular you want to avoid contracting cerebral malaria, which can be fatal in 24 hours. Self-diagnostic kits, which can identify malaria in the blood from a finger prick, are available in the West and are a worthwhile investment.

The risks from malaria to both mother and foetus during pregnancy are considerable. Unless good medical care can be guaranteed, travel in malarial areas while pregnant should be discouraged unless essential.

MENINGOCOCCAL MENINGITIS

Meningococcal infection is spread through close respiratory contact and is more likely in crowded situations, such as dormitories, buses and clubs. Infection is uncommon in travellers. Vaccination is recommended for long stays and is especially important towards the end of the dry season. Symptoms include a fever, severe headache, neck stiffness and a red rash. Immediate medical treatment is necessary.

The ACWY vaccine is recommended for all travellers in sub-Saharan Africa. This vaccine is different from the meningococcal meningitis C vaccine given to children and adolescents in some countries; it is safe to be given both types of vaccine.

POLIOMYELITIS

Polio is generally spread through contaminated food and water. It is one of the vaccines given in childhood and should be boosted every 10 years, either orally (a drop on the tongue) or as an injection. Polio can be carried asymptomatically (ie showing no symptoms) and could cause a transient fever. In rare cases it causes weakness or paralysis of one or more muscles, which might be permanent.

RABIES

Rabies is spread through the bite or lick of an infected animal on broken skin. It is always fatal once the clinical symptoms start (which might be up to several months after an infected bite), so post-bite vaccination should be given as soon as possible. Post-bite vaccination (whether or not you've been vaccinated before the bite) prevents the virus from spreading to the central nervous system. Animal handlers should be vaccinated, as should those travelling to remote areas where a reliable source of post-bite vaccine is not available within 24 hours. Three preventive injections are needed over a month. If you are infected and have not been vaccinated, you will need a course of five injections starting 24 hours, or as soon as possible, after the injury. If you have been vaccinated, you will need fewer post-bite injections and will have more time to seek medical help.

SCHISTOSOMIASIS (BILHARZIA)

This disease is spread by flukes (minute worms) that

are carried by a species of freshwater snail. The flukes are carried inside the snail, which then sheds them into slow-moving or still water. The parasites penetrate human skin during paddling or swimming and then migrate to the bladder or bowel. They are passed out via stool or urine and could contaminate fresh water, where the cycle starts again.

Paddling or swimming in suspect freshwater lakes (including many parts of Lake Malawi) or slow-running rivers should be avoided. Although parts of Lake Malawi might be low risk, other areas (including some popular tourist destinations) bring a risk of contracting bilharzia.

In some cases there may be no symptoms; in others there may be a transient fever and rash. Advanced cases might have blood in the stool or urine. Long-term effects can be very harmful; it is essential that you have a check-up for the disease when you get home or reach a place with good medical services.

Be sure your doctor is familiar with bilharzia, and be aware that the disease may have a long incubation period and may not be initially apparent, so you might need more than one test. A blood test can detect antibodies if you have been exposed and treatment is then possible in specialist travel or infectious-disease clinics. If not treated the infection can cause kidney failure or permanent bowel damage. It is not possible for you to directly infect others.

TRYPANOSOMIASIS (SLEEPING SICKNESS)

Spread via the bite of the tsetse fly. It causes a headache, fever and eventually coma. There is an effective treatment.

TUBERCULOSIS (TB)

Tuberculosis is spread through close respiratory contact and occasionally through infected milk or milk products. BCG vaccination is recommended for those likely to be mixing closely with the local population, although it gives only moderate protection against TB. It is more important for long stays than for short-term stays. Inoculation with the BCG vaccine is not available in all countries. It is given routinely to many children in developing countries. The vaccination causes a small permanent scar at the site of injection, and is usually given in a specialist chest clinic. It is a live vaccine and should not be given to pregnant women or immunocompromised individuals.

TB can be asymptomatic, only being picked up on a routine chest X-ray. Alternatively, it can cause a cough, weight loss or fever, sometimes months or even years after exposure.

TYPHOID

Typhoid is spread through food or water contaminated by infected human faeces. The first symptom is usually a fever or a pink rash on the abdomen. Sometimes septicaemia (blood poisoning) can occur. A typhoid vaccine (typhim Vi, typherix) will give protection for three years. In some countries, the oral vaccine Vivotif is also available. Antibiotics are usually given as treatment and death is rare unless septicaemia occurs.

YELLOW FEVER

Zambia, Mozambique and Malawi all require you to carry a certificate of yellow-fever vaccination only if you are arriving from an infected area (a requirement that is vigilantly enforced). However, a certificate is still often requested at points of entry, including for travellers coming from Tanzania into Mozambique and those going from Zambia into South Africa, and vaccination is recommended for almost all visitors by the Centers for Disease Control & Prevention (www.cdc.gov).

Yellow fever is spread by infected mosquitoes. Symptoms range from a flu-like illness to severe hepatitis (liver inflammation), jaundice and death. The yellow-fever vaccination must be given at a designated clinic and is now considered to be valid for life. However, many countries still adhere to the previous validity period of 10 years, so if your vaccination is older than this, it's worth checking with the relevant embassy or at least travelling with a copy of the updated regulations from the World Health Organization (see www.who.int/ith/updates/20160727/en/). Note that yellow fever is a live vaccine and must not be given to immuno-compromised or pregnant travellers.

Traveller's Diarrhoea

Although it's not inevitable that you will get diarrhoea while travelling in the region, it's certainly likely. Diarrhoea is the most common travel-related illness and sometimes can be triggered by simple dietary changes.

To help prevent diarrhoea, avoid tap water, only eat fresh fruit and vegetables if cooked or peeled, and be wary of dairy products that might contain unpasteurised milk. The small plastic bags of water sold on street corners are best avoided. Take care with fruit juice, particularly if water may have been added. Milk in many smaller restaurants is made from reconstituted milk powder, which is safe if it's been made with boiled or mineral water.

With freshly cooked food, plates or serving utensils might be dirty, so be selective when eating food from street vendors and make sure that cooked food is piping hot all the way through.

If you develop diarrhoea, drink plenty of fluids, preferably an oral rehydration solution containing water (lots), and some salt and sugar. A few loose stools don't require treatment, but if you start having more than four or five stools a day, start taking an antibiotic (usually a quinoline drug, such as ciprofloxacin or norfloxacin) and an anti-diarrhoeal agent (such as loperamide) if you are not within easy reach of a toilet. If diarrhoea is bloody, persists for more than 72 hours or is accompanied by fever, shaking chills or severe abdominal pain, seek medical attention.

TAP WATER

Don't drink tap water unless it has been boiled, filtered or chemically disinfected (such as with iodine tablets). Don't drink from streams, rivers and lakes. It's also best to avoid drinking from pumps and wells; some bring pure water to the surface, but the presence of animals can contaminate supplies. Bottled water is widely available, except in very remote areas, where you should carry a filter or purification tablets.

AMOEBIC DYSENTERY

Contracted by eating contaminated food and water, amoebic dysentery causes blood and mucus in the faeces. It can be relatively mild and tends to come on gradually, but seek medical advice if you think you have the illness as it won't clear up without treatment (which is with specific antibiotics).

GIARDIASIS

This, like amoebic dysentery, is also caused by ingesting contaminated food or water. The illness usually appears a week or more after you have been exposed to the offending parasite. Giardiasis might cause only a short-lived bout of typical travellers' diarrhoea, but it can also cause persistent diarrhoea. Ideally, seek medical advice if you suspect you have giardiasis, but if you are in a remote area you could start a course of antibiotics.

Environmental Hazards

HEAT EXHAUSTION

This condition occurs following heavy sweating and excessive fluid loss with inadequate replacement of fluids and salt, and is particularly common in hot climates when taking unaccustomed exercise before full acclimatisation. Symptoms include headache, dizziness and tiredness. Dehydration is already happening by the time you feel thirsty; aim to drink sufficient water to produce pale, diluted urine. Self-treatment: fluid replacement with water and/or fruit juice, and cooling by cold water and fans. The treatment of the salt-loss component consists of consuming salty fluids, as in soup, and adding a little more table salt to foods than usual.

HEATSTROKE

Heat exhaustion is a precursor to the much more serious condition of heatstroke. In this case there is damage to the sweating mechanism, with an excessive rise in body temperature; irrational and hyperactive behaviour; and eventually loss of consciousness, then death. Rapid cooling by spraying the body with water and fanning is ideal. Emergency fluid and electrolyte replacement is usually also required by intravenous drip.

INSECT BITES & STINGS

Mosquitoes might not always carry malaria or dengue fever, but they (and other insects) can cause irritation and infected bites. To avoid these, take the same precautions as you would for avoiding malaria. Use DEET-based insect repellents. Excellent clothing treatments are also available; mosquitoes that land on treated clothing will die.

Bee and wasp stings cause real problems only to those who have a severe allergy to the stings (anaphylaxis). If you are one of these people, carry an 'epipen' (an adrenaline (epinephrine) injection), which you can give yourself. This could save your life.

Sandflies are found in some areas. They usually only cause a nasty, itchy bite, but they can carry a rare skin disorder called cutaneous leishmaniasis. Prevention of bites with DEET-based repellents is sensible.

Bedbugs are often found in hostels and cheap hotels. They lead to very itchy, lumpy bites. Spraying the mattress with crawling-insect killer after changing bedding will get rid of them.

Scabies is also frequently found in cheap accommodation. These tiny mites live in the skin, particularly between the fingers. They cause an intensely itchy rash. The itch is easily treated with malathion and permethrin lotion from a pharmacy; other members of the household also need treating to avoid spreading scabies, even if they do not show any symptoms.

SNAKE & SCORPION BITES

Don't walk barefoot, or stick your hand into holes or cracks. However, 50% of people bitten by venomous snakes are not actually injected with poison (envenomed). If bitten by a snake, don't panic. Immobilise the bitten limb with a splint (such as a stick) and apply a bandage over the site, with firm pressure (similar to bandaging a sprain). Do not apply a tourniquet, or cut or suck the bite. Get medical help as soon as possible so antivenin can be given if needed.

Scorpions are frequently found in arid areas. They can cause a painful bite that is sometimes life-threatening. If bitten, take a painkiller. Seek medical treatment if collapse occurs.

Language

English is the official language in Malawi and is widely spoken. Chichewa, one of the many languages in Malawi, is used throughout the country as a lingua franca.

Portuguese is the official language of Mozambique. It is widely spoken in larger towns, less so in rural areas. Mozambique's numerous African languages, all of which belong to the Bantu family, can be divided into three groups: Makhuwa-Lomwe languages, spoken by more than 33% of the population, primarily in the north; Sena-Nyanja languages in the centre and near Lake Niassa; and Tsonga languages in the south. The exact number of languages spoken in Mozambique has not been established, but it is estimated that there are at least nine, and perhaps as many as 16. Outside southern resorts and the areas bordering Zimbabwe and Malawi, English is not widely spoken. In northern Cabo Delgado and Niassa provinces near the Tanzanian border, Swahili is frequently heard and may be more useful than Portuguese.

In Zambia, English is the official language and is widely spoken. Of the scores of local languages spoken in Zambia, the main four are covered in this chapter: Bemba, Lozi, Nyanja and Tonga. Zambians place much emphasis on the relationship between speakers and it's very important to use the correct forms of address, particularly with the Lozi. There are often two different ways to say 'you' and to greet people, depending on their social status. The informal mode is used for children, friends and peers. The polite mode is used for strangers, elders and adults of equal or higher status. In this chapter the abbreviations 'inf' for informal and 'pol' for polite are included where required.

WANT MORE?

For in-depth language information and handy phrases, check out Lonely Planet's *Africa Phrasebook*. You'll find it at **shop.lonelyplanet.com**, or you can buy Lonely Planet's iPhone phrasebooks at the Apple App Store.

BEMBA

Bemba is spoken widely in Lusaka and in the Copperbelt, Luapula, Central and Northern Provinces of Zambia. When addressing elders, add *bashikulu* (grandfather) for a man and *bamama* (grandmother) for a woman. You can generally get by using English numbers for prices and times.

Basics

Hello.	*Muli shani.*
Greetings!	*Uli shani?* (inf) *Mwapolenipo mukwai!* (pol)
Goodbye.	*Shalapo.* (inf) *Shalenipo mukwai.* (pol)
Good morning.	*Wabuka shani?* (inf) *Mwashibukeni?/ Mwabuka shani?* (pol)
Good evening.	*Icungulupo/ Mwatushenipo mukwai.*
Good night.	*Icungulopo.*
Please.	*Mukwai.*
Thank you./ Excuse me.	*Natasha./Natotela./ Banjeleleko.*
Yes.	*Ee (mukwai).*
No.	*Awe./Teifyo.*
How are you?	*Uli shani?* (inf)/ *Muli shani?* (pol)
I'm fine.	*Ndifye bwino.*
Good./Fine./OK.	*Chawama./Chilifye./ Chisuma./Chilifye bwino.*
I don't understand.	*Nshumfwile bwino.*
What's your name?	*Niwe nani ishina?* (inf) *Nimwe banani ishina?* (pol)
My name is ...	*Ishina lyandi ni ne ...*

How much?	*Shinga?/Nishinga?*
toilets	*ifimbusu*
men	*baume*
women	*banakashi*
today	*lelo*
tomorrow	*mailo*
tomorrow (early)	*mailo ulucelo*
yesterday	*mailo yafumineko*

Eating & Drinking

Please bring me ...	*Ndetele niko ...*
bananas	*nkonde*
beans	*cilemba*
beer	*bwalwa*
bread	*umukate*
cassava	*kalundwe*
chicken	*inkoko*
coffee	*kofi*
eggs	*amani*
fish	*isabi*
fruit	*icisabo/ifisabo* (sg/pl)
meat	*inama*
milk	*umukaka*
mushrooms	*ubowa*
oranges	*amachungwa*
peanuts	*mbalala*
potatoes	*ifyumbu*
tea	*chai*
vegetables	*umusalu*
(drinking) water	*amenshi (yakunwa)*

CHICHEWA

Keep in mind when using this list that you may not be speaking 'proper' Chichewa. Importantly, though, you'll be understood, and locals in Malawi will be pleased to hear a visitor using their language.

Basics

Mazungu means 'white person', but is not a derogatory term. *Bambo* literally means 'father' but is a polite way to address any Malawian man. The female equivalent is *Amai* or *Mai*. Chichewa speakers talking together will normally use English for numbers, prices and expressing time.

Hello.	*Moni.*
Goodbye.	*Tsala bwino.* (if leaving) *Pitani bwino.* (if staying)
Good night.	*Gonani bwino.*
Please.	*Chonde.*
Thank you.	*Zikomo.*
Excuse me.	*Zikomo.*
Yes./No.	*Inde./Iyayi.*
How are you?	*Muli bwanji?*
I'm fine.	*Ndili bwino.*
Good./Fine./OK.	*Chabwino.*
What's your name?	*Dzina lako ndani?*
I don't understand.	*Sindikunva.*
How much?	*Ntengo bwanji?*
I want ...	*Ndifuna ...*
I don't want ...	*Sindifuna ...*
to buy	*kugula*
to sleep	*kugona*
men	*akuma*
women	*akazi*
today	*lero*
tomorrow	*mara*
tomorrow (early)	*m'mara*
yesterday	*dzulo*

Eating & Drinking

Please bring me ...	*Mundi passe ...*
to eat	*kudya*
bread	*buledi*
chicken	*nkhuku*
coffee	*khofi*
eggs	*mazira*
fish	*somba*
fruit	*chipasso/zipasso* (sg/pl)
lake perch	*chambo*
meat	*nyama*
milk	*mkaka*
potatoes	*batata*
tea	*ti*
vegetables	*mquani*
water	*mazi*

LOZI

Lozi is spoken mainly in Zambia's Western Province. If greeting royalty or aristocrats, use *Ba lumele Malozi, sha*. English numbers are usually used to express time.

Numbers – Lozi

1	*il'ingw'i*
2	*z'e peli or bubeli*
3	*z'e t'alu or bulalu*
4	*z'e ne or bune*
5	*z'e keta-lizoho*

Basics

Hello.	*Eeni, sha.* (general) *Lumela.* (inf) *Mu lumeleng' sha.* (pol)
Goodbye.	*Siala (foo/hande/ sinde).* (inf) *Musiale (foo/hande/ sinde).* (pol)
Good morning.	*U zuhile.* (inf) *Mu zuhile.* (pol)
Good afternoon/ evening.	*Ki manzibuana./ U tozi.* (inf) *Mu tozi.* (pol)
Good night.	*Ki busihu.*
Please.	*Sha.*
Thank you (very much).	*N'itumezi (hahulu).*
Excuse me.	*Ni swalele.* (inf) *Mu ni swalele.* (pol)
Yes.	*Ee.* (inf) *Eeni.* (pol)
No.	*Awa.* (inf) *Batili.* (pol)
How are you?	*U cwang'?/W'a pila?/ W'a zuha?* (inf) *Mu cwang'?/Mw'a pila?/ Mw'a zuha?* (pol)
I'm fine.	*N'i teng'./N'a pila./ N'a zuha.*
Good./Fine.	*Ki hande.*
OK.	*Ku lukile.*
I don't understand.	*Ha ni utwi.*
What's your name?	*Libizo la hao ki wena mang'?* (inf) *Libizo la mina ki mina bo mang'?* (pol)
My name is ...	*K'i na ...*
How much?	*Ki bukai?*
toilets	*bimbuzi/limbuzi*
men	*banna*
women	*basali*
today	*kachenu*
tomorrow	*kamuso*
tomorrow (early)	*kamuso kakusasasa/ ka mamiso*
yesterday	*mabani*

Eating & Drinking

Use Ndate (sir) or Ma (madam) to denote 'please'.

Please bring me ...	*Ndate/Ma, ha mu ni fe ...*
banana	*likonde/makonde* (sg/pl)
beans	*manawa*
beef	*nama ya komu*
beer	*bucwala/mutoho* (sg/pl)
bread	*sinkwa*
chicken	*kuhu*
coffee	*kofi*
egg	*lii/mai* (sg/pl)
fish	*tapi*
food	*licho/sicho*
freshwater bream	*papati*
fruit	*tolwana/litolwana* (sg/pl)
gravy	*mulo*
meat	*nama*
milk	*mabisi*
mushrooms	*mbowa*
peanuts/cashews	*ndongo*
pork	*nama ya kulube*
potatoes	*makwili*
rice	*raisi*
salt	*lizwai*
sweet	*munati*
tea	*tii*
vegetable	*miloho/muloho* (sg/pl)
(drinking) water	*mezi (a kunwa)*

NYANJA

Nyanja is widely spoken in Lusaka and in the Central and Eastern Provinces of Zambia. You can generally get by using English numbers for prices and times.

Basics

Hello.	*Bwanji.*
Good morning.	*Mwauka bwanji.*
Good afternoon.	*Mwachoma bwanji.*
Good night.	*Gonani bwino.*
Goodbye.	*Pitani bwino/salani bwino.*
Thank you./ Excuse me.	*Zikomo.*
Thank you very much.	*Zikomo kwambiri.*
Yes./No.	*Inde./Iyai.*
How are you?	*Uli bwanji?* (inf) *Muli bwanji?* (pol)

I'm fine.	*Ndili bwino.*
Good./Fine./OK.	*Chabwino.*
I don't understand.	*Sindimvera.*
What's your name?	*Dzina ianu ndani?*
My name is ...	*Dzina ianga ndine ...*
How much?	*Ndizingati?*
toilets	*chimbuzi*
men	*amuna*
women	*akazi*
today	*lelo*
tomorrow	*mawa*
tomorrow (early)	*m'mawa*
yesterday	*dzulo*

Eating & Drinking

Please bring me ...	*Ndifuna kukhala ndi ...*
beans	*kaela*
beef	*nyama ya ng'ombe*
beer	*mowa*
bread	*buledi*
chicken	*nkuku*
coffee	*khofi*
eggs	*ma egesi*
fish	*nsomba*
fruit	*cipatso/zipatso* (sg/pl)
meat	*nyama*
milk	*mukaka*
pork	*nyama ya nkumba*
potatoes	*mapotato*
sweet potato	*kandolo*
tea	*tiyi*
vegetables	*mbeu zaziwisi*
(drinking) water	*mandzi (yo kumwa)*

PORTUGUESE

Most sounds in Portuguese are also found in English. The exceptions are the nasal vowels (represented in our pronunciation guides by ng after the vowel), which are pronounced 'through the nose'; and the strongly rolled *r* (rr in our pronunciation guides). Also note that the symbol zh sounds like the 's' in 'pleasure'. The stressed syllables are indicated with italics. Masculine and feminine forms of nouns and adjectives are provided in the following phrases where necessary, indicated with 'm' and 'f' respectively.

Basics

Hello.	*Olá.*	o·*laa*
Goodbye.	*Adeus.*	a·de·*oosh*
How are you?	*Como está?*	*ko*·moo shtaa
Fine, and you?	*Bem, e você?*	beng e vo·*se*
Excuse me.	*Faz favor.*	faash fa·*vor*
Sorry.	*Desculpe.*	desh·*kool*·pe
Yes./No.	*Sim./Não.*	seeng/nowng
Please.	*Por favor.*	poor fa·*vor*
Thank you.	*Obrigado.* / *Obrigada.*	o·bree·*gaa*·doo (m) / o·bree·*gaa*·da (f)
You're welcome.	*De nada.*	de *naa*·da

What's your name?
Qual é o seu nome? — kwaal e oo *se*·oo *no*·me

My name is ...
O meu nome é ... — oo *me*·oo *no*·me e ...

Do you speak English?
Fala inglês? — *faa*·la eeng·*glesh*

I don't understand.
Não entendo. — nowng eng·*teng*·doo

Directions

Where's (the station)?
Onde é (a estação)? — *ong*·de e (a shta·*sowng*)

What's the address?
Qual é o endereço? — kwaal e oo eng·de·*re*·soo

Could you please write it down?
Podia escrever isso, por favor? — poo·*dee*·a shkre·*ver* ee·soo poor fa·*vor*

Can you show me (on the map)?
Pode-me mostrar (no mapa)? — *po*·de·me moosh·*traar* (noo *maa*·pa)

Eating & Drinking

What would you recommend?
O que é que recomenda? — oo ke e ke rre·koo·*meng*·da

I don't eat ...
Eu não como ... — e·oo nowng *ko*·moo ...

I'd like (the menu).
Queria (um menu). — ke·*ree*·a (oong me·*noo*)

Cheers!
Saúde! — sa·oo·de

That was delicious.
Isto estava delicioso. — *eesh*·too *shtaa*·va de·lee·see·o·zoo

Please bring the bill.
Pode-me trazer a conta. — *po*·de·me tra·*zer* a *kong*·ta

Emergencies

Help!	*Socorro!*	soo·*ko*·rroo
Go away!	*Vá-se embora!*	*vaa*·se eng·*bo*·ra
Call ...!	*Chame ...!*	*shaa*·me ...
a doctor	*um médico*	oong *me*·dee·koo
the police	*a polícia*	a poo·*lee*·sya

I'm lost.
Estou perdido. shtoh per·*dee*·doo (m)
Estou perdida. shtoh per·*dee*·da (f)

I'm ill.
Estou doente. shtoh doo·*eng*·te

Where is the toilet?
Onde é a casa de banho? *ong*·de e a *kaa*·za de *ba*·nyoo

Shopping & Services

I'd like to buy ...
Queria comprar ... ke·*ree*·a kong·*praar* ...

How much is it?
Quanto custa? *kwang*·too *koosh*·ta

It's too expensive.
Está muito caro. shtaa *mweeng*·too *kaa*·roo

There's a mistake in the bill.
Há um erro na conta. aa oong e·rroo na *kong*·ta

Time & Numbers

What time is it?
Que horas são? kee o·rash sowng

It's (10) o'clock.
São (dez) horas. sowng (desh) o·rash

Half past (10).
(Dez) e meia. (desh) e *may*·a

morning	*manhã*	ma·*nyang*
afternoon	*tarde*	*taar*·de
evening	*noite*	*noy*·te
yesterday	*ontem*	*ong*·teng
today	*hoje*	o·zhe
tomorrow	*amanhã*	aa·ma·*nyang*
1	*um*	oong
2	*dois*	doysh
3	*três*	tresh
4	*quatro*	*kwaa*·troo
5	*cinco*	*seeng*·koo
6	*seis*	saysh
7	*sete*	*se*·te
8	*oito*	*oy*·too
9	*nove*	*no*·ve
10	*dez*	desh
20	*vinte*	*veeng*·te
30	*trinta*	*treeng*·ta
40	*quarenta*	kwa·*reng*·ta
50	*cinquenta*	seeng·*kweng*·ta
60	*sessenta*	se·*seng*·ta
70	*setenta*	se·*teng*·ta
80	*oitenta*	oy·*teng*·ta
90	*noventa*	no·*veng*·ta
100	*cem*	seng
1000	*mil*	meel

Transport

boat	*barco*	*baar*·koo
bus	*autocarro*	ow·to·*kaa*·roo
plane	*avião*	a·vee·*owng*
train	*comboio*	kong·*boy*·oo
... ticket	*um bilhete de ...*	oong bee·*lye*·te de ...
one-way	*ida*	*ee*·da
return	*ida e volta*	*ee*·da ee *vol*·ta

I want to go to ...
Queria ir a ... ke·*ree*·a eer a ...

What time does it leave/arrive?
A que horas sai/chega? a ke o·rash sai/*she*·ga

TONGA

Tonga is spoken mainly in Zambia's Southern Province. You can generally get by using English numbers for prices and time.

Basics

Hello.	*Wabonwa/Wapona.* (inf) *Mwabonwa/Mwpona.* (pol)
Goodbye.	*Muchale kabotu.*
Good morning.	*Mwabuka kabotu.*
Good evening.	*Kwa siya.*
Good night.	*Kusiye kabotu.*
Please.	*Ndalomba.*
Thank you/excuse me.	*Amuninjatile.*
Thank you very much.	*Twalumba kapati.*
Yes.	*Ee.*
No.	*Pepe.*
How are you?	*Muli buti?*

MOZAMBIQUE'S LOCAL LANGUAGES

While Portuguese will greatly facilitate your travels in Mozambique, a few greetings and basic phrases in one of the local languages will be warmly received. Changana (also called Tsonga) is one of the most useful languages in Maputo and southern Mozambique.

Good morning.	*lixile* ('li-shee-le')	**Good afternoon.**	*lipelile*
Goodbye.	*salani*	**Thank you.**	*kanimambo*

In the far north near Lake Niassa, most people speak Nyanja.

Good morning.	*mwaka bwanji*	**Good afternoon.**	*mwalongedza*
Goodbye.	*ine de likupita*	**Thank you very much.**	*zikomo kwambile*

The main languages in central Mozambique are Sena and Ndau. To greet someone in Sena, say *magerwa*. In Ndau, it's *mawata*. In and around Chimoio, you will also hear Manyika with the greeting *mangwanani*.

In much of Nampula and Cabo Delgado provinces, where major languages include Makonde and Makhuwa, the most useful greeting is *salaam'a*.

In northern Cabo Delgado Swahili is useful; here are some basic phrases in Swahili.

Hello.	*Jambo./Salama.*	**1**	*moja*
Goodbye.	*Kwa heri.*	**2**	*mbili*
How are you?	*Habari?*	**3**	*tatu*
I'm fine, thanks.	*Nzuri.*	**4**	*nne*
Yes.	*Ndiyo.*	**5**	*tano*
No.	*Hapana.*	**6**	*sita*
Please.	*Tafadhali.*	**7**	*saba*
Thank you (very much).	*Asante (sana).*	**8**	*nane*
You're welcome.	*Karibu.*	**9**	*tisa*
Excuse me.	*Samahani.*	**10**	*kumi*

I'm fine.	*Ndi kabotu.*
Good./Fine./OK.	*Mbubo.*
What's your name?	*Ndiweni izyina?*
My name is ...	*Izyina iyangu ndime ...*
I don't understand.	*Tandileteleli.*
How much?	*Mali nzi?*
toilets	*chimbuzi*
men	*ba lumi/mulombwana*
women	*ba kaintu*
today	*tunu*
tomorrow	*chifumo*
yesterday	*ijilo*

Eating & Drinking

Please bring me ...	*Mu ndetele ...*
beans	*bunyanga*
beef	*nyama ya ng'ombe*
beer	*bukoko*
bread	*chinkwa*
chicken	*nkuku*
coffee	*nofi*
eggs	*ma gee*
fish	*inswi*
meat	*nyama*
milk	*mukupa*
onion	*hangisi*
potatoes	*mapotato*
pumpkin leaves	*lungu*
rice	*laisi*
sweet potato	*chibwali*
tea	*tii*
tomatoes	*lunkomba*
vegetables	*cisu mani*
(drinking) water	*menda (a kumwa)*

4WD – four-wheel drive; locally called 4x4

ablutions block – found at camping grounds and caravan parks: a building that contains toilets, showers and washing-up area; also known as an amenities block

aldeamento – fortified village complex (Mo)

ANC – African National Congress

assimilados – a colonial-era population classification, referring to those Mozambicans who adopted Portuguese customs and ways (Mo)

baía – bay (Mo)

bairro – neighbourhood, area or section of town (Mo)

baixa – the lower-lying area of a city or town; in coastal Mozambique this often means the part of the city near the port, and the *baixa* is frequently synonymous with 'commercial district' (Mo)

bakkie – utility or pick-up truck (pronounced 'bucky')

barraca – market stall or food stall; also a thatched shelter at camping grounds, often with plug points (Mo)

biltong – a chewy dried meat that can be anything from beef to kudu or ostrich

BIM – Banco Internacional de Moçambique

boma – town (Ma, Z)

braai – a barbecue

buck or **bok** – any kind of antelope

buhobe – staple made from maize, millet or cassava flour (Lozi) (Z)

bushcamp – a small and exclusive place to stay deep in a national park, usually dismantled in the wet season, then rebuilt next dry season

busunso – any sauce used with buhobe (Z)

camião, camiões – truck(s) (Mo)

camp (noun) – a place to stay, but not necessarily one that entails 'camping', or even budget accommodation; throughout Africa, many places with 'Camp' in the name are upmarket establishments – effectively small hotels in or near national parks but retaining the feel of being out in the bush

capitania – port authority (Mo)

capulana – a colourful cloth worn by women around their waist (Mo)

casa de cultura – literally, 'house of culture'; cultural centre found in each provincial capital. The *casas de cultura* exist to promote traditional culture and are good sources of information on traditional music and dance performances in the area (Mo)

casal – room with a double bed (Mo)

cascata – waterfall (Mo)

casita – bungalow (Mo)

CBD – Central Business District; city centre or downtown area

cerveja – beer (Mo)

chambo – a fish of the tilapia family, commonly eaten in Malawi

chapa – any public transport that is not a bus or truck; usually refers to converted minivans or pick-ups

chibuku – local style mass-produced beer, stored in tanks and served in buckets, or available in takeaway cartons (mostly in Malawi) and plastic bottles known as *scuds* (Ma, Z)

chiperone – damp misty weather that affects southern Malawi (Ma)

chitenje– multicoloured piece of material used as a scarf and sarong

correios – post office (Mo)

dagaa – small, sardine-like fish (Ma, Mo)

dagga – (pronounced da-kha) Southern African term for marijuana, not to be confused with *dagaa*

dambo – area of grass, reeds or swamp alongside a river course (Z, Ma)

dassies – herbivorous gopher-like mammals of two species: *Procavia capensis*, also called the rock hyrax, and *Dendrohyrax arborea* or tree hyrax; these are not rodents but thought to be the closest living relatives of the elephant

dhow – Arabic sailing vessel that dates from ancient times

dia da cidade – city or town day; a holiday commemorating the town's founding, often celebrated with parades and song-and-dance performances (Mo)

difaqane – forced migration by several Southern African tribes in the face of Zulu aggression; also known as *mfecane*

djembe – a type of hand drum

donga – steep-sided gully caused by soil erosion

donkey boiler – a water tank positioned over a fire and used to heat water for showers and other purposes

drift – a river ford; most are normally dry

duplo – room with two twin beds; see also casal

EN1 – Estrada Nacional 1; the main south–north highway in Mozambique; also often N1.

EN6 – Estrada Nacional 6; the highway running from Beira west towards Chimoio and the Mozambique–Zimbabwe border; also often N6.

estrada – road, highway (Mo)

euphorbia – several species of cactus-like succulents that are endemic in Southern Africa

feira – trading fair (Mo)

flotty – a hat for canoe safaris, with a chin-strap and a bit of cork in a zippered pocket to ensure that it floats in case of a capsize

fortaleza – fort (Mo)

Frelimo (Frente da Libertação de Moçambique) – Mozambique Liberation Front

fynbos – fine bush, primarily proteas, heaths and ericas

galabiyya – man's full-length robe

game – formerly used for any animal hunted, now applied to all large, four-footed creatures

GMA – Game Management Area

igini – magic charm used by witches; other magic charms are also known as *inkuwa* (Z, Ma)

ilha – island (Mo)

ilya – a delicacy of very thin corn porridge mixed with yogurt and sugar (Lozi) (Z)

indígenas – literally, 'indigenous people', refers to a colonial-era population classification (Mo)

inselberg – isolated ranges and hills; literally 'island mountains'

Izzit? – rhetorical question that most closely translates as 'Really?' and used without regard to gender, person or number of subjects; therefore, may also mean 'Is it?', 'Are you?', 'Is he?', 'Are they?', 'Is she?', 'Are we?' , etc; also 'How izzit?', for 'How's it going?'

jesse – dense, thorny scrub, normally impenetrable to humans

just now – refers to some time in the future but implies a certain degree of imminence; it could be half an hour from now or two days from now

kalindula – modern Zambian style of music involving a blend of Congolese rumba and more gentle indigenous sounds (Z)

kampango – catfish (Ma)

kankobele – thumb piano; consists of narrow iron keys mounted in rows on a wooden sound board (Ma)

kapenta – an anchovy-like fish (*Limnothrissa mioda*) caught in Lake Kariba

KK – popular nickname for Kenneth Kaunda (not derogatory) (Z)

kotu – king's court (Z)

kwacha – Zambian and Malawian currency

kwasa kwasa – Congo-style rhumba music

lago – lake (Mo)

LAM – Linhas Aéreas de Moçambique; Mozambique's national airline

litunga – king (Z)

LMS – London Missionary Society

lupembe – wind instrument made from animal horn

lutindzi – type of grass

mabele – sorghum (Z, Ma)

machamba – small farm plot (Mo)

machibombo – bus (Mo)

makishi – a dance performed in Zambia featuring male dancers wearing masks of stylised human faces and with grass skirts and anklets (Z)

makwaela – a type of dance characterised by *a cappella* singing accompanied by foot percussion

Malawi shandy – non-alcoholic drink made from ginger beer, Angostura bitters, orange or lemon slices, soda and ice

mapiko – masked dance of the Makonde people; also refers to the wooden masks worn by the dancer (Mo)

marginal – beach road (Mo)

marimba – African xylophone, made from strips of resonant wood with various-sized gourds for sound boxes

marrabenta – Mozambique's national music, with an upbeat style and distinctive beat

matola – pick-up or van carrying passengers (Ma)

mbira – thumb piano; consists of five to 24 narrow iron keys mounted in rows on a wooden sound board

mealie meal or **mielie pap** – maize porridge, a dietary staple throughout the region; known as *xima* in Mozambique (Z, Ma)

mercado – market (Mo)

metical, meticais – Mozambican currency

mielies – cobs of maize

migração – immigration (Mo)

minas (minas de terra) – land mines (Mo)

mfecane – see *difaqane*

miombo – moist open woodland, also called *Brachystegia* woodland; comprises mainly mopane and acacia *bushveld*

monte(s) – mountain(s) (Mo)

mopane worms – the caterpillar of the moth *Gonimbrasia belina*, eaten as a local delicacy throughout the region

mpasa – lake salmon (Ma)

murunge – see *mzungu*

muti – traditional medicine

mzungu – white person, especially in Zambia and Malawi

nganga – fortune teller

nalikwanda – huge wooden canoe that is painted with black and white stripes and carries the *litunga* (Z)

ncheni – lake tiger fish (Ma)

now now – definitely not now, but sometime sooner than *just now*

nshima – filling maize porridge-like substance eaten in Zambia; known as nsima in Malawi and *xima* in Mozambique

nyanga – panpipes; also the name of a dance in which the dancer plays the panpipes (Mo)

pan – dry flat area of grassland or salt, often a seasonal lake-bed

parque nacional – national park (Mo)

participation safari – an inexpensive safari in which clients pitch their own tents, pack the vehicle and share cooking duties

pastelaria – shop selling pastries, cakes and often light meals as well (Mo)

Pedicle, the – the tongue of Democratic Republic of Congo territory that almost divides Zambia into two

peg – milepost

pensão, pensões – inexpensive hotel(s) (Mo)

photographic safari – safari in which participants carry cameras rather than guns

pint – small bottle of beer or can of oil (or similar), usually around 300ml to 375ml (not necessarily equal to a British or US pint)

piri-piri or **peri-peri**– hot pepper sauce (Mo)

potjie – (*poy*-kee) a three-legged pot used to make stew over an open fire; also refers both to the stew itself and to a gathering at which the stew forms the main dish

pousada – hotel or inn, usually a step up from a *pensão* (Mo)

praça – square (Mo)

praia – beach (Mo)

prazeiro – prazo holder (Mo)

prazo – privately owned agricultural estates allocated by the Portuguese crown; the prazo system was used by the Portuguese between the 17th and early-20th centuries in an attempt to strengthen their control in Mozambique (Mo)

refresco – soda, soft drink (Mo)

régulo – chief, traditional leader (Mo)

relish – sauce of meat, vegetables, beans etc eaten with boiled *mielie* meal (*nsima*, *nshima* etc)

Renamo (Resistência Nacional Moçambicana/Mozambican National Resistance) – the main opposition party in Mozambique

reserva – reserve (Mo)

robot – traffic light

rondavel – round, African-style hut

rooibos – literally 'red bush' in Afrikaans; herbal tea that reputedly has therapeutic qualities

rua – street (Mo)

sangoma – witchdoctor; herbalist

slasher – hand tool with a curved blade used to cut grass or crops, hence 'to slash' means 'to cut grass'

sungwa – a type of perch (Ma)

tackies – trainers, tennis shoes, gym shoes

tambo – fermented millet and sugar drink

TDM (Telecomunicações de Moçambique) – the national telecommunications company

timbila (plural of mbila) – type of marimba or xylophone used by the Chopi people (Mo)

toasties – toasted sandwiches

township – indigenous suburb, typically a high-density black residential area

tufo – a dance of Arabic origin, common on Mozambique Island and along the northern Mozambican coast (Mo)

veld – open grassland (pronounced 'felt'), normally in plateau regions; lowveld, highveld, bushveld, strandveld, panveld

vlei – (pronounced 'flay') any low open landscape, sometimes marshy

watu – dugout canoe used in western Zambia (Z)

xima – maize- or cassava-based staple, usually served with a sauce of beans, vegetables or fish; also known as upshwa in some areas (Mo)

zol – see *dagga*

Behind the Scenes

SEND US YOUR FEEDBACK

We love to hear from travellers – your comments keep us on our toes and help make our books better. Our well-travelled team reads every word on what you loved or loathed about this book. Although we cannot reply individually to your submissions, we always guarantee that your feedback goes straight to the appropriate authors, in time for the next edition. Each person who sends us information is thanked in the next edition – the most useful submissions are rewarded with a selection of digital PDF chapters.

Visit **lonelyplanet.com/contact** to submit your updates and suggestions or to ask for help. Our award-winning website also features inspirational travel stories, news and discussions.

Note: We may edit, reproduce and incorporate your comments in Lonely Planet products such as guidebooks, websites and digital products, so let us know if you don't want your comments reproduced or your name acknowledged. For a copy of our privacy policy visit lonelyplanet.com/privacy.

OUR READERS

Many thanks to the travellers who used the last edition and wrote to us with helpful hints, useful advice and interesting anecdotes:

Andy Craig, Bas Geelen, Carole Plan, Cristobal Vega, Daniel Hager, Dominic Frei, John Schelesnak, John Seaman, Kathleen Kearns, Katie Belshaw, Mark Rowlatt, Mike Paredes, Suzanne van Hooff

WRITER THANKS

Mary Fitzpatrick

Many thanks to all those who helped me during this project, especially to Rafael Holt in Tofo for the excellent background information; to Sidney Bliss in Maputo for updates on the latest Mozambique happenings; and to the staff at Maputo Special Reserve and at Limpopo National Park. My biggest thanks go to Rick, Christopher, Dominic and Gabriel for their company, patience, good humour and support in Mozambique and back home.

James Bainbridge

Believe the hype about Malawian friendliness: this really is the Warm Heart of Africa. *Zikomo*, then, to pretty much everyone for being so awesome, and in particular to the many folk, too numerous to mention, in lodges from Mzuzu to Mulanje. My research trip was considerably more fruitful and fun with your local knowledge and sociable bottles of Green.

Trent Holden

First up, thanks to Matt Phillips for commissioning me on Zambia, as well as all the production staff for putting it all together. A huge thanks to Kim Phippen for taking the time to help out in all manners, much appreciated! To my good friend Lacken 'Lucky' Banda for the epic road trip, as well as Giacomo in facilitating this; the team from African Parks for their assistance in helping me get around Liuwa Plain National Park; David Julian Wightman for taking the time to take me on the 'salaula experience' and helping out with info; Ian Murphy for a copy of his awesome books; finally lots of love to my family, especially Kate who allows me to travel to such far-flung, exotic places.

Brendan Sainsbury

Thanks to all the untold taxi drivers, chefs, hotel receptionists, tour guides, and innocent bystanders who helped me during this research. Special thanks to Jasper and Bart in Pemba, the guys at Cinco Portas on Ibo Island, Peter at Pensão Gurúè, and the wonderful staff at Gorongosa National Park.

ACKNOWLEDGMENTS

Climate map data adapted from Peel MC, Finlayson BL & McMahon TA (2007) 'Updated World Map of the Köppen-Geiger Climate Classification', Hydrology and Earth System Sciences, 11, 163344.

Cover photograph: Lion cubs, South Luangwa National Park, Zambia; Steve Bloom Images/Alamy

THIS BOOK

This 3rd edition of Lonely Planet's *Zambia, Mozambique & Malawi* guidebook was researched and written by Mary Fitzpatrick, James Bainbridge, Brendan Sainsbury and Trent Holden, and curated by Mary. The Victoria Falls chapter was curated by Anthony Ham. The previous edition was written by Mary Fitzpatrick, Michael Grosberg, Trent Holden, Kate Morgan, Nick Ray and Richard Waters. This guidebook was produced by the following:

Destination Editor Matt Phillips

Product Editors Bruce Evans, Kate Kiely

Senior Cartographer Diana Von Holdt

Book Designer Mazzy Prinsep

Assisting Editors Sarah Bailey, Imogen Bannister, Pete Cruttenden, Rosie Nicholson, Victoria Smith

Assisting Cartographers Julie Dodkins, Corey Hutchison

Cover Researcher Naomi Parker

Thanks to Jennifer Carey, David Carroll, Daniel Corbett, Tony Wheeler

Index

Map Pages **000**
Photo Pages **000**

Map Pages **000**
Photo Pages **000**

Map Legend

Sights

- Beach
- Bird Sanctuary
- Buddhist
- Castle/Palace
- Christian
- Confucian
- Hindu
- Islamic
- Jain
- Jewish
- Monument
- Museum/Gallery/Historic Building
- Ruin
- Shinto
- Sikh
- Taoist
- Winery/Vineyard
- Zoo/Wildlife Sanctuary
- Other Sight

Activities, Courses & Tours

- Bodysurfing
- Diving
- Canoeing/Kayaking
- Course/Tour
- Sento Hot Baths/Onsen
- Skiing
- Snorkelling
- Surfing
- Swimming/Pool
- Walking
- Windsurfing
- Other Activity

Sleeping

- Sleeping
- Camping

Eating

- Eating

Drinking & Nightlife

- Drinking & Nightlife
- Cafe

Entertainment

- Entertainment

Shopping

- Shopping

Information

- Bank
- Embassy/Consulate
- Hospital/Medical
- Internet
- Police
- Post Office
- Telephone
- Toilet
- Tourist Information
- Other Information

Geographic

- Beach
- Gate
- Hut/Shelter
- Lighthouse
- Lookout
- Mountain/Volcano
- Oasis
- Park
- Pass
- Picnic Area
- Waterfall

Population

- Capital (National)
- Capital (State/Province)
- City/Large Town
- Town/Village

Transport

- Airport
- Border crossing
- Bus
- Cable car/Funicular
- Cycling
- Ferry
- Metro station
- Monorail
- Parking
- Petrol station
- S-Bahn/Subway station
- Taxi
- T-bane/Tunnelbana station
- Train station/Railway
- Tram
- Tube station
- U-Bahn/Underground station
- Other Transport

Note: Not all symbols displayed above appear on the maps in this book

Routes

- Tollway
- Freeway
- Primary
- Secondary
- Tertiary
- Lane
- Unsealed road
- Road under construction
- Plaza/Mall
- Steps
- Tunnel
- Pedestrian overpass
- Walking Tour
- Walking Tour detour
- Path/Walking Trail

Boundaries

- International
- State/Province
- Disputed
- Regional/Suburb
- Marine Park
- Cliff
- Wall

Hydrography

- River, Creek
- Intermittent River
- Canal
- Water
- Dry/Salt/Intermittent Lake
- Reef

Areas

- Airport/Runway
- Beach/Desert
- Cemetery (Christian)
- Cemetery (Other)
- Glacier
- Mudflat
- Park/Forest
- Sight (Building)
- Sportsground
- Swamp/Mangrove

OUR STORY

A beat-up old car, a few dollars in the pocket and a sense of adventure. In 1972 that's all Tony and Maureen Wheeler needed for the trip of a lifetime – across Europe and Asia overland to Australia. It took several months, and at the end – broke but inspired – they sat at their kitchen table writing and stapling together their first travel guide, *Across Asia on the Cheap*. Within a week they'd sold 1500 copies. Lonely Planet was born.

Today, Lonely Planet has offices in Franklin, London, Melbourne, Oakland, Dublin, Beijing and Delhi, with more than 600 staff and writers. We share Tony's belief that 'a great guidebook should do three things: inform, educate and amuse'.

OUR WRITERS

Mary Fitzpatrick

Mozambique Originally from the USA, Mary spent her early years dreaming of how to get across an ocean or two to more exotic locales. Following graduate studies, she set off for Europe. Her fascination with languages and cultures soon led her further south to Africa, where she has spent the past two decades living and working as a professional travel writer all around the continent. She focuses particularly on East and Southern Africa, including Mozambique and Tanzania. Mary has authored and co-authored many guidebooks for Lonely Planet, including *Mozambique*; *Tanzania*; *South Africa, Lesotho & Swaziland*; *East Africa*; *West Africa*; and *Egypt*.

James Bainbridge

Malawi James is a British travel writer and journalist based in Cape Town, South Africa, from where he roams the globe and contributes to publications worldwide. He has been working on Lonely Planet projects for over a decade, updating dozens of guidebooks and TV hosting everywhere from the African bush to the Great Lakes. The managing author of several editions of Lonely Planet's *South Africa, Lesotho & Swaziland*, *Turkey* and *Morocco* guides, his articles on travel, culture and investment appear in the likes of *BBC Travel*, the UK *Guardian* and *Independent*, *Condé Nast Traveller* and *Lonely Planet Traveller*.

Trent Holden

Zambia, Victoria Falls Trent has worked for Lonely Planet since 2005. He's covered 30-plus guidebooks across Asia, Africa and Australia. With a penchant for megacities, Trent's in his element when assigned to cover a nation's capital – the more chaotic the better – to unearth cool bars, art, street food and underground subculture. On the flipside he also writes books to idyllic tropical islands across Asia, in between going on safari to national parks in Africa and the subcontinent. You can catch him on Twitter @hombreholden.

Brendan Sainsbury

Mozambique Born and raised in the UK in a town that never merits a mention in any guidebook (Andover, Hampshire), Brendan spent the holidays of his youth caravanning in the English Lake District and didn't leave Blighty until he was 19. Making up for lost time, he's since squeezed 70 countries into a sometimes precarious existence as a writer and professional vagabond. In the last 11 years, he has written more than 40 books for Lonely Planet about places from Castro's Cuba to the canyons of Peru.

Published by Lonely Planet Global Limited
CRN 554153
3rd edition – Sep 2017
ISBN 978 1 78657 043 7

10 9 8 7 6 5 4 3 2 1
Printed in China